Langmaker

Langmaker:
Celebrating Conlangs

by Jeffrey Henning

YONAGU BOOKS

Yonagu • Chicago • 2020

Edited by Mark Rosenfelder

© 1995-2005, 2020 by Jeffrey Henning.
All rights reserved, including the right to reproduce this book or portions thereof in any form whatsoever, except for review purposes.

ISBN 9781661715571

ed. 1.0

Contents

PREFACE	7
INTRODUCTION	9
MODEL LANGUAGES PREFACE	13
MODEL LANGUAGES	15
A NAMING LANGUAGE	20
GYMNASTICS WITH ONOMASTICS	38
POSSIBILITIES AND PURPOSES	46
MEANING CHANGE	50
MEANING	67
RELATIVE TERMS FOR RELATIVES	76
THE CASE FOR CASES	86
ON TOLKIEN	92
EMULATING TOLKIEN: ALVISH	103
BARSOOMIAN	112
LAPINE	124

DUBLEX	127
FITH	146
ILISH	171
INTERMYTHIC ENGLISH	177
KALI-SISE (PITAKESULINA)	181
KARKLAK (GNOME TONGUE)	206
MINHYAN	210
ROXHAI	229
SIMPENGA	261
TEV'MECKIAN (GALAXY QUEST)	267
DENJU	283
CONLANGS AT A GLANCE	291
INDEX	384

Preface

By David J. Peterson

If you were a conlanger with an internet connection in the early 2000s you knew Langmaker.com. You may not have been a member of the Conlang Listserv; you may not have had a username on the Zompist Bulletin Board; you may never have participated in a conlang relay. But if you ever so much as typed "new language" into AltaVista, you were aware of Langmaker, and were a frequent visitor.

In its heyday, Langmaker was something like Reddit plus Wikipedia, but devoted exclusively to conlanging. If something was happening in the world of conlanging, it was on the front page of Langmaker. If there was a conlang you wanted to know more about, you could find a short description plus links on Langmaker's list of conlangs. There were grammatical descriptions, short articles on conlanging topics and specific conlangs, created writing systems, Babel texts, wordlists, a Top 200 conlangs list that every conlanger longed to be on… It was, without a doubt, the single greatest conlanging resource that existed at that time.

Even so, the best thing about Langmaker was its universality. From the beginning, conlanging and the conlang community have been prone to factionalism (cf. the Conlang-Auxlang schism of 1996). Langmaker somehow transcended that. Every conlanger from every conlang community—or from no conlang community—was welcome there, and every conlanger found value in it. It was the Rick's of conlanging.

To have your translation of the Babel Text up on Langmaker meant something—not because it was particularly exclusive, but because you knew *everyone* would see it. How Jeffrey Henning, founder and curator of Langmaker, managed to engender and maintain that sense of benevolent neutrality I'll never know. But I do know that it is sorely missed today, when there's no similar website or service to bind together all the various conlang communities—or the ever growing number of conlangers who have no conlanging home at all, coining words and filling declension tables out in the wilds of social media.

Towards the end of Langmaker's run, I served as the editor of new Babel texts submitted to the site. As editor, I didn't do much actual editing—I mainly performed a cursory check to ascertain that the submission was a sincere translation of the Babel text, that all the sentences had been translated, and that there were no obvious translation errors—but it felt good to help introduce a new conlang to the world. Back then, showing off a translation of the Babel text was the conlanger's way of premiering their new language. Nowadays, that practice has fallen by the wayside largely because even if one completes a new Babel text translation, where does one share it? The Conlang Listserv? The ZBB? The Conlang Facebook group? The Conlangs Subreddit? CALS? FrathWiki? Twitter? Tumblr? Instagram...? Whatever the choice, the audience is limited, because there's no Rick's of conlanging any longer—there is no Langmaker.

Though nothing could replace Langmaker, it's wonderful that Mark Rosenfelder has decided to publish a collection of Jeffrey Henning's conlang work. No book could contain everything hosted on Langmaker, but this book has some of Jeffrey's best stuff—including one of the most original engelangs I've ever seen in Fith; his groundbreaking essay on naming languages; and his page on Tev'Meckian, which, I'm ashamed to admit, tricked me into believing that there had been a *Galaxy Quest* TV series in the 1980s that I had somehow missed. Though reading Jeffrey's work on the printed page is nothing like reading it on a non-HD computer screen with a 14.4k dialup connection and a minutes-long pageload, I invite you to enjoy this wonderful collection!

Introduction

By Mark Rosenfelder

This book collects the best of Jeffrey Henning's work on Langmaker.com, the conlanging site he founded in 1998.

- The guides he created for the *Model Languages* newsletter, distributed by e-mail in 1995-6
- His own conlangs, including the stack-based Fith, the conlanging game Dublex, and the playful Tev'Meckian
- Reviews of pioneering conlanging by J.R.R. Tolkien, Edgar Rice Burroughs, Richard Adams, and others
- A database of over a thousand conlangs available on the web at the time

This wasn't by any means all that was on the site. If you were interested in conlanging in the early 2000s, you checked it frequently for news and reviews, put your conlang or Babel Text translation into the database, suggested a neologism, maybe borrowed some of the wordlists or used the LangMaker software, which included a word generator and sound change applier.

Jeffrey encouraged interactivity, and even had a small staff to find and review submissions. For the record, these included David J. Peterson, Kevin Athey, Aaron Morse, Ethan Dickey, C.J. Sproson, Felix Wan, David Solly, Robert Jung, and Matthias Persson.

By 2004, Langmaker had over 20,000 unique visitors a month.

The chapter on cases was written for a book project. That and the sketch of Denju have not been published before.

What to look for

Now, maybe you're read my *Language Construction Kit*, and wonder what this book will add to your life, or to your conlanging.

First, you might learn something! Jeffrey is an enthusiastic guide to both languages and conlanging, and his essays on naming languages, meaning change, kinship terms, and place names are full of neat facts and useful info.

Second, Jeffrey's conlanging interests are extremely broad. I've concentrated on naturalistic languages, which means diving deep into how human languages work. But there are other approaches, which Jeffrey talks about and provides examples of:

- PHILOSOPHICAL LANGUAGES, which attempt to organize concepts rather than assigning words haphazardly— see Roxhai
- LOGICAL LANGUAGES or LOGLANGS, which reject the irrationality and miscellaneity of natural languages, often with the aim of teaching or allowing us to think better— see Fith
- AUXILIARY LANGUAGES or AUXLANGS, which make things as simple as possible in order to serve as a universal seeond language— see Kali-Sise
- Experimental or TOY LANGUAGES, which simply play with a neat idea in a way no 'natural language' does— see Ilish or Intermythic English

All of these have a long history— it can be said that conlangs of the 17th and 18th century tended to be philosophical or logical, while those of the 19th and early 20th century tended to be auxiliary languages.

Though conlanging tends to be a solitary pursuit, it turns out that one of the major motivations of many a conlang is to do it better than some other conlang. Though perhaps every auxlanger *kind of hopes* that their language will be chosen as The One, the motivation is often to *improve Esperanto*, or Interlingua, or Ro, or Solresol.

Jeffrey is also an indefatigable word-builder. He notes, perhaps drily, that he decided to publish the Fith lexicon once it had reached 10,000 words. The Kali-sise lexicon is over 5,000.

Watch how he does it— some derivational morphology here, some word generation there, and above all the patience to just *finish it all*, going far beyond the Swadesh List. And occasionally, just for fun, a bravura performance in non-naturalism, such as Fith's words for the numbers 1 to 144 each being a distinct root.

Our history

Conlanging has its own long history, perhaps best known from appendices to books on particular conlangs— Mario Pei's *One Language for the World* (1958), Pierre Janton's *Esperanto: Language, Literature, and Community* (1992), Arika Okrent's *In the Land of Invented Languages* (2010).[1]

This book is a part of that history. It serves as a snapshot of the conlanging community around 2000-2005: what was visible, what sort of information it was looking at, what conlangs people were eager to share.

The *Model Languages* material looks back further, to a time when the hobby had no accepted name and was scattered over mailing lists and early websites, and further back yet, when the beginning conlanger had to be satisfied with scrutinizing anything that looked like a conlang: Tolkien, Barsoomian, Lapine, even Furbish.

While we're talking about the historical record, you probably want to know: what happened to Langmaker? Well, the database broke down in 2008. Due to his main job and a burgeoning family, he had limited time, and this was not sufficent to get it fixed. So, sadly, the site was lost as a resource and as a community. Besides, Jeffrey's new obsession is making board games.

Some notes on presentation

We've taken the opportunity to edit and reformat the text, regularize the typography, use IPA symbols, and correct some errors. If it's entirely new to you, this book mostly uses these symbols:

ʃ	sh as in *shot*
ʒ	zh as in *vision*
x	kh as in *Bach, khan*
ð	voiced th as in *then*
θ	voiceless th as in *thick*

---

[1] Okrent's own list of conlangs very quirkily chooses Ilish and Nunihongo from Jeffrey's work. (Nunihongo was "what Japanese might look like if half of its vocabulary were derived from English", but was never finished.)

For English vowels, compare these English words

```
          front      central    back
high   ┌ peat                    boot ┐
        \      pit        put        |
closed   \ pate       uh       boat  |
          \                putt      |
open       \     pet            bought|
low         └ pat          pot       ┘
```

with the IPA symbols for their values:

```
          front      central    back
high   ┌ i                        u  ┐
        \      ɪ          ʊ          |
closed   \ e            ə         o  |
          \                          |
open       \    ɛ           ʌ     ɔ  |
low         └ æ             a        ┘
```

When a technical term is introduced, it's printed in SMALL CAPS. Among other things, this means that you can use it yourself, and that you can search the term for more information.

Jeffrey's work from Langmaker (that is, excluding other contributors') ran to over 2000 pages. To get this material down to a book you can hold, I've removed some of the less developed languages, and some other material that hasn't aged well. Mostly I removed those beautiful but bulky wordlists. However, I've placed the lexicons for Fith and Kali-sise here:

> http:/www.zompist.com/lm/

With some regret, I've omitted Oðblgshezi, a listing of 362 words which could be formed by writing on an old-style calculator and turning the display upside-down. (The name is 1234567890.) I'll just note some of the better finds: BELIZE, BESIEGES, BIGGISH, BOLSHOI, ELIGIBLE, HOBBIES, HOGGISH, LESOTHO, OBSESSES, SIZZLES, THIGHS.

So, read and enjoy, and then go make your own!

Model Languages Preface

This how-to guide is based on a newsletter I wrote in 1995 and 1996. This is the original introduction.
— Jeffrey, 6/30/01

One of the reasons I've started the newsletter is to increase awareness of the hobby of MODEL LANGUAGES and to provide a banner for language enthusiasts to rally around. There is little awareness about model languages as a hobby; in fact, no one is quite sure what to call it, with Tolkien referring to it as private languages; and others calling it constructed languages or imaginary languages. I've chosen to call them model languages because models are not intended to be full-scale replicas, but miniaturized versions that provide the essence of something, even if certain details have to be skipped over. In the same way, no one can construct a complete language, but a model of a language can be very useful. Additionally, as much of the joy is in building the languages as in actually using them; one of my colleagues is into model airplanes, and he and his son spend more time building them than flying them, a passion I understand completely.

Language modelers do not gather together in local clubs or display the results of their craft. Many look at their model languages as private experiments that they would be too self-conscious to discuss with others. Inventing model languages is an unusual hobby, though really it is no different than the hobbies of those who write poems or short stories.

The hobby has a disparate group of adherants that do not communicate with one another. Model languagers or language modelers can be found among writers, game players, computer game designers, science-fiction and fantasy fans, professional linguists and teachers. The community of hobbyists is a large one, with approximately 40,000 people in the United States having invented their own languages and some 250,000 having used model languages such as Esperanto, Quenya and Klingon.

It is my personal goal to increase public awareness of model languages as a legitimate hobby. One day, when somebody asks me what my interests are, I'd like to be able to say model languages and have them know what I'm talking about. I also have this fantasy where there is enough interest in the topic to be able to publish a small monthly magazine dedicated to it.

To help achieve these goals, I encourage you to spread the word about model languages. Please feel free to post sample issues of *Model Languages* to groups, forums or mailing lists that you think would be interested; myself, I've posted the newsletter to the TOLKLANG and CONLANG Internet mailing lists and to RPGAMES, WRITERS, FLEFO, SFMEDI and SFLIT on Compuserve. Please forward issues to friends, and mention this newsletter to writers, gamers, linguists, science fiction lovers, and anyone else you think might share your interest in model languages.

Feel free to drop me a note at any time to discuss questions you might have or issues you might like to see covered, or stories or knowledge you would like to share with other subscribers. If you want to start general discussions for others to join in on, I suggest you join CONLANG (CONstructed LANGuages).

Best regards,

Jeffrey

> *What range of accomplishment there is among these hidden craftsmen, I can only surmise — and I surmise the range runs, if one only knew, from the crude chalk-scrawl of the village schoolboy to the heights of palaeolithic or bushman art (or beyond). Its development to perfection must none the less certainly be prevented by its solitariness, the lack of interchange, open rivalry, study or imitation of others' technique.*
>
> J.R.R. Tolkien, "A Secret Vice"

> *We were listening to somebody lecturing on map-reading, or camp-hygeine, or the art of sticking a fellow through without (in defiance of Kipling) bothering who God sent the bill to; rather we were trying to avoid listening, though the Guards' English, and voice, is penetrating. The man next to me said suddenly in a dreamy voice: 'Yes, I think I shall express the accusative case by a prefix!'*
>
> J.R.R. Tolkien, "A Secret Vice"

Model languages

Volume I, Issue 1 — May 1, 1995

An introduction to the hobby of model languages

Some people build model airplanes, some craft model trains and some... well, they invent model languages. MODEL LANGUAGES can be everything from a few words of made-up slang to a rigorously developed system of interrelated imaginary tongues. It is not a hobby many people know about, since model languages cannot be flown in the park like a model airplane or displayed in full glory in the basement like a model railroad. Model languages exist on paper or in computer files and may be shared only with a few close friends or may be used to give depth to imaginary worlds read or watched by millions.

Millions of people have created model languages of some small scope. Many children invent their own secret vocabularies to share with friends, while teenagers may develop their own private slang to talk about the opposite sex. If few adults seem to create model languages, it is only because schools teach us that language is a formal structure, not a casual, informal world to be explored. The teaching of rigid dictionary definitions, sentence parsing and grammar dry up our interest in the wellspring of language.

Model languages demystify and demythologize the study of language. For too often, our desire to learn to express ourselves with language, to create new words, has been suppressed in favor of rigid conformance to the norm.

People now regard creating new words as a magical and distant process, yet it is something that we all engage in, though we may not even realize it at the time. While working as a market researcher, my boss once told me to "take the executive summary and bulletize it," offhandedly inventing the word *bulletize* to describe the act of paring paragraphs down to phrases preceded by • bullets. Over breakfast one morning, my wife asked me if I wanted *an English*, inadvertently inventing a new, shortened form of *English muffin*. During her pregnancy, we adopted the word *soogob* (*bogus* pronounced backwards) to describe how she was feeling. After our twins were born, we used the word *mouthies*, as in "Alex is making mouthies," to refer to the sucking motion each of the boys would make with their mouths when hungry.

Not one of these words will end up in the dictionary, but each serves a purpose and each demonstrates that we are all constantly inventing words, in a more carefree fashion than we might imagine. Lexicographers might decry the creation of many of these barbarisms, but it is from such coinages that the English language adapts to our times and needs. Millions of speakers provide a check and balance to ensure that only the most useful or needed of these coinages gains wide currency.

Different types of model languages

Why invent a model language? Someone might craft a language as a personal code, shared with a few companions. A fiction writer might want to add depth to an imaginary place or world, creating a language for inventing character names and place names or even for translating a few key proverbs or poems. A person who designs their own setting for a role-playing game might create a language for the same reason, or a person might invent a language to gain a better understanding of how true languages are structured and evolve. For a few, creating a language can be an almost spiritual effort, intended to close the gap that separates man from the Word of God. People create model languages for a myriad of other reasons — to create a universal language, to create a language for programming computers, or to simply learn more about how real languages work.

Even as a model railroad can vary in complexity from a simple loop to a switching yard to a railroad empire, a model language can be small or large. At its smallest, a model language might consist of a few coined words used in a short story. For instance, a science-fiction story I once wrote used the words *reconsat*, *moby* and *etlang* to describe a reconnaissance satellite, a cetacean alien and an extraterrestrial language, respectively.

Model Languages

A larger model language might be an entire dialect or slang, based on English. In *A Clockwork Orange*, Anthony Burgess writes the entire book in **Nadsat**, a slang used by teenagers in a near-future Britain. A sample:

> *Oh, it was gorgeosity and yumyumyum. When it came to the Scherzo I could viddy myself very clear running and running on like very light and mysterious nogas, carving the whole litso of the creeching world with my cutthroat britva. And there was the slow movement and the lovely last singing movement still to come. I was cured all right.*

The reader finds herself learning the language as she reads each page — learning by immersion. Nadsat has about 300 words.

Even more ambitious is the creation of a FICTIONAL LANGUAGE: a unique language, to add verisimilitude to a world. Harry Harrison in his book *West of Eden* had a linguist, T.A. Shippey, create a language for his saurians, the ruling race of an alternative earth where the dinosaurs evolved into sentient beings. An example:

> **Enge hantèhei, agatè embokèka lirubushei kakshèsei, hèawahei; hevai'ihei, kaksheintè, enpelei asahen enge.**
> To leave father's love and enter the embrace of the sea is the first pain of life — the first joy is the comrades who join you there.

Shippey did not create an entire language, of course, but outlined a structure and then created a simple grammar and skeletal lexicon to give the impression of a full language.

More ambitious still is a model language that is actually meant to be used to communicate. Such a language requires a vocabulary of at least 1,000 to 2,000 words and a detailed grammar. The most famous such language is **Esperanto**. Dr. Zamenhof invented Esperanto as a universal language to enable everyone to communicate without having to use any one social group's language. Esperanto was seen as perfect for a country like India, which has over 150 languages, with speakers of different languages separated by centuries-old hatreds.

Finally, the most ambitious language involves the creation of an entire DIACHRONIC language system — an imaginary language descended from other real or imaginary languages, based on principles of sound change and semantic shift. J.R.R. Tolkien, in *The Silmarillion*, created an entire language system with two primary languages and five secondary languages descended from a common root tongue. Thus primitive *galadaa*, "tree", became *alda* in **Quenya** and *galadh* in **Sindarin**. Such a system is so detailed that it can enthrall someone for a lifetime, and Tolkien never finished his system (though completion was not one of his goals).

This newsletter's goals

> *The Kings Heath house backed on to a railway line, and life was punctuated by the roar of trains and the shunting of trucks in the nearby coal-yard. Yet the railway cutting had grass slopes, and here [the young Tolkien] discovered flowers and plants. And something else caught his attention: the curious names on the coal-trucks in the sidings below, the odd names which he did not know how to pronounce but which had a strange appeal to him. So it came about that by pondering over Natyglo, Senghenydd, Blaen-Rhondda, Penrhiwceiber, and Tredegar, he discovered the existence of the Welsh language.*
>
> *Later in childhood he went on a railway journey to Wales, and as the station names flashed past him he knew that here were words more appealing to him than any he had yet encountered, a language that was old and yet alive.*
>
> Humphrey Carpenter, *Tolkien: A Biography*, p. 28

If you've read this far, model languages intrigue you, and you might even try your hand at creating your own. Alternatively, perhaps language in general fascinates you, and you want to understand better how languages work. In either case, this newsletter will introduce you to the basic principals that undergird real languages and will show you how to create your own languages, whether of a few words or a complete historic system.

The purpose of this newsletter is to teach you just enough about linguistics to be able to create your own model languages. It is not meant as a formal survey of the entire field of linguistics. Linguistics is too often presented in a dry manner, when it can be a source of endless wonder. It is no coincidence that a linguist created one of the most amazing novels of the twentieth century (Tolkien and *The Lord of the Rings*). This newsletter is meant to evoke the playfulness of linguistics and to give us an opportunity for hands-on training, as it were.

Issues of this newsletter will discuss how languages use sound and sound representation, how they form words, shapes meanings, and represent grammar. It will also outline how each of these characteristics of a language change over time. It will provide practical guidance on how to create your own languages, how to coin words and how to use language to add verisimilitude to imagined worlds. *Model Languages* will also examine published model languages and critique their effectiveness.

This newsletter is for those who want to learn more about language. You may have a fascination with words, wondering where they came from and how they ended up in today's most natural sounding forms. This newsletter is intended for writers, for entry-level linguistic students, for word lovers and for role-playing game players.

One of the great advantages of model languages as a hobby is that it requires so little investment. Unlike model railroading, which requires costly equipment and paraphernalia, model languages require little more than pen and paper... and imagination.

Subscribe to *Model Languages*, and soon you will be combining sounds into new words, like an engineer hitching up the cars of a train to an engine. Soon you will be laying the track of a linguistic system.

A Naming Language

Volume I, Issue 2 — June 1, 1995

Inventing a language for naming people and places

> "My name is Alice, but-"
>
> "It's a stupid name enough!" Humpty Dumpty interrupted impatiently; "What does it mean?"
>
> "Must a name mean something?" Alice asked doubtfully.
>
> "Of course it must," Humpty Dumpty said with a short laugh: "my name means the shape I am — and a good handsome shape it is, too. With a name like yours, you might be any shape, almost."
>
> Lewis Carroll, *Through the Looking Glass*

Despite Humpty Dumpty's comment, Alice could not be just any shape — her name actually summons forth an image of someone who is simple and proper, according to surveys conducted to determine the impressions people have of different names. All names have perceptions attached to them.

Etymologically speaking, Alice's name is from Germanic "nobleness". Most American and European names have become simple labels, their original meanings forgotten. How many people realize that a name like *Jeffrey Henning*, if translated literally, means "Godpeace Meadowlark"? Meanwhile, Native American names like "Dances With Wolves" (to take a bad example) wear their etymologies on their sleeves.

If you are fascinated by the origins of names, then you will be happy to learn that a NAMING LANGUAGE is one of the most useful types of model languages to create — and one of the easiest, making a great first language for the hobbyist. A naming language can be less complex than other model languages, since it does not need a detailed grammar and since it can get by with a small vocabulary: with just 150 words, you can generate millions of names for imaginary people and places. Once you've read this issue, you'll be able to create two or three naming languages in as little as a half hour, though you'll end up fascinated by your creations and will spend many more hours on them.

To begin creating any type of model language, you must be able to create words in that language. To create words, you need to understand sounds, meaning, sound change and so forth. This issue will introduce you to the basic aspects of language; subsequent issues of *Model Languages* will explore each one in more depth.

Language change

The vocabulary of languages is constantly changing, as technology changes and as our understanding changes. Twenty years ago no one talked of *faxes*, *PCs* or being *on-line*. No one had heard of *perestroika*. Things were still *groovy*, *nizza*, *happening*. Besides adding and retiring words, languages put new spins on old words: *gay* now primarily refers to "homosexuality", not "happiness"; *liberal* now is almost a curse, referring to "favoring governmental power" when it once meant "favoring governmental power to promote social progress". These word changes are not surprising. Any of us can look over the linguistic landscape of our lives and see how the terrain has changed. If you project this forward a thousand years, it is easy to see how the shape of a language's vocabulary will go through major upheaval.

It's harder to see that the grammar of the language, the way we put words together, will change too. While saying *hopefully* is still frowned upon, it is no longer viewed as completely ungrammatical. The pronoun *they* is often used to refer to one person, rather than the plural it is formally meant to refer to; in casual conversation and writing, *they* is now the gender-indifferent alternative to *he or she* (incidentally, as it was four hundred years ago, before pedantic grammarians — yes, *them* — stepped in). Looking a thousand years out, other grammatical distinctions will have been leveled, revealing new horizons behind them.

Finally, it can be hard to realize that the very sounds we use for words change. It's not hard to believe the occasional word changes, such as knowing that *cupboard* is now pronounced *cubboard*, the [p] sound having assimilated to the following [b]. It is harder to believe that English words that now begin with [p] and date from Indo-European all began with [b] in Indo-European times. Such systemic changes, where a sound changes throughout the entire vocabulary, happen gradually.

To imagine how it happens, think of a dialect, such as the Bostonian's "idear about whether the cah is pahked in Hahvahd yahd". Sound changes systematically when these dialectal differences become emulated and become the new accepted pronunciations. Imagine an alternate universe where JFK served out 8 years as the U.S. President, and was succeeded by 8 years of RFK, who was followed by 8 years of Teddy (it had to happen in some universe!). No doubt in that universe the Bostonian accent became American English's new standahd.

Basic sound changes do not happen suddenly like earthquakes buckling the landscape, but gradually like water eroding a shoreline. Language change is for the most part slow, since change is on the whole discouraged. The whole point of language is for people to be able to make themselves understood to each other, and this happens best in an environment where the language changes no faster than the land at the water's edge.

Language change is important because it shows the best way for you to invent a model language — by making changes to an existing language (whether natural or a model).

An ancestral language — the grandmother tongue

Every person alive today has or had a mother. Similarly, every mother tongue spoken by all these people had an ancestral language that it evolved out of. Even Proto-Indo-European, the reconstructed ancestor language of hundreds of European and Indian languages, had an ancestral language it evolved out of: Nostratic, which some linguists hypothesize was also the ancestor to five other PROTO-LANGUAGES. Since Nostratic itself is most likely descended from another language, records of the first language are no more knowable than records of Adam.

The ramifications for the language modeller are that the language he or she creates should not spring fully armed from the head of Zeus like Athena, but should derive from its own parent language. Most model languages are unknown orphans, when a pedigree would not have been hard to provide. Tolkien is one of the few modelers to actually create an ancestor tongue, which he used to derive many different Elvish languages for *The Lord of the Rings*, of which the best known are Quenya and Sindarin.

"Wait a minute," you might be thinking, "are you saying that to create a model language I first have to create another model language? Where does that language come from? When does it end?" Tolkien again provides the best example; he created root words in a proto-language; he imagined that the elves would have reconstructed their ancestral language, much as Europeans reconstructed Indo-European. Proto-languages are elaborate hypothetical constructions and, as hypotheses, are fuzzy around the edges: nothing but the bones of an extinct dinosaur, while the exact color of its flesh can never be known. A proto-language, therefore, can be a simpler form of model language.

The benefit of creating a proto-language is that it makes it easier to create sister languages to the model language you are chiefly interested in (what, more languages?!), enabling you to formulate new words based on regularly sound changes (more on this in it a minute). It also makes it easier to coin words in your desired model language, providing a rich system of root words to use to derive new words. So creating a proto-language can save you time.

The easiest way to save time on your first model language is to use an existing language as the proto-language. I once worked on a science fiction story set aboard a colony whose original settlers had been 20th- century Italians and Spaniards, who — through centuries of living together — had created a new, simpler language. By using Italian as the ancestor language, with many borrowings from Spanish, I not only made it easier to create a new language but I taught myself some Italian and Spanish as well!

If you are writing about a story that has taken place in the last 10,000 years and is set in Europe or India, you might even use Proto-Indo-European as the ancestral language for your languages. Check out *The Roots of English* by Robert Claiborne for an easily readable discussion of Indo-European roots, or check out the appendix to *The American Heritage Dictionary of the English Language*, published by Houghton Mifflin; both works are biased toward emphasizing roots from which English words descended, but make good starting points for devising a language.

Sound

To create your language, you need to decide which sounds you want speakers to distinguish. Basically, while it would be easy to think that the sound [t] is always the same, [t] actually describes a range of sounds, all closely approximating one another. The way you position your tongue when saying [t] will vary depending on what other sounds you say before or after it, but we articulate these [t] sounds similarly enough to recognize them as the same thing.

There is no objective reference that says a language must have any particular sound. For instance, Old English did not distinguish between the sounds [f] and [v] or [s] and [z]. The plural of [hoof] was pronounced [hoovz] but it was not until later times that speakers treated the /f/ sound in the singular as different from the /f/ sound in the plural. In Old English times, there could be no word [vat] different from [fat] — such a distinction was just not made. Gradually, the sounds came to be heard as distinct.

So when creating the sounds of your language, you need to realize that they will only approximate English sounds, not exactly match them, and might not reflect distinctions currently made in English. The [hw] sound in *whale* might be regarded by your speakers as the same as the [w] sound in *wail* (if you do pronounce these differently— not all English speakers do so).

You can certainly include in your language sounds that are not part of English, say the French vowels [y ø œ], pronounced with the lips rounded, or the expectorating [x] of Hebrew and Yiddish, let alone the clicking sounds of Khoisan. However, you should refrain from having too many unusual sounds in your language; you want your readers to be able to pronounce your words without too much difficulty. Simply having regular sounds combined in unique ways (e.g., *sretan*, or *tsedet*) will be enough to convince them it is a unique language anyway.

Languages are very strict about PHONOTACTICS, how sounds are combined. English, for instance, allows words to begin with [sn-], but never [zn-]. The rules English uses could fill pages, but as a modeler you want to just hint at complexity. You may want to have a combination that is unusual in English and make it frequent in your language: for instance, have some words begin with [sr-], [kn-], [kθ-], [tl-], but here again restraint is the order of the day.

As you specify how sounds can be combined, you may want to outline valid syllables. Your language might only allow syllables of CVC (Consonant+Vowel+Consonant) or just CV or VC. Some languages, like Japanese or Korean, have very strict limits on how syllables can be formed, making it possible to list all the valid syllables of the language. But where Hawaiian allows just 162 different syllables, Thai has 23,638 syllables.

Two languages can have the exact same consonants and vowels and yet sound very different, depending on the syllable patterns and on the frequency of the consonants and vowels. You may want to list the sounds that occur most often. By paying rigorous attention to this when developing the proto-language, you can relax a little more during creation of the descendant language, which will carry on many of the same frequency patterns, though applied to different sounds as the sounds change.

Many languages have very simple vowel systems. Eskimo-Aleut has just three vowels, while Spanish and Japanese each have five vowels. The typical language has between 5 and 7 vowels, but Indo-European languages usually have more: English has 12, and German has 14. The African language !Xũ has the record with 24 vowels.

Languages have been observed to have anywhere from six consonants (Rotokas) to 95 (!Xũ), with an average of 22.8 consonants. The typical language has twice as many consonants as vowels. The most common consonants include [p], [b], [t], [d], [k], [g], [x], [f], [s], [ʃ], [m], [n], [ŋ], [w], [l], [r], [j] and [h].

For a great discussion of the sound structure of languages, check out *The Cambridge Encyclopedia of Language* by David Crystal.

Sound change

Over time, sounds gradually change in certain circumstances. John F. Kennedy, like many Bostonians, would drop his last [-r] from words like [car], except before vowels, leading to inserted r's elsewhere ("my idear is..."). As alluded to before, had enough Americans adopted this, it would have been considered a regular sound change and many other words might have undergone this change. Or listen to the dialect of Brooklyn, where [bird] becomes [bojd]; someday all English speakers might pronounce [ir] as [oj]. No doubt, through the rise of one dialect in Old English, the sound [sk] changed to [ʃ].[2]

Over great periods of time, these changes become more pronounced. Literally and figuratively.

Here are some common ways consonants evolve into one another:

    b ↔ gw, p, v
    ch ↔ kw
    d ↔ g, t, th
    f ↔ p, v
    g ↔ k, w, y, z
    gw ↔ gu, b, g, k, ku, kw, v, y, zh

---

[2] Common IPA symbols are defined in the introduction. Confusingly, English *y* is IPA [j]. —MR

h ↔ hy, k, s, y
hw ↔ hv, kw, p
k ↔ g, gw, h, kw, s, th, kw
kw ↔ gw, ku, ch, hw, k, kh, kv, p, sh, t
l ↔ r
p ↔ b, f, hw, pf
r ↔ l
s ↔ h, k, kw
t ↔ d, th
th ↔ d, k, t
v ↔ b, f, gw
w ↔ g, v
y ↔ g, gw, h, z
z ↔ g, t, y
zh ↔ gw

This list is not meant to be all inclusive, just representative of changes that occurred in Indo-European.[3]

Likelihood Of Sound Change

Number of IE Languages where IE initial consonant changed:

gh	12						
kw	11						
d	4						
l	1						
gw	12	g	9	s	4	r	1
gwh	12	w	9	p	3	m	0
bh	11	k	7	t	2	n	0
dh	11	b	4	y	2		

You can use the above table as a rough guide to determine which consonants are more likely to undergo change. It is not representative of all languages, being an analysis of 12 languages descended from Proto-Indo-European and showing the number of languages where the consonant in

---

[3] Most of these changes are forms of LENITION. E.g. voiceless stops /p t k/ become voiced /b d g/ or fricatives /f θ x/ at the same place of articulation, or weaken entirely to /h/. /kw/ → /p/ combines the stop feature from /k/ and the labial place of articulation from /w/. —MR

the word-initial position changed. The languages analyzed were Armenian, Avestan, Common Germanic, Greek, Hittite, Latin, Lithuanian, Old Church Slavonic, Old Irish, Old Persian, Sanskrit, and Tocharian.

The nasals, [n] and [m], are fairly stable, as are the liquids [l] and [r]. The stops [p], [t] and their voiced counterparts [b] and [d] change in only a third of the languages. All aspirated consonants changed in every language analyzed, being markedly unstable; [k] and [g] and their glide forms [kw] and [gw] were also more likely to change than not.

Sound changes actually vary by position, with a sound change applying to different places – the [s] might become [h] at the beginning of a word, [k] in the middle of a word and [z] at the end of a word (though this is an extreme example). For simplicity's sake, you may just want to apply the same changes regardless of position.

Environmental changes

Besides these phonetic changes, there are often ENVIRONMENTAL changes in words, where sounds change because of the sounds they are near. The following examples illustrate the major types of sound change.

ASSIMILATION: a sound is influenced by adjoining sounds.

> REGRESSIVE or ANTICIPATORY: a sound is influenced by the following sound. English [kupbord] became [kubbord]; the word *assimilation* is itself an example: Latin *adsimulāre* became *assimulāre*, since [ad-] regularly assimilated to [as-] before [s].
>
> PROGRESSIVE: a sound is influenced by a preceding sound. E.g. Germanic *wulnō > *wullō > wool.
>
> COALESCENT or RECIPROCAL: two neighboring sounds influence one another: Sanskrit *ātman* > Middle Indic *appan* 'self'.

DISSIMILATION: a sound moves away from the pronunciation of neighboring sound: French *marbre* became English *marble* as the second [r] changed to contrast with the first.

SPLIT: a sound becomes regarded as two distinct sounds, such as Old English [s] compared to Modern English [s] and [z]. Old English's failure to distinguish between the sounds is one of the reasons many Modern English words are written with 's' when we say [z],

METATHESIS: two sounds change places, *third* from Old English *thridda*.

CLUSTER SIMPLIFICATION: one of a cluster of consonants is omitted. English *cnoccian* > *knock* [nak]; [kubbord] > [kubord].

ELISION: loss of an unstressed vowel or syllable: *elementary* becomes [elementri] when the final schwa sound [ə] is elided.

LOSS: a sound disappears from the language altogether, as the velar fricative [x] (and the final sound of Scottish *loch*), did in English, with only a vestige remaining in English spelling: the silent *gh* of English words like *light, night, sight*, which were once pronounced [lixt], [nixt] and [sixt].

HAPLOLOGY: the loss of a sequence of sounds because of similarity of neighboring sounds: Latin *nutrītrīx* > *nutrīx* 'nurse'. Should this ever be called *haplogy* it will have undergone haplology itself.

SYNCOPE: the loss of medial sounds, as *boatswain* lost the [t] sound as it was shortened to [bosən].

APOCOPE: the loss of final sounds, as in the silent 'e' in words like *love* and *hate*. Of course, the silent 'e' used to be pronounced.

PROTHESIS: introduction of an extra initial sound, as occurred in Spanish and Old French, which frequently inserted an [e] sound before an initial [s] + C: for instance, Latin *specialis* became Spanish *especial.*

EPENTHESIS: introduction of extra medial sound, as Old English *bræmel* became *braembel* (modern *bramble*). This is not just random; [m] and [b] are similar, both being labial stops.

LIAISON: Sometimes a sound is mostly lost, but reappears in some contexts. The Bostonian's "ideah" becomes "idear" when the next word begins with a vowel.

You can quickly generate more than one language by inventing **different sound change rules for each language**. So perhaps the Dilbertian [d] becomes [t] in Dogbertian, whereas it becomes [ð] in Dinobertian. Or take a look at how the names *James, John* and *Katherine* have evolved in seven different languages:

English	James	John	Katherine
French	Jacques	Jean	Catherine
German	Jakob	Johann	Katharina
Italian	Giacomo	Giovanni	Caterina
Spanish	Jaime	Juan	Catalina
Swedish	Jakob	John, Johan	Karin, Katarina

Yiddish   *Dzheymz*   *Yohan*   *Katerine*

Webster's Third New International Dictionary

Names vary idiosyncratically and do not always evolve according to the regular sound changes that affect other words. Thus the English towns of *Luton* and *Leyton* are — despite their differences — both derived from the same word, *Lygetun*, "farm by the river Lea" (the river Lea, incidentally, may either mean "bright one" or may represent the name of a river god, Lugus).

Names get shortened frequently; for instance, *Johann, Giovanni* and *Yohan* all indicate that there used to be an [a] sound after before the [n] in *John* and that the silent [h] in *John* used to be pronounced, and still is in German, Swedish and Yiddish.

Spelling

When inventing your own language, you can go all out — inventing your own alphabet or even hieroglyphs to accompany it. You can have spellings that represent scholarly thinking about how the word derived, so that the word sounding like [gramilt] is actually spelled '*kramillid*', for instance, because lexicographers believe the word [gramilt] used to be pronounced [kramillid]. You can invent new symbols or use old symbols to represent sounds, so that *pra@t!so>r* is pronounced... oh, never mind.

Or, you can spare users of your language a lot of difficulty; you can strive for a system of spelling that is phonetic. Since learning a new language is difficult enough, this is the course I recommend. Yes, I'm hooked on phonics.

Be warned, however, that even a phonetic representation can present difficulties, if you yourself are mistaking English spellings and conventions for actual pronunciations. For instance, if you were representing English phonetically, you might think that you could specify that the plural was regularly formed by adding [-s] to the end of a word. While this is true for [cat], it is not true for *dog*, whose plural is actually pronounced [dogz]; *church*, for its part, has a plural of [tʃurtʃez]. So make sure your phonetic spelling really describes the sound you want.

One problem with phonetic spelling is that words are pronounced differently in different circumstances: the word a can be pronounced [ei] or as [ə] (schwa), and can be pronounced [ənd], [ən] or [n], depending on whether or not the speaker is placing emphasis on them.

While you can use special characters for sounds, it will be easier on your readers if you transcribe them using conventional letters. The letter 'h' is great for forming digraphs; you might say that 'rh' represents a trilled [r] sound, or that 'mh' might be an aspirated [m] (sounding similar to [v]), or that 'dh' represents the voiced th [θ] in *then*, while 'th' represents the unvoiced th [ð] in *thin*.

Your spelling may even reflect a regular sound change of the language. For instance, in German, the final 'b' in a word sounds like [p], the final 'd' like [t], and the final 'g' like [k], so *Korb* is pronounced [korp], *Band* [bant] and *Tag* [tak].

Words

Once you have created sounds, you can begin generating words. Words are nothing more than sounds arbitrarily linked to meanings. ONOMATOPOEIA refers to sounds that are imitative, such as *arf, bark* or *bow-wow* for the sounds a dog makes. Most words are not onomatopoetic. Tolkien once remarked that he found *cellar door* to be an incredibly beautiful series of sounds, though the meaning was not worthy of it.[4] So don't slave over matching sounds to words. If you spend all your time thinking about the exact sound each word should have you'll never flesh out your vocabulary.

Grammar

It can make learning new words somewhat easier if they have to follow specific patterns depending on parts of speech. Your language might require the root form of all verbs to end in [-r] and all nouns might end in a vowel.

A naming language does not need a complex grammar. The only grammatical decision you really need to make is how to form compound words: should the modifier proceed or follow the word being modified. Assume you have a language with the word *kwan* for "dog" and *kooz* for "house". Does the phrase *kwan kooz*, then, mean "doghouse" or "house dog"?

---

[4] Being English, he presumably said [sɛlaːdɔː]. —MR

Proper names

Many common names were formed from surprisingly few elements. If you coin just 150 words in a model language, you will be able to generate millions of distinct names.

I analyzed about 300 common English and European names to come up with the following tables of common meanings underlying these names.

Adjectives for proper names

bear-like	beloved	bitter	blessed	brave
chief	compassionate	constant	desired	divine
eagle-like	earnest	falcon-like	famous	flowering
fortunate	fox-like	free	hallowed	happy
industrious	laughing	lion-like	loyal	manly
mighty	noble	northern	patriotic	peaceful
powerful	praiseworthy	prayerful	protecting	pure
ready	sharp	shining	small	strong
strong-willed	swift	valiant	victorious	war's
wealthy	wise	wolf-like	worthy	young

Nouns for proper names

arrow	battle	bearer	brightness	counselor
crown	defender	dweller	earth	farmer
father	fighter	forest	gate	gift
giver	God	guardian	hammer	harvester
healer	helper	home	horse	keeper
laurel	leader	lily	lover	maid
man	pearl	people	protector	rock
rose	ruler	runner	smith	son
spear	staff	steward	stranger	stronghold
sword	traveler	twin	warrior	wolf

You can use these tables to generate names in the following ways:

- **adjective**: "Pure" (*Katherine*)
- **adjective + adjective**: "Noble and Shining" (*Alberta*)
- **adjective + noun**: "Chief Protector" (*Howard*)
- **noun + noun**: "Elf Ruler" (*Avery*)

- **adjective + adjective + noun**: "Noble, Brave Warrior" (*Gunther*)
- **adjective + noun + noun**: "Strong Warrior Twin"
- **adjective + adjective + noun + noun**: "Young Bear-like Battle Hammer"

You can use these tables to generate almost all the names you need. Theoretically you could use these tables to generate 6.3 million names.

Feel free to use a few elements that you like in many different names; for example, "famous" in Anglo-Saxon was represented by *hroth* and is contained in the names *Rodney* ("famous"), *Robert* ("famous brightness"), *Roland* ("most famous of the land"), *Roderick* ("famous ruler"), *Rudolph* ("famous wolf") and *Roger* ("famous spear"). *Roger*, incidentally, was spelled *Hrothgar* in Old English, and is the name of the beleaguered king in *Beowulf*.

You can easily flesh out the above tables to better represent the culture of the people who will speak your model language. For instance, islanders would not name people after wolves and foxes, but after predators peculiar to their locale, such as sharks and octopuses. Their names would reflect people's relationship to the sea: sailors, divers, swimmers and beachcombers. The tools they would refer to would not be swords and spears, but tridents and hooks. The adjectives they would use would likewise reflect their environment: *unsinkable, seaworthy* and *foamy*.

If you want to add additional words to these tables, check out the etymologies of real names; one good source is *The Baby Boomer's Name Game* by Christopher Andersen, which includes an etymological dictionary of 2,500 common names.

Place names

The names of people and places are intimately related. For instance, *Winslow* (a town in Buckinghamshire, England) is named after *Wine* (an Old English name meaning "friend") and means something like "Wine's hill", "Wine's burial mound" or perhaps even "Wine's estate at the burial mound". In turn, *Winslow* is a man's first name and means "from Winslow". Many place names become first or last names in this way, and these in turn might inspire new place names; some other town of Winslow might be named after a fellow named Winslow — and so it goes.

Most names refer to a natural feature, such as a river, a hill or a forest, or to a man-made construction, such as a fort, a road or a burial mound.

Naming Languages

Place names are very seldom taken from an event that may have happened there, such as a battle or a coronation, but do sometimes take names from recurring events — a field where people are regularly executed or married (I'll refrain from comparing these activities!) might have a name like the *Hangingfield* or the *Weddingfield*. For instance, the village of "*Kingstone*" is not likely to be so named because some king drew a sword from a stone there, but rather because many monarchs have been coronated there (or stoned there, depending on the kingdom's traditions!).

Place names in the British Isles tend to be formed from 50 basic root meanings, which are given below. These 50 meanings can be combined to give 2450 different names, and can be combined to form millions more when combined with names involving people (e.g., *Boston*, "Botwulf's stone"; the ending is not *-ton*, "town", but *-ston*).

Meaning	*English/Irish/Welsh word element*
abbey	Abbey-
bridge	Pont-, -bridge
castle	Castle
church	Eccle(s)-, Kil(l)-, Kirk-, Llan-, -church
cottage	-cot
dwelling	-wich, -wick
enclosure	Lis-, -wardine, -worth
estate	-land
farm	-ton, -by
field	-field
ford	-ford
fort	Caer-, -b(o)rough, -burgh, -bury
fort(old fort)	-caster, -c(h)ester
fort(ring fort)	Rath-
height	Ard-
highland	Blaen-, -head
hill	Bryn-, Dun-, -don
hilltop	Pen-
holy place	-stead, -stede, -stow
home farm	-hampton
homestead	Bally-, -ham(stead), -hampstead
island	Ennis-, -ey
lake	Loch-
meadow	Clon-
monastery	-minster
moor	-more, -moor

mountain peak	Ben-
new	New-
pass	-gate
people of	-ing(s)
place	Stock-, Stoke-
pond	-mer(e)
port	Port-, -port
resort	-ville
river mouth	Aber-, Bel(la)-, Inver-, -mouth
riverside	-side
rock	Carrick-
secondary settlement	-stock, -stoke, -thorpe
stone	-ston(e)
stream	-b(o)urne, -well
town	Ballin(a)-
tree	-tree, -try
upper	Auchter-
valley	Glen-, Strath-, -dale
valley (narrow)	-combe
valley (wooded)	-den
village	Tre-
wood	Rhos-, Ros-, Ross-, -wood
wooded angle of land	-shot(t)
woodland	-ley, -le, -leigh

After Adrian Room, *Dictionary of Place Names in the British Isles*

Place names can be formed from combinations of the affixes listed above and from other place names and proper names:

- **affix + affix**: "New Town" (*Newton*)
- **affix + affix + affix**: "New Town on the Moor" (*Newtonmore*)
- **affix + affix + placename**: "New Town in Mearns [a county]" (*Newton Mearns*)
- **placename + affix**: "Newton-of-the-Abbey" (*Newton Abbot*)
- **placename + propername**: Newton Stewart [after William Stewart]
- **propername + placename**: "Hynca's Enclosure" (*Hinxworth*)

Often when you analyze a place name, you will find that a river runs through it: *Exeter* (from *Exchester*) means "fortification on the river Exe", *Exmoor* is "moorland along Exe", *Exmouth* is at the mouth of Exe, while *Exwick* is a "farm by the Exe".

Exe itself means simply "water", from the British Celtic *isca*. (This may seem boring, but *isca* is part of "the water of life" that entered English — through Scottish Gaelic — as *whiskey*!) Many names of rivers, mountains and other features of the landscape come from general words. Imagine an Englishman pointing to a river and asking, "What do you call that?" The native Celt might have simply said *teme*, "river", since to him or her it was "the river", the prominent river in the area and hence not in need of its actual name in typical conversation. And thereby a noble river such as the *Thames* would have been christened.

To create the name of a city on a river then, you'll have to name the river first — and that name might derive from another language, as the Thames shows.

Place names often incorporated terms from other languages. For instance, the Celtic city of *Eborakon* — meaning "place of *Eburos* (the yew man)" — had its name Romanicized to *Eburacum*. This name was meaningless to the invading Saxons, who Anglicized it as *Eofor* ("boar", which had a similar sound) and appended *wīc* ("dwelling place"), to give it the name of *Eoforwīc*. When the Vikings invaded, they misconstrued *wic* as *vi-k* (which meant "bay" and was inappropriate to the inland city but stuck anyway); since *Eofor* was meaningless to them, there was no pressure to keep the first syllables recognizable, and the name was gradually shortened to *Jarvik*. This in turn was later shortened to *York*, the name as it stands today and as it may stand until the city is invaded again. York's name was not directly affected by the fall of England to the Normans, the only conquerors not to leave their mark on it. If the Normans' ancestors, the Vikings, had had as little effect on the city's name, York's modern name might very well be *Everwick*.

The history of the name York reveals five waves of occupation (Celtic, Roman, Saxon, Viking, English) and so tells a lot about the fortunes of the city. While you do not want to go into as much detail for each name in your own imaginary world, this history is worth creating for the most important place names. To rival the history of York, you'd have to invent five model languages!

In the same way you're best prepared to write a poem if you studied a lot of poems, you're best prepared to coin a place name by studying how other people have coined place names. To this end, I definitely recommend reviewing an etymological dictionary like *Dictionary of Place Names in the British Isles*, which covers over 4,000 place names. Each name tells a story, as the name of York shows.

Example - quickly create your own naming languages

The following quick sketch of three languages — Nagada, Makata and Negasi — will show you how you can quickly create your own naming systems.

The consonants of **Nagada** are [b], [d], [g], [s], [m], [n], [l], [r] and [h]. The vowels are [a], [e] and [u]. The vowels differ greatly in frequency: [a] is used about twice as often as [e], which is used slightly more often than [u]. All syllables in Nagada follow the form CV (Consonant+Vowel).

The language of **Makata** is descended from Nagada and showed the following sound changes: [b] > [p], [d] > [t], [g] > [k], [m] > [n] and [n] > [m].

The language of **Negasi** went through different changes from Nagada. The only consonantal change was that of [d] > [t] > [s]. Vowels changed depending on the syllable they appeared in:

Vowel	First syllable	Final syllable
[a]	[e]	[i]
[e]	[u]	[a]
[u]	[a]	[o]

For instance, the Nagada word *naba* became *nebi* in Negasi.

All words in the three languages are spelled phonetically. All three languages put the modifier before the word being modified (e.g., "doghouse" means "the house for dogs").

Here are the root words of Nagada and how those words appear in Makata and Negasi.

	Nagada	*Makata*	*Negasi*
"bearer"	ba	pa	be
"beloved"	naba	mapa	nebi
"blessed"	luma	peta*	lami
"divine"	luma	luna	luna*
"giver"	ge	ke	gu
"healer"	dala	tala	seli
"lily"	hama	hana	heni
"pearl"	rele	rele	rula
"shining"	dube	tupe	saba
"swift"	sahu	sahu	seho

Naming Languages

There was not room in this short introduction to cover borrowing or meaning change or any of the other factors that can override direct descent from a parent language, and I will give only one example here: Negasi borrowed *luna* from Makata to distinguish between the meanings of "divine" and "blessed", which were both reflected by the single word *luma* in Nagada. Makata, for its part, coined the word *peta* for "blessed" to distinguish between the two concepts.

Based on these words, here are some common names in the three languages.

	Nagada	*Makata*	*Negasi*
"blessed pearl"	Lumarele	Petarele	Lamirula
"divine healer"	Lumadala	Lunatala	Lunaseli
"swift healer"	Sahudala	Sahutala	Sehoseli
"lily giver"	Hamage	Hanake	Henigu
"pearl bearer"	Releba	Relepa	Rulabe

The above table assumes the meanings of the names were kept current (like "Dances With Wolves") rather than fossilized. If the meanings were instead forgotten, then the Makata and Negasi forms would have been shaped simply by changing the sounds of the words. So Nagada *Lumarele* would be Makata *Lunarele*, rather than *Petarele*.

If I was actually going to use these names in a story, I would spend much more time refining them to develop an affinity between the sound of a name and the character I wanted to represent. However, taking the words as they are can provide insights into the imagined people. I think *Lumarele* is a great name for an island princess, and I can picture *Sahudala*, the impotent witch doctor who wants her hand in marriage, but the name of her jealous sister *Hamage* carries with it the stench of lilies, rather than their sweet aroma...

Gymnastics with Onomastics

Volume I, Issue 3 — July 1, 1995

Where the last issue of *Model Languages* described in detail how to create model languages for generating names, this issue specifically elaborates on how different languages and cultures form names.

Here are some useful terms to describe the study of names:

- ONOMASTICS - the study of names (in general)
- ANTHROPONOMASTICS - the study of personal names
- TOPONOMASTICS - the study of place names.

Structure of names

There are many different ways a culture can structure a name, and the people who speak your language may use any of the following, or a different way besides:

[given name] - *Jeffrey*

[given name] [family name] - *Jeffrey Henning* (American)

[family name] [given name] - *Mao Zedong* (Chinese)

[given name] [home town's name] - *John Zamoyski* (Polish, from town of Zamosc; toponymic)

[given name] [occupation name] - *John Smith* (English)

[given name] [maiden name] [husband's family name] - *Karen Flynn Henning* (American)

[given name] [middle name] [family name] - *Jeffrey Alan Henning* (American) [given name] [middle name] [confirmation name] [family name] - *Karen Lee Kristina Flynn* (Catholic Irish)

[given name] [family name] [occupation name] - *Mark Jones-the-petrol* (Welsh)

[given name] [father's name] ["son"] - *Bjørnstjerne Bjórnson* (Norse)

[given name] [father's name] ["daughter"] - *Vigdís Finnbogadøttir* (Norse)

[given name] [father's name + "child of"] [family name] - *Mikhail Sergeyevich Gorbachev* (Russian)

[given name] [middle name] [maternal grandfather's family name] [paternal grandmother's family name] [paternal grandfather's family name] — *Eliana Marcia Villela Gomes Soares* (Brazilian)

[given name] [middle name] [maternal grandfather's family name] [paternal grandfather's family name] [husband's mother's name] [husband's father's name] — *Maria Beatriz Villela Soares Veiga de Carualho* (Brazilian)

[given name] [father's family name] y [mother's family name] - *José Aguilar y Fernández* (Spanish)

[given name] [father's family name] de [husband's father's name] - *María Álvarez de Aguilar* (Spanish)

["father of"] [eldest son] — *Abu Hamid* (Arabic)

[given name] [father's given name] - *Tafari Makonnen* (Amharic)

This list is in no means exhaustive, with the possibility of variations even within a tradition. My friend Steve and his wife recently named their baby Joshua Patrick Lewis LaFrance Weissman: *Joshua Patrick* because they liked the Old and New Testament ring, *Lewis* after Steve's grandfather, *LaFrance* after his wife's surname, and *Weissman* because ... well, because!

Throughout much of history, when most people never traveled far from home, a given name sufficed, with use of a nickname in case there were two Davids in the village, for instance. As people were exposed to more and more people, the family name was added to differentiate people, then the middle name was added for the same purpose. As mass communications and the Internet expose people to that many more individuals, it would not be surprising if people begin making more prominent use of their middle names and begin adding extra middle names, like my friend Steve did for his son.

In Britain and the U.S., the first name, the given name, is the one the person regularly goes by. This is not so in Germany, where many people go by their middle names, so that *Helmut Michael Schneid* is likely to be called *Michael* by his friends, not *Helmut*.

Of course, many East Asian languages put the family name before the given name, reversing the regular order of Occidental names. Thus, *Mao Zedong* is known as Chairman Mao, not Chairman Zedong. Hungarian is another language that puts the family name first.

English names are unique in one respect — no other language has a construct similar to the *Sr.* ("Senior") that gets appended to the names of fathers who have sons with the same names, so that Carl Glenn Henning's eponymous father is known as *Carl Glenn Henning, Sr*. As for the *Jr.* appellation, it is used in English, Spanish and Portuguese names, among others, though not the Roman numeral designations II, III, IV and so on. Brazilian names have analogous structures to Jr., where *Neto* is to "grandson" and *Sobrinho* is to "nephew" as Júnior is to "son".*

Some languages, such as Russian, add gender endings to the family name, so that it is Mr. *Molotov*, but Mrs. *Molotova*. The Japanese routinely append an HONORIFIC to a person's name, such as *-san*; or *-sama*, a superhonorific; or *-kun*, for someone familiar or subordinate; or *-chan*, a term of endearment reserved for children.

Patronymics: in the name of the father

One of the more common elements of names is a PATRONYMIC, a reference to a person's father.

Language	Affix	Example
English	-son	Stevenson
Greek	-poulous	Cosmopoulus
Irish	O'-	O'Leary
Polish	-ski	Jaruzelski
Scots	Mac-, Mc-	MacDougal
Welsh	Ap	Ap Gwilym

Related to this, *Fitz-* (as in Fitzgerald) is Old French for "son of", though it was typically used to mean "illegitimate son of". (So the next time you're angry with some idiot, but your kids are listening, call him a "son of a Fitz".)

Amharic (a language of Ethiopia) no longer has a separate word for its patronymic, so a name is simply formed from the child's given name plus the father's given name (as if Robert Stevenson was just *Robert Steven*).

While English has fossilized its patronymic, so that for all we know Robert Louis Stevenson's father may have been named *Joe*, many languages — including Arabic, Hebrew and Icelandic — give a new patronymic to each generation. In such a culture, Robert Louis Stevenson's son Jeffrey would be known as *Jeffrey Robertson* and *his* son Thomas would be known as *Thomas Jeffreyson*, and so on, with each son given a different last name from his father.

The Russians use patronymics in such a way that children still have the same family name as their parents. In Russian, the patronymic is the middle name, so Ivan's son has the middle name of *Ivanovich*, while Ivan's daughter has the middle name of *Ivanovna*.

The Spanish and Portuguese are more fair to the people who carry these children for nine months. Both languages form last names from the family names of both the mother and father. In Brazilian, the name of the mother precedes the father's, so that the mother of *Eliana Marcia Villela Gomes Soares* has a surname of *Villela*, while Eliana's father had the surname of *Gomes Soares* (*Gomes* being the family name of his mother). Spanish reverses the order, putting the name of the father first.

Related to patronymics, but different altogether, is TEKNONYMY or PAEDONYMY, where the parent is named after the child. In Arabic, the parent would be known as "father of" or "mother of" the eldest son.

Constructing names

Forming first names first

The story is told, perhaps apocryphally, of a tribe in Nyassaland, Africa, that took its names from a publisher's book catalog that had found its way into their hands. The chief christened himself *Oxford University Press*. Ox, as his friends may have called him, had chosen his name in one of the more unusual ways. Typically, first names are formed from compounds, from saints' names, from places, from personal traits — in fact, from many things other than publisher's book catalogs.

German and Celtic frequently formed compounds (see the previous chapter). Examples of this style of first names include *Baldwin*, "bold friend", and *Gilbert*, "shining pledge".

The first name is often, especially in Britain, called the Christian name, because after the Norman Conquest the first name was frequently taken from that of a Christian saint (Matthew, Mark, Luke and others). Other traditions would name children after places (*Norton*, "from the northern village"; *Glenna*, "from the glen"), personal characteristics *(Joy; Kent,* "handsome"; *Kevin,* "kind") and even animals (I'm not going to mention "Dances With Wolves" again).

Arabic and Semitic, and many other languages, feature THEOPHORIC names, names referring to God, such as Arabic *Abdallah*, "servant of Allah", or Hebrew *Daniel*, "God is the judge", and *Michael*, "God-like". Anglo-Saxon names also referred to God, as in *Godfrey* referring to "God's peace" (and surviving in the more common name descended from Godfrey, *Jeffrey*). The Anglo-Saxons had not always been Christian, and older names made frequent use of *Alf-*, "elf", the elves being divine spirits, so that *Alfreda* meant "counselled by elves" and *Elvira* meant "elf-like" (making it a suitable name for the host of a horror-movie show).

Since the elves, if not appeased, might take a baby and leave a changling in its place, it was hoped that a child named after elves would be left alone by them. Other cultures take the fear of evil spirits further. If a mother had already lost a child to disease, she might be likely to name her next child after something vile, to keep evil spirits away. So her baby might be given an APOTROPAIC name like "Ugly" or "Misshapen".

A name like "Ugly" would not be accepted in many European countries. France, Germany and Scandinavia all have lists of approved first names; a baby must be given an approved name, or the child will not be legally recognized. (Perhaps a superstitious Norwegian will name his child "Illegal" in the hopes of keeping those modern evil spirits, lawyers, away.)

Incidentally, many languages do not have separate names for men and women, as if all names were like the English neuter names of *Chris, Alex, Lee* and *Kelly*. Other languages often use regular inflections for grammatical gender to indicate the gender of names, so that *John* and *Jane*, for instance, which are both from the same Hebrew name, are represented as *Johann* and *Johanna* in German, *Giovanni* and *Giovanna* in Italian and *Juan* and *Juana* in Spanish.

Forming family names

In America, melting pot of the world, there are over 1.2 million last names, according to an analysis of the Social Security rolls. In an analysis of my own business address book, consisting of 4,240 U.S. computer professionals, I found 2,936 unique names, ranging from Abate to Zytniak. Choosing any individual at random revealed a 48% chance that no one else in the address book had the same last name as them — this is simply an amazing diversity, representing the hundreds of cultures who have seen citizens migrate to the United States.

Koreans, in contrast, have just a few principal last names, such as Kim, Pak and Yi, though they have different spelling variations (Yi is also spelled Li, Lee, I and Rhee). Because ancestry is so important to Koreans, they have been culturally adverse to changing their last names; in fact, family names are so important that women do not change their family names upon getting married. As a result, Koreans have preserved the last names of the three major families that first settled the present-day Korean peninsula.

Like the Koreans, the Welsh also have few family names. So to tell apart all the people named Jones, Price or Evans, the Welsh tend to distinguish people with 'by-names', so that Welsh *Mark Jones-the-petrol* is distinguished from *Mark Jones-the-gardener*.

Many family names derived from such a casual use of referring to people by their occupations: farmer, weaver (e.g., *Webster*), baker. One of the most prestigious occupations in ancient times was that of the blacksmith, who forged swords into ploughshares in time of peace, and pikes into pole-arms in time of war. In fact, blacksmiths were among the most influential members of community, which is why the most common family name in many cultures is "Smith":

Arabic	*Haddad*
English	*Smith, Smythe*
French	*La Fèvre, La Forge*
German	*Schmidt*
Hungarian	*Kovács*
Portuguese	*Ferreiro*
Russian	*Kuznetsov*
Spanish	*Ferrer, Herrera*

Besides occupations and patronymics, other sources of family names include places (*Henning*, for instances, means "the meadow filled with larks"), colors (*White, Brown, Green*) and virtues (*Good*).

Forming names of nations

Many groups of people (races and nations) see themselves as "the people" of the world. If they are isolated from other tribes or realms, they are even more likely to name themselves "the people", as the Inuit (Eskimos), the Bantu (an African tribe) and the Illeni Indians (for whom Illinois is named) did; also the Germans (*Deutsch*). The Chinese name themselves after their ancient dynasty, the Han— though in English we name them for the *preceding* dynasty, the Qin.

The more different realms a group of people are aware of the more likely they are to name themselves after the place where they live: the Canadians live in Canada, the English live in England, the Germans live in Germany. But the Jews live in *Israel* (the name of one of their greatest ancestors).

If your imaginary people are imaginative enough to call themselves something besides "the people" or "the people of [place]", they will nonetheless give themselves a flattering name, something like "the people of God" or "the blessed people" or "the people of [person]", where the person is any suitably noble patriarch or matriarch.

So how did the English get to be called the *English*? Well, in the fifth and sixth centuries AD, the Angles, Saxons and Jutes migrated from northern Germany to southern Britain. The Angles' name was related to their word *angel*, "hook", and is assumed to refer to hook-shaped stretches of the German coast. By the ninth century, *Englaland* was used to describe the island all three tribes had settled, and the form of the name was quickly shortened (not by happenstance, but by haplology) to *England*.

Cultural attitudes towards names

> *No one knows a man's true name but himself and his namer. He may choose at length to tell it to his brother, or his wife, or his friend, yet even those few will never use it where any third person may hear it. In front of other people, they will, like other people, call him by his use-name, his nickname — such a name as Sparrowhawk, and Vetch, and Ogion which means 'fir-cone'. If plain men hide their true name from all but a few they love and trust utterly, so much*

> *more must wizardly men, being more dangerous, and more endangered. Who knows a man's name, holds that man's life in his keeping.*
>
> Ursula K. Le Guin, *A Wizard of Earthsea*

Names are invested with a power. Many cultures have private names, or true names, that are only to be used by family and close friends, with a public name used regularly instead. The fear is that a wizard or witch will learn their true name and so be able to cast a spell over them.

In Múharafic, the model language spoken by desert nomads in an exceptionally dry science fiction novel a friend and I once wrote, each person's name exerts power over them. The most powerful person in the clan is the watersinger, who names each child upon ascension to adulthood, and therefore knows the names of everyone in the clan. The watersinger can declare a person outcast by announcing his true name to everyone. Alternatively, a person can *gnomifesi*, "confide one's true name to another", to give themselves in marriage to their partner.

The Todas of India are not afraid to have their names known, but they will not themselves pronounce their own names. When an individual is introduced to someone new, she asks a companion to say her name.

As David Crystal writes in *The Cambridge Encyclopedia of Language*, "People in the 20th century may find it easy to dismiss such attitudes, but things have not greatly changed. It is unlikely that popular opinion would ever allow a new ship to be named *Titanic*."

> *Thanks to personal correspondence (January 6, 2005) from Mauro Mello Jr. for clarification on the use of Jr. in South America.*

Possibilities and Purposes

Volume I, Issue 3 (2/2) — July 1, 1995

> *Nobody believes me when I say that my long book [The Lord of the Rings] is an attempt to create a world in which a form of language agreeable to my personal aesthetic might seem real. But it is true. An enquirer (among many) asked what the L.R. was all about, and whether it was an allegory. And I said it was an effort to create a situation in which a common greeting would be* elen si-'la lu-'menn omentielmo *['A star shines on the hour of our meeting'], and that the phrase long antedated the book.*
> Letter from J.R.R. Tolkien to Christopher Tolkien, Feb. 21, 1958

Model languages come in many different sizes and types. You can classify a model language both for its scope and for who is intended to speak it.

Classifying by scope

For different scales, a model language might be used for jargon, names, proverbs, conversations or literature. Each layer of complexity requires a more detailed lexicon and grammar, ranging from a jargon consisting of a handful of words and a way of forming plurals to a complex language that can be used to carry on a conversation or support a literature.

Most of the model languages that have gained recognition have been intended for use as true languages, but many other model languages of smaller scale exist within works of fiction. Few writers can create an entire language, as Tolkien or Anthony Burgess did; few writers need that much detail in the first place.

When trying to decide what model language to create, you should not be intimidated by the magnitude of the works accomplished by Tolkien or Burgess — that would be like fearing to write a short story because you had read *War and Peace*.

Creating a language for jargon simply means you are only interested in having a few words to convey the flavor of another culture. A model jargon is rarely even dignified with a name, since it is so small. A science-fiction author might coin a few words for unusual aliens and new technologies. For instance, I do not recall much linguistically about Larry Niven's *Ringworld*, other than to remember that he coined the word *tanj*, "there ain't no justice", as the curse word used by his characters; no doubt he had coined other words to reflect the technology and topography of Ringworld and to enhance its ambience.

Classifying by time-frame of speakers

Besides classifying a model language by its use, you can classify a language by whether the people who speak it are alive today or are an imagined people of the past or future. A model language might be intended to represent the language of a people who lived in the remote past. It might be intended as a linguistic experiment, showing how a language might have evolved if the past had been changed (alternate past). A model language is commonly something intended for use in the present, such as Esperanto. Finally, it might be set in a future world, such as Burgess' Nadsat or Marc Okrand's Klingon.

Ideas for model languages

What follows are some ideas drawn from across the above classification matrix, to encourage you to create your own model language.

Naming languages

A naming language is a model language created primarily for the purpose of naming people, places and things in an imaginary country or world. It is the simplest type of language to create, since it doesn't need a detailed grammar.

Alternate languages

Science fiction contains a sub-genre of literature known as the alternate history, which postulates worlds that never existed, but might have. What if William the Conquerer, instead of Harold, had fallen at Hastings? What if the French Quebecois and their English neighbors had assimilated? What if the Moors had not stopped at Spain but had conquered England? Alternate universes such as these suggest languages that might have emerged but didn't — these alternate universes are ripe for the creation of model languages.

If William the Conqueror and his Norman troops had failed to conquer the Anglo-Saxons, the English language would have taken a different course altogether. English would have retained much more of its vocabulary, which instead was largely displaced by Norman French. Since an Anglo-English would have retained much of its vocabulary, it might have proven more resistant to borrowing foreign terms. Anglo-English syntax would depend more on inflections, for English lost the Anglo-Saxon inflectional endings under pressure from Norman French, which had a different system of inflections altogether. Anglo-English would be a fascinating language indeed. (If anyone out there wants to be the Ivar Aasen of English, let me know.)

If the French- and English-speaking people of Quebec had been less interested in preserving their own backgrounds and more interested in building a community together, a new Gallic-English might have evolved as the two languages merged. This new language would have an even simpler grammar than English, as speakers concentrated on the distinctions that French and English had in common.

The Moors expanded from North Africa to conquer much of the Iberian Peninsula. Had al-Mansur been able to forge a kingdom that would have survived his death (rather than degenerate into quarelling taifas), the Moors might have tried to invade England, giving rise to a Moorish English.

Alternative languages are fun to think about, and you should always be able to come up with one moor version of English.

Future languages

The model linguist need not stop at the past or imagined alternate pasts. He can move to the future, postulating languages that might come to exist.

For instance, the Roman Empire spread Latin across Europe. As the Empire declined, the farflung local speakers of Latin slowly changed the language they had learned from Rome. As a result, Latin evolved into Italian, French, Spanish, Portuguese, Romanian, Sardinian, Catalan, Rhaetian, Occitan and Dalmatian (now extinct). A different type of empire has risen today, the cultural empire of English. English is now spoken as the mother tongue in Britain, the United States, Canada, Guyana, Australia and New

Zealand. Over time, the dialects of English spoken in these areas may diverge as much as Italian, Spanish and French diverged from Latin, giving rise to new languages, based on English, but different from it. English has already given rise to new Englishes, such as Krio (an African creole) and Singlish (Singaporean English).

The great thing about constructing a future English is that you already know English! You have already mastered its vocabulary and grammar and can postulate how you would like to see those evolve in a future descendant of English.

Auxiliary languages

Anyone who has traveled extensively through foreign countries wishes there was one language she could learn that people everywhere could speak. English comes close, but carries with it a cultural baggage that many find oppressive or offensive. From Volapük to Esperanto to Interlingua, people have struggled to create languages to make it easier to bring people together. Nor are these efforts in the past. For instance, Phil Hunt is creating Eurolang, which he hopes to position as the common language of the European Union.

It is easy to think of situations where simplified bridge languages would be beneficial to people — to Quebec and to the U.S./Mexico border, to give two North American examples. While the practical steps required to see that an auxiliary language establishes a significant community of speakers are daunting, you can always choose to create such a language as simply a fascinating linguistic exercise, rather than a new social movement.

The possibilities for model languages are endless. Timothy Miller has been entertaining CONLANG subscribers with his Monkey Language, and he is also developing a Ferengi language for *Star Trek* fans (the Ferengi are the big-eared aliens, in case you didn't know). The possibilities are endless, so get working on your language today!

Meaning Change

Volume I, Issue 4 — August 1, 1995

Silly are the goddy tawdry maudlin for they shall christgeewhiz bow down before him: bedead old men, priest and prester, babeling a pitterpatternoster: no word is still the word, but, a loafward has become lord.

Ronald Suffield, "The Tenth Beatitude"

This subtle poem by the English philologist Ronald Suffield is actually written at two levels. For Suffield intends that the reader hold in mind not just the current meanings of these words but the original meanings as well. For the meaning of a word changes over time. The example everyone knows is *gay*, which originally meant "merry", but because some people are a little too merry came to mean "wanton", and because some people are a little too wanton came to mean "homosexual", which is the sense almost exclusively used now.

A model language that you develop will have words that are descended from words with quite different meanings. Some of the words used in Suffield's poem will be used to demonstrate how words change through time.

Pejoration

PEJORATION is the process by which a word's meaning worsens or degenerates, coming to represent something less favorable than it originally did. Most of the words in Suffield's poem have undergone pejoration.

For instance, the word *silly* begins Suffield's poem and meant in Old English times "blessed", which is why Suffield calls his poem a *beatitude* (Christ's beatitudes begin with "blessed are the..."). How did a word meaning "blessed" come to mean "silly"? Well, since people who are blessed are often innocent and guileless, the word gradually came to mean "innocent". And some of those who are innocent might be innocent because they haven't the brains to be anything else. And some of those who are innocent might be innocent because they knowingly reject opportunities for temptation. In either case, since the more worldly-wise would take advantage of their opportunities, the innocents must therefore be foolish, which of course is the current primary meaning of the word *silly*.

The word *goddy* in the poem is a METAPLASMUS (artful misspelling) of *gaudy*. The word *gaudy* was derived from the Latin word *gaudium*, "joy", which was applied to praying (as a type of rejoicing). Because the most common prayers in Middle English times were the prayers of the rosary, Middle English *gaude* came to be associated with the rosary and came to mean "an ornamental rosary bead". Unfortunately, not all who prayed with the rosary were genuinely pious; many were like the Pharisees of old and just wanted to be seen praying — religion for them was ornamental rather than functional. As a result, modern English *gaudy* gradually acquired its current meaning of tasteless or ostentatious ornamentation.

A related word to *gaudy*, which is not explicitly referenced in Suffield's poem but is implied, is *bead* (in the poem, *bedead* is probably an anagrammatic play on *beaded*). In Middle English times, *bead* (then spelled '*bede*') referred only to a rosary bead. Middle English *bede* was itself descended from Old English *gebed*, prayer. The phrase *telling one's beads* was literally "saying one's prayers", with each rosary bead used to keep count of the number of prayers said. In the days when all English-speaking Christians were Catholics, using the rosary was such a common practice that it was only natural for the word for prayer to become the word for the bead used to say a prayer.

In this way, Suffield is arguing, deep spiritual communication has been trivialized into a trinket. Modern English *bead* has come so far from its original center that its sphere of meaning no longer includes prayer — but does include other small round objects, such as beads of sweat.

The word *rosary*, incidentally, originally was Latin for "a rose garden", which was applied as a metaphorical description of the prayer cycle, which was "a rose garden of prayers", with the rose garden symbolizing both the Garden of Eden (or *paradise*, which originally meant, well we could go on forever...) and the rose of the Virgin Mary.

A word that has shown similar semantic degeneration to *gaudy* is *tawdry*. In the eighth century, Æthelthýrth, Queen of Northumbria, abdicated her office and renounced the pleasures of the flesh, having her marriage to the King of Northumbria annulled to become abbess of a monastery on the Isle of Ely. This act of sacrifice and her subsequent holiness prompted others to revere her as a saint. Legend has it that she died of a disease of the throat, a disease that she regarded as judgment upon the vanity of her youth, when she loved to wear beautiful necklaces in court. Eventually, Æthelthýrth was beatified, and — as by this time phonetic change had simplified her name to *Audrey* — she was known as St. Audrey. An annual fair was held in her memory each October 17th, and at the fair were sold cheap souvenirs, including a neck lace called *St. Audrey's lace*. In England, the initial [s] of saints' names is often elided (for instance, the town of St. Albans in Hertfordshire is locally pronounced as [talbans] by some). As a result of this process, by the 1800s, the necklaces were called *tawdry laces*. It wasn't long before *tawdry* was applied to the other cheap souvenirs sold at the annual fair, with the result that *tawdry* became a general adjective meaning "gaudy and cheap in appearance".

The word *tawdry* is not the only eponymous word to degenerate: the last word in Suffield's first stanza, *maudlin*, is short for *Magdalene*. Mary Magdalene was the reformed prostitute who wept at Christ's tomb that first Easter morning; this weeping has been memorialized in innumerable medieval paintings and stain-glass windows. As a result, her name came to be used to describe anyone who was weeping, and from there the meaning radiated out to "excessively sentimental." *Magdalene* came to be pronounced *maudlin* through gradual phonetic change; in fact, *Magdalen College* at Oxford University is locally known as *Maudlin*. Silly are the goddy tawdry maudlin.

Moving on to the next line of Suffield's poem (*for they shall christgeewhiz bow down before him*), we find another religious figure, of greater stature than Mary Magdalene or St. Audrey, who has had his name spawn many new words. Of course, this is Jesus Christ, whose name has become an oath. Because swearing is considered inappropriate in polite society, people slightly changed the sound of the invective. *Damn it!* became *darn it!*, *shit!* became *shoot!*, *Jesus!* became *gee, gee whiz* and *geez* and *Jesus Christ!* became *Jiminy Crickets*, among others. These euphemistic changes are called minced oaths.

The final word in Suffield's poem to undergo pejoration is *paternoster*, which is descended from the Latin *pater noster*, which represents "Our Father", the first words of the Lord's Prayer. As a result of this relationship, the words came to be known as another name for the Lord's Prayer and came to mean one of the large beads on a rosary on which the Paternoster was recited (those beads again!). As its meaning radiated outward from "large bead", it even came to mean "a weighted fishing line with hooks connected by bead-like swivels". The word *paternoster* also came to mean any word-formula spoken as a prayer or magic spell. Since the

MEANING CHANGE 53

Paternoster was in Latin, and in Medieval times Latin was no longer the native language of any of the reciters, the prayer was often recited quickly and with little regard for the sense of the words. Because of this, *paternoster* came to mean meaningless chatter, words empty of meaning — this sense of the word gave rise to the form *patter*. (The word *pitter-patter*, though used by Suffield in his poem, is actually etymologically unrelated to the word *patter* with this meaning.)

Patter has the sense of meaningless words, and sharp words can become rounded and dull. But although Suffield laments that no word is still the Word [of God], some words do assume a dignity they had not before possessed.

Amelioration

AMELIORATION is the process by which a word's meaning improves or becomes elevated, coming to represent something more favorable than it originally referred to.

Two words that have undergone amelioration are *priest* and *prester*. Both words (along with *presbyter*) are descended from the Greek word *presbuteros*, "older man, elder", a comparative form of the word *presbus*, "old man". Because churches of most religions are headed by elders and not youth, and because age is often equated with wisdom, the Greek word gradually acquired the meaning of "church leader, priest". The different forms represent borrowings made at different times, with *priest* being the oldest English form, followed by *prester*, followed by the learned borrowing of *presbyter*.

In what for Suffield is the greatest example of amelioration, the early Old English word *hláfweard*, which if translated using its descendant words would be *loafward*, meant "the keeper of the bread" and was applied to the head of a household. Although "keeper of the bread" might bear witness to the importance of that most basic of foodstuffs to early Anglo-Saxons, alternatively one might argue that it had no more literal sense than *bread* does in the modern word *breadwinner*. The word *hláfweard* has been shortened over time, first to *hláford* and then to *lord*. Over time, the word has been used of not just any head of household but of princes and nobility; this sense was extended to include the Prince of Light, God. For Suffield, this extension of lord makes a fitting appellation for Christ, given that Christ was the keeper of the bread of communion. The word *lord*, which ends the poem, stands in start contrast to the demeaning phrase *christgeewhiz* used earlier in the poem as an example of pejoration.

By ending the poem with the word lord, Suffield offers a hope for redemption for all words.

Clearly the poet Suffield believes that man has taken the meaning out of God's words, reducing *pater noster* to *patter* and God's son's name to a curse. Yet if he is extreme in his view of pejoration as an example of man's trivialization of God and rejection of divine meaning, the process of semantic change is almost universally condemned by teachers, scholars and other concerned language speakers. In fact, semantic drift is as natural as continental drift and almost as inexorable. The meanings of words change, sometimes for the worse, but sometimes providing useful distinctions. Some words, like *lord*, are even inspired.

Categories of semantic change

As the above discussion shows, many people view semantic change with strong emotions. Some, like Suffield, may even perceive it as an almost diabolical force. The discussion of meaning change is often emotionally charged, with the meanings perceived as "improving" (amelioration) or "worsening" (pejoration) over time. This next section will attempt to provide a more clinical overview of how words change meanings.

Try this: flip through the dictionary and look at random for a word with four or more meanings, preferably a word you think you know. Chances are you will find that it has an unlikely hodge-podge of meanings, at least one of which will surprise you. Here's what I found when I tried this myself: *daughter* has these senses, among others:

- One's female child.
- A female descendant.
- A woman thought of as if in a parent/child relationship: *a daughter of Christ*.
- Something personified as a female descendant: the Singer sewing machine is the *daughter* of the loom.
- Physics. The immediate product of the radioactive decay of an element.

The last sense makes me want to write a short story, *The Daughter of Fat Man*, in which I could use the word *daughter* in at least three of its senses. How does a word come to have such broad, often very different, meanings?

At the simplest level, words do undergo only two types of meaning change, not amelioration and pejoration, but generalization (a word's meaning widens to include new concepts), and specialization (a word's meaning contracts to focus on fewer concepts).

Generalization

Also known as extension, GENERALIZATION is the use of a word in a broader realm of meaning than it originally possessed, often referring to all items in a class, rather than one specific item. For instance, *place* derives from Latin *platea*, "broad street", but its meaning grew broader than the street, to include "a particular city", "a business office", "an area dedicated to a specific purpose" before broadening even wider to mean "area". In the process, the word place displaced (!) the Old English word *stow* and became used instead of the Old English word *stede* (which survives in *stead, steadfast, steady* and — of course — *instead*).

Generalization is a natural process, especially in situations of "language on a shoestring", where the speaker has a limited vocabulary at her disposal, either because she is young and just acquiring language or because she is not fluent in a second language. A first-year Spanish student on her first vacation in Spain might find herself using the word *coche*, "car", for cars, trucks, jeeps, buses, and so on. When my son Alexander was two, he used the word *oinju* (from orange juice) to refer to any type of juice, including grape juice and apple juice; *wawa* (from water) referred to water and hoses, among other things.

Some examples of general English words that have undergone generalization include:

Word	Old Meaning
pants	"men's wide breeches extending from waist to ankle"
place	"broad street"

Specialization

The opposite of generalization, SPECIALIZATION is the narrowing of a word to refer to what previously would have been but one example of what it referred to. For instance, the word *meat* originally referred to "any type of food", but came to mean "the flesh of animals as opposed to the flesh of fish". The original sense of *meat* survives in terms like *mincemeat*, "chopped apples and spices used as a pie filling"; *sweetmeat*, "candy"; and *nutmeat*, "the edible portion of a nut". When developing your model language, it is meet to leave compounds untouched, even if one of their morphemes has undergone specialization (or any other meaning change).

For an example from another language, the Japanese word *koto* originally referred to "any type of stringed instrument" but came to be used to refer only a specific instrument with 13 strings, which was played horizontally and was popular in the Edo Period.

Other examples of specialization, from the development of English, include:

Word	Old Meaning
affection	emotion
deer	animal
forest	countryside
girl	a young person
starve	to die

A taxonomy of semantic change

All other semantic change can be discussed in either terms of generalization or specialization. This section describes different subtypes of meaning change.

A shift in meaning results from the subsequent action of generalization and specialization over time: a word that has extended into a new area then undergoes narrowing to exclude its original meaning. In the unlikely event that all the senses of *place* except for "a business office" faded away, then *place* would be said to have undergone a shift.

Generalization

Metonymy

METONYMY is a figure of speech where one word is substituted for a related word; the relationship might be that of cause and effect, container and contained, part and whole. For instance, Shakespeare's comment "Is it not strange that sheep's guts should hale souls out of men's bodies?" (from *Much Ado About Nothing*) uses "sheep's guts" to refer to the music produced by harpstrings. Had *guts* come to mean "music", then the meaning would have shifted due to metonymy.

The Greek word *dóma* originally meant "roof". In the same way English speakers will metonymically use roof to mean "house" (as in "Now we have a roof over our heads"), the Greeks frequently used *dóma* to refer to "house", so that that is now the standard meaning of the word. A Russian word will provide a similar example: *vinograd*, "vineyard", was so frequently used to refer to "grapes", as in "Let's have a taste of the vineyard" that it has come to mean "grapes".

Metaphorical extension

Grace Murray Hopper, the late Admiral and computer pioneer, told a story of an early computer that kept calculating incorrectly. When technicians opened up its case to examine the wiring, which physically represented the machine's logic, a huge dead moth was found, shorting out one of the circuits and causing the faulty logic. That moth was the first of its kind to achieve immortality. Because of it, software is now frequently plagued with *bugs*.

The use of *bug* to refer to an error in computer logic was a metaphorical extension that became so popular that it is now part of the regular meaning of bug. The computer industry has a host of words whose meaning has been extended through such metaphors, including *mouse* for that now ubiquitous computer input device (so named because the cord connecting it to the computer made it resemble that cutest of rodents).

Metaphorical extension is the extension of meaning in a new direction through popular adoption of an originally metaphorical meaning. The *crane* at a construction site was given its name by comparison to the long-necked bird of the same name. When the meaning of the word *daughter* was first extended from that of "one's female child" to "a female descendant" (as in daughter of Eve), the listener might not have even noticed that the meaning had been extended.

Metaphorical extension is almost a natural process undergone by every word. We don't even think of it as meaning change. In its less obvious instances, we don't even see it as extending the meaning of a word. For example, the word *illuminate* originally meant "to light up", but has broadened to mean "to clarify", "to edify". These meanings seem so natural as to be integral parts of the words, where senses such as "to celebrate" and "to adorn a page with designs" seem like more obvious additions.

A few specific metaphors are common to many different languages, and words can be shown to have undergone similar, if independent, developments. Thus the Welsh word *haul* and the Gaelic word *súil*, both meaning "sun", have both come to mean "eye." Nor is this metaphor a stranger to English, where the daisy was in Old English originally a compound meaning "day's eye", from its yellow similarity to the sun.

More often, languages will differ in the precise correspondences between words, so that some languages have broad words with many meanings, which must be translated into multiple words in another language. A word like *paternoster*, discussed earlier, with senses ranging from the "Lord's Prayer" to "a magic spell" to "a large bead" to "a weighted fishing line" will have to be translated into four different words in another language (though I challenge you to find an English-to-language-of-your-choice dictionary that indicates the four meanings of *paternoster*).

Word	Old Meaning
illuminate	"to light up"

Radiation

RADIATION is metaphorical extension on a grander scale, with new meanings radiating from a central semantic core to embrace many related ideas. The word *head* originally referred to that part of the human body above the rest. Since the top of a nail, pin or screw is, like the human head, the top of a slim outline, that sense has become included in the meaning of head. Since the bulb of a cabbage or lettuce is round like the human head, that sense has become included in the meaning of *head*. Know where I'm headed with this? The meaning of the word *head* has radiated out to include the head of a coin (the side picturing the human head), the head of the list (the top item in the list), the head of a table, the head of the family, a head of cattle, $50 a head. But I'll stop while I'm ahead.

Other words that have similarly radiated meanings outward from a central core include the words *heart*, *root* and *sun*.

Specialization

The only specific subtype of specialization that I have identified is contextual specialization.

Contextual specialization

The word *undertaker* originally meant "one who undertakes a task, especially one who is an entrepreneur". This illustrates contextual specialization, where the meaning of a word is reshaped under pressure from another word that had frequently co-occured with it: thus *undertaker* acquired its meaning from constant use of the phrase *funeral undertaker*; eventually, under the pressure towards euphemism, the word *funeral* was dropped.

Another example of contextual specialization is *doctor*, which originally meant "a teacher" and then later "an expert", where it came to be used in the phrase *medical doctor*; now of course this is redundant and medical is omitted, with the primary sense of *doctor* having become more specialized.

Word	Old Meaning
undertaker	entrepreneur
doctor	teacher

Shift

> *I heard an American student at Cambridge University telling some English friends how he climbed over a locked gate to get into his college and tore his pants, and one of them asked, 'But, how could you tear your pants and not your trousers?'*
> Norman Moss, *British/American Language Dictionary*

SHIFTS occur when the sense of a word expands and contracts, with the final focus of the meaning different from the original. For some reason, words describing clothing tend to shift meanings more frequently than other words, perhaps because fashion trends come and go, leaving words to seem as old fashioned as the clothing they describe. Who today wants to wear *bloomers, knickers* or *pantaloons*?

The word *pants* has an interesting history. It's ultimate etymon is Old Italian *Pantalone*. In the 1600s, Italy developed *commedia dell'arte*, a style of comedy based on improvisation using stock characters. *Pantalone* was a stock character who was portrayed as a foolish old man wearing slippers and tight trousers. Through regular metyonmy, speakers of Old French borrowed his name to describe his Italian trousers. Their word was then borrowed into English as *pantaloon*, which in time was shortened to *pants* and came to mean trousers in general. British speakers of English have modified the meaning again to the sense of "underpants", resulting in the confusing situation described in Norman Moss' quote above.

Cast like discarded laundry along the divide separating British and American English are quite a few words for clothing, as the following table shows.

jumper
Etymon: English dialect *jump*
Original: loose jacket
American: pinafore

British: light pullover

knickers
Etymon: *knickerbockers*
Original: breeches banded below knee
American: boy's baggy trousers banded below knee
British: bloomers, old-fashioned female underpants

pants
Etymon: *pantaloon*, from Old French *pantalon*
Original: men's wide breeches extending from waist to ankle
American: trousers
British: underpants

suspenders
Etymon: *suspend*
Original: straps to support trousers
American: (unchanged)
British: garter

tights
Etymon: Etymon:
Original: *tight* (adj.)
 snug, stretchable apparel worn from neck to toe; typica worn by dancers or acrobats
American: (that, or tight pants of the same material)
British: pantyhose

vest
Etymon: Etymon:
Original: Old French *veste*, Lat. *vestis*
 clothing
American: waistcoast
British: undershirt

Amelioration

Suffield's poem gave many good examples of amelioration, including priest from "old man". A complementary term, *pastor*, likewise underwent amelioration, originally meaning "shepherd" (a sense surviving in the word *pastoral*), but coming to mean its current sense of "minister" by the extensive Christian references to "the Lord is my shepherd" as a call to ministry.

Meaning Change

The following table shows other examples, including *pluck* in the sense of "He has a lot of pluck."

Word	Old Meaning
enthusiasm	abuse
guts ("courage")	entrails
pastor	shepherd
pluck ("spirit")	act of tugging
queen	woman

Pejoration

King James II called the just completed St. Paul's Cathedral *amusing, awful and artificial*. Call the just completed rock and roll museum in Cleveland *amusing, awful and artificial*, and you may be accurate but you will mean something quite different from King James. When he lived, those words meant that the cathedral was "pleasing, awe-inspiring and artful" respectively. The meaning of each word has grown more negative with time. People seem much more likely to drag words down than to lift them up, to build museums instead of cathedrals, as the following examples may demonstrate.

Word	Old Meaning
crafty	strong
cunning	knowing
egregious	distinguished, standing out from the herd
harlot	a boy
notorious	famous
obsequious	flexible
vulgar	popular

Semantic reversal

Occasionally a word will shift so far from its original meaning that its meaning will nearly reverse.

Word	Old Meaning
counterfeit	an original
garble	to sort out
manufacture	to make by hand

Contronyms

A CONTRONYM is like a word that has undergone semantic reversal, only the tension has not eased: the word still preserves its original meaning, along with a contradictory — if not exactly counterposed — meaning.

Word	Meanings
bimonthly	"happening every other month", "happening twice monthly"
biweekly	"happening every other week", "happening twice weekly"
ravish	"to overwhelm with force, especially rape"*, "to overwhelm with emotion, enrapture"
sanction	"authoritative measure of approval"*, "coercive measure of disapproval of nation against nation"
table	Brit. "to put on the table for discussion", Amer. "to set aside a motion rather than discuss it"

*The older of the two senses given

Interestingly, *biannual* means only "twice each year", with no recorded sense of "every other year" in *Webster's II New Riverside University Dictionary.*

The word *cleave* (meaning "to split or separate" or "to adhere or cling") is actually two different words, both from the Old English (*cleofan* and *cleofian* respectively) but by changes in pronunciation, these words have evolved the same current form.

Meaninglessness

The nadir of semantics is meaninglessness. The final semantic change. The death of meaning. The defeat of *sigor.*

The word *sigor* is Old English for "victory". It is now meaningless to almost all English speakers, except for those familiar with Old English or with German (where its cognate survives in *Sieg*).

Few now know what *sigor* means. Is this a change in its meaning or a change in the very state of the word? Is death part of life?

Meaning change across languages

Imagine for a moment that *sigor* had survived. It might have been changed to *siyor*, and its meaning could have generalized to "success". It would then stand in contrast to the German *Sieg*.

Sister languages, or dialects of a language, often have the same basic word with different meanings. These word pairs then become known as "false friends" to speakers trying to learn the other language. For instance, German *Lust* means "pleasure", which is in fact the original meaning of the English word, which comes from the same common ancestor as *Lust*. In English, *lust* underwent specialization and pejoration, as speakers associated it with only one type of pleasure. The British and American English clothing terms also show how related languages can send words off in different directions over time.

As you develop your model languages, you should have words in related languages undergo different semantic changes. Situations where a word's meaning changes the same way in two related languages are relatively rare, the example of the Irish and Gaelic words for "sun" evolving into "eye" notwithstanding.

When languages borrow words, they frequently change the meanings of those borrowings, typically making generic words more specific, in the same way that one language's place names often grew out of another language's generic words for concepts such as "hill", "river" and "town". Take the history of the Low German word *spittal*, derived from a generic Romance word for "hospital" but then restricted to "a hospital for lepers".

Meaning change through time

Future meaning change

Words are slowly changing in meaning even now, though the changes happen at the speed of continental drift rather than with the sudden jolt of earthquakes. To conclude this issue, and to summarize the types of meaning change discussed here, I have extrapolated how some words might change meanings in the next 25 years.

Generalization: *entrepreneur*, "small-business owner or worker" (because of its favorable connotations, this word was widely adopted as a label, even by those who were not risk takers).

Metonymy: *sun-cell*, "electric car" (so called because of the prominent solar cell on the roof of the vehicle).

Metaphorical Extension: *surfaced*, "checked all Internet messages, including e-mail, voice mail and video mail" (originally popularized in the phrase "I just surfaced from checking my flood of e-mail"; given added cachet under the influence of *surf*, which see).

Radiation: *Internet*, "Internet, narrowcast television, narrowcast radio, virtual reality, videoconferencing" (because it all was added onto the 'Net).

Specialization: *surf*, "navigate the Internet" (traditional "water surfing" becomes sea-*boarding*).

Contextual Specialization: *candidate*, "political candidate" (the word *contestant* began to be used instead of *candidate* for non-political contexts).

Shift: *fax*, "point-to-point e-mail" (e-mail gradually superseded fax). *post-modern*, "modern" (by calling everything modern post-modern, this change was inevitable).

Amelioration: *temp*, "specialist".

Pejoration: *liberal*, "idiot" (this term was used as an insult as early as 1988 and was gradually abandoned as a label by the Democrats it originally described). *job*, "drudgery".

Semantic Reversal: *modern*, "obsolete" (thanks to the change in meaning of post-modern). *putrid*, "cool" (slang).

Contronym: *communism*, "communism, capitalism" (courtesy of the Hong Kong communists).

Meaninglessness: *perestroika* (this word was used only by historians interested in how the Russian economy followed that of Sicily).

If you want to create a slang or jargon, besides coining new words you should change the meanings of current words, much as these examples did. Just be aware that it is easier for an outsider to pick up new words than old words whose meaning has changed, since the outsider will bring all his assumptions from past experience to bear, so that when he hears a teenager call something *putrid*, he will assume that it is putrid.

The history of meaning change

> *To say that Bilbo's breath was taken away is no description at all. There are no words left to express his staggerment, since Men changed the language that they learned of elves in the days when all the world was wonderful. Bilbo had heard tell and sing of dragon-hoards before, but the splendour, the lust, the glory of such treasure had never yet come home to him.*
>
> J.R.R. Tolkien, *The Hobbit*

If the history of semantic change had to be summed up as one process, it would be that of specialization. The Anglo Saxons 1500 years ago made do with perhaps 30,000 words in their complete vocabulary, while Modern English has anywhere from 500,000 to a million words, depending on whether or not scientific vocabularies are included.

"In the beginning was the Word, and the Word was God, and the Word was with God." It could be argued that originally there was one word, from which all others have sprung. The origins of language will never be known, but the first language probably had a vocabulary of a few hundred words, providing a rich enough vocabulary for a primitive people who had few materials and fewer abstract concepts. Many of the words of the first languages had very broad senses of meaning.

For instance, the word *inspire* is from the Latin *inspirare*, which literally means "to breathe into". Its archaic meaning is "to breathe life into", with newer meanings like "to be the cause of", "to elicit", "to move to action", "to exalt" and "to guide by divine influence". Now if a minister were to speak of Adam as *dust inspired*, he might mean by that not just that the dust is having life breathed into it (the original etymological meaning), but also that the dust is being exalted and given form, that it is being moved to action, and that it is being divinely guided (these are the metaphorical or extended meanings). In other words, this minister might not mean just one of the definitions of inspired but all of them simultaneously.

The extended meanings are branches that have split off from the trunk, and our hypothetical minister has simply traced them back to the root.

If you seek to create a language from an earlier time, you should probably develop a small vocabulary, with it words having much more overlapping of meaning than the vocabularies of modern languages. Imagine a word *spiratholmos* — an ancient ancestor to Latin *inspirare* — meaning "wind, breath, voice, spirit." A speaker who used the word *spiratholmos* would regard the wind in the trees as the breath of the earth, the voice of God, the spirit animating each of us.

This is different way of looking at words, and prompted Tolkien to write, "There are no words left to express his staggerment, since Men changed the language that they learned of elves in the days when all the world was wonderful." What Tolkien's elves might have expressed in one word, resonant with meaning, Tolkien's diminutive man cannot express at all.

Semantic change can be viewed dispassionately as a natural process, but it can also be invested with a spiritual significance, as Tolkien and Suffield have done. A model language is an art form and its crafting can even convey this theme of spiritual isolation. As Ronald Suffield wrote, "no word is still the word, but, a *loafward* has become *lord*."

Meaning

Volume I, Issue 6 – October/November 1, 1995

I won't use words again
They don't mean what I meant
They don't say what I said
They're just the crust of the meaning
With realms underneath
Never touched
Never stirred
Never even moved through
If language were liquid
It would be rushing in

Suzanne Vega, "Language"

If language were liquid, we could enter a submersible and use sound waves to reveal the subterranean terrain. For each word floats like a buoy, anchored to some unseen spot far below. The meanings of the word *brother* seem easy to pick out from the waters, but in fact the possible meanings stretch deeper than you might expect, ranging from "full brother" to "any kinsman" to "any fellow human" to "anything related" (as in the brother vices of greed and selfishness). Since we can't use sonar, how can we sound out the meanings of words?

Semantic primitives

It used to be thought that any word could be described in terms of semantic primitives. For instance, Manfred Bierwisch, writing in 1970, said that semantic features do not differ from language to language, but are instead part of the general human capacity for language, forming a universal inventory used in particular ways in individual languages.

According to this theory, every word can be broken up into primitive kernels of meaning, called SEMANTEMES (also called semantic features or semantic components). Some sample definitions using semantemes:

Word	Semantemes
father	male + parent
mother	female + parent
son	male + offspring
daughter	female + offspring
brother	male + sibling
sister	female + sibling

The process of breaking words down into semantemes is known as COMPONENTIAL ANALYSIS and has been most often used to analyze kinship terms across languages. The components are often given in more detail. For instance, kinship terms like those shown above might have three components: *sex, generation, lineage*. Sex would be male or female; generation would be a number, with 0 = reference point's generation, -1 = previous generation, +1 = next generation; lineage would be either direct, colineal (as in siblings) or ablineal (as in uncles and aunts).

This is obviously a highly technical way to define words we all know and use without overdue consideration, but — by using these components — you can concisely define a variety of English kinship terms.

Word	Generation	Lineage	Sex
mother	-1	Direct	Female
father	-1	Direct	Male
aunt	-1	Ablineal	Female
uncle	-1	Ablineal	Male
sister	0	Colineal	Female
brother	0	Colineal	Male
daughter	1	Direct	Female
son	1	Direct	Male
niece	1	Ablineal	Female
nephew	1	Ablineal	Male

This can be the starting point of a more detailed analysis of English terms. One advantage of isolating and identifying each component is that it then becomes possible to identify holes in a language's vocabulary, areas for which it lacks a direct term. For instance, English lacks a genderless word for an aunt or uncle; you can't fill in the blank for the statement "parent is to mother and father, as ___ is to aunt and uncle". You can still express this concept in English (we typically refer to *aunts and uncles* but you can more formally refer to *parents' siblings*), but you will likely express it less often than you would if there was a word for it.

Meaning

Another gap is the lack of words for either "male cousin" or "female cousin". The paradigm *parent/mother/father, sibling/sister/brother* is just not carried out for cousin. This is unlike other Germanic languages, including Danish (*Faetter* and *Kusine* for male and female cousins respectively), Dutch (*neef* and *nicht*) and German (*der Vetter* and *die Kusine*). Old English probably also made this distinction, but replaced it with Norman French *cosin* — ignoring the feminine form *cosine*.

The following table more fully fleshes out the distinctions English does make in kinship terms.

Word	Generation	Lineage	Sex
parent	-1	Direct	x
mother	-1	Direct	Female
father	-1	Direct	Male
[parent's sibling]	-1	Ablineal	x
aunt	-1	Ablineal	Female
uncle	-1	Ablineal	Male
sibling	0	Colineal	x
sister	0	Colineal	Female
brother	0	Colineal	Male
cousin	0	Ablineal	x
[female cousin]	0	Ablineal	Female
[male cousin]	0	Ablineal	Male
child, offspring	1	Direct	x
daughter	1	Direct	Female
son	1	Direct	Male
[niece or nephew]	1	Ablineal	x
niece	1	Ablineal	Female
nephew	1	Ablineal	Male

There are many more "holes" or gaps in the vocabulary than those labeled here. What about terms where the generation is not specified? Where the lineage is not specified?

The combination of {Generation 0, Lineage Direct} is meaningless (except for some backwater place — choose your own to make fun of — where brothers marry their sisters and people can be their own fathers). Since the sense of {Lineage Colineal} only applies to a generation of 0, it could be thought of as the manifestation of Direct in that area. (The term Ablineal can apply to any generation.)

A fuller componential analysis (yes, fuller) of kinship terms is presented in the next chapter.

While componential analysis is useful for some exercises, it is not a representation of how language works: no linguist has ever been able to develop a complete list of semantic primitives. Invariably, some of the primitives identified are actually molecules that can be broken down into new atoms. For instance, *parent*, *offspring* and *sibling* are all interrelated terms; the word *parent* can be defined as "a person who has offspring" and *sibling* can be defined as "a person with a parent who has other offspring". If semantic primitives were to exist, they would number in the thousands and would resemble a mathematical logic system more than the mind's loom of language.

The bother of brother

While Suzanne Vega sings of language being liquid, the rigidity of componential analysis makes language seem like frozen liquid: ice cubes. While semantemes have their place, especially to compare and contrast languages' lexicons, they do not indicate how we actually define terms in our minds.

One of the problems with semantemes is that they assume words have a single basic meaning. Take *brother*, which was defined above first as "male sibling" and then as {Generation 0, Sex Male, Lineage Colineal}. The English word actually has a much broader meaning than either of these definitions, with many degrees of brother-ness radiating out from a core meaning of "male sibling", as shown below in a no-means exhaustive list.

- brother-german
- half brother
- stepbrother
- kinsman
- comrade
- fraternity member
- co-religionist
- lay person
- racial brother
- fellow man

Defining these labels in more detail we have:

1. A male having the same biological parents as another person: *brother-german*
2. A male having one biological parent in common with another person: *half brother*
3. The son of one's stepparent by a previous spouse or lover: *stepbrother*
4. A male with the same ancestor as another person: *kinsman*
5. A male friend who is loved as if he were a biological brother: *comrade*
6. A male friend who belongs to the same fraternity: *fellow fraternity member*
7. A man who follows the same religious beliefs: *co-religionist*
8. A male lay member of a religious order: a monk or lay person
9. A person of the same race or nation
10. A fellow man
11. Something that closely resembles another in kind

Even this radius of meaning is not exhaustive: a *brother* can mean a "brother-in-law", a *brother* can be an adopted son raised by your parents, a *brother* can be used in the strict sense of "a fellow African American". The gender of a brother does not even have to be male — *we must help our brothers in the Fatherland* uses *brother* to include both men and women (as illustrated in meaning #9 above).

As this example shows, people think of words not as fixed definitions composed of semantic primitives, but as examples or PROTOTYPES. The prototypical brother has the same biological parents as another person and has an emotionally close relationship with his siblings. On a scale of brother-ness from 0 to 100 the prototype is 100. A 90 might be a brother who was twenty years older than another person and as a result was never close to him, or the brother who was abusive and was disliked — even though these examples are biologically brothers, they do not share in that emotional closeness of true brother-ness. A best friend can be considered a brother on the basis of emotional closeness, rather than kinship. The brother virtues of love and charity are considered brothers only because they resemble one another — this is a metaphorical use of the primary sense of brother, scoring perhaps a 10 out of 100 on our hypothetical scale of brother-ness.

The word brother, then, is defined not in terms of semantic primitives, but in terms of a network of associations with other words. The human brain recursively defines words by words (just like a dictionary).

Translations (meanings across languages)

When you decide to translate *brother* into your model language, you will have to decide which of its many meanings you wish to convey. Too often we assume that an English word has exact counterparts in other languages. We say that English *brother* = Spanish *hermano*, when in fact *hermano* has different connotations. For one thing, *hermano* is the expression of a root form *herman-* with a masculine ending; give it a feminine ending and you have *hermana*, "sister"; *hermano* has less of a distinctively masculine connotation than *brother* does.

Rather than considering the breadth of the meaning of *brother*, let's take a simpler example. It is tempting to say that *casa* in Spanish equals *house* in English, like 1+1=2.

casa = house

In fact, *casa* also equals *home*, since Spanish does not distinguish between *house* and *home* with separate words. (Spanish does make a similar distinction, but it does so syntactically, by saying *la casa*, "the house", contrasted with *casa*, "home".)

casa = home

Of course, in English *house* and *home* are different.

house ≠ home

If this is so, then:

casa ≠ casa.

Clearly, semantics can never be reduced to an algebra of translation.

As further evidence that words with common meanings are not exactly equivalent, review some double-translations. The story is told of an American in the USSR who received a telegram, *Your daughter was hung for juvenile crimes*. In fact, the Soviet censor had translated the telegram into Russian, and then back into English. The original English telegram read *Your daughter was suspended for delinquency*. The words *suspended* and *delinquency* had different prototypes (different spheres of meaning) than the Russian words they were paired with.

Words in other languages will make different distinctions. Some will encompass a wider range of meanings than corresponding English words.

For instance, Rick Harrison's planned language Vorlin has some interesting words: the basic sense of the word *bat* is "a ball-hitting tool", with its radiated meanings including "bat, hockey stick, and tennis racket", while the word *sop* means "soup" and "stew". Other Vorlin words cover a smaller range of meanings, so that *for*, "form, shape", does not include other senses of English form like "a paper document to be filled in", "a molding to be filled with concrete" or "manners or conduct".

As you determine what the words in your model language mean, you have to keep in mind that they will not exactly equal English words. But, as a practical matter, you probably don't want to create words for each separate meaning of *brother* and have each word assigned only to that meaning, like the following English words: *brother german* ("full brother"), *half-brother, stepbrother, brother-in-law, comrade, fellow, kinsman, fraternity member, coreligionist.* Doing so loses much of the flexibility of *brother*.

As an example, here's how I translated the different realms of brother into the model language Negasi.

> **nemi** A brother, ranging from the meanings of a full biological brother to a distantly related kinsman, but excluding the broader senses of fellow man, fraternity member, or coreligionist. [Nagada *nama*]
>
> **sanami** A half-brother, a stepbrother or a brother-in-law. [Nagada *du + nama*, "near brother"]
>
> **henami** A comrade, fellow or kinsman. [Nagada *ha + nama*, "far brother"]
>
> **sanemi** A best friend. [*sa + nemi*, "near brother"]
>
> **lunanemi** A coreligionist, though for this imagined culture it would refer to a specific religion. [*luna + nemi*, "divine brother"]

Translating the English word *comrade* into Negasi *henami* will result in totally different associations. The Negasi view comrades as close to kin, and their word that would be translated comrade of course has no taint of communism. So the word *henami* has a stronger familial association than English *comrade* does. While an English-to-Negasi dictionary might list *henami* = *comrade*, this oversimplifies the relationship between the prototypes represented by each word. The words intersect; they are not mutually inclusive.

As an aside, note the difference between *sanami* and *sanemi*. The word *sanami* was coined in the Nagada language, so its literal meaning of "near brother" has been forgotten, since it underwent sound change differently than *sa nemi* — "near brother" as two words — did. This allowed the literal meaning "near brother" to be used to coin a new word in Negasi, in this case referring to "a best friend", a previously absent meaning.

Prototypes for the birds

Another useful example to describe semantic PROTOTYPES or semantic stereotypes is birds: the prototypical *bird* has feathers and wings and can fly. Yet penguins, ostriches and Big Bird are considered birds, even though they can't fly. A duck-billed platypus, on the other hand, isn't considered a bird, despite the fact that it lays eggs and has a beak; it is not considered a bird since it has no feathers, no wings and can't fly.

Prototypes are also a more useful way to describe meaning than semantic primitives, because prototypes embrace the connotations of a word, rather than just the denotations. The notion of prototypes can be used to show how words overlap. For instance, the following table roughly summarizes different types of body builds:

Above-average
    fat   obese

             chubby

             plump

Average weight

Below average
    thin   skinny

            scrawny

The words *skinny* and *scrawny* are subsets of *thin*; *plump*, *chubby* and *obese* are subsets of *fat*. Noticeably absent are any words for average weight. English, like many languages, rarely has words to describe midpoints, only extremes.

Words are often grouped together like this in semantic networks. However, these word sets can be exceedingly complicated. For instance, the words used to describe body builds each have complex connotations as part of their prototypes: *plump* is used more often to describe food such as meat and fruits than *fat* is; similarly, *chubby* is more often used for little boys (or girls) than *fat* is. The word *scrawny* also suggests "bony"; there are other words not shown on this list that also have connotations and specific uses, like *lean*, which suggests "muscular", and *slim*, which suggests "tall", and *slender*, which suggests "graceful". Connotations are not specified in dictionaries and are rarely articulated.

Besides connotations, there are habits governing what other words to use with a word. The synonyms *pursue* and *chase* are almost interchangeable, except that *pursue* is preferred when the object to be chased is highly desirable - *pursue* truth, wisdom, happiness, but *chase* a thief, a bus, a fox. You could write an essay on the difference between *he pursued love* and *he chased love*.

Obviously, it is very difficult to translate these prototypes from one language to another. Failure to properly account for the radius of meaning of a word often has comical results, as evidenced by this sign in a Bucharest hotel lobby: *The lift is being fixed for the next day. During the time we regret that you will be unbearable*. Historically speaking, the word *unbearable* had began with a strict literal meaning, but over time its radius of meaning had expanded to include a figurative sense as well. The combinations of connotations and detailed usage preferences for any word are not articulated, but mastering them is one of the hallmarks of literary writing.

Conclusion

Meaning is therefore a combination of prototypical examples. The important thing to keep in mind, when creating your own languages, is that the words you invent will not exactly equal the English words you define them as. While, for practical purposes, you will define most words very straightforwardly in English, you will want to highlight the unique culture of your language's speakers by noting how the range of meanings and the range of possible uses distinguishes your invented lexicon from English words.

No wonder Suzanne Vega sang, "I won't use words again. They don't mean what I meant. They don't say what I said."

Relative Terms for Relatives

Volume I, Issue 6 – October/November 1995

Kinship terms have been widely analyzed across languages, which often make quite different distinctions. I broke English kinship terms down into Generation, Sex and Lineage earlier, but to translate terms from other languages we will need to add additional semantic components.

I will outline KinDEEP (KINship Distinctive Elements, Exhaustive Profile) here, a detailed framework for defining kinship terms from different languages. KinDEEP has semantic components for Generation, Lineage, Sex, Side Of Family, Relative Birth Order and Person.

Generations

The value for Generation is any number, with 0 indicating the base or current generation, negative numbers indicating ancestors of the base generation, and positive numbers indicating descendants.

One of the more unusual kinship terms in the world is *maili*, from Njamal, an Australian aborigine language. The word *maili* means "any relative two generations distant", such as a father's father (two generations before) or a daughter's son's wife's sister (two generations after). KinDEEP expresses this as simply {Generation: +2}{Generation: -2}.

Lineage

As described in the last chapter, Lineage can be either Direct, Colineal or Ablineal.

Sex

Sex is either Male, Female or Corresponding.

The atom Corresponding is necessary to analyze some Hawaiian terms. For instance, the Hawaiian word *kaikaina* means "younger sibling of the same sex as the referent". So a man's *kaikaina* would be his younger brother; a woman's *kaikaina* would be her younger sister.

Side of family

Languages often make distinctions between the sides of a family, such as maternal, paternal, step- and half-. The semantic component of Side of Family can take any of these values: {Maternal}, {Paternal}, {Step}, {Half} and {Honorary}.

Maternal/paternal

One difference might be as simple as distinguishing between a mother's brother and a father's brother, as Latin and many other European languages do. Latin has two different words for "uncle" depending on the exact relationship, *avunculus* for "mother's brother" and *patruus* for "father's brother". Thus Latin lacks one word to collectively describe what we think of as "uncle" (how did schoolchildren cry "surrender!" we wonder?) or — for that matter — "aunt". Like Old French, other Romance languages lost this distinction, adopting the maternal terms to refer to either side of the family; thus, Modern French has *oncle* and *tante*, which were adopted into English as *uncle* and *aunt* respectively, displacing the Old English tradition of referring to this generation as "father's brother", "mother's sister", etc.

Just as Latin has no single words for either "uncle" or "aunt", Swedish has no single words equivalent to either "grandmother" or "grandfather", but must specify which side of the family the relationship is through. Swedish does this concisely, using *far* to mean "father", *mor* to mean "mother", for:

- *mormor*, "mother's mother, maternal grandmother"
- *farmor*, "father's mother, paternal grandmother"
- *morfar*, "mother's father, maternal grandfather"
- *farfar*, "father's father, paternal grandfather"

Interestingly, however, Swedish does not use *mor* and *far* by themselves for "mother" and "father" respectively, using *moder* and *fader* for that instead. No sense taking logic too far in a natural language! (I am not aware of any other European language that distinguishes between maternal and paternal grandparents.)

The family's dark side

Besides referring to the maternal or paternal side of a family, it is also possible to refer to other blood distinctions, especially those regarding re-marriage. English uses the prefix *step-* to refer to relatives related only by re-marriage, not blood, as in the evil stepmother (which is not redundant) and the ungrateful stepdaughter, for instance. English uses the suffix *-in-law* to refer to relatives related by marriage, as in the evil mother-in-law and the ungrateful daughter-in-law. When all this familial love becomes too much to bear, English uses *ex-* in front of many or all the other terms, so that you can refer to your *ex-husband*, your *ex-stepdaughter*, your *ex-mother- in-law*, even your *ex-great-grandfather-in-law*. But you're not likely to hear the terms *ex-mother* or *ex-brother* to describe estranged relatives...

English also uses the prefix *half-* to refer to children who share only one parent (*half-brother* and *half-sister*) but the term is not used to refer to other relatives (no *half-mother, *half-grandson).

The family's bright side

Families often have unofficial members, as English recognizes by encouraging the use of *Aunt* and *Uncle* for close family friends of the same generation as a child's parents. I have an Uncle Bill and Aunt Jill, close friends of my parents' from their college days, who were the only honorary parentsibs that I had. To support this almost metaphoric use of *Aunt* and *Uncle*, KinDEEP uses the value {Honorary} as part of the semantic component of Side Of Family.

Relative birth order

Japanese also makes distinctions of another variety, distinguishing between younger and elder siblings. For instance, *ane*, "older sister"; *ani*, "older brother"; *otōto*, "younger brother"; *imōto*, "younger sister". Of course, these words also have first- and second-person forms.

In total, therefore, Japanese has six words for "brother", with separate words making the following distinctions:

- "older brother"
- "younger brother"
- "my older brother"
- "my younger brother"
- "your older brother"

RELATIVE TERMS   79

- "your younger brother"

KinDEEP has the semantic component {Relative Birth Order}, with values for {Older} and {Younger}.

In natural languages, this distinction is almost always used for siblings, but KinDEEP extends it for the common siblings of any generation, making it easy to express terms such as "younger uncle", for instance.

Person

The Japanese are strongly oriented around family and ancestry, and accordingly their language is richer in kinship terms than English. One of the distinctions Japanese makes is that it has separate forms for "my relative" and "your or other's relatives". For instance, *mago* is "my grandson"; *omagosan* is "your grandson". Think of this as a combination pronoun/kinship term, with the term specifying either first person ("my") or second person ("your"). All of Japanese' second-person forms end in the *-san* suffix or a variant of it. The base word may be different, as in *haha* for "my mother" but *okāsan* for "your mother" (rather than *hahasan).

Therefore, KinDEEP recognizes the semantic component Person, with values of {First} and {Second}. It would be easy to suggest a third-person form — e.g., "their mother" — but I am not aware of any language that makes this distinction.

Kindeep examples

The following table provides a framework to present the kinship terms of many different languages.

When you create your own model language, you can decide which components you want to include. A typical minimal profile involves just three components, as in English's use of Generation, Lineage and Sex, though it is easy to imagine a language that does not distinguish between terms based on sex.

KinDEEP is actually exhausting, rather than exhaustive! For instance, it fails to have terms that have been enabled by reproductive science: the *womb-mother* (she carried the child of another in her womb), the *egg-donor* (she provided the egg that was fertilized and carried by the womb-mother), the *caretaker-mother* who actually raised the child but was not biologically related, the *sperm donor* and *caretaker-father*!

Table of kinship terms

L Language: D = Danish, E = English, H = Hawaiian, J = Japanese, L = Latin, M = Malay, N = Njamal (Australia), P = Pitjanjatjara (Australia), S = Swedish
Gen Generation
Ln Lineage: A = ablineal, C = colineal, D = direct
Sx Sex: F = female, M = male, S = corresponding
Sd Side of Family: M maternal, P paternal, ½ half, S step, H honorary
Per Person: 1 = first, 2 = second
B Relative Birth Order: O = older, Y = younger

L	Term, Translation	Gen	Ln	Sx	Sd	Per	B
E	great great grandparent	-4	D				
E	great grandparent	-3	D				
E	great aunt	-2	A	F			
S	*mormor*, maternal grandmother	-2	D	F	M		
S	*farmor*, paternal grandmother	-2	D	F	P		
E	grandmother	-2	D	F			
S	*morfar*, maternal grandfather	-2	D	M	M		
S	*farfar*, paternal grandfather	-2	D	M	P		
E	grandfather	-2	D	M			
E	grandparent	-2	D				
L	*matertera*, maternal aunt	-1	A	F	M		
P	*kurntili*, paternal aunt	-1	A	F	P		
L	*amita*, paternal aunt	-1	A	F	P		
E	aunt	-1	A	F			
J	*haha*, my mother	-1	D	F		1	
J	*okásan*, your mother	-1	D	F		2	
E	mother	-1	D	F			
P	*ngunytju*, mother or mother's sister	-1	D,A	F	M		
E	"uncle", man of father's generation	-1	A	M	H		
P	*kamura*, maternal uncle	-1	A	M	M		
L	*avunculus*, maternal uncle	-1	A	M	M		
L	*patruus*, paternal uncle	-1	A	M	P		
E	uncle	-1	A	M			
E	father	-1	D	M			

P	*mama*, father or father's brother	-1	D,A	M	P			
E	father or uncle	-1	D,A	M				
E	parent's sibling	-1	A					
E	parent	-1	D					
D	*kusine*, female cousin	0	A	F				
E	stepsister	0	C	F	½			
E	stepsister	0	C	F	S			
J	[N/A], my sister	0	C	F		1		
J	[N/A], your sister	0	C	F		2		
J	*ane*, older sister	0	C	F			O	
J	*imōto*, younger sister	0	C	F			Y	
E	sister	0	C	F				
D	*fætter*, male cousin	0	A	M				
E	stepbrother	0	C	M	½			
E	stepbrother	0	C	M	S			
J	[N/A], my brother	0	C	M		1		
J	[N/A], your brother	0	C	M		2		
J	*ani*, male older brother	0	C	M			O	
J	*otōto*, male younger brother	0	C	M			Y	
E	brother	0	C	M				
H	*kaikaina*, younger sibling of my gender	0	C	S			Y	
E	(first) cousin	0	A					
E	sibling	0	C					
M	[N/A], sibling or cousin	0						
E	daughter	1	D	F				
E	son	1	D	M				
E	cousin, first cousin once removed	1	A					
E	offspring	1	D					
E	granddaughter	2	D	F				
J	*mago*, my grandson	2	D	M		1		
J	*omagosan*, your grandson	2	D	M		2		
E	grandson	2	D	M				
E	grandchild	2	D					
E	family, parents and siblings	[-1,0]	D,C					
E	ancestor	[						
E	descendant	[>0]						
N	*maili*, anyone two generations removed	[2,-2]						

E	*cousin*, relative from common ancestor*		A	
E	*cousin*, member of kindred group		Hn	
E	*cousin*, relative by blood or marriage			
E	relative			
E	kin			

*English *cousin* is a relative descended from a common ancestor by two or more divergent steps, so KinDEEP does not offer a perfect translation, since it includes uncle and aunt.

Sen:esepera kinship terms

For my model language Sen:esepera, which is designed to fulfill the role of an interlanguage for use by people of all the world's linguistic backgrounds, I chose a maximally expressive way of forming kinship terms. All kinship terms are compounded from roots representing each symantic component and its atoms, as shown in the following table.

Person			Sen:esepera
		my	*imun*
		your	*tun*
Sex			
		male	*eman*
		female	*fem*
		corresponding	*sim*
Side			
		paternal	*pam*
		maternal	*fam*
		half-	*duen*
		step-	*tepim*
		honorary	*belim*
Generation			
		-3	*intensin*
		-2	*inten*
		-1	*in*
		0	*u*
		1	*dim*
		2	*dimin*
		3	*diminten*
Order			

Relative terms   83

	older	*tempan*
	younger	*im:tempan*
Lineage		
	direct	*pa*
	ablineal	*ta*
	colineal	*sa*
	unspecified	*coganta*

[*afo:*] before *intensin, diminten* means "great-"

[*afo:*] before *in, dim* means "all" (e.g., "*afo:in*" means "all ancestors")

Thus an English speaker can talk about his cousin, *u:ta* in Sen:esepera, if that is the term he is most comfortable with, while a Dutch speaker can talk about her *nicht* ("female cousin"), *fem:u:ta* in Sen:esepera, if that is the term she is most comfortable with. The word *fem:u:ta* will stand out to the English-speaker reading Sen:esepera, who does not habitually make the distinction of sex for cousin, but he will immediately know the meaning of the word.

Sen:esepera	**gloss**	Gen	Sx	Ln	Sd	Per	B
afo:intensin:pa	great great grandparent	-4		D			
intensin:pa	great grandparent	-3		D			
fem:inten:ta	great aunt	-2	F	A			
fem:fam:inten:pa	maternal grandmother	-2	F	D	M		
fem:pam:inten:pa	paternal grandmother	-2	F	D	P		
fem:inten:pa	grandmother	-2	F	D			
eman:fam:inten:pa	maternal grandfather	-2	M	D	M		
eman:pam:inten:pa	paternal grandfather	-2	M	D	P		
eman:inten:pa	grandfather	-2	M	D			
inten:pa	grandparent	-2		D			
fem:fam:in:ta	maternal aunt	-1	F	A	M		
fem:pam:in:ta	paternal aunt	-1	F	A	P		
fem:pam:in:ta	paternal aunt	-1	F	A	P		
fem:in:ta	aunt	-1	F	A			
imun:fem:in:pa	my mother	-1	F	D		1	
tun:fem:in:pa	your mother	-1	F	D		2	
fem:in:pa	mother	-1	F	D			

fem:fam:in:ta:pa	mother or mother's sister	-1	F	D,A	M		
eman:belim:in:ta	man of father's generation	-1	M	A	Hn		
eman:fam:in:ta	maternal uncle	-1	M	A	M		
eman:fam:in:ta	maternal uncle	-1	M	A	M		
eman:pam:in:ta	paternal uncle	-1	M	A	P		
eman:in:ta	uncle	-1	M	A			
eman:in:pa	father	-1	M	D			
eman:pam:in:ta:pa	father or father's brother	-1	M	D,A	P		
eman:in:ta:pa	father or uncle	-1	M	D,A			
in:ta	parent's sibling	-1		A			
in:pa	parent	-1		D			
fem:u:ta	female cousin	0	F	A			
fem:duen:u:sa	stepsister	0	F	C	½		
fem:tepim:u:sa	stepsister	0	F	C	S		
imun:fem:u:sa	my sister	0	F	C		1	
tun:fem:u:sa	your sister	0	F	C		2	
fem:u:tempan:sa	older sister	0	F	C			O
fem:u:im:tempan:sa	younger sister	0	F	C			Y
fem:u:sa	sister	0	F	C			
eman:u:ta	male cousin	0	M	A			
eman:duen:u:sa	stepbrother	0	M	C	½		
eman:tepim:u:sa	stepbrother	0	M	C	S		
imun:eman:u:sa	my brother	0	M	C		1	
tun:eman:u:sa	your brother	0	M	C		2	
eman:u:tempan:sa	male older brother	0	M	C			O
eman:u:im:tempan:sa	male younger brother	0	M	C			Y
eman:u:sa	brother	0	M	C			
sim:u:im:tempan:sa	younger sibling of my gender	0	S	C			Y
u:ta	child of aunt or uncle	0		A			
u:sa	sibling	0		C			
u:coganta	sibling or cousin	0					
fem:dim:pa	daughter	1	F	D			
eman:dim:pa	son	1	M	D			
dim:ta	first cousin once removed	1		A			
dim:pa	offspring	1		D			

Relative terms

fem:dimin:pa	granddaughter	2		F	D	
imun:eman:di-min:pa	my grandson	2		M	D	1
tun:eman:dimin:pa	your grandson	2		M	D	2
eman:dimin:pa	grandson	2		M	D	
dimin:pa	grandchild	2			D	
in:ta:o:u:sa	parents and siblings	[-1,0]			D,C	
afo:in:coganta	ancestor	[				
afo:dim:coganta	descendant	[>0]				
inten:dimin:coganta	anyone two generations removed	[2,-2]				

ta	relative from common ancestor
belim:coganta	member of kindred group or nation
coganta	relative by blood or marriage; kin

The Case for Cases

Most of the languages you've probably studied are analytical languages: English, German, Spanish, French, Italian. Most modern Romance languages have lost their inflections over time. This means they've lost their case system; instead of saying *vir urbis*, "man of the city", they say *vir de urbem*. A case system is just a way of directly marking nouns to indicate their role in the sentence, rather then preceding them with a preposition (or following them with a postposition).

While learning Latin makes most Catholic high schoolers clench up, the difficulty isn't that it has a nominative, genitive, dative, accusative, ablative and vocative case, but that it forms them five different ways (five DECLENSIONS), with different forms for the singular and the plural, plus it has irregular words.

After all, if all you had to learn was that *-us* was nominative, *-i* was genitive, *-o* was dative and ablative, *-um* was accusative and *-e* was vocative, that wouldn't be so hard, but instead you have to learn five declensions with up to 12 forms each. (Hey, India's ancient prestige language beats Europe's here: Sanskrit has 10 declensions with three genders and three numbers (singular, dual, plural) across 8 cases.)

The advantage of using cases is that you can omit the prepositions and have much more concise phrases. In a language like English, prepositions are among the most frequently used words. If you replace prepositions with cases, you get short phrases like *vir urbis* instead of "man of the city". In fact, 9.2% of English words in the British National Corpus were prepositions that could have been omitted had English possessed a case system, as the following table indicates.

The Case for Cases

Preposition	Frequency	Rank	Case
of	2.9%	3	Genitive
in, inside	1.8%	6	Inessive
to	0.9%	12	Terminative
for	0.8%	15	Ablative
with	0.7%	18	Comitative
on	0.6%	19	Adessive
by	0.5%	25	Instructive
at	0.5%	26	Locative
from	0.4%	29	Ablative

Adam Kilgarriff, "English word frequency list"

Cases are easiest for a native English speaker to understand if they are simply seen as replacements for prepositions. Of course, languages often have a hundred or so prepositions – far more than any language has cases – so cases end up being paired with prepositions. For instance, a language with just one locative case instead of the six locative cases of Finnish might assume an unmarked locative word indicated "at" and would precede the word with a locative preposition ("in", "inside", "on", "by", "above", "below") when needed to clarify.

Moreover one case, such as the ablative in Latin, can become the catch-all case used with almost any preposition; in fact, it is because prepositions are often used with cases that the cases themselves end up being redundant and fall out of use in favor of prepositions.

Case Systems

The simplest case system has just two cases:

- Subject case – the category of nouns serving as the grammatical subject of a verb
- Oblique case – any grammatical case other than the nominative

English has three cases

It is a common misconception that English **nouns** have a genitive case, marked by the possessive " 's " ending. Linguists however have shown that the English possessive is no longer a case at all, but has become a CLITIC, an independent particle which is always written and pronounced as part of the preceding word. This can be shown by the following example:

The King of Sparta's wife was called Helen.

If the English *'s* were a genitive, then the wife would belong to *Sparta*; but the *'s* attaches not to the word *Sparta* but to the entire phrase *King of Sparta*. Clitic *'s* can even attach to things that aren't nouns:

That boy of yours's impudence knows no bounds.

But English **pronouns** have three cases: e.g. nominative *I*, accusative *me*, genitive *my*. In fact, if you're wondering when to use the nominative or accusative, thinking of English pronouns should give you the answer.[5]

Number of cases

The number of cases in a language varies widely.

Language	Number of Cases
Anglo-Saxon	5
English	3 (pronouns only)
Estonian	14
Finnish	15
French	4 (pronouns only)
German	4
Hindi	3
Indo-European	8
Latin	4 to 7 (see below)
Latvian	7
Polish	7
Quechua	13
Sanskrit	8

Possible cases

While cases are often given obfuscative names, you can name them anything you want. The following table defines some commonly used cases.

Case	Type	Definition
ABESSIVE	Essive	"without"
ABLATIVE-1	Locative	location "from" or "from out of"

---

[5] But not if you have a conjunction. Many people would say *John and I* where they would say *me*; others say *John and me* where they would say *I*. —MR

ABLATIVE-2	Objective	instrument or manner or place of the action described by the verb
ACCUSATIVE	Objective	direct object of a verb
ADESSIVE	Locative	location "on"
ALLATIVE	Locative	location "onto"
CAUSAL	Other	cause ("because of")
COMITATIVE	Other	a companion role ("in company with", "together with")
DATIVE	Objective	indirect object of a verb
DISTRIBUTIVE	Other	"to each one of X"
ELATIVE	Locative	location "(from) out of"
ESSIVE	Essive	a temporary state of being ("as a ..."); the day something happens
GENITIVE	Genitive	ownership, especially inalienable possession (*my nose* is inalienable; *my pencil* is alienable)
ILLATIVE	Locative	location "into"
INESSIVE	Locative	location "in"
INSTRUCTIVE	Instrumental	means of accomplishing an action ("by means of")
INSTRUMENTAL	Instrumental	instrument achieving the action described by the verb
LIMITATIVE	Other	"only X", "nothing but X"
LOCATIVE	Locative	final location of action or the time of the action
NOMINATIVE	Nominative	grammatical subject of a verb
PARTITIVE		partialness ("some (of), any (of)")

POSSESSIVE	Genitive	alienable possession (*my nose* as opposed to *my pencil*)
PROLATIVE	Instrumental	"by way of"
TERMINATIVE	Locative	location indicating where the action ends
TRANSLATIVE	Essive	undergoing a change of state ("becoming", "changing to")
VOCATIVE	Other	referent of the noun is being addressed

You can, of course, make up your own cases. For instance, Jesse Bangs invented the *contradative* case for Yivrian. The contradative case indicates action against or to the harm of something, making it the opposite of the dative.

Latin

Here are the declensions for "lord" and "island".

	s	pl	s	pl
nominative	dominus	dominī	īnsula	īnsulae
accusative	dominum	dominōs	īnsulam	īnsulās
genitive	dominī	dominōrum	īnsulae	īnsulārum
dative	dominō	dominīs	īnsulae	īnsulīs
ablative	dominō	dominīs	īnsulā	īnsulīs
vocative	domine	dominī	īnsula	īnsulae

How many cases does Latin have? It depends on the word! The vocative only occurs for words ending in -*us* (which are very common). For neuter nouns, there is no separate accusative — you use the nominative instead. And the locative exists only for geographical names— e.g. *Rōma* "Rome" becomes *Rōmae* "at Rome".

German

German nouns have four cases. Here are the declensions for "book" and "name".

	s	pl	s	pl
nominative	Buch	Bücher	Name	Namen
accusative	Buch	Bücher	Namen	Namen
dative	Buch(e)	Büchern	Namen	Namen

The Case for Cases

| genitive | Buch(e)s | Bücher | Namens | Namen |

The forms show a good deal of SYNCRETISM — re-use of endings.

Quechua

The languages we've looked at so far have separate endings for singular and plural — e.g. the Latin ending *-ārum* is both genitive and plural. Quechua uses the same endings for singular and plural; the plural suffix *-kuna* appears before the case suffix. So "of the house" is *wasipa;* "of the houses" is *wasikunapa*.

nominative	(no suffix)
accusative	**-ta**
dative	**-man**
ablative	**-manta**
genitive	**-pa**
benefactive	**-paq**
instrumental	**-wan**
locative	**-pi**
terminative	**-kama**
transitive	**-nta**
causal	**-rayku**
limitative	**-pura**
distributive	**-nka**

Finnish

Finnish is worth a look for its six locative cases. There are three cases each for "in" and "at". Within each set, there are case for movement into, location (without movement), and movement out.

illative	majaan	into the house
inessive	majassa	in the house
elative	majasta	out of the house
allative	majalle	to the house
adessive	majalla	at the house
ablative	majalta	from the house

On Tolkien

Growing up with language

The Shakespeare of model languages is J.R.R. Tolkien. His best-selling fantasy novel, *The Lord Of The Rings*, now considered a literary classic, achieved much of its believability from the depth of its invented languages: Quenya, Sindarin, Adûnaic and others. The following article provides a broad overview of Tolkien's seminal work with model languages.

Tolkien was exposed to languages to a remarkable degree. He learned Latin, German and French from his mother. At school, he learned or taught himself Middle English, Old English, Finnish, Gothic, Greek, Italian, Old Norse, Spanish, modern Welsh and medieval Welsh. He had an amazing working knowledge of languages, and was familiar with Danish, Dutch, Lombardic, Norwegian, Russian, Swedish and many ancestral Germanic and Slavonic languages. It would have been no surprise to his mother that he became a professional philologist.

He even had a part-time job as a lexicographer for the original *Oxford English Dictionary* — the *New English Dictionary*, as it was known then. He worked for the dictionary in 1919-1920 and learned more about language than in any comparable period of his life. For instance, he had to develop the etymologies of words like *water, wick* and *winter*, and in so doing had to cite comparable forms in other languages like proto-Teutonic, Old Teutonic, Old Saxon, Middle Dutch, Modern Dutch, Old High German, Middle High German, Middle Low German, Modern German, Old Slavonic, Lithuanian, Russian and Latin. He did this commendably well; the head of the Dictionary, Dr. Henry Bradley, said of Tolkien, "His work gives evidence of an unusually thorough mastery of Anglo-Saxon and of the facts and principles of the comparative grammar of the Germanic languages. Indeed, I have no hesitation in saying that I have never known a man of his age who was in these respects his equal."

These were the natural languages that Tolkien learnt, and they served as an inspiration for his model languages.

As a child, Tolkien was first exposed to model languages when he learned a language his cousins had invented, called Animalic, which primarily consisted of English animal names. For instance, *Dog nightingale woodpecker forty* meant "You are an ass." Animalic served as an inspiration for Tolkien to create not just words, but his own language. He and one of his cousins created a more involved language than Animalic called Nevbosh (meaning New Nonsense) based on disguised pieces of English, Latin and French.

Nevbosh was his first attempt at creating an entire language. Already, when learning Greek, he had made up pseudo-Greek words, but Nevbosh went beyond that. Later, in his adolescence, Tolkien recalled Nevbosh and resolved to invent a serious language, one richly developed to model a natural language.

It is not surprising that Tolkien as a teenager attempted such an ambitious undertaking, given his already established love of language. As Tolkien's biographer, Humphrey Carpenter, writes, "If he had been interested in music, he very likely would have wanted to compose melodies, so why should he not make up a personal system of words that would be, as it were, a private symphony?" Since Tolkien's education had been intensively centered around language, when he began to create, those creations took a linguistic form.

Tolkien's first serious model language was called Naffarin. It was strongly influenced by Spanish, but with its own phonology (sound structure) and grammar. Tolkien chose Spanish because his guardian (he had been orphaned at the age of twelve) was half-Spanish and had lent him books on that language, which Tolkien found attractive.

Naffarin was but the first of many model languages that Tolkien would create. His next language began after he had purchased a Gothic primer from a friend and become captivated by that language. Years later, in a letter to W.H. Auden, Tolkien wrote, "I discovered in it [Gothic] not only modern historical philology, which appealed to the historical and scientific side [of me], but for the first time the study of a language out of mere love: I mean for the acute aesthetic pleasure derived from a language for its own sake, not only free from being useful but free even from being the vehicle of a literature."

Since little of Gothic's vocabulary survives in its small corpus, Tolkien soon found himself inventing words to fill in the gaps. This in turn inspired him to create a hypothetical historical Germanic language, one hitherto never discovered but with established relationships to Old English, Gothic and other Germanic tongues.

From Naffarin and Neo-Gothic, Tolkien went on to create a new model language, inspired by Finnish. He had been studying for exams in the Exeter College library at Oxford when he first encountered Finnish. Years later, he compared the experience to tasting a fine wine: "It was like discovering a complete wine-cellar filled with bottles of an amazing wine of a kind and flavour never tasted before. It quite intoxicated me; and I gave up the attempt to invent an unrecorded Germanic language, and my own language — or series of invented languages — became heavily Finnicized in phonetic pattern and structure." This was to become Quenya, his principal Elvish language, but elves had not yet entered the picture.

The chronological development of Tolkien's principal model languages:

- Nevbosh (inspired by English, French and Latin)
- Naffarin (inspired by Spanish)
- Neo-Gothic (filling holes in Gothic's vocabulary)
- "Unrecorded Germanic" (unnamed language related to Old English, Gothic and other Germanic tongues)
- Quenya (inspired by Finnish, influenced by Latin and Greek)
- Primitive Eldarin
- Sindarin (inspired by Welsh)

Tolkien had devoted considerable efforts to fleshing out Quenya, when he realized that he could not continue to create the language without knowing something of the people who spoke it. He had written poems in this language, but now he found himself needing to creating a history for these people, whoever they might be.

It so happened, at the age of 21, that he had an epiphany. He read for the first time the Old English religious poem *Crist of Cynewulf*. In it, he encountered two lines that were to fire his imagination for years: *Eala Earendel engla beorhtast ofer middengeard monnum sended*. "Hail Earendel, brightest of angels, above middle earth sent unto men." The words seemed to hint at something beautiful and remote. While the Old English dictionary recorded Earendel as a ray of light, Tolkien interpreted it literally as the star that heralded the dawn's light (Venus) and figuratively as John the Baptist, presaging Christ. In fact, Earendel heralded the light that would be diffused into the Two Trees, the Silmarils and the vial of

Galadriel: all prominent works of light in his fiction. Tolkien wanted to discover the truth behind these two Old English lines, and he began to conceive of a greater story, involving a mariner. From this simple line about Earendel, the line itself "a leaf caught in the wind", Tolkien began to discover the great tree of his mythology, which would pass through many seasons, growing from "The Lay of Earendel" to *The Book of Lost Tales* to *The Silmarillion*, *The Hobbit* and *The Lord of the Rings*.

As Tolkien wrote in his allegorical story "Leaf By Niggle", about a painter with a painting too detailed to ever finish:

> *There was one picture in particular which bothered him. It had begun with a leaf caught in the wind, and it became a tree; and the tree grew, sending out innumerable branches, and thrusting out the most fantastic roots. Strange birds came and settled on the twigs and had to be attended to. Then all round the Tree, and behind it, through the gaps in the leaves and boughs, a country began to open out; and there were glimpses of a forest marching over the land, and of mountains tipped with snow.*

From that first leaf caught in the wind, that first glimpse of Earendel, Tolkien then discovered elves, who were very different from the fairy folk he had once composed poems about. Elves possessed grandeur and dignity, being in fact — in Tolkien's mind — Un-Fallen Man. He realized that the language he had created was in fact spoken by these elves. As a result, he began to spend more time composing the stories of this imaginary world, "middle earth" (which was a common name for the world in Old English times, setting earth between heaven and hell). Still, the languages and name-making occupied as much of his time as the actual writing, since the writing of the history was for Tolkien but a subset of the act of language creation (or subcreation, to use his word for it, as he explicitly defined himself in relation to the Creator).

By 1917, Tolkien had expanded Quenya to many hundreds of words and had even outlined its ancestral tongue, Primitive Eldarin. Primitive Eldarin then gave rise to another prominent elvish language, Sindarin, which was modelled on the Welsh language that had fascinated Tolkien from boyhood and which he had finally begun to study at Oxford.

While Quenya was originally patterned on Finnish, it was later influenced by Latin and Greek. Quenya and Sindarin were both intended to be of a European kind in style and structure (but not in specifics) and both were meant to satisfy Tolkien's aesthetic taste in sound structure. Sindarin, or

Grey-elven, resembles Welsh phonologically and has a similar relationship to Quenya, or High-elven, as exists between British (meaning Celtic languages at the time of the Roman invasion) and Latin (both descended from Proto-Indo-European, as both Quenya and Sindarin were descended from Primitive Eldarin). The creation of Primitive Eldarin enabled Tolkien to later outline many other elvish languages, primarily as a backdrop for Quenya and Sindarin.

Tolkien had started out to create a language. He was now creating languages, peoples and a world.

Tolkien would often create a word by first starting with the needed meaning, then coming up with the forms as they would exist in Quenya and Sindarin. Other times, he would just make up a name in the heat of writing; later, he would either try and determine how the name had reached such a form or he would dismiss the form and come up with a new name. He viewed his languages as real languages that he was discovering, rather than inventing, and in one of his unfinished novels, *The Lost Road*, he has the protagonist, a philologist, gradually discover the lost words of a previously unknown tongue (Quenya or Sindarin), before being transported back into time towards the source of those words.

Characteristics of the Middle-Earth languages

Tolkien once said that he wrote *The Lord of the Rings* simply to create a world in which "A star shines on the hour of our meeting" (*Elen síla lumenn' omentielvo*) was a common salutation. While this exaggerates's motivation (*The Lord of the Rings* was originally conceived of simply as a sequel to capitalize on the commercial success of *The Hobbit*), it does highlight how interrelated writing and linguistic invention were for Tolkien.

Tolkien developed a very elaborate linguistic background for *The Lord of the Rings*, for it both as a hypothetically historical document and as an imagined world. He wrote the book as if it were the translation of an ancient manuscript, which he called the *Red Book*. The *Red Book* was written in a language called Westron, which was the tongue of the hobbits who narrated the tale. Tolkien decided that languages related to Westron would have to be translated into languages with equivalent relationships to English. The result is two layers of linguistic invention.

Model language	*Represented as*
Westron	English
Hobbit Westron	"Hobbit English"
"Rohirrimic"	"Rohirrimic Old English"

"language of Dale"   Old Norse
Sindarin   Sindarin
Quenya   Quenya (transliteration reflects Latin)

Hobbit English is the imaginary dialect of English that Tolkien chose to translate the hobbits' language into. This language differs somewhat from English, adapting some archaisms to its needs (reflecting the fact that Hobbit Westron was a dialect of Westron):

- The word *mathom* is used for a gift of dubious usefulness that one is reluctant to discard; Tolkien adapted it from the Old English *māþum*, "treasure".
- Another example is *Thane*, an inherited title of the leader of the Took clan of hobbits, adapted from the Old English *þegn*, a title for a noble who served an earl.
- The word *orc* is used to describe goblins and is from the Old English *orc* "demon", a word used in *Beowulf*.

One of the most interesting parts of Hobbit English isn't even used in the text of *The Lord of the Rings*, but is reserved for the appendices. Tolkien posed a linguistic what-if question: What if the Latin calendar's names for months hadn't supplanted the Anglo-Saxon names? What would the names of months look like in English then? The result is names like *Afteryule* for January and *Blotmath* for October, names true to the original forms. The fact that such details had to be crammed into an appendix illustrates how — even though Tolkien was primarily interested in the languages — he could subordinate that material to the story when appropriate, including it as notes rather than cluttering the story.

Month names in Hobbit English

Hobbit English	*Old English*	*English*
Afteryule	*aeftergēola* "afteryule"	January
Solmath	*solmōnaþ* "mire-month"	February
Rethe	*Hrēþ* "fierce, furious"	March
Astron	*Easter-mōnaþ* "Easter-month"	April
Thrimidge	*thrimilce*	May
Forelithe	*līþa*, "midsummer (June, July)"	June
Afterlithe	*aefter-līþa*	July
Wedmath	*weod* "mild, gentle"	August
Halimath	*hālig-mōnaþ* "holy-month"	September
Winterfilth	*winter-fylleth* "winter fall"	October
Blotmath	*blōtmōnaþ* "blood-month"	November
Foreyule	*gēola* "Yule"	December

In ancient times, the hobbits lived near the riders of Rohan, whose language had changed little from those times. With Hobbit Westron now translated as English, to convey this relationship Tolkien translated the language of the Rohirrim (in the hypothetical manuscript) into words and names that were similar, though not exactly like, Old English words and names.

Since Tolkien conceived of the language of Dale and the Long Lake (regions in Middle Earth) as somewhat more removed from the hobbits' language, he represented it as Old Norse in a few names, primarily that of the dwarves. While dwarves had their own language, they considered their names private and adopted outward names that were common among the people they dwelt by.

Westron is descended from the human Adûnaic language, but almost all of the names in Gondor are Elvish, as a result of the long alliance between the men of Gondor and the elves in their wars against the dark powers.

The Elvish languages were of course the source of most of Tolkien's energies when it came to the creation of model languages. For these languages, Tolkien created a vocabulary of incredible detail. By 1938, he had prepared a base vocabulary of 800 root words of Primitive Eldarin, from which he could derive many other words for many other languages. For instance, the root *bes- meant "wed" and had descendents *besnó, "husband"; *bessé, "wife"; and *besú, "husband and wife, married pair"; and *bestá, "matrimony". Each of these roots then had different descendants in different languages; the six known descendents of just *besno, "husband" are shown below.

Sample cognate Elvish words:

Language	Word	Meaning
Primitive Eldarin	*besnó	"husband"
Quenya	verno	"husband"
Old Noldorin	benno	"husband"
Exilic Noldorin	benn	"man"
	[Replacing in ordinary use the old word dîr (< *der-, "adult male")]	
Exilic Noldorin	hervenn	"husband"
	[< her- (< *kher-, "rule, govern, possess") + benn, counterpart to hervess, "wife"]	
Ilkorin	benn	"husband"
Danian	beorn	"man"

> [Blended with *ber(n)ó, "man" (< *ber-, "valiant man")]
> J.R.R. Tolkien, *The Lost Road and Other Writings*

Incidentally, the asterisk is a common philological symbol to indicate that there is no direct extant evidence that such a form existed but it is assumed to exist based on reconstruction from the available descendents. The asterisk is frequently used to indicate Indo-European roots, from which most European languages are descended. Tolkien used it to indicate that the root forms had been reconstructed by Elvish scholars.

Tolkien developed a regular system of sound change to govern how words were typically modified from Primitive Eldarin to the descendent languages. Sometimes these regular sound changes were overridden, as in Danian *beorn*, whose form developed idiosyncratically under the influence of *ber(n)ó, which had come to mean "man" by semantic change, broadening its meaning from "valiant man". Such an instance of semantic change demonstrates how richly Tolkien developed his model languages in order to make them more true to real life linguistic processes. As his son Christopher Tolkien — close confidant and later editor of many of his father's papers — was to phrase it:

> *He did not, after all, invent new words and names arbitrarily: in principle, he devised them from within the historical structure, proceeding from the bases or primitive stems, adding suffix or prefix or forming compounds, deciding (or, as he would have said, finding out) when the word came into the language, following through the regular changes of form that it would thus have undergone, and observing the possibilities of formal or semantic influence from other words in the course of its history. Such a word would then exist for him, and he would know it. As the whole system evolved and expanded, the possibilities for word and name became greater and greater.*
> Christopher Tolkien, *The Lost Road and Other Writings*, p. 342

Or as Tolkien himself put in when writing about Niggle: "He used to spend a long time on a single leaf, trying to catch its shape, and its sheen, and the glistening of dewdrops on its edges. Yet he wanted to paint a whole tree, with all of its leaves in the same style, and all of them different."

As the cognate terms of *besnó* imply, Tolkien had conceived of a complex tree of interrelated languages.

Tree of tongues: interrelationship of elvish languages

+ dead language

    Valarin
        Valinorian
            Ingwiquenya +
            Quenya (Elf-latin) +
        Quendian
        Lembian
            many dialects
        Danian
            Taliskan +
                tongues of Western men +
            Leikvian (East Danian) +
            Ossiriandic
        Eldarin
            Koreldarin
                Lindarin
                Kornoldorin (Finrodian)
                Noldirin (in Beleriand) +
            Telerin
                Telerin (in Valinor)
            Beleriandic
                Doriathrin

J.R.R. Tolkien, *The Lost Road and Other Writings*, p. 196

This is just one of Tolkien's conceptions (circa 1937) of the interrelationships of the Elvish languages. He often revised it and reconsidered it. However, the two principal languages were always Quenya and Noldirin (the earlier name of Sindarin).

Tolkien invented the most elaborate model language system ever published as part of a work of fiction. What had started out quite simple had grown. Yet, again and again, Tolkien failed to prepare a final grammar and lexicon for any of his languages. His goal was not to create a finished language system, but to simply delight in creating words and linguistic shapes in the fabric of an imagined time. The joy was in the finding.

Here is the most well known of Tolkien's Elvish poems. This is a hymn to Elbereth that was sung in the house of Elrond in *The Fellowship of the Ring*:

    A Elbereth Gilthoniel

> *silivren penna miriel*
> *o menel aglar elenath!*
> *Na-chaered palan-díriel*
> *o galadhremmin ennorath*
> *Fanuilos le linnathon*
> *nef aear, si nef aearon!*
>
> O Star-queen, Star-kindler,
> glittering down and sparkling like jewels
> from the firmanent's glory of the host of stars!
> To remote distance after having gazed
> from tree-woven middle-earth,
> Snow-white, to thee I will chant,
> on this side of the ocean, here on this side of the great ocean!

For Tolkien, inventing model languages was an intellectual exercise of great seriousness, yet he realized how unusual these activities were. While he felt many children created simple languages, as he and his cousins had done, he was not aware of many others who took inventing languages as seriously as he did. Indeed, while he found his "private lang." activities to be a source of constant amusement, he would dismiss these activities when discussing them, calling it "a mad hobby" when talking to friends or "my nonsense fairy language" when talking about it with his wife.

Yet for him his model languages were an almost spiritual exercise as he followed his love of language and myth. He viewed his creation of languages as a Christian art, an act of subcreation that assisted the Lord in creating the world, perhaps creating even a part of heaven.

Tolkien's Niggle, once he had completed his "long" and "distasteful" journey (an allegory for death), at last found his way to a new country:

> *Before him stood the Tree, his Tree, finished. If you could say that of a Tree that was alive, its leaves opening, its branches growing and bending in the wind that Niggle had so often felt or guessed, and had so often failed to catch. He gazed at the Tree, and slowly he lifted his arms and opened them wide.*
>
> *"It's a gift!" he said.*

For further reading

"Leaf By Niggle", in J.R.R. Tolkien, *Poems and Stories*, Houghton Mifflin: Boston, 1994.

Tolkien, Christopher; Ed. *The Lost Road and Other Writings: Language And Legend Before 'The Lord of the Rings'*. Houghton Mifflin: Boston, 1987. — About 50 pages of etymologies for Primitive Eldarin and its daughter tongues, providing a unique behind-the-scenes look at Quenya and Sindarin.

Carpenter, Humphrey. *Tolkien: A Biography*. Ballantine Books: New York, 1978.

Carpenter, Humphrey; Ed. *The Letters of J.R.R. Tolkien*. Houghton Mifflin: Boston, 1981. Tolkien discusses his languages and approach to creating them in some of these letters. One example, from a letter to Naomi Mitchison, 4/25/1954:

> *Two of the Elvish tongues appear in this book... They are intended (a) to be definitely of a European kind in style and structure (not in detail); and (b) to be specially pleasant. The former is not difficult to achieve; but the latter is more difficult, since individual's personal predilections, especially in the phonetic structure of languages, varies widely, even when modified by the imposed languages (including their so-called native tongue).*
>
> *I have therefore pleased myself. The archaic language of lore is meant to be a kind of Elven-latin, and by transcribing it into a spelling closely resembling that of Latin (except that y is only used a consonant as y in E. Yes) the similarity to Latin has been increased ocularly. Actually it might be said to be composed on a Latin basis with two other (main) ingredients that happen to give me phonaesthetic pleasure: Finnish and Greek. It is however less consonantal than any of the three. This language is High-elven or in its own terms Quenya (Elvish).*

I bought *J.R.R. Tolkien: The Man Who Created "The Lord of the Rings"* (Michael Coren, 2004) for one of my sons. It is a good children's biography of our king of langmakers. While it doesn't discuss his language invention in any detail (Humphrey Carpenter's biography is better for that), it provides a detailed look at his life and at his two most popular works, *The Hobbit* and *The Lord of the Rings*.

Emulating Tolkien: Alvish

When learning a craft, whether writing, sculpting or creating model languages, it always helps to begin by purposefully copying a master's style. This enables you to begin creating and gives you time to experiment prior to developing your own style. For instance, my first poetry slavishly followed e.e. cummings. My first attempt at a children's book faithfully echoed the voice of Dr. Seuss. Interestingly, my first attempt at a model language did not emulate Tolkien, but copied Clyde Heaton's Orcish, a language he published in an article called "Even Orcish is logical" (*Dragon* magazine, July 1983), which started me on this hobby.

One of the language families I have tinkered with the longest is meant to be spoken by elves, like Tolkien's Quenya and Sindarin; my Alvish and Old Alvish languages date back some 13 years now. My first attempt at Alvish was patterned closely on Anglo-Saxon, and the language existed as little more than a source language for Karklak, then the principal language I was working on. About five years ago, I revamped Alvish to resemble ancient Greek, which I first thought gave the language a noble sound. When that did not meet my fancy, I revamped the language again and developed a 3000-word vocabulary for it. Some sample vocabulary, from Alvish III:

age, n.	**thufpaxef**, neut. (thoofPAHKSef)
age, v.	**thufpaxere**, neut. (thoofpahksEre)
agree, v.	**cupfuscrifere**, neut. (koopfooskriFEre)
agreement, n.	**cupfuscrifep**, neut. (koopfoosKRIfep)
agriculture, n.	**mudolrelep**, neut. (moodolRElep)
ahem, interj.	**ixax** (IKSahks)
ahoy, interj.	**esathnebis** (eSAHTHnebis)
aid, v.	**ethere**, neut. (Ethere)
air, n.	**tusef**, neut. (TOOSef)
alarm, v.	**esadadere**, neut. (esahDAHdere)
alas, interj.	**frithfrith** (FRITHfrith)
alienate, v.	**apadere**, neut. (ahpahDEre)

alignment, n.	**fadap**, f. (FAHdahp)
all, adj.	**quafeth**, neut. (QUAHfeth)
all, adv.	**quaferemi**, neut. (quahFEremi)
all, n.	**quafep**, neut. (QUAHfep)
alleluia, interj.	**ipipneb** (Ipipneb)

I have no idea what I was aiming for, but the result is undeniably ugly. *Ipipneb? Frithfrith?*

Recently, I have decided to try and pattern Alvish more closely on Quenya and Sindarin, inspired in part by a recent discussion on the CONLANG mailing list, where David Bell discussed his language Amman-lar, originally a Tolkien clone, before Bell found his own voice.

Before creating Alvish IV, I closely studied the Quenya and Sindarin words published in *The Silmarillion*. I decided that what sounded pleasing to me was the emphasis on sounds produced towards the front of the mouth (e.g., /p/, /b/, /f/, /v/, /i/, /e/, /a/). Additionally, syllables in Sindarin and Quenya typically followed the style CV or CVN, where N was a nasal (/m/ or /n/), lateral (/l/) or approximant (/r/). Based on this insight, I then produced the following definition of the PHONOTACTICS (sound and syllable structure) for Old Alvish, the ancestor of Alvish:

    (Con1) Vwl (Con2)

where

    Con1 = p, b, f, v, t, d, c, g, y, w, ch, gh
    Vwl = i, a, o, u, uu
    Con2 = m, l, n, r, s

The /c/ is pronounced as in *cat*, /ch/ as in *loch* (IPA x), /gh/ is a voiced /ch/ (IPA ɣ). Each of the above lists of phonemes is roughly arranged with those sounds pronounced closest to the front of the mouth listed first. Sounds are listed in declining order of occurrence in actual Old Alvish words.

A further restriction to possible combinations of phonemes is that whenever there are two adjacent vowels (e.g., the /i/ and /o/ are in separate syllables in *dios*, /di-os/) they can only be one of the following: i-o, i-uu, i-a, u-o, u-i, u-a, o-i. So, for example, *diis* is not a valid Old Alvish word, since /i-i/ is not a valid combination. (The dash - is used to indicate syllable breaks.)

ALVISH

Some sample Old Alvish words and phrases:

> *anim*
> *basuus*
> *buci*
> *chi gicuu*
> *dafon*
> *ghis*
> *gibas*
> *ogus dian*
> *toman*
> *vafus*

The sound system for Old Alvish is less flexible than that of Tolkien's languages. Words like *Aglarond, Amarth, Bragollach* and *Minas Tirith* could not be formed in Old Alvish, due its different syllable structure, but would be probably be borrowed in forms like *Agelaronde, Amarte, Beragolcha* and *Minas Tirti*.

But Old Alvish's sole purpose in my design is to provide a source for Alvish. I designed Old Alvish to have an elegant structure, which has become more complicated (and therefore more flexible) in Alvish.

I decided that Alvish developed from Old Alvish according to the following steps. First, Middle Alvish was distinguished from Old Alvish by the following sound shifts, designed to give the language even more front sounds:

> /c/ > /th/
> /g/ > /h/
> /ch/ > /c/
> /gh/ > /g/
> /a/ > /e/
> /uu/ > /o/
> /o/ > /a/

This had the net effect of giving Middle Alvish three sounds that it did not have before (/th/, /h/ and /e/) while eliminating three sounds that it had had (/ch/, /gh/ and /uu/).

Some examples:

> MA *buthi* < OA *buci*
> MA *ci hitho* < OA *chi gicuu*

MA *defan* < OA *dafon*
MA *gis* < OA *ghis*

As this example should illustrate, you can quickly generate your own languages, based on a source language, simply by preparing tables of sound correspondences such as the one above. A phoneme can gradually become pronounced as any "neighboring" sound, where a "neighborhood" consists of similar physical points of articulation. By this measure, the shift of /c/ to /th/ is unlikely, as the physical positions of the two sounds are far apart, but this can be explained away by positing an intermediate step; e.g., the sound /c/ came to be pronounced as /t/ (as in OA *buci* becoming Early Middle Alvish *buti*), before the /t/ phonemes so produced came to be pronounced as /th/ (MA *buthi*).

The next series of sound shifts distinguishes Middle Alvish from Alvish and is more complex. In this series, there are no straightforward one- to-one correspondences, where one occurrence of a phoneme always becomes another phoneme. In the transition to Alvish, sounds changed only because of their environment (the other sounds they are pronounced near). While the notation used to describe these can grow quite complex, inventing sound changes like the following is not difficult. Basically, I spent a lot of time trying to make sure that Alvish words fit my preconceptions of what words I found aesthetically pleasing, and I then formulated rules to give me a way to get from the strict phonotactics of Old Alvish to something looser.

The main changes from Alvish to Old Alvish are in the phonotactics. An Alvish word can begin or end with any consonant, but the consonants in the middle must follow similar patterns to Old Alvish.

FIRST SYLLABLE	(ConWI) Vwl (ConSF)
INTERNAL SYLLABLES	(ConSI) Vwl (ConSF)
TERMINAL SYLLABLE	(ConSI) Vwl (ConWF)
ONE-SYLLABLE WORD	(ConWI) Vwl (ConWF)

where

ConWI = p, b, f, v, t, d, c, g, y, w, th, h, m, l, n, r, s, sp, st, sc
ConSI = p, b, f, v, t, d, c, g, y, w, th, h, s, sp, st, sc
Vwl = i, e, a, u, o
ConSF = m, l, n, r
ConWF = p, b, f, v, t, d, c, g, y, w, th, h, m, l, n, r, s

Clearly, this sort of mapping out of all sound combinations can grow much more complex than you want or need for a model language, but the complexity of Alvish phonotactics pales in comparison to the phonotactics of English, which would take a small book to describe in detail (e.g., the only time an English word can begin with three consonant sounds the first consonant has to be /s/, as in *spring*, not something like *zbring*).

The rules for deriving Alvish words from Middle Alvish are:

/ti/ > /thi/

/a-i/ > /i-a/ (eliminating the only vowel pair to begin with /a/; e.g., /thi-al-fu/ < MA /tha-il-fu/)

/s-/ > /-s/ (removing /s/ from being a possible final consonant for internal syllables; e.g., /i-san/ > MA /is-an/)

/-sX/ > /-X/ where X ≠/a/,/e/,/i/,/o/,/u/,/p/,/t/,/c/ (any /s/ that migrated before an X is omitted; e.g., /pa-fu/ < MA /pas-fu/)

/-DVC#/ > /D#/ where D=/t/,/d/; V is a vowel, C is consonant and # indicates the end of a word (this rule indicates that final syllables that begin with /t/ or /d/ move the dental phoneme to the end of the previous syllable and truncate the remaining syllable; e.g., /alt/ < MA /al-ten/)

/mD#/ > /nD#/ (any final /md/ or /mt/ formed by the previous rule replaces /m/ with /n/)

/#V1T-V2/ > /#TV2/ where T=/m/,/n/,/l/,/r/,/s/ (any word that begins with a vowel and is followed by a syllable-terminating consonant and a following vowel — starting a new syllable — drops the initial vowel and moves the consonant to the next syllable; e.g., /nim/ < MA /en- im/).

One thing I've ignored when doing sounds shifts is whether a phoneme was in a stressed or unstressed syllable. Contrast English /ob-JECT/ ("I object, your honor") to /OB-ject/ ("the object of the game is this"). In English, the vowel /o/ has become a schwa in the unstressed syllable in /ob-JECT/ but not in the stressed syllable in /OB-ject/. Rather than deal with the issue of stress (which in the Alvish languages always falls on the penultimate — next-to-last — syllable), I decided that elves are more fastidious in their pronunciation and blur sounds less in unstressed syllables than mere mortals do... It's a cop out, but this is supposed to be fun, right?

I won't formally describe the rules for forming compound words in Alvish. But forming compounds does have a number of twists, mainly designed to make sure that the resulting word matches the phonotactics of Alvish defined above. The rules:

- For the first of the two words compounded, anytime a vowel immediately follows another vowel (e.g., /e/ in /i-e/), that vowel is dropped.
- When the first word ends in a vowel and the second word begins with a vowel, those vowels change into an acceptable vowel pair (if they're not already); e.g., i-a, i-o, i-e, u-a, u-i, u-e.
- When the first word ends in a consonant, that consonant can be only /m/, /n/, /l/ or /r/, otherwise it moves to the front of the second word (if the second word begins with a vowel) or it is deleted.
- This process is inverted when the second word *begins* with a consonant; since that consonant cannot be /m/, /n/, /l/ or /r/, the consonant moves to the end of the first word, unless the first word ends in a consonant, in which case it is dropped altogether. Whew!

Based on all these rules, I derived some sample words for Alvish. These words have no assigned meanings, since I have just been experimenting to make sure that I like the resulting sounds of the words generated.

a-hu-di-en [< a-hus di-en < OA o-gus + di-an]
a-pun [< OA o-pun]
alt [< MA al-ten < OA ol-tan]
as [< OA os]
ban-u [< OA bon-u]
be [< OA ba]
be-sos [< MA bes-os < OA bas-uus]
bel [< OA bal]
bet [< MA be-tu < OA ba-tu]
bi-al [< MA ba-il < OA bo-il]
bi-hi-bes [< OA bi + gi-bas]
bi-om [< OA bi-uum]
bo-ses [< MA bos-es < OA buus-as]
bol-i-e-ba [< bol-e e-ba < OA buul-a + a-bo]
bot [< MA bo-thar < OA buu-cor]
bul-a-sim [< bu-el a-sim < MA bu-el as-im < OA bu-al + os-im]
but [< MA bu-thi < OA bu-ci]
ci-hit [< MA ci hi-tho < OA chi + gi-cuu]

de-fan [< OA da-fon]
di-os [< OA di-uus]
di-si [< di-as i < OA di-os + i]
dir-a-bi-en [< di-ar-a bi-en < OA di-or-o + bi-an]
du-an [< OA du-on]
du-ha [< OA du-go]
e [< OA a]
e-bun-bid [< MA e-bun bi-da < OA a-bun + bi-do]
e-pa-tam-en [< OA a-po + tom-an]
em-ho [< OA am-guu]
fa-po [< OA fo-puu]
far [< OA for]
fe-pu [< OA fa-pu]
fe-vin-ve-fus [< OA fa-vin + va-fus]
fel-im-fon-et [< fel-i-am fon-et < MA fel-a-im fon-e-tul < OA fal-o-im + fuun-a-tul]
fes [< OA fas]
fir-o [< OA fir-uu]
fu-en [< OA fu-an]
gi-su [< gis u < OA ghis + u]
hit [< MA hi-tan < OA gi-ton]
i-ba [< OA i-bo]
i-fen-pur [< OA i-fan-pur]
i-san [< MA is-an < OA is-on]
ir-u-se [< MA ir us-e < OA ir + us-a]
ni [< MA on-i < OA uun-i]
nim [< MA en-im < OA an-im]
nur [< MA en-ur < OA an-ur]
o-fam [< OA uu-fom]
pa-fu [< MA pas-fu < OA pos-fu]
pa-fu [< OA po-fu] (arrived at the same form as the previous word but by a different route)
pe-yil [< OA pa-yil]
pi-em-do [< OA pi-am-duu]
pi-fem [< OA pi-fam]
pi-sun-bi-as [< MA pis-un ba-is < OA pis-un + bo-is]
pir-di-fus [< pi-ar di-fus < OA pi-or + di-fus]
po-fu [< OA puu-fu]
po-vi [< OA puu-vi]
pod [< MA po-des < OA puu-das]
pom-i [< OA puum-i]
pu-em [< OA pu-am]
pu-il [< OA]

pul-on [< OA pul-uun]
ran [< MA er-an < OA ar-on]
te [< OA ta]
ter-in [< OA tar-in]
the-wom-o [< OA ca-wuum-uu]
thi [< OA ci]
thi-al-fu [< MA tha-il-fu < OA co-il-fu]
thi-as [< OA ci-os]
thin-o [< thi-on no < MA thi-on an-o < OA ci-uun + on-uu]
tho-pa [< OA cuu-po]
thot [< MA tho-tol < OA cuu-tuul]
ti-po-dom-pi [< OA ti-puu + duum-pi]
ti-vol [< OA ti-vuul]
tim-vul-po-wim [< OA tim-vul + puu-wim]
tin [< OA]
to-por [< OA tuu-puur]
tu-es [< OA tu-as]
u-fi [< OA]
u-va [< OA u-vo]
um [< OA]
urt [< MA ur-thi < OA ur-ci]
ut [< MA u-tho < OA u-cuu]
va [< OA vo]
val-i [< OA vol-i]
vam [< OA vom]
vem [< OA vam]
vi-al [< MA va-il < OA vo-il]
vi-fom-fe-hu [< OA vi-fuum + fa-gu]
vim-u [< OA]
vo-fi [< OA vuu-fi]
vod [< MA vo-di < OA vuu-di]
wil-pe [< OA wil-pa]
ya-wir-os [< OA yo-wir-uus]
yar-o [< OA yor-uu]
ye-bon [< OA ya-buun]
yed [< MA ye-dum < OA ya-dum]
yi-si-pu [< yis i-pu < OA yis + i-pu]
yo [< OA yuu]
yu-es [< OA yu-as]
yu-pi [< OA]

Some sample sentences (really just random sequences of words):

Ut ofam tivol pomi fes te pafu firo vial fevinvefus.
Bihibes fepu yupi be thopa biom ahudien vali yed puem.
Vifomfehu wilpe iba apun iruse piemdo thino duha bulasim fapo.
Ut tipodompi dirabien boses bial e terin yebon ufi ni.
Vam va dios thewomo thi defan urt bot ifenpur uva.
Fuen pofu vem as nur bet pirdifus ebunbid tin bel.
Pifem hit isan epatamen tues nim duan bolieba vofi pisunbias.
Disi vimu banu cihit pod thialfu pulon yawiros besos yaro.
Yo pafu ran peyil timvulpowim puil alt thias topor um.
Yisipu be felimfonet thot emho vod povi yues far gisu.

So there you have the sounds of Alvish.

Barsoomian

Background

John Carter was the first human in history to visit Mars. His travels and those of his compatriots have been recorded in Edgar Rice Burroughs's eleven volumes about Barsoom, as the natives call the Red Planet. These books include:

> *A Princess Of Mars*
> *The Gods Of Mars*
> *The Warlord Of Mars*
> *Thuvia, Maid Of Mars*
> *The Chessmen Of Mars*
> *The Mastermind Of Mars*
> *Fighting Man Of Mars*
> *Swords Of Mars*
> *Synthetic Men Of Mars*
> *Llana Of Gathol*
> *John Carter Of Mars*

The following descriptions of the Barsoomian language were recorded by Captain John Carter in *A Princess Of Mars*:

> *This power [telepathy] is wonderfully developed in all Martians, and accounts largely for the simplicity of their language and the relatively few spoken words exchanged even in long conversations. It is the universal language of Mars, through the medium of which the higher and lower animals of this world of paradoxes are able to communicate to a greater or less extent, depending upon the intellectual sphere of the species and the development of the individual.*

> *The Martian language, as I have said, is extremely simple, and in a week I could make all my wants known and understand nearly everything that was said to me. Likewise, under Sola's tutelage, I developed my telepathic powers so that I shortly could sense practically everything that went on around me.*
>
> *'In the name of my first ancestor, then,' she continued, 'where may you be from? You are like unto my people, and yet so unlike. You speak my language, and yet I heard you tell Tars Tarkas that you had but learned it recently. All Barsoomians speak the same tongue from the ice-clad south to the ice-clad north, though their written languages differ. Only in the valley Dor, where the river Iss empties into the lost sea of Korus, is there supposed to be a different language spoken, and, except in the legends of our ancestors, there is no record of a Barsoomian returning up the river Iss.'*

These excerpts, excepting a few others that repeat information shown in these, are all the direct comments we have concerning the nature of Barsoomian. Captain Carter's failure to explore these matters in more depth indicates his lack of linguistic background; he did not realize how unusual Barsoomian was compared to Earth languages. Barsoomian differs in the following main ways:

- The language is closely tied to telepathy. Words can either be telepathically projected or spoken, with the majority of words apparently projected (Carter writes "relatively few spoken words [are] exchanged even in long conversations").
- The language has a strong biological basis (no doubt tied to the telepathic capability), being known across species and races of men. Where on Earth *homo sapiens* is the only species to develop linguistic capabilities, Barsoomians apparently first developed a language long ago in a primal species; this capability has then evolved while maintaining compability across species. (Little is known about the language of Dor.)
- The language changes slowly. Given that the different races are separated by vast distances and had in many cases become isolated from one another, yet still speak the same language, it is clear that some influence — probably biological — keeps the language from changing at the same pace as the languages of Earth humans. One factor in this conservatism has to be the long lifespans of the races of Martian men, who can live up to a thousand years if not killed in battle. If Earthly humans lived on average a thousand years (compared to the average of 20 years at the

time of Christ), Terran languages might have changed 50 times slower than they did (1000 divided by 20 = 50).
- The Barsoomian language can be learned very quickly. While this was no doubt exaggerated for convenience of the narrative, the grammar and vocabulary must be significantly more regular than most Earth languages.

Phonology and Orthography

Because the only field notes we have for Barsoomian came from a soldier who was untrained in linguistics, we do not have an accurate understanding of how Barsoomian is pronounced. To further complicate things, John Carter's manuscript used hieroglyphics to represent Barsoomian words; Edgar Rice Burroughs, who prepared John Carter's manuscripts for publication, then spelled these words as he heard John Carter pronounce them. For instance, in a footnote discussed the use of the word *radium* in *A Princess Of Mars*, Burroughs writes, "In Captain Carter's manuscript it [radium] is mentioned always by the name used in the written language of Helium and is spelled in hieroglyphics, which it would be difficult and useless to reproduce."

Burroughs transcribed all words as if they were English words; thus *zode*, for instance, is probably pronounced with a silent 'e' (to rhyme with *lode*), but we cannot be sure.

Burroughs used the following vowel symbols: A, AI, E, EE, I, O, OO, U.

He used the following consonant symbols and digraphs: B, C, D, DJ, DW, F, G, H, K, L, LL, M, N, NG, PT, QU, R, S, SK, ST, SS, T, TH, TZ, V, X. Two digraphs are used only in dialects - LL is used only in Okarian, while SS is used only in the valley Dor.

The exact sounds of all of these symbols are currently unknown. For instance, without further field study, we cannot know whether 'th' was voiced or unvoiced, whether 'dj' was pronounced [dy] or [dʒ].

The following consonant clusters may be treated as single consonants in the morphology: DJ, DW, PT, QU, SK and ST. This is still being investigated.

We do not know why John Carter chose to use the letter 'c' instead of 'k'; perhaps this was colored by the knowledge of one of the Barsoomian writing systems. Barsoomian races had many different methods of writing, ranging from pictographs to ideographs and perhaps even to consonantal alphabets. More likely, this was simply an arbitrary decision of John Carter's part. Our analysis of the vocabulary shows no instances where Carter's use of 'c' or 'k' distinguishes two words (e.g., there is no word *kalot* as distinct from *calot*). Therefore, we feel that 'c' and 'k' both represent the same underlying sound /k/. (The only words using 'c' are *calot* and two proper nouns: *Bar Comas* and *Carthoris*.)

Phonotactics

Phonotactics is the sequential arrangements of phonemes that are possible in a language. Acceptable syllables seem to be V, CV, CVC, CVCC, and CCVC.

- There do not seem to be significant restrictions on the final consonant in CVC syllables.
- For final clusters, we see *lk nth pt rk rd rn rt rs rth rz tz*. It seems that r+C is freely allowed.
- We see final *ss ll*, though it's not clear if these are geminate, or reflect a difference in the vowel, or even a separate phoneme.
- For initial clusters, we see *dw pt qu sk st thr*, a much more limited but also very miscellaneous set.

A fuller explanation awaits more field work.

The form *thurds* does not fit, but is likely to be Barsoomian *thurd* plus the English plural.

Grammar

Little is known about Barsoomian grammar, though it must have been a comparatively simple grammar for John Carter to have been able to learn it so quickly. The following are all hypotheses about the grammar:

- Barsoomian lacks number distinctions, articles and noun declensions.
- Barsoomian does not conjugate verbs or mark them for tense. For instance, *sak* is translated both as "jump!" (imperative) and "to jump" (infinitive).
- Sentences follow the SVO order - Subject, Verb, Object.
- Questions have the same sentence form as statements, but end in a question word, such as "who", "what", "when", "why", or "maybe". The sentence "When will we enjoy the death throes of the red one? or does Lorquas Ptomel, Jed, intend holding her for

ransom?" would have a literal translation of "We has joy of death pains of red woman when? or Lorquas Ptomel, Jed, put her up for ransom, maybe?"
- The language has a second person pronoun contrast between formal and familiar (translated by Carter as "thee" or "thou"). It is assumed it had pronouns for first, second and third person. If most words are unmarked for part of speech, the language may have had no special forms for possessive pronouns.

Word Sets

This section looks at word sets such as proper names, numbers and military terms.

Proper Names

Naming practices differ significantly from culture to culture on Barsoom. In many culture's, a father's name is often incorporated into the name of his son, either as the first or second element:

- Mors Kajak, son of Tardos Mors (of Helium)
- Djor Kantos, son of Kantos Kan (of Helium)
- Sab Than, son of Than Khosis (of Zodanga)
- Hal Vas, son of Vas Kor (of Dusar)

Among the green men, once a green Martian kills his first warrior, he takes that warrior's second name as his own. John Carter, when he lived among the green men, earned the name *Dotar Sojat* by slaying two warriors.

Numerals

> *Another subject of interest is that of Barsoomian numbers. Little information is available, our main source being those hormads created by Ras Thavas, who were identified by number (in* Synthetic Men of Mars*). This has helped in drawing up a table, but unfortunately only five hormads are so designated:* Tor-dur-bar = *four million eight (SMM/4),* Teeaytan-ov = *eleven hundred seven (SMM/4),* Aymad = *one man (SMM/11),* Il-dur-en = *? million ? (SMM/11),* Durdan = *million ? (SMM/15).*
>
> *Even here we have three unknowns:* il, en *and* dan. *Assuming they are primary numbers, they could be any of the primary numbers two, three, five, six and nine.*

> - Roy, John Flint. *A Guide To Barsoom*, pp. 122-124. 1976. New York: Del Rey.

The following table is an expansion of Roy's table, with unattested forms marked and with more hypothetical forms proposed.

Number	Barsoomian	Source
1	*ay*	*ay-mad*, "one man" (SMM/chapter 11)
4	*tor*	*tor-dur-bar*, "four million eight" (SMM/4)
7	*ov*	*teeaytan-ov*, "eleven hundred seven" (SMM/4)
8	*bar*	*tor-dur-bar*, "four million eight" (SMM/4)
10	*tee*	*teepi*, "ten money-units" (LG/2-11)
11	*teeay*	*teeaytan-ov*, "eleven hundred seven" (SMM/4)
14	**teetor*	[assumed on analogy with *teeay*]
17	**teeov*	[assumed on analogy with *teeay*]
18	**teebar*	[assumed on analogy with *teeay*]
40	**tortee*	[assumed]
70	**ovtee*	[assumed]
80	**bartee*	[assumed]
100	*tan*	*tanpi*, "100 money-units" (LG/2-11)
400	**tortan*	[by analogy with *teeaytan*]
700	**ovtan*	[by analogy with *teeaytan*]
800	**bartan*	[by analogy with *teeaytan*]
1,000	**dar*	*dar*, "a military unit with 1,000 men"
1,000	**teetan*	[by analogy with *teeaytan*]
1,100	*teeaytan*	*teeaytan-ov*, "eleven hundred seven" (SMM/4)
1,400	**teetortan*	[by analogy with *teeaytan*]
1,700	**teeovtan*	[by analogy with *teeaytan*]
1,800	**teebartan*	[by analogy with *teeaytan*]
10,000	**mak*	back-formation from *umak*, "a military unit with 10,000 men", on analogy with *utan*, "a military unit with 100 men"
1,000,000	*dur*	*tor-dur-bar*, "four million eight" (SMM/4)

Military Titles & Units

The military titles are all attested, but most of the names of military units are conjecture. But if we assume that **u-* [< *utan* and *umak*] is a prefix meaning "military unit" joined to a number word (*tan* and *mak* are both attested), we can interpolate **utee* and **udur* (where *dur* is "million", used figuratively). The term *dar* is assumed to have the following etymology:

< *udar < *u- + dar, "ten thousand". The *ujed and *ujeddak terms are pure conjecture.

Title	Unit	Size of Unit
padwar	*utee	10 soldiers
dwar	utan	100 soldiers
teedwar	dar	1,000 soldiers
odwar	umak	10,000 soldiers
jedwar	*udur	army
jed	*ujed	armies of country or principality
jeddak	*ujeddak	armies of empire

*unattested

Lexicon

The following lexicon has been adapted from the glossary at the end of *Thuvia, Maid Of Mars*. Unfortunately for those trying to translate texts, most of the lexicon consists of proper nouns.

The lexicon lists the Barsoomian term, an educated guess of its division into syllables (using ˙), its meaning, and the book it was first mentioned in, using the following abbreviations:

1. *A Princess Of Mars* (APOM)
2. *The Gods Of Mars* (TGOM)
3. *The Warlord Of Mars* (TWOM)
4. *Thuvia, Maid Of Mars* (TMOM)

Aa˙an˙thor - A dead city of ancient Mars. - TMOM

apt - An huge, white-furred Arctic monster. - TMOM

As˙tok - Prince of Dusar. - TMOMg

banth - A fierce beast of prey that roams the low hills surrounding the dead seas of ancient Mars. - TGOM

Bar Com˙as - Jeddak of Warhoon. - APOM

Bar˙soom - Mars - APOM

ca˙lot - A dog. About the size of a Shetland pony and has ten short legs. - APOM

Car˙thor˙is - Son of John Carter and Dejah Thoris, his name a combination of theirs. - TGOM

Dak Kov˙a - Jed among the Warhoons (later jeddak). - APOM

dar´seen - A chameleon-like reptile, that can change its color. - APOM

da´tor - Title for chief or prince of the First Born. - TGOM

De´jah Thor´is - Princess of Helium, daughter of Mors Kajak of Helium. - APOM

Djor Kan´tos - Son of Kantos Kan; padwar of the Fifth Utan. - TGOM

Dor - Valley of Heaven, river valley of Iss. - APOM

Do´tar So´jat - John Carter's Martian name, from the surnames of the first two warrior chieftains he killed. - APOM

Du´sar - A Martian kingdom. - TMOM

dwar - A captain, leader of a utan. - TGOM

ersite - A kind of stone. - TMOM

Gozava - GO ZA VA Tars Tarkas' dead wife. - APOM

Gur Tus - Dwar of the tenth utan. - TGOM

haad - Martian mile. - TMOM

Hal Vas - Son of Vas Kor the Dusarian noble. - TMOM

Hastor - A city of Helium. - TGOM

Hek´ka´dor - Title of Father of Therns (Matai Shang). - TGOM

He´li´um - The empire of the grandfather of Dejah Thoris. A leading nation of red men. - TMOMg

Hor Vas´tus - Padwar in the navy of Helium. - TMOM

Hor´tan Gur - Jeddak of Torquas. - TMOM

Horz - Deserted city; Barsoomian Greenwich for time. - TMOM

Ill´all - The most remote city of Okar. - TMOM

Iss - River of Death. A sacred river. - TMOM

Iss´us - Goddess of Death, whose abode is upon the banks of the Lost Sea of Korus. - TMOM

Jav - A Lotharian. - TMOM

jed - King. - TMOMg

jed´dak - Emperor. - TMOM

Kab Kad´ja - Jeddak of the Warhoons of the south. - TMOM

Ka´da´bra - Capitol city of Okar. - TMOM

ka´dar - Guard. - TMOM

Kalk·sus - Cruiser; transport under Vas Kor. - TMOM

Kan·tos Kan - Padwar in the Helium navy. - TMOM

Ka·ol - A Martian kingdom in the eastern hemisphere. Isolated and surrounded by Japan. - TMOM

kaor - The greeting used principally by red Martians - TGOM

Kar Ko·mak - Odwar of Lotharian bowmen. - TMOM

kar·ad - Martian degree. - TMOM

Ko·mal - The Lotharian god; a huge banth. – TMOM

Kor·ad - A dead city of ancient Mars. - TMOM

Kor·us - The Lost Sea of Dor. - TMOM

Ku·lan Tith - Jeddak of Kaol. - TMOM

La·kor - A thern. - TWOM

Lar·ok - A Dusarian warrior; artificer. - TMOM

Lor·quas Ptom·el - Jed among the Tharks. - TMOM

Lothar - The forgotten city. - TMOMg

Mar·en·tin·a - A principality of Okar. - TMOM

Mat·ai Shang - Father of Therns. - TGOM

Mors Ka·jak - A jed of lesser Helium, son of Tardos Mors of Helium. - APOM

No·tan - Royal Psychologist of Zodanga. - APOM

Nut·us - Jeddak of Dusar. - TMOM

Od - Martian foot. - TMOM

O·dwar - A commander, or general. - TMOM

O·kar - Land of the yellow men. - TWOM

O·mad - Man with one name. - TMOM

O·me·an - The buried sea. - TGOM

Or·luk - A black and yellow striped Arctic monster. - TWOM

Otz - Mountains near Iss, surrounding the Valley Dor and the Lost Sea of Korus. - TGOM

Pa·dwar - Lieutenant. - APOM

Pan·than - A soldier of fortune. - TMOM

Par·thak - The Zodangan prison guard who brought food to John Carter in the pits of Zat Arras. - TGOM

Phai·dor - Daughter of Matai Shang. - TGOM

pim·al·i·a - PIM AL I A
Gorgeous flowering plant. - TGOM

Ptarth - A Martian kingdom of red men. - TGOM

Ptor - Family name of three Zodangan brothers. - APOM

Sab Than - Prince of Zodanga. A jed of Zodanga, son of Than Khosis. - APOM

saf·ad - A Martian inch. - TMOM

sak - To jump, to leap. - APOM

Sa·len·sus Oll - Jeddak of Jeddaks, ruler of Okar. - TWOM

Sar·an Tal - Carthoris' major-domo. - TMOMg

Sar·ko·ja - A green Martian woman. - APOM

Sa·tor Throg - A Holy Thern of the Tenth Cycle. - TGOM

Sha·dor - An isle on northern shore of Sea of Omean used as a prison. - TGOM

sil·i·an - Slimy reptiles inhabiting the Sea of Korus. - TGOM

sith - Hornet-like flying monster that dwells in Kaolian jungle. - TWOM

skeel - A Martian polishable hardwood, used for the deck of an airship. - TGOM

So·la - A young green Martian woman. Of Thark. - APOM

So·lan - An official of the palace. A man of secrets, in Kadabra. - TWOM

som·pus - A kind of tree. - TMOM

sor·ak - A little pet animal among the red Martian women, about the size of a cat. Used as an insult. - APOM

Sor·an - Overlord of the navy of Ptarth. - TMOM

sor·a·pus - A Martian hardwood used for ship cabins; has large succulent fruits. - TGOM

Sor·av - An officer of Salensus Oll. Commander of the forces of the palace of Kadabra. - TWOM

tal - A Martian second. One 200th of a *xat* (unit of measuring time). - TGOM

Tal Ha·jus - Jeddak of Thark. - APOM

Tal'u - Rebel Prince of Marentina. - TWOM

Tan Ga'ma - Warhoon warrior. - TGOM

Tar'dos Mors - Grandfather of Dejah Thoris and Jeddak of Helium. - APOM

Tar'i'o - Jeddak of Lothar. - TMOMg

Tars Tar'kas - A green man, chieftain of the Tharks. - APOM

Tha'bis - Issus' chief. An old woman. - TGOM

Than Kho'sis - Jeddak of Zodanga - APOM

Thark - City and name of a green Martian horde. - APOM

thern - A priest of the cult of Issus. Typically known as Holy Therns. - TGOM

thoat - A ten-foot-high steed of the green Martians. - APOM

Thor Ban - Jed among the green men of Torquas. - TMOMg

Tho'r'ian - Chief of the lesser Therns. - TGOM

Throx'us - Mightiest of the five oceans. - TMOMg

Thurds - A green horde inimical to Torquas. - TMOMg

Thur'i'a - The nearer moon. - TGOM

Thur'id - A black dator. - TGOM

Thu'van Dihn - Jeddak of Ptarth. - TWOM

Thu'vi'a - Princess of Ptarth. - TGOM

Tor'ith - Officer of the guards of the First Born at submarine pool. - TGOM

Tor'kar Bar - Kaolian noble; dwar of the Kaolian Road. - TWOM

Tor'quas - A green horde. - TMOMg

Tur'jun - Carthoris' alias. - TMOMg

u'tan - A company of one hundred men (military). - TGOM

Vas Kor - A Dusarian noble. - TMOMg

War'hoon - A community of green men; enemy of Thark. - APOM

Wool'a - A Barsoomian calot. - TMOMg

xat - A Martian minute; one fiftieth of a zode (unit of measuring time). - TGOM

Xa'var'i'an - A Helium warship. - TGOM

Xo·dar - Dator among the First Born. - TGOM

Yer·sted - A First Born, commander of the submarine. - TGOM

Zad - Tharkian warrior. - APOM

Zat Ar·ras - Jed of Zodanga. - TGOM

Zith·ad - Dator of the guards of Issus. - TGOM

zit·i·dar - A heavy (mastodonian) draft animal of the green men. - APOM

Zo·dan·ga - Martian city of red men. Capitol of Helium's chief enemies among the red men. - APOM

zode - A Martian hour; one tenth of a Martian day (unit of measuring time). - TGOM

Martian Proverbs

"Blessed be your ancestors for this meeting." — common

"In the name of the Ninth Ray!" — common

"Only our first ancestor knows." — common

"A warrior may change his metal, but not his heart." - Dejah Thoris

"Blessed be the shell of thy first ancestor." — First Born saying

"Man builds naught that man may not destroy." — Larok

"Leave to a Thark his head and one hand and he may yet conquer." — Tars Tarkas

"By your first ancestor!" — Thuvia

"May my ancestors have mercy on me." — Thuvia

"May the white apes take us all!" — Thuvia

"Praised be to our first ancestor!" — Thuvia

"The intellects of our ancestors are with us." — Thuvia

Lapine

Richard Adams' *Watership Down* (New York: Macmillan, 1972) is one of the classic works of xenofiction (the fiction set in strange cultures, real or imagined), placed as it is among and between the warrens of rabbits in the English countryside. Lapine, the language he sketches for his rabbits, is arguably the best naming language ever created, and is a minimalist virtuoso performance, a haiku of a language compared to the sonnet of Sindarin.

The following documentation of the language is derived from Adams' own appendix to *Watership Down*, but is reconstructed as extensively as possible from the limited examples. All hypothetical reconstructions are preceded by an *asterisk.

Vocabulary from the sequel has been deliberately left out, as the point of this example is how much can be accomplished with how little. Lapine went a long way towards establishing the verisimilitude of the rabbits' culture.

??? Translated by Adams as "Lapine", meaning the language and religion of the rabbits. Whether Lapine actually has a word for Lapine is unknown. [From English *lapin* n. Rabbit fur, especially when dyed to imitate a more expensive fur; ultimately from French *lapin* 'rabbit']

??? The Lapine word is unknown, but Adams translates it as "bob stones" and calls it a traditional game among rabbits.

Crixa A crossroads, the center of Efrafa, located at the crossing point of two bridle paths.

Efrafa A warren founded by General Woundwort.

El-ahrairah The legendary rabbit folk hero [*elil hrair rah*, Prince with a Thousand Enemies]

***eli** Enemy of rabbits [hypothetical reconstruction of the singular. Could also be **ela*]

elil Enemies of rabbits.

embleer Stinking, as in the smell of a predator, esp. a fox.

fa Watcher? Augmentative? [Reconstruction from Owslafa]

flay Food, especially grass or other edible plants.

flayrah Lettuce, or other unusually good food ['food-prince']

Frith The sun god of the rabbits.

Frithrah An exclamation ['sun-prince']

fu After, afterwards.

fu inlé After moonrise.

***hain** Meaning uncertain: either blackbird or song. [Reconstructed from Nildro-hain, "Blackbird's song"]

hlao Any dimple or depression formed in the grass, such as that formed by a daisy plant or a thistle, which can hold moisture

Hlao The name of Pipkin in Lapine.

Hlao-roo A nickname of Pipkin [with diminutive]

hlessi (pl. **hlessil**) An outcast rabbit, living above ground, without a regular hole or warren

homba (pl. **hombil**) A fox

hrair Any number over four, a great many, an uncountable number. Loosely translated as "a thousand."

Hrairoo The name of Fiver in Lapine, so called for being the last in a litter of five or more rabbits. ['thousand' + dim]

hraka Droppings, excretions.

hrududu (pl. **hrududil**) A motor vehicle such as a car or tractor.

***hy(z)** To shine. [Reconstruction from Hyzenthlay]

Hyzenthlay The name of a doe who lived in Efrafa [*hy(z) *zen(th) thlay, "Fur Shining Like Dew"]

Inlé Literally, the moon or moonrise. Figuratively, darkness, fear and death.

lendri A badger.

li Head (body part).

marli Literally, a doe. Figuratively, a mother.

m'saion "We meet them."

narn Pleasant to eat.

***ni** Time? High or highest? [Reconstructed from ni-frith]

ni-frith Noon.

***nildro** Meaning uncertain: either blackbird or song. Probably blackbird.

Nildro-hain The name of a doe who lived in Efrafa. ["Blackbird's Song"]

Owsla The strongest rabbits in a warren. The elite rulers.

Owslafa Council Police. A term only used in Efrafa.

Pfeffa A cat.

Rah A prince, leader or chief. Usually suffixed, dropping the 'r' when following an 'r'.

roo A diminutive, usually affectionate. Suffixed.

sayn Groundsel.

silf Outside, not underground.

silflay To go above ground to feed.

silflay Food available above ground (outside the warren). [*silf flay*]

tharn Literally hypnotized with fear (think of the "deer caught in the headlights" only with a rabbit), stupefied, distraught. Figuratively, foolish, forlorn or heartbroken.

Thethuthininang The name of a doe who lived in Efrafa. ["Movement of Leaves"]

thlay Fur.

Thlayli A nickname ['fur head']

threar A rowan tree or mountain ash.

Threarah Lord Threar.

u Similar to "the" in English.

U Hrair The Thousand (Enemies)

vair To excrete.

yona (pl. **yonil**) A hedgehog.

***zen(th)** Dew [Reconstruction from *Hyzenthlay*]

zorn Destroyed, murdered; suffered a catastrophe.

Dublex

Dublex is a langmaking game — think of it as Scrabble for people who like to invent words. Rather than the letter tiles of Scrabble, Dublex has 400 word tiles. You combine the word tiles two at a time to come up with new words. For instance:

> **vocsist** /vohk-SEEST/ [voc+sist, "word system"]
> *language* — *a systematic means of communicating by the use of sounds or conventional symbols*
>
> **jamadbin** /zhah-mahd-BEEN/ [jamad+bin, "frozen building"]
> *igloo* — *an Eskimo hut built of blocks (usu. sod or snow) in the shape of a dome*
>
> **cafazmuh** /kah-fahz-MOOSH/ [cafaz+muh, "jumping rodent"]
> *rabbit, bunny, coney, cony*
>
> **pedmest** /pehd-MEHST/ [ped+mest, "foot place"]
> *pedestal* — *an architectural support or base for a statue*
>
> **cisdesir** /kees-deh-SEER/ [cis+desir, "story desire"]
> *story hunger* — *an emotional need for fulfillment through narrative fiction in any form (book, television sitcom, movies, etc.)*

You are encouraged to adapt definitions from the WordNet database. It's completely appropriate to invent words without any English equivalents, such as *cisdesir*, "story hunger", above.

The heart and soul of the Dublex game is the Dublex language, the language invented for the 400 word tiles.

The name Dublex is a combination of *dub* ("to give a name to facetiously or playfully; to nickname") and *lex* (from Greek 'lexis', "word", as in 'lexicon'). It's also a play on *duplex* ("twofold; double") since the Dublex words you create have two parts: e.g., *sihbin*, "health building = hospital", *nassens*, "nose sense = smell".

Wordmaking — How To Combine Roots

You can coin new Dublex words using the following techniques:

- simple compounding
- suffixing
- coining phrases
- forming acronyms

Simple compounding

The simplest method of word creation is simply to place a modifier before the word being modified. Thus *darg+vic = dargvic*, "road +vehicle = car", and *fon+sens = fonsens*, "sound + sense = hearing". You can string together as many compounds as is reasonable, as in *lun+col+vic = luncolvic*, "lunar + wheeled + vehicle = lunar rover". As a result, you can incorporate other people's coined words into your own words.

Suffixing

A small set of Dublex words follow the word they modify. Most of these are scalars, which are words that describe an end point on a scale, such as *term*, "hot temperature", and *dens*, "dense object". So *vattermmest* is "water + hot + place = hot springs", and *furtcisid* is *furt+cisid*, "acidic fruit", which might refer to the lemon, lime or kumquat. All the scalars are marked in the Dublex root-word dictionary.

Five suffixes that aren't scalars are *ses* "female"; *mas* "male"; *ton* {augmentative}; *let* {diminutive}; and *con* "opposite". Sample words are *tigerses* "tigress", *bacarmas* "bull", *lunton* "full moon", *lunlet* "crescent moon", and *succon* "unhappiness".

The advantages of having a few of the most common roots be suffixes including having alphabetical lists with related terms close to one another (e.g., *bacar* "bovine"; *bacarmas* "bull"; *bacarses* "cow") and having clearer structure in words with three or more roots.

Coining Phrases

English and many languages have set phrases, called IDIOMS, whose meaning is not obvious from the words used. For example, the *White House* is not just a house that is white. Dublex phrases are formed using the part-of-speech marker *-i*, which means, in effect, that this word idiomatically modifies the word after it, so "White House" might be

> **nieri fambin**
> white + {idiom} + house(family+building)

You can also simply write this *nierfambin*, of course, but marking words as idiomatic is useful for indicating the scope of a modifier: *nieri* "white", clearly modifies *fambin* "house", where *nierfambin* could be read as "white family's building" or "white family-building".

Forming Acronyms

Really long phrases or words can be truncated into acronyms. For instance, *vatdartpart*, "watery dirt part = mud part = brick", could be shorted to *vadapart* or *vadap*. The rule for forming acronyms is that you use only the initial CV from each word except the last word, which you can either append in full (as in *vadapart*) or truncate to the initial consonant (as in *vadap*).

However, acronyms can't conflict with one of the 400 roots or 3 pronouns (*von*, *nin* and *tan*, the first-, second- and third-person pronouns, respectively); therefore, *voltdarg*, "electric road, monorail", cannot be shortened to *vod*, which is a root meaning "body of water", but would have to be shortened to *vodarg*.

Pronounciation

Dublex, as a language for use in a game, has a simplified sound system that should be easy for you to learn.

Vowels

Dublex has just five vowels, each written by a single letter.

> a - as in father
> e - as in pet
> i - as in pizza
> o - as in Poe or poet

u - as in tutu

Consonants

Voiceless	Voiced
Stops	
p - as in pot	b - as in bought
t - as in tot	d - as in dot
c /k/ - as in cot	g - as in got
Fricatives	
f - as in fought	v - as in vote
s - as in sought	z - as in zit
h /ʃ/ - as in shot	
j /ʒ/ - as in vision	
Liquids	
l - as in lap	
r - as in rap	
Nasals	
m - as in map	
n - as in nap	

All consonants may begin or end a syllable.

Guidelines For English Speakers

As an experienced English speaker, you will need to get used to the following:

The letter **c** is always pronounced /k/. In English, **c** has several different sounds associated with it, the most common of which is /k/ as in *cat* and the next most common is /s/ as in *city* or *cent*. In Latin (and we are using the Latin alphabet), **c** was originally always pronounced /k/, but over time came to be pronounced /s/ in front of /i/ or /e/; English borrowed this pronounciation when it borrowed Latin vocabulary. The Dublex way is simpler for speakers of other languages, but requires a bit of unlearning for the English speaker.

The letter **h** is always pronounced /ʃ/. This is odd, certainly, but Latin lacked the /ʃ/ sound altogether and the *sh* way of writing it was cobbled together by Norman monks. Since the /h/ sound itself does not occur in

Dublex, this letter was adopted to represent /ʃ/. So when you see the Dublex word *hazar*, "tree", remember that it is pronounced *shah-ZAHRR*.

The letter **j** is always /ʒ/ as in *vision*. The /ʒ/ sound does occur in English, but it written many different ways — few of them *zh*[6]! The regular *j* sound, as in English *just*, is actually a /d/ sound followed by /ʒ/, a combination rarely permitted in other languages. Since the /dʒ/ (English *j*) combination isn't used in Dublex, the letter **j** has been pressed into service for /ʒ/ (which, like /ʃ/, never occured in Latin).

The letter **r** is actually a trilled /r/ as in Spanish *carro*. If you pronounce it as in English, though, your fellow Dublexians are not likely to be bothered.

Every consonant is pronounced, so *comb* is pronounced /komb/ (to practice, try pronouncing *combat* without *-at*), and *ruch* is /rukʃ/ ("rough object").

Schwa Insertion

When consonants occur together in a Dublex word, you may — if you find pronouncing the consonant cluster difficult — insert an indeterminate vowel between the consonants. The indeterminate vowel or schwa is a mid-central neutral vowel [ə], typically occuring in unstressed syllables in English, such as the final vowel in *sofa*. Schwa insertion is something native speakers of Polynesian languages and Chinese dialects will find especially helpful, since consonant clusters do not occur in those languages. As a speaker of English, you will need it less often than they would, but may find it helpful when pronouncing words with doubled consonants: for instance, *vissens* /vis-sens/ or /vis-ə-sens/.

Stress & Syllables

If a Dublex word ends in a consonant, its last syllable receives the stress. If a word ends in a vowel, its next-to-last (PENULTIMATE) syllable receives the stress. So *comun* ("communication") is pronounced /ko-MUN/, with the emphasis on the final syllable, and *comunu* ("to communicate") is pronounced /ko-MU-no/, with the emphasis on the penultimate syllable. This keeps the basic sound of the root word the same, regardless of

---

[6] It appears in Russian transliterations, e.g. WWII's Marshal Zhukov. And **j** for /ʒ/ should be familiar from French. —MR

the part-of-speech ending. (The final consonant always begins the syllable with the part-of-speech ending.)

Design Notes

The phonology was based on a simplification of Lojban's vocabulary, as the Lojban database of words in Arabic, Chinese, English, Hindi, Russian and Spanish was the first source of Dublex words. While ease of pronunciation was considered somewhat important, Dublex's voiced fricatives are not among the 20 most common phonemes in the world's languages. In this case, the fact that these sounds were used in the source languages was more important, and the learner only has to master the distinction between voiceless and voiced fricatives to acquire three new sounds. Because /v/ was used, /w/ was omitted, since many speakers have difficulty contrasting the two.

The letters *k, q, w, x* and *y* are not used in Dublex words.

Lexicon Design

Morphotactics

The most important goal in structuring the lexicon for Dublex was to have it always be obvious when a word is a compound form or a root form. To this end, almost all Dublex words begin and end with consonants and exclude consonant clusters from the beginning of syllables. So root words are of the forms:

> CVC (Consonant-Vowel-Consonant) *muh* /muʃ/ "rodent"
> CVCC *sist*, "system"
> CVCVC *catoh* /ka-TOʃ/ "cat"
> CVCVCC *malact* /ma-LAKT/ "milk"
> CVCVCVC *hocolat* /ʃo-ko-LAT/ "chocolate"

A root like *plant* is not permitted, since initial consonant clusters are not allowed, and the word *campus* /kahm-POOS/ could not be a root but would be a compound of the roots *cam+pus* ("shirt" + "usage"). The word patterns make it easy to tell where one root begins and one ends (for instance, *duvsir* is clearly *duv+sir* and *mentvoc* is clearly *ment+voc*). All final vowels make up their own morpheme, marking the part of speech (for instance, *vissensu* is *vis+sens+u*).

The set of consonants was specifically chosen so that each consonant can occupy any place within a morpheme: initial, medial or final.

While the word patterns (phonotactics) of Dublex may seem artificial, many languages have much greater restrictions on possible word forms than Dublex does. For instance, Polynesian languages typically allow only V and CV syllables; Chinese syllables are typically CV or CVC. This means that when roots are borrowed into these languages, they undergo a lot of change, such as when English 'pocket monster' becomes Japanese *pokemon*. In Dublex, English *plant* (from Latin) is present as *palt*, since neither *plant nor *palnt are valid roots.

Recognizable Forms

Which brings us to the primary design tension of Dublex. On the one hand, root words must fit strict syllable patterns, but on the other hand root words should be as recognizable as possible to speakers of any language.

Since it was not feasible to analyze thousands of languages for common forms, Dublex focused in on words from six of the most spoken languages in the world: Arabic, Chinese, English, Hindi, Russian and Spanish (called the six cardinal languages). The primary source of these natural-language words was the Lojban etymological dictionary, which presented phonetic information about 1200 words. Where possible, forms in other languages were also considered, especially forms in German, Dutch, Italian, Esperanto and Novial, as derived from Rick Harrison's *Universal Language Dictionary*.

How recognizable are Dublex words? It is rare that you will have a Dublex word like *motor* "motor", which — as a technical term derived from Latin — has found its way into all the cardinal languages (though, in Mandarin Chinese, it takes the form *mădá*). More typical is something like *cafaz* "jump", from the Arabic *kafaz*, a form which won out because it fit the word structure of Dublex best and because its initial /k-/ was reinforced by Hindi /kud/. Matching the initial sound was considered quite important, as it has been demonstrated to be a strong mnemonic, and a high correspondence of word-initial sounds from Dublex to the speaker's native tongue makes Dublex sound "more natural".

While early attempts were made to systemize word formation, these methods were rejected and it was done on ad hoc basis. The priority was to take any form more or less as is, if it were present in two of the cardinal languages. If it were a particular high-frequency form, it might be truncated to one syllable, such as *per* from Latin *persona*, extant in Romance (Spanish, Italian, et al), Germanic (English, German, et al) and Russian, and reinforced by Hindi *puruc*. If no forms matched, but some matched on an initial letter, one of those forms was chosen.

In some cases, conflicts with other words changed the available form: *cat* in Dublex means "cut" as this form is supported in more cardinal languages than the form *cat* for "cat"; therefore something longer than /kat/ was needed for "feline" and the selection was *catoh*, taking the /-osh/ from Russian *koshk*, with the *-ato-* reinforced by the Romance form *gat(t)o*.

While word forms could have been generated randomly by computer, looking to natural languages for inspiration provided some needed realism to the language — and makes remembering the vocabulary a little easier, especially for English speakers.

The 400 Dublex Roots

To save space, etymologies are limited to one line giving the closest form. For more information, see the original list on the web. The URL is in the introduction.

bac - alphabet [< a, b, c fit into phonotactics]
bacar - bovine, cow, bull [Arabic *bakar*]
bad - body part — any part of an organism such as an organ or extremity [Arabic & Hindi *badan*]
bah - outside [Hindi *bahar*]
bamub - bamboo [Malay *bambu*]
banc – reserve, supply (*not* the financial institution) [Old High German *banc* "moneychanger's table"]
baner - flag, banner [Vulgar Latin *bandaria*]
bar - bar, rod, rail [English and Spanish]
barc - lightning [Arabic *bark*]
bazar - market —[Persian *bazar*]
bez - absence [Russian /bez/]
bin - building, edifice [Arabic *bin/*, with initial /b-/ in English 'building']
bir – barley [from its most popular by-product, *beer*]
bomb - an explosive device [Italian *bomba*']
bud - future [Russian *budush*]
bur - brown [Russian & Hindi *bur*]
cact – action [Latin *actum*, with initial /k-/ from Hindi *karni*]
caf – coffee [Italian *caffe*]
cafaz - jump [Arabic *kafaz*]
cah – abstraction [Russian *kashestv*]
cal - feces, excrement [Russian *kal*]
calc – peripheral, auxiliary device [Latin *calculare*]

DUBLEX   135

calot - dog, canine [Arabic *kalb* and Hindi *kuta*]
cals - class, kind, type [Latin *classis*]
cam – garment, article of clothing [Dublex *camis* "shirt"]
camel – camel [Greek *kamelos*]
camer - room, chamber [Late Latin *camera*]
camis – shirt [Late Latin *camisa*]
camp – field [Latin *campus*]
canc – shell, outer covering [Latin *cancer* "crab"]
cand - hole— an opening into something but not through it; contrast *hubac* [Hindi *kandra* "cave"]
canon – cannon [Old Italian *cannone*]
cant – fastener [Hindi *kant*]
canun – law, rules [Arabic & Hindi *kanun*]
cap – head [Indo-European **kaput-*]
capt – leader [Late Latin *capitaneus* "chief"]
caras – love [Welsh *cara* and Latin *cārus*]
carb - carbon, C [French *carbone*]
carc - sharp object [scalar] [Esperanto *akra* and Latin *acutus*]
card – heart [Greek *kardia*]
carn – flesh [Latin *caro, carn-*]
cars – cross [Hindi *kras*]
cart – card [Greek *khartes*]
cat - cut, cutting [English *cut*, Arabic *qaṭa*, etc]
catoh – cat [Arabic *kat* + Russian *koshk*]
caz - cause [Latin *causa*]
celeb - play, diversion [Hindi *kel*, Arabic *laib*, Latin *celebrare*]
ciber – cyberspace [English *cyber-*]
cirv – curve [Latin *curvus*, altered due to clash with Russian "whore"]
cis - story, tale [Hindi & Arabic *kisa*]
cisid – acid Russian *kisl* + Latin *acidus*]
citab – book [Arabic and Hindi *kitab*]
cog – knowledge [Latin *cognitio*]
cohol – alcohol Arabic *kuhul*]
col – wheel [Russian *koliso*]
coleb – oscillation, swinging movement Russian *koleb*]
color – color [Latin]
comanj – eating [Spanish *comer* + Old French *mangier*]
comar – comparison [Latin *comparare*]
comb - fight, combat, conflict [Late Latin *combattere*]
comp – computer [Latin *computare*]
comun – communication [Latin *communicare*]
con - opposite extreme [Latin *contra*]
cond - condition, state, status [Latin *conditio*]

cont - control [English]
conus – cone [Russian *konus*]
cop - copy, a duplicate [Medieval Latin *copia*]
corb – edge, boundary [Hindi *kor* + Germanic *bor*]
cord - string, thread [Greek *khorde*]
corect – correct [Latin]
cos – cooking, food preparation [Spanish *cocer*]
cost – bone [Russian *kost*]
cov – cover [English]
cozom - outer space [Greek *kosmos*]
cub - cup [Arabic *kub*]
cumah - cloth, fabric [Arabic *kumash*]
curl – violence [French *cruel*]
curs – run, fast movement [Indo European *kers*-]
dab - pressing, pressure [Hindi *dab*]
dal – diagonal, inclined [Hindi *dal*]
dar – stripe [*dar*]
darg – road, route [Arabic *darb* + Hindi *marg*]
dart - dirt, ground [Hindi *darti*]
datun – same or identical things [Arabic *datu* + Mandarin *tun*]
delc - claim, assertion [Latin *declarare*]
dend – debt [Hindi *dendar,* Spanish *deuda*]
debt — the state of owing money
dens – dense [Latin *densus*]
dent – tooth [Indo-European *dent-*]
des = ten to the power of— forms large number words, as *desduv* 10^2, *dester* 10^3, *dessis* 10^6 [Latin *decem* 'ten']
desir - desire, wish, want [Latin *desiderare*]
dev – god, deity, divinity [Indo-European *deiwos*]
dif – difficult task [Latin *difficultas*]
din – day [Hindi *din,* Russian *dyen*]
dinar money [Latin *denarius*]
direct - direction, orientation [Latin *directio*]
dis – separation [Latin *dis-*]
dit – digit [Italian *dito*]
doj – precipitation: rain, snow, etc. [Russian *dozhd*]
don – gift [Latin *donum*]
dun – east [Mandarin *dong*]
dur – long event [Medieval Latin *duratio*]
duv = two [Indo-European *dwo-*]
fab – creation [Latin *fabricare* 'make']
fac – obscenity— appended to a word to make it obscene, e.g., *duvpig* is "buttocks", but *duvpigfac* is "ass" [English]

fam – family [Latin *familia*]
fan – art [Arabic *fan*]
farc – difference [scalar] [Turkish *fark*]
farh – fraction [Latin *fractio*]
fas – decay, something rotten [Arabic *fasad*]
fer – iron, Fe [Latin *ferrum*]
ferc – frequent [Latin *frequentia*]
fest - celebration, rejoicing, jubilee [Latin *festivalis*]
fib – amphibian [New Latin *Amphibia*]
fil – file, esp. computer file [English]
fin – ending, conclusion [Latin *finis*]
foc – fire [Latin *focus*]
fon – sound [From Dublex *telfon*, more univeral than *son-*]
font – front, forward part [Latin *front-*]
forl – flower, bloom, blossom [Latin *flora*]
form – form, two-dimensional shape [Latin *forma*]
fort – strong thing [scalar] [Latin *fortis*]
furt – fruit [Spanish *fruto*]
galc – throat, pharynx [Hindi *gal* + Arabic *halk*]
gan – agent [Mandarin *gan*]
gard – scale (of quantity) [Latin *gradus*]
garm – communication unit, as in 'telegram' [Greek *gramma*]
gars – grass [Indo-European **ghre-so-*]
gas – gas [Dutch *gas*]
ger – all sides, all around [Hindi *ger* "surround"]
germ – sibling, brother or sister [Latin *germanus*]
gid – food [Arabic *gida*]
gitar – guitar [Spanish *guitarra*]
gov – government [Romance *govern-*]
gulb – deep object [Russian *glubok*]
gurn – grains, cereal [Mandarin *gu* + Spanish *grano*]
gurp – group [Germanic]
habil – ability [Latin *habilitas*]
hacar – form, three-dimensional shape [Arabic *shakl* + Hindi *akar*]
hafer – blade [Arabic *shafr*]
halt – high object [English *height* + Latin *altus*]
hand – hand [Germanic]
har – four [Hindi *car*]
harl – square [Dublex *harlinform* "four-line-form"]
hasal - event, occurrence, happening [Arabic *hasal*]
haz – fun [Dublex *hazil* 'comedy']
hazar – tree [Arabic *shazar*]
hazil – comedy [Arabic *hazli* + Hindi *hasya*]

herc – sphere [Dublex *sirchacar* 'circle-3.d.form']
hical – frame [Arabic *haikal*]
hild – shield [English]
him – tool, utensil, implement [Hindi *shimta*]
hir – bird [Hindi *shiryi*]
hisan – horse [Arabic *hisan*]
hocolat – chocolate [Nahuatl *xocolatl*]
hor – hour [Latin *hora*]
horc – wide object [scalar] [Russian *shirok* + Hindi *shaur*]
horz – horizontal [Latin *horizon*]
hubac – opening, aperture [Arabic *shubak*]
hucar – thanks [Hindi *shukra*, Mandarin *xie*]
human – human being [English]
hun – choice [Hindi *shuna* + Mandarin *xuan*]
jam – tuber [Mandingo *ñambu* 'yam']
jamad – freezing [Arabic *jamad*]
jamil – beauty [Arabic *jamil*]
jant = animal, beast [Hindi *zhantu*, Russian *zhivotna*]
jeb – pocket [Arabic *jib*]
jel – yellow [Russian *jelt*]
jib – task, work, chore [English *job*]
jor – connection, joint [Hindi *zhor*]
lam – intensity, emphasis [Arabic *lami*]
lamp – lamp [Greek *lampas*]
lan – face [Mandarin *lian*]
lang – long object [Germanic *langaz*]
lans – spear, lance [Latin *lancea*]
lant – fall, drop [Mandarin *luo*]
lav – washing [Latin *lavatio*]
lern – learning [English]
let – little, small; diminutive [Romance *-el, -et, -elet*]
lev – left (side) [Russian *lyev*]
lib – freedom, liberty [Latin *libertas*]
lic – liquid [Latin *liquidus*]
lin – line [Latin *linea*]
loc – location, position [Latin *locus*]
luc – allium— onion, garlic, leek [Russian *luk*, Engish *leek*]
luft – air [German *Luft*]
lum – light [Latin *lumen*]
lun – moon [Latin *luna*]
mahin – machine [French]
mal = disparagement, pejoration [Latin *malus* 'bad']
malact – milk [Russian *moloko* + Greek *galaktos*]

malc – possession [Hindi *malak*]
mam – mammal [Late Latin *mammalis*]
mand – command, instruction [Latin *mandare*]
mans – meat [Sanskrit *mānsa-*, Russian *myaso*]
map – parent [Blend of English *ma* & *pa*]
mar – ocean, sea [Latin *mare*]
marc – mark [English etc.]
mas – male, masculine [Latin *mas*]
mat – adult [Latin *maturus*]
mater – matter, material, substance [Latin *materia*]
med – middle, center [Indo-European **medhyo-*]
meh – sheep [Hindi *mesh*]
memb – item, member [Latin *membrum*]
ment – mind [Indo-European **mn-ti*]
mer – measure, measurement [Russian *myer*]
mest – site [Russian *myest*]
metal – metal [Greek *metallon*]
metod – way, manner [Greek *methodos*]
micor – tiny object or event [diminutive] [Greek *mikro-*]
milit – military [Latin *militaris*]
min – fish [Hindi *min*]
mir – world [Russian *mir*]
mirg – deer, cervid [Hindi *mrig*]
miz – corn, maize [Spanish *maíz*, from Cariban]
mob – furniture [Spanish *muebles*]
molot – hammer [Russian *molot*]
mont – mount, mountain [Latin *montanus*]
mort – death [French]
mosam – weather [Hindi *mausam*]
mot – fat [Hindi *mota*]
motiv – target, goal [*motive*]
motor – motor, engine [Latin]
mov – movement [Latin *movere*]
muc – mouth [Hindi *muk*]
muh – rodent [Hindi *mushik* 'mouse']
mulp – performance [Dublex *multpercact*, "multiple-person activity"]
mult - multiplication [Latin *multiplicare*]
mum – whatchmacallit, a word the speaker can't remember [*mumble*]
murl – wall [Latin *muralis*]
music – music [Greek *musikē*]
nahar – source, origin [Russian *nashin* + Arabic *shara*]
nam – name [Indo-European **no-men-*]
narm – soft object [Hindi *naram*]

nas – nose [Indo-European *nas-*]
nasc – birth [Latin *nascens*]
nat – nature [Latin *natura*]
natin – nation, country, state [French *nation*]
nen – nine [Indo-European *newn*]
ner – black, blackness [Italian *nero*]
nest – house, lair, den [*nest*]
net – net [English]
nic – worker, seller, professional [Russian *-nik*]
nil – blue [Sanskrit *nila*, Spanish *añil*, etc.]
nobil – noble [Latin *nobilis*]
nod – base, node, station [Latin *nodus* 'knot']
nog – limb [Russian *noga*]
nomer – number, numeral [Indo-European *nom-eso-*]
nomin – noun [Latin *nomin-*]
nont – negation [Latin *non* + Germanic *n-t*]
nort – north [Indo-European *nr-t(r)o-*]
nun – present, now [Indo-European *nu-*, Esperanto *nun*]
nupt – marriage, matrimony [Latin *nuptiae*]
pacar – hold [Hindi *pakar*]
pant – plant [Latin *planta*]
pap – paper [Greek *papuros*]
part – part [English, French]
parv – truth [Russian *pravda*]
pas – past [English]
patuln – pants, trousers [French *pantalon*, Hindi *patalun*]
ped – foot [Indo-European *ped-*]
pel – interval [Hindi *pel* 'range']
pelm – pome, fleshy fruit such as an apple or pear [Germanic etc. *apel* + Turkic *elma*]
pen – five [Indo-European *penkwe*]
pens – stylus, pen [*pencil*]
per – person, individual [Latin *persona*]
perm – permanent object [scalar] [Latin *permanens*]
pict – picture, image [Latin *pictura*]
pig – buttock, cheek [Mandarin *pigu*]
pin – plane, surface [Mandarin *pingmian*, Latin *planus*]
pir – feather [Russian *pir*, Hindi *par*]
pird – object, thing [Russian *pridmyet*]
politic – politics [Greek *politikos*]
poln – full container [Russian *poln*]
polv – dust [Spanish *polvo*]
pors – question, query [Persian *pors*, Russian *vapros*]

DUBLEX 141

porv – provision, supply [Latin *providere*]
pos – position [Latin *positio*]
post – mail [Vulgar Latin *posta* 'station']
pub – people group, public [Dublex *pubilc*]
pubilc – public good, common good [Latin *publicus*]
pus – use, usage [Hindi *upiog* + Russian *primin-* + Latin *usare*]
rad – radio [English]
ran – injury, damage, harm [Russian *ran*]
rast – increase [Russian *rasti-* 'grow']
raz – time, instance, occasion [Russian *raz*]
reg – rule, regulation [Latin *regula*]
rep – repetition [Latin *repetare*]
rept – reptile, reptilian [Latin *reptare* 'creep']
resp - responsibility, liability, accountability [Spanish *responsabilidad*]
rest – remainder, remnant [Latin *restare*]
rezon - reason, explanation, justification, rationale [French *raison*]
ris – rice [Italian *riso*]
risp – reciprocity [Latin *reciprocus* + Hindi *apsi*]
rival – competition [Latin *rivalis*]
roc – rock, stone [Vulgar Latin **rocca*]
ruch – rough object [Hindi *ruksh*]
run – red [Hindi *arun*]
sac – sack [Greek *sakkos*]
sadits – sitting position [Russian *sad* + English *sit*]
safar – journey, trip, travel [Arabic *safari*]
safid – copulation, sexual intercourse [Arabic *safid*]
sah – favorableness [Hindi *sahayak*]
sahab – companion, associate; with, accompanied by [Arabic *sahab*]
sal – salt [Indo-European **sal-*]
sald – vegetable [Romance *salada* 'salad'; this is much more international than any root for vegetable]
salf – old object [scalar] [Arabic *salaf*]
sanj – bread [*sandwich*, more international than any word for 'bread']
sart – side, flank [Russian *starana*]
sat – satisfaction [Latin *satisfactio*]
seb – self [Russian *seb*]
secop – watcher, observer [Dublex *telsecop* and *micorsecop*]
sem – seven [Indo-European **septm*]
senor – Mr., Mrs., Ms., Miss [Spanish *señor*, Latin *senior*]
sens – sense, sensation [Latin *sensus*]
sent – emotion, feeling [Indo-European **sent-yo-*]
ser – series, sequence [Latin *series*]
serc – secret [Latin *secretus*]

ses – female, feminine [Russian *sistra* 'sister', Romance *-esse*]
set – set [Engish]
sezon – season [French *saison*]
sic – search [English *seek* + Russian *isk-*]
sih – health [Arabic *siha*]
silc – silk [Mandarin *si*]
sint – science [Latin *scientia*]
sir – zero [Arabic *sifr* + English *zero* etc.]
sirc – circle [Latin *circulus*]
sis – six [Indo-European **s(w)eks-*]
sisp – insect [Dublex *sisped* 'six-feet']
sist – system [Latin *systema*]
sol – Sun [Latin]
som – sleep [Latin *somnus*]
subect – subject [Latin *subjectus*]
suc – happiness [Hindi *suki*]
sucar – sugar [Arabic *sukar*]
sud – suddenness, abruptness [*sudden*]
suh – meaning [Hindi *sushit*]
sulal – offspring [Arabic *sulala*]
sum – total, sum [Latin *summa*]
sup – readiness [Dublex *subpus* 'sudden use']
super – superlative [Latin *super* over']
supt – step [Russian *stup*, English *step*]
sur – something above [French 'over']
surc – safety, security [Hindi *surkshit*]
sust – substitute [Spanish *sustitución*]
sut – thread, filament [Sanskrit *sutram*]
suvin – pig, hog [Indo-European **sue-ino-*]
tabac – tobacco [Spanish *tabaco*]
tabul – board [Latin *tabula*]
tact – touch [Latin *tactus*]
tajar – exchange, trade [Arabic *tajar*]
tam – expensive object [scalar] [Arabic *taman* + Hindi *dam*]
tamat – tomato [Nahuatl *tomatl*]
tar – star [Hindi *tar*, English *star*]
tard – something late or tardy [Vulgar Latin *tardivus*]
tarn – change, transformation [Latin *trans*]
tat – taut, tight [*taut*]
tel – far object [From *telfon, telvis, telsecop*]
temp – time [Latin *tempus*]
tend – tendency, propensity [Latin *tendere*]
ter – three [Indo-European *trie*]

term – hot object [Greek *therme*]
teror – fear [Latin *terror*]
tiger – tiger [Greek *tigris*]
tigun – offer [Mandarin *tigong*]
tint – ink [Latin *tinctus*]
tol – heavy object [Hindi *tol*]
tols – thick object [scalar] [Russian *tolst*]
tom – atom [Greek *atomos*]
ton – much [Romance augmentative *-on(e)*]
top – top [English]
tub - tube [Latin *tubus*]
tufan – storm [Arabic *tufan*]
val – worthiness [Latin *valere*]
vam – plant organ [Hindi *vamspat* 'plant']
van – one [English *one*, Arabic *wahid*]
vas – container [Latin *vas* 'vessel']
vat – water [Germanic **water*]
vav - removal, subtraction [Hindi *vyavakaln-*]
veb – World Wide Web [English]
vel – fast object [scalar] [Latin *velocitas*]
vend – sale [Latin *vendere*]
vent – wind (weather) [Latin *ventus*]
verb – verb [Latin *verbum*]
vert – vertical [Latin *verticalis*]
vic – vehicle [Latin *vehiculum*]
vid – glass [Spanish *vidrio*]
vih – excess [Russian *vish*]
vis – sight, vision [Dublex *telvis,* since 'television' is more international than any root for 'vision']
voc – word [Latin *vocalis*]
voct – eight [Russian *vosem,* Indo-European **okto-*]
vod – body of water [Russian *voda* 'water']
volm – loud object [Spanish *volum-*]
vols – hair [Russian *volas*]
volt – electricity [after Alessandro Volta]
vosp – arachnid, spider [alteration of Dublex *voctped* 'eight feet']
vov – egg [Latin *ovum*]
vuh – weapon [Mandarin *wuqi*]
zad - deficit, shortfall, insufficiency[Dublex *ziad* < Arabic *aziad*]
zard- risk — something involving hazard or uncertain danger [*hazard*]
zup – off [Mandarin *zai* 'at' + English *upon*]

Dublex Game Rules

Solitaire

For solitaire play, choose any seven Dublex words at random, then begin to combine them to form new words. The object is to coin as many words as possible. You decide what the words mean. It's just for fun, but if you want to compete with yourself, keep track of how many words you can coin from any seven Dublex words and strive to improve your personal best. It's not just 7 times 7 or 49 words, since you can string more roots together (*vocsistlet* "language (diminutive) = dialect"), create phrases and even create acronyms (*vadap* "watery dirt part = mud part = brick").

Two-Player play

Two players each choose seven different Dublex words (at random or by choice) and try to form the most words from them in a given time period — say, five minutes. The winner is the player with the most words coined.

Three or more players

When you have three or more players, there's an even better way to play (come on, play Dublex with a few friends and spread the joy of conlanging!). Choose seven Dublex root words at random. For five minutes, everyone tries to coin words from these roots. When the five minutes are up, each player reads his list. Any time two or more players have the same word form with the same basic meaning, they each get one point. Whoever has the most points wins the hand, and you can play up to 50 points a game. The goal is to create as many consensus word compounds as possible with your fellow players. Whoever succeeds in this best wins. In effect, you and your fellow players are creating a common language together.

Acknowledgments

Ray Brown - Thanks to Ray for his suggestions for simplying the sound system of Dublex.

Ivan Derzhanski - Thanks to Ivan for his comments and corrections on natural language sources of Dublex vocabulary.

David Dynes - Thanks to our past summer intern David Dynes for all his help compiling the Dublex dictionary.

Rick Harrison - Thanks to Rick for designing the Universal Language Dictionary, and for overseeing the compilation of it, which proved an invaluable reference for coining Dublex words and for deciding which core concepts needed to be included in the Dublex dictionary.

Lojbanistas - Thanks to all the Lojbanistas who contributed to the six-language etymological lexicon.

Mark McGrath - Thanks to Mark for insisting on schwa insertion.

Rick Morneau - Thanks to Rick for his article on morphotactics, which prompted me to design the morphotactics of Dublex, and especial thanks for his magnum opus, "Lexical Semantics", which influenced the grammar of Dublex significantly.

Leo Moser - Thanks to Leo for sharing generously of his research for his Acadon system and for his detailed feedback on the internationality of proposed root words. It was at Leo's passionate suggestion and insistence that 'c' was adopted in all places for the /k/ sound.

John Cowan, Mark Shoulson, BPJ, et al - Thanks to everyone who helped me refine the Dublex vocabulary and provided valuable feedback.

Others - If I left you out, please forgive me..

Fith

The Alien Language With A LIFO Grammar

A LIFO ("last in first out") stack can be thought of as a deck of cards. In Fith, every card is a different word or set of words. Some words — like nouns — typically just get added to the stack.

Let's say we're processing the string *zhong hong lin lo*. We process words one item at a time. The first word — **zhong** "nation" — is a noun, so it's placed on the stack:

>   *zhong*

The next word, **hong** ("man"), is placed on top of it.

>   *hong*
>   *zhong*

The next word is an adjective, **lin** "loyal." Adjectives modify the noun or phrase on top of the stack. We can represent this as *hong^{lin}* "loyal man", and add it back to the stack. (A stack entry can be a phrase.) So the stack now looks like:

>   *hong^{lin}*
>   *zhong*

Next is the postposition **lo** "of". This is a relationship between two items: <top of stack> *of* <next item down>. We can represent this as in predicate calculus, or a computer language, and put it back on the stack:

>   *lo(zhong, hong^{lin})*

This means "loyal man of the nation".

The notation could be different, but the important thing is to emphasize the **processing** done at each step: we know that *lin* modifies *hong* and we know the relation <hong lin> **of** <zhong>.

A trickier example

To really show off the language, we need to look at a more complicated example. Strap in.

> **Sren shi du shtring shoungh ke dhlinm shlo ke sthem lonh shen emn dyainmh meeñ o**
> language you *dup people vice the private swap-of the join *counterrotate *swap a makes when !
> *Share the secret vice— invent a language!*

Sren is a noun, so it's added to the stack.

> *sren* 'language'

Shi is a 2nd person (masculine) pronoun. Add it to the stack.

> *shi* 'you'
> *sren* 'language'

Du is a command to duplicate the top item on the stack.

> *shi* 'you'
> *shi* 'you'
> *sren* 'language'

Shtring and **shoungh** are nouns and are placed on the stack. Yes, the stack is getting kind of full!

> *shoungh* 'vice'
> *shtring* 'people'
> *shi* 'you'
> *shi* 'you'
> *sren* 'language'

Ke is the definite article. We can consider this a modification of the top noun.

> *shoungh*^{ke} 'the vice'
> ...

Dhlinm is a modifier — "private, secret". It modifies the top stack item.

> *shoungh*^{ke,dhlinm} 'the private vice'
> ...

Shlo has the same meaning as *lo* 'of', but takes the arguments in the opposite order. Instead of <top> of <next>, it means <next> of <top>.

> *shlo(shtring, shoungh*^{ke,dhlinm}*)* 'people of the private vice'
> *shi* 'you'
> *shi* 'you'
> *sren* 'language'

This is getting hard to read, so let's replace it with <vice-people>. This is not a Fith operation; it's just a way to make the exposition clearer!

> <vice-people>
> ...

Ke is the definite article again, so the top item becomes '**the** people of the private vice.'

> <vice-people>^{ke} 'the vice people'^e
> *shi* 'you'
> *shi* 'you'
> *sren* 'language'

Sthem is a verb ('join'). The top two items on the stack are its object and its subject. We replace them with a representation of the entire clause.

> *sthem(shi,* <vice-people>^{ke} *)* 'you join the vice people'
> *shi* 'you'
> *sren* 'language'

Lonh is a command which rearranges the stack: it takes the top item on the stack and pushes it down to #3 position.

> *shi* 'you'
> *sren* 'language'
> *sthem(shi,* <vice-people>^{ke}*)* 'you join the vice people'

Shen swaps the top two stack positions.

> *sren* 'language'
> *shi* 'you'

sthem(shi, <vice-people>^{ke}) 'you join the vice people'

Emn is the indefinite article, and modifies the top item on the stack.

sren^{emn} 'a language'
shi 'you'
sthem(shi, <vice-people>^{ke}) 'you join the vice people'

Dyaimh is the verb 'make'. Again, the object is the top of the stack, and the subject is right below that.

dyaimh(shi, sren^{emn}) 'you make a language'
sthem(shi, <vice-people>^{ke}) 'you join the vice people'

Meeñ is a conjunction, 'when'. The conjoints are the two items below.

meeñ(dyaimh..., sthem...)

I'm abbreviating a lot by now, but the meaning of this item is "when you make a language, you join the people of the private vice". No punctuation, though — we don't know if this is a statement, a question, or what.

Finally, **o** is an exclamation mark. It expects to find an entire sentence on the stack, which is just what we have, and removes it. This tells us to interpret the clause we have as an exclamatory statement.[7]

Syntactic Device: Lingering

A rhetorical device used in Fith is to mention subjects that are then left to linger on the stack before being used. This can serve as introduction or indirection. The whole time a Fithian is talking these unused words (typically nouns) are in the back of the listener's mind, as it were, coloring all that is said after. A short example (examples of this can be much longer):

> As we all love the pouch that bore us, we all love the clan who raised us. As we all love the clan who raised us, so must we love this nation that sacrificed for us. - Tsho Ming Sun Do.

There is not room in this language overview to present the whole translation here, other then to say that it begins with the words "nation clan

---

[7] Instead of ad hoc devices like superscripts, the processing could be represented by creating syntactic trees. This is much like top-down parsing of a context-free grammar, as in the *Syntax Construction Kit*, p. 213. Operations like *shen* correspond to transformations, though the notation is quite different! —MR

pouch". Thanks to the stack-based grammar, the word "nation" *zhong* can be introduced first, even though it is not used until four clauses later! (Obviously politicians find this device to be a great way to seem to answer an opponent.)

One popular parody of Tsho Ming Sun Do's famous statement (popular among the enemies of the Tsho nation anyway) begins with the words *Lu lu lu lu...* "Us us us us...". (The parody is perfectly grammatical, if impossible for humans to understand in real time.)

Parts of Speech

Fith is isolating, with no words modified by inflections or derivational affixes. The following analysis of the parts of speech is heavily influenced by Western European languages; this is not at all how a Fithian would describe the language.

Nominals

Nouns - A noun is placed on the stack as is and does not affect items already on the stack. Noun forms themselves are not marked for number, gender or case. Articles are optional, in which case the precise meaning is determined from context (e.g., *zhong hong lo* typically means "A man of THE nation").

Articles - The articles *ke* ("the"), *emn* ("a, some") and *zhenh* ("in general, as a class") are optional. When they are used, they occur after a noun or noun phrase: e.g., *hong fthong shlo emn*, "man people of a" → "a man of the people." An example of *zhenh* is

> **yumn zhenh tra humh vai e.**
> human [as a class] Terra from be sentence
> *Humans, as a rule, are from Terra.*

Plural Markers - The plural markers *ku* ("singular", default), *wa* ("dual", used less often than in Middle Fith texts) and *a* ("plural") do not affect the stack but indicate that all subsequent nouns and pronouns are of the number indicated. Plural markers can occur anywhere.

Pronouns - The 18 pronouns can be singular or plural depending on the plural marker in effect.

E.g. *lu* is "I" or "we" (masculine); *go* is "you (one or more females, as agent of the action)"; *ta* is "his", "its", or "theirs".

	agent		patient		possessive	
	m	*f*	*m*	*f*	*m*	*f*
1	lu	fi	ba	im	zha	ro
2	shi	go	de	na	ong	su
3	za	hu	em	pe	ta	un

Predicates

Verbs - A two-argument verb removes a subject and an object and replaces them with a clause on the stack. Verbs are not marked for tense, number, gender or person; this is assumed from context or made explicit by modifiers. A three-argument verb removes a subject, object and focus from the stack, replacing them with a clause. The special noun *vo* ("it", as in "It is raining") is used when the subject, object or focus is unspecified.

Tense Markers - The tense markers *zroe* ("present", default), *yan* ("past") and *shti* ("future") do not affect the stack but indicate that all subsequent verbs are of the tense indicated. Like plural markers, tense markers can occur anywhere.

Others

Modifiers - A modifier can be used as an adjective or adverb: an adjective if the stack top is a noun or noun phrase, an adverb if the stack top is a verb or verbal phrase. A modifier always removes the stack top and replaces it with a phrase. For instance:

> **hong lin**
> man loyal
> *loyal man*

> **hong shi vin um lin**
> man you follow still loyal
> *The man still loyally follows you*

Postpositions - These have a similar function to English prepositions:

> **fthong hong lo**
> people man of
> *man of the people*

Fith has two classes of POSTPOSITIONS: traditional postpositions such as *lo*, where the object of the postposition is the second item from the top of the stack, and the swap postpositions, where the object of the postposition is the top of the stack:

> **hong fthong shlo**
> man people of{swap}
> *man of the people*

The swap postpositions were originally all contractions of *shen* and a traditional postposition (e.g., *shlo* is a contraction of *shen lo*) though unrelated forms have since emerged (*sre*, "up", and *zhomn*, "[swap] up").

Stack Conjunction

A stack conjunction is a word with the primary purpose of directly manipulating the mental stack. The following sections cover the key stack conjunctions and their meanings.

(In the sample stacks, the top is to the right. E.g. if the stack is given as X Y Z, the topmost item is Z.)

Placeholder Conjunctions

This type of operator searches the stack down to the first occurrence of the placeholder *nyun*. Every subsequent element of the stack is then put in a series representing the relationship glossed (e.g., "and", "or", "nor").

> *drumh* (*nyun* X Y Z → "X, Y and Z") marks a simple series of nouns.

> *tuumnh* (*nyun* X Y Z → "either X, Y or Z") marks an *either...or* series of nouns

> *dwoumnh* (*nyun* X Y Z → "neither X, Y nor Z") marks a *neither...nor* series of nouns.

Copying Conjunctions

The following copying conjunctions add one or more items to the top of the stack, based on the existing contents of the stack.

> *du* (n1 → n1 n1) makes a copy of the top stack item. [called "dup", for duplicate, in English grammars]

> *kuu* (n1 n2 → n1 n2 n1 n2) copies the top two stack items. [called "redup"]
>
> *voi* (n1 n2 → n1 n2 n1) copies the second stack item to the top of the stack. [called "dupover"]
>
> *dzhi* (*nyun* X Y Z → *nyun* X Y Z X) copies the stack item above *nyun* to the top of the stack. [called "pick"]

For instance, *hong lin du* produces the stack <*hong lin*> <*hong lin*>. The phrase *hong lin du lo* translates as "most loyal man of loyal men" (the superlative is determined from context in this instance).

Another example: the phrase *zhong hong kuu* produces the stack *zhong hong zhong hong*, "nation man nation man".

Stylistically, it is considered poor form to repeat a recently said word when a stack conjunction could easily be used instead.

Ordering Conjunctions

The following ordering stack conjunctions rearrange the position of the items on the stack:

> *shen* (X Y → Y X) exchanges the stack positions of the top two stack items. [called "swap"]
>
> *ronh* (X Y Z → Y Z X) moves the third stack item to the top, pushing down the first two stack items. ["rotate"]
>
> *lonh* (X Y Z → Z X Y) moves the top stack item to the third item, pushing the second and third items up. ["counterrotate"]

The word *shen* is used to rearrange the order of the top two items of the stack. For example, compare

> **Hong ke rumn ke vith e**
> man the robot the see sentence
> *The man saw the robot.*
>
> **Hong ke rumn ke shen vith e**
> man the robot the swap see sentence
> *The robot saw the man.*

The swap rearranged the order of the subject and object. Swap, rotate and counterrotate conjunctions enable Fithian word order to be pretty free, despite the fact that verbs require subject-object word order. What follows illustrates this and is a good example of *lonh*:

> **zhong hong kuu non lonh lo shen krai e**
> nation man redup without counterrotate of hate sentence
> *The man with a nation is hated by the man without a nation.*

The first two nouns are copied to the stack, and *kuu* copies both of them. This has the same result as saying *zhong hong zhong hong*, but it's better style.

> *hong* 'man'
> *zhong* 'nation'
> *hong* 'man'
> *zhong* 'nation'

Non creates a prepositional phrase:

> *non(zhong, hong)* 'man without nation'
> *hong* 'man'
> *zhong* 'nation'

Lonh moves the top of the stack two items down:

> *hong* 'man'
> *zhong* 'nation'
> *non(hong, zhong)* 'man without nation'

The preposition *lo* replaces the top two items with *lo (hong, zhong)* 'man of nation'. Then *shen* reverses the two prepositional phrases, giving us

> *non(hong, zhong)* 'man without nation'
> *lo(hong, zhong)* 'man with nation'

Finally the verb *krai* takes the top of the stack as the object and the next item as the subject.

Contrast this with

> **zhong hong non zhong hong lo krai e**
> nation man without nation man with hate sentence
> *The man without a nation hates the man with a nation.*

Here things are put on the stack and then consumed in the same order by the verb. The pragmatic effect of using *lonh* and *shen* here is similar to the use of the passive in English.

The effect of *ronh lonh* is to rotate the top three items, then restore them to their original order, in effect leaving the stack unchanged. As a result, Fithian speakers use *ronh lonh* as a filler sound like English "um" when hesitating while talking.

Destructive Conjunctions

The following conjunctions remove items from the stack:

>*frong* (n1 → ø) removes the top item from the stack. [called "drop"]

>*bom* (n1 n2 → n2) nips the second item from the stack. [called "nip"]

>*skuunh* (n1...nn → ø) removes all items from the stack. [called "drop all"]

Here is an example of *skuunh*: the phrase *shi vum vai e* ("you were an egg", lit. "you egg be") is a dire insult, roughly equivalent to "f— you" in English (and is a reference to the pestilent monotreme rodents native to the planet Fithia). However, the phrase *shi vum vai skuunh* is the equivalent of "shucks" or "you goof"; it is the mildest of oaths, said by parents to their children and lovers to one another. (Imagine saying "f— you never mind" to your child!)

Stop Stack Operators

The following stop operators remove items from the stack as sentences.

>*e* removes the top item from the stack as a sentence

>*i* removes the top item from the stack as a sentence introducing detail (translated to English with a colon as punctuation)

>*o* removes the top item from the stack as an exclamation

>*u* removes the top item from the stack as a question

The operators *e* and *frong* have different semantic meanings (while sharing the same syntactical function). The word *e* ends an utterance, popping the stack top off the stack. It is like a period ending a sentence in written discourse, but in Fith it is always spoken. The word *frong*, on the other hand, like *bom*, has the sense of "forget I mentioned that".

Synchronization Conjunction

The synchronization conjunction *strunh* [called "synch"] is used to remind the listener how deep their mental stack should be. It requires that a number already be on the mental stack. For instance, *kyuunh strunh* means "two [synch]". Such a phrase has the sense of, "You should still have two items on your stack [after *kyuunh* has been removed], and I'll be getting to them shortly. If you don't, let me know and I'll clarify."

It is frequently used when talking in a noisy environment (the communal showers, for instance) and is used less often otherwise.

Further Usage Notes

Fith often uses the stack conjunction *du* [*dup] as a type of third-person pronoun. For example: *Hong du* produces the following stack in the mind of the listener: *hong hong*, "man man". E.g.:

> **rumn ke vainm du vonh e hong ke shen shkrung e.**
> robot the red (dup) jump. Man the (swap) deactivate.
> *The red robot jumped. The man deactivated it.*

The difficult part of this for English speakers is that you have to call attention to the fact that you will be referring to something later by saying *du*. In other words, you have to know that you are going to refer to something with a pronoun before you actually do so, marking the antecedent. This makes it harder to use (for humans) than a third-person pronoun.

The *shen* (*swap conjunction) is required to place the nouns in correct order for the verb *shkrung*, "deactivate". The subject has to go on the stack first, followed by the object. The swap-conjunction places the items <*hong ke*> "the man"> and <*rumn ke vainm*> "the red robot" in the correct order on the stack. Without *shen*, the meaning of the last sentence would be, "The red robot deactivated the man."

Phonology

The vocal tract of the Fithians is similar to that of humans, but different enough to make it impossible for humans to exactly pronounce Fithian sounds. And then there is the matter of the hand signals, some of which require the use of two thumbs... As a result, all humans speak Fith with a marked speech impediment (an uncharitable Fithian considers human pronunciation to be a parody), but the following guidelines allow us to come as close to the original sounds and signals as humanly possible.

Phonotactics

A word is formed from the following components:

    (I) V (F) H

    I = Initial consonant or consonant cluster (optional)
    V = Vowel or diphthong
    F = Final consonant or consonant cluster (optional)
    H = mandatory hand signal or word representing a hand signal

Initial consonants

Single Consonants - 25

    p t k
    b d g
    tsh
    dzh
    f th s sh h
    v dh z zh xh
    m n ng
    l
    r y w

h = velar voiceless [x], **xh** = velar voiced [ɣ]; **sh** = [ʃ], **zh** = [ʒ].

tsh and **dzh** are counted as single consonants, since they combine with other consonants in the same manner as single consonants, but they are of course actually consonant clusters /tʃ/ and /dʒ/.

The "single consonants" can then be clustered with other consonants as follows:

    add -r (20)
        pr tr kr
        br dr gr
        tshr
        dzhr

fr thr sr shr hr
vr dhr zr zhr xhr
mr nr

add -l (20)
    pl tl kl
    bl dl gl
    tshl
    dzhl
    fl thl sl shl hl
    vl dhl zl zhl xhl
    ml nl

add -y (12)
    py ty ky
    by dy gy
    fy sy
    vy zy
    my ny

add -w (12)
    pw tw kw
    bw dw gw
    fw sw
    vw zw
    mw nw

add -th (2)
    fth sth

prefix s- (5)
    sp st sk
    sf sth

prefix s-, add -r (5)
    spr str skr
    sfr sthr

prefix sh- (3)
    shp sht shk

prefix sh-, add -r (3)
    shpr shtr shkr

This totals 106 possible initial consonants or clusters (/sth/ occurs twice). It equals 107 possible word beginnings when you include the fact that you can omit a consonant altogether.

Vowels

    a - pat

ai - pay
e - pet
ee - bee
i - pit
ie - pie
o - pot
oe - toe
oi - noise
ou - out
u - cut
uu – boot

These vowels can be either nasalized or non-nasalized, but are almost always nasalized. The one exception is when no final consonant is indicated in the English transcription of a word (see next section).

Final Consonants And Consonant Clusters

The most common endings are the five nasals:

n
m
ng (as in sing)

mn (pronounced with no vowel between, as in *dumn*, "down"; try pronouncing *human* as one syllable)

nm (also pronounced with no vowel between, as in *vainm*, "red"; try pronouncing *venom* as one syllable)

Any of these nasals may be aspirated (actually, the process creates a geminate of the final nasal, which is followed by a clearly audible puff of breath):

nh
mh
ngh
mnh
nmh

The last final "consonant" is -ñ, the vestige of the nasal ending /ɲ/. In English transliterations, it is written as a consonant but in fact it is not pronounced, instead having the effect of keeping the vowel nasalized, thereby distinguishing *hoñ* ("to talk") from *ho* ("to lie"). The vowel is only not nasalized when it is not followed by a transliterated consonant.

There are 107 x 12 x 12 (15,408) possible unique word forms.

Cultural Notes

Names

The name of a Fith is four words long: the name of his nation, followed by the name of his clan, followed by the name of his mother, followed by the name his mother gave him. (Why do I use the pronoun *his*? Because 80% of Fithian births are to males, meaning men outnumber women four to one.)

> **Tsho Ming Sun Do**
> *Do, of the mother Sun, of the clan Ming, of the nation Tsho*

Among family and among friends of the same clan, only the given name (e.g., *Do*) is used. Among other members of the same clan, the mother's name is also used (e.g., *Sun Do*). Among members of another clan belonging to the same nation (even presuming friendship), the clan name is used (e.g., *Ming Sun Do*). Everyone else uses the full name. Occasionally, a Fithian's best friend will be of another nationality: those two will go through life calling each other by their full names.

Because clans often change allegiances, a Fithian's national name may change two or three times during his life. Tsho Ming Sun Do was born *Lom Ming Sun Do*, before the Ming clan joined the Tsho nation. (Tsho Ming Sun Do eventually led the Tsho nation to complete victory over the Lom nation, entirely conquering it.)

The words that are used as names have no other meaning (no names like Grace or Joy) and are chosen from a set that has become fixed by tradition. There are now just 144 possible given names, and 12 times that many clan names. The name of a nation is taken from the name of its preeminent clan.

Numbers

The Fithians use a number system based on 144. They have unique words for the numbers 0 through 144, then express greater numbers using 144 as the base.

FITH

0. sing
1. an
2. kyuunh
3. tshun
4. noengh
5. nguñ
6. staimh
7. mrongh
8. tloumn
9. meengh
10. hliem
11. vwuunm
12. hlemnh
13. shrengh
14. swangh
15. tloeñ
16. ngim
17. sprengh
18. riengh
19. sreeñ
20. shum
21. zrienh
22. nrou
23. roumnh
24. syou
25. gwuunm
26. pumnh
27. tweenh
28. langh
29. dhu
30. vlenmh
31. shtronmh
32. zhliemh
33. shtinmh
34. tshuung
35. staing
36. foimnh
37. swuuñ
38. tshe
39. loinm
40. tiemnh
41. dzhaing
42. sreen
43. fleenmh
44. dwemn
45. skroung
46. pluunm
47. shtaimn
48. dzhaingh
49. nlaimh
50. dwanmh
51. hluu
52. sfaimnh
53. pangh
54. krimn
55. thlaim
56. thlung
57. tim
58. tshlonmh
59. pree
60. dzhonm
61. nwainh
62. shkoñ
63. lainmh
64. pwaimnh
65. syiemnh
66. mring
67. pliengh
68. stheenm
69. vwimn
70. myimn
71. kloim
72. spoum
73. menm
74. tleeng
75. sproemh
76. vwiemn
77. shtang
78. fainm
79. hrieñ
80. soin
81. banmh
82. hlinh
83. nweenmh
84. stimn
85. meenm
86. dzhlomnh
87. ranh
88. frinh
89. brounm
90. sthoenm
91. keemn
92. tshluu
93. dzhlaingh
94. sriem
95. wonh
96. mram
97. gwuunh
98. pwang
99. ki
100. truñ
101. puumh
102. soen
103. myaimh
104. byañ
105. prem
106. bloing
107. vyoum
108. xhon
109. syeemh
110. bronm
111. tyemnh
112. shproimnh
113. bwaingh
114. zroen
115. shkang
116. glomh
117. kromh
118. fliemnh
119. kroeng
120. fweemnh
121. nlu
122. lee
123. ftham
124. dhloemnh
125. gyai
126. mrungh
127. skuumn
128. blumh
129. shproinm
130. gwuuñ
131. dyin
132. gienh
133. vreenmh
134. sproimn
135. zhoing
136. teemnh
137. zhloimnh
138. mwuung
139. thouñ
140. femh
141. dzhloimnh
142. syienm
143. zhluumh
144. mang

When a number is mentally processed, the Fithian checks the stack top to see if that is a number as well. If it is, it multiplies that number by 144 and adds its own value. Thus *an kyuunh* would be 1 x 144 + 2 = 146, while *mang an* would be 144 x 144 + 1 = 20,737.

Numbers are otherwise treated as nouns. To use a noun as an adjective requires using the postposition *tshon* "of" (but used only for numbers). Thus:

> **yan lu hong kyuunh tshon vilh e**
> past I man two of see sentence
> *I saw two men.*

Partings

The most common parting is

> **Song ke duun**
> Friend the go-away-with-the-intention-of-returning
> *The friend departs but will come again.*

Fith Lexicon

This is as much of the Fith-English lexicon as has so far been documented. We made the decision to publish once we reached 10,000 words. Issues to be addressed in future editions:

Many of the verbs have not yet been properly identified as either two-argument or three-argument (Fith speakers know this innately - it is not listed in their dictionaries); for now, assume "v" indicates possible three-argument verbs. An unknown number of irregular verbs require the object to proceed the subject; those have not all been identified yet.

Few compound words have been given in this initial lexicon. They do exist, though they are possibly more transient and polysemous than the common one-syllable words given here.

The class of Siamese words has only just begun to be studied. Apparently, Siamese words place two nouns on the stack, which are not treated as a phrase. For instance, there is a word that places "clan" and "mother" on the stack. If the next word were a verb, say "misses", then the sentence would be "Mother misses the clan." The component words could be used as subjects, objects, prepositional objects: they could be used in any way that saying the words "clan mother" could.

The Fithians have a rich vocabulary for discussing politics and alliances, and this has yet to be fully documented.

Etymologies documenting the evolution from multiple-syllable Old Fith words to the vowel-harmonized roots of Middle Fith and the monosyllables of Modern Fith have not yet been researched. Old Fith had 14 vowels, with /oo/ (took) and /ah/ (father) used, but they were the least frequently used sounds and were gradually abandoned in favor of a system that fit *den zhaimn ke* ("the golden twelve", the belief that twelve is the right number to have of something, meaning literally "the green twelve" in Fith, since green has the positive connotations the color of gold has for us). Also because of *den zhaimn ke*, four final consonant clusters of Old Fith (/l/, /lh/, /r/, and /rh/) were abandoned in favor of the "the golden twelve" endings (10 nasals, the vowel, and the non-nasalization of the vowel).

No font for the Fithian writing system has been developed yet. The Fithian writing system is a combination of an alphabet, a syllabary (for want of a better word) and an ideography. The initial consonant cluster of a word is represented alphabetically. Each unique combination of vowel and final consonant (the rime of a syllable, comprising 160 forms in Fith) has a unique symbol: so /oi/ is written differently than /oin/, which is written differently than /oimn/. And as if that wasn't enough, about the thousand most common words (actually it has been formalized at 12*144, *hlemnh sing*) have unique symbols. And the 144 digits (0 to 143) have unique symbols. So Fithians have to learn close to 2000 symbols to represent their language. Their brains are well suited to this; where humans using ideographic systems (Chinese, for instance) take decades to master all their symbols; a young Fithian can learn their writing system is about two Terran years.

Word	POS	Meaning
a	p	
ai	n	clique, coterie, ingroup, inner circle, pack, camp — an exclusive circle of people with a common purpose
aim	n	trustworthiness, trustiness — the trait of deserving trust and confidence
aimh	n	place, station — proper or designated social situation:
aimn	n	spat — a young oyster or other bivalve
aiñ	c	(clan name)
aingh	m	optical — of or relating to or involving optics;
ainh	n	hater — a person who hates
ainmh	n	ownership — the state or fact of being an owner

amn	m	psychic, psychical — pertaining to forces or mental processes outside the possibilities defined by natural or scientific laws
an	#	1
añ	m	intensive — tending to give force or emphasis;
ang	c	(clan name)
angh	n	subculture — a social group within a national culture that has distinctive patterns of behavior and beliefs
anmh	n	game — a single play of a game;
ba	n	first-person male patient pronoun
bai	n	chain, chemical chain — a series of linked atoms (generally in an organic molecule)
baimn	n	ectropy — the opposite of entropy: increasing order (as resulting from growth and development)
baimnh	v	travel, go, move, locomote — change location; move, travel, or proceed
bain	n	sortie, sally — a military action in which besieged troops burst forth from their position
baing	n	warning — a message informing of danger
baingh	c	(clan name)
bainm	c	(clan name)
bam	n	improvement — a condition superior to an earlier condition
bamn	n	stability — a stable order
bamnh	v	act, behave, do — behave in a certain manner; show a certain behavior; conduct or comport oneself
bañ	n	multitude, masses, mass, hoi polloi, people — the common people generally
bang	n	ring, ringing, tintinnabulation — the sound of a bell ringing
banm	n	differentia — a distinguishing characteristic esp in different species of a genus
banmh	#	81
be	c	(clan name)
bee	n	design, designing — the act of working out the form of something (as by making a sketch or outline or plan)
beem	n	procession — a collection of things moving ahead in an orderly manner
beemh	n	forfeit, forfeiture — something that is lost or surrendered as a penalty

beemn	m	pyrotechnic, pyrotechnical — of or relating to the draft of making fireworks
beeñ	n	committee, citizens committee — a self-constituted organization to promote something
beeng	c	(clan name)
beengh	n	prophylaxis — the prevention of disease
beenm	n	zooplankton — animal constituent of plankton; mainly small crustaceans and fish larvae
bem	n	aggression — deliberately unfriendly behavior
bemnh	n	square matrix — a matrix with the same number of rows and columns
beñ	n	surprise — a sudden unexpected event
benh	n	group action — action taken by a group of people
benmh	n	craft, trade — people who perform a particular kind of skilled work
bi	n	urgency — the state of being urgent; an earnest and insistent necessity
bie	n	grasping, taking hold, seizing, prehension — the act of gripping something firmly with the hands
biemh	m	biennial, biyearly — occurring every second year
biemn	n	pool — an organization of people or resources that can be shared
bien	n	acquisition — something acquired
bieñ	c	(clan name)
bieng	c	(clan name)
biengh	v	afford, open, give — afford access to
bienm	n	coven — an assembly of witches; usually 13 witches
bim	n	psychedelia — the subculture of users of psychedelic drugs
bimh	c	(clan name)
bimn	n	unwritten law — law based on customary behavior
bin	c	(clan name)
biñ	n	rationing — the act of rationing
bing	n	history — the continuum of events occurring in succession leading from the past to the present
bingh	c	(clan name)
binmh	n	confusion, mix-up, confounding — a mistake that results from taking one thing to be another
bla	n	concurrence — agreement of results or opinions
blai	c	(clan name)

blaim	n	seaworthiness, fitness — fitness to traverse the seas
blaimnh	c	(clan name)
blaiñ	n	meekness — the feeling of patient submissive humbleness
blainmh	n	vibes, vibrations — a distinctive emotional atmosphere; sensed intuitively
blam	n	pain, painfulness — emotional distress; a fundamental feeling that people try to avoid
blamh	n	garden — the flowers or vegetables or fruits or herbs that are cultivated in a garden
blamn	n	helplessness — a feeling of being unable to manage
blang	m	comparative — relating to or based on or involving comparison
blanh	v	bring on — cause to appear;
blanm	m	elemental — relating to or being an element
blanmh	n	food
ble	n	back — the position of a player on a football team who is stationed behind the line of scrimmage
blee	c	(clan name)
bleem	n	autotelism — belief that a work of art is an end in itself or its own justification
bleemn	n	scandal, outrage — a disgraceful event
bleemnh	c	(clan name)
bleen	n	period — the interval taken to complete one cycle of a regularly repeating phenomenon
bleeñ	n	noise conditions — the condition of being noisy (as in a communication channel)
bleeng	n	sorption — the process in which one substance takes up or holds another (by either absorption or adsorption)
bleengh	c	(clan name)
bleenh	n	speech act — the use of language to perform some act
bleenm	m	equatorial — of or relating to or at an equator
blem	n	devotion — (usually plural) religious observance or prayers (usually spoken silently)
blemh	n	agitation — the feeling of being agitated; not calm
blemn	c	(clan name)
blen	n	balance, equilibrium, equipoise, counterbalance — equality of distribution

bleñ	n	personification — one who personifies an abstract quality
bleng	n	welcome — the state of being welcome;
blengh	n	anastomosis, inosculation — a natural or surgical joining of parts or branches of tubular structures
blenh	n	payroll, paysheet — the total amount of money paid in wages
blenm	n	authorization, authorisation, empowerment — the act of authorizing
blenmh	n	default judgment, judgment by default — a judgment entered in favor of the plaintiff when the defendant defaults (fails to appear in court)
blie	n	zing — a brief high-pitched buzzing or humming sound
bliemn	n	summit, summit meeting — a meeting of heads of governments
bliemnh	n	space age — the age beginning with the first space travel
blieñ	m	royal — of or relating to or indicative of or issued or performed by a king or queen or other monarch
blienh	n	halogen — any of the chemical elements fluorine or chlorine or bromine or iodine or astatine
blim	n	public library — a nonprofit library maintained for public use
blimn	m	personal — of or arising from personality;
blimnh	v	oppress, suppress, crush — come down on
bling	m	agricultural — relating to or used in or promoting agriculture or farming
blingh	n	buzz — a confusion of activity and gossip;
blinh	c	(clan name)
blo	c	(clan name)
bloemh	m	liturgical — of or relating to or in accord with liturgy
bloemn	n	leap, jump — an abrupt transition
bloen	n	democracy, republic, commonwealth
bloeñ	n	fuel, combustible, combustible material — a substance that can be burned to provide heat or power
bloengh	m	tactical — of or pertaining to tactics

Translations into Fith

David J. Peterson collects translations of a specific poem he wrote in Sheli.

He asked me to do a translation into Fith, and given all the help he has provided me by helping edit Langmaker.com submissions, I can't refuse him! But this is a sad, sad poem for a race of alien herbivores to recite.

> **Teng limnh mwu**
> **a breengh lo somnh nlienm vreemh e**
> **ku bluunh shen zlumnh lo skingh byom lo vo dyem e**
> **a ke spoem stum dzheen ronh lo sthingh kweemnh e.**
> limb-stump mast tree-stump
> *plural shank of midair andante cut .
> *singular container *swap without of rock ocean of it absorb .
> *plural the predator horn brown *rotate of marketplace remove .
> *Tree stumps of shanks cut midair andante. A container without a mast absorbs a rock of the ocean. Predators take the brown horns from the stumps to the marketplaces.*

Fith poems, like Fith speeches, introduce words sentences before they are used. This poem begins ominously, "stump, mast, stump", where *teng* is the stump of a limb or tooth and *mwu* is the stump of a tree. These three stark images of truncated objects color the rest of the poem.

Speaking of color, I had to translate "red" as "brown", because in my interpretation of David's poem the red is the red of blood, but in that context Fiths refer instead to brown, the color of dried blood.

Of course, Fith, as the language of aliens, divides its lexicon in odd ways. For instance, there's no general word for "leg" or "limb", but there is one for "shank" (the part of the leg from the knee to the ankle); there's no general word analogous to "glide", as in "glide through the ocean" in David's original, so I reached for "absorb" as an ironic alternative; there's no general word for "boat" either, let alone "barge", which led to the need to translate "barge" as "container without a mast", which was a fortunate circumlocution, since it provided me the initial image of the poem.

The words used:

a - plural marker
bluunh - container: something that holds things, especially for transport or storage

breengh - shank: the part of the human leg between the knee and the ankle
byom - ocean: a large body of water constituting a principal part of the hydrosphere
dyem - absorb, suck, imbibe, soak up, sop up, suck up, draw, take in, take up: be able to take in, as of liquids
dzheen - brown
e - sentence marker
ke - definite article
ku - singular marker
kweemnh - remove, take, take away: remove something concrete, as by lifting, pushing, taking off, etc.; or remove something abstract
limnh - mast: a vertical spar for supporting sails
lo - of
mwu - stump, tree stump: the base part of a tree that remains standing after the tree has been felled
nlienm - andante: a moderately slow tempo (a walking pace)
ronh - *rotate (stack conjunction)
shen - *swap (stack conjunction)
skingh - rock, stone: a lump of hard consolidated mineral matter
somnh - midair: some point in the air; above ground level
spoem - predator, predatory animal: any animal that lives by preying on other animals
sthingh - market, marketplace: the world of commercial activity where goods and services are bought and sold
stum - horn, tusk
teng - stump: the part of a limb or tooth that remains after the rest is removed
vo - it (argument placeholder)
vreemh - cut: make an incision or separation
zlumnh - without, with no ..., lacking

The Langmaker motto

When I first translated the Langmaker motto into Fith, I made the typical human mistake of translating every word:

> **Shi shtring shoungh ke lo plaiñ lo ke sthem shi sren emn vo dyainmh meeñ o**
> you people vice the of concealing of the join you language a (it) makes when !
>
> *Share the secret vice— invent a language!*

In Fithian discourse, it is considered poor style to reuse a recent word. Fith imperatives require the pronoun "you" (e.g., "You run!" not "Run!"), but it was poor form for me to repeat the pronoun, *shi*, for both sentences when it can easily be accessed using a stack conjunction. Additionally, it is good Fithian style to begin a paragraph with the last prominent noun (in this case, *sren* "language"). Accordingly, I had to retranslate as follows:

> **Sren shi du shtring shoungh ke dhlinm shlo ke sthem lonh shen emn dyainmh meeñ o**
>
> language you *dup people vice the private swap-of the join *counterrotate *swap a makes when !
>
> *Share the secret vice— invent a language!*

Acknowledgments

Thanks to Mark Reed for a LIFO Introduction.

Thanks to Jim Henry for suggesting that perhaps each word in Fith "could end with a sort of CRC code"; that suggestion inspired the creation of *strunh*.

Thanks to Jörg Rhiemeier for the invention of Shallow Fith.

Ilish

From the *Encyclopedia Fithica*

One of the more unusual species of creatures on Fithia (by Terran standards) is the **il**, a deep-sea-dwelling, omnivorous "fish" with its own capability for language (the intelligence of ils is somewhere between that of Terran canines and three-year old humans). The ilian languages (known as the Ilish language family) may have originally evolved from the unusual reproductive cycle of the il.

The female of the species ejects its fertilized eggs over the face of the male il; these eggs completely cover the sonar-emitting and -receiving "eyes" of the male il, eventually rendering the male il "blind" (unable to use sonar) as the eggs take root and develop. The eggs derive sustenance from the male by literally sucking its eyes out. For the three months of incubation and the month of regeneration of the sonar tissue, the male il depends upon the female il to tell it the location of prey, predators and obstacles. Without language, the male il would starve and the propagation of the species would cease.

The female il communicates with the male by sending the male il electric shocks. Each electric signal acts as a word, with collections of signals forming sentences. The male il can respond in kind, interrogating the female by generating its own electric signals. These signals show arbitrary symbolism; they are not inherited but vary, with the precise schemes differing among il living in different regions of Fith's oceans. Both the male and female il teach their language to their offspring, as the young il (called *ilts*) are blind for several months after detaching themselves from their father.

Fithian scientists have removed the ilts from their biological parents (speaking one dialect or language) to an adoptive couple speaking a different dialect or language, and in all cases where the ilts have survived, the ilts have learned the language of their adopted parents rather than the language of their biological parents; this is a sure sign that the ilian communication system is in fact language based. (Unfortunately, in early experiments, the adopted ilts were devoured by the adopting parents; only when all of the original offspring of the adopted parents were removed would the ils be content to raise the adopted ilts.)

Because only one il can talk to another at a time, they sometimes form speaking-chains, with the first il (typically the mother), sending a signal to the second il, which relays it to the third, and so forth.

Pronouns

One last interesting fact about the ilian languages: each language has an elaborate system consisting of thousands of pronouns, with no nouns at all. Each pronoun system in the different ilian languages arbitrarily represents common coordinates on a three-dimensional spatial system, where the speaker (actually, the emitting il) is the origin of the coordinating system. Thus there are arbitrary signals for concepts such as the following:

> (0,0,0) - speaker ("I, me")
>
> (1,1,1) - that thing removed one unit from the speaker upwards, one unit to the left, one forward
>
> (-1,-1,-1) - that thing removed one unit from the speaker downwards, one unit to the right, one backward
>
> (0,0,1), (0,1,0), (0,1,1), etc.

The units are logarithmic, so coordinates that represent ever further distances away include ever larger areas, going up to eleven units away in some dialects (which would be 12,167 coordinate cells).

For the nearer coordinates, there is no relationship between the amplitude of the electric signals and the coordinate system; it is as arbitrary as any sound-sense correspondence in the pronoun system of a human language. Pronouns for coordinates more than two away in any distance are formed from compounds.

Interestingly, as an il swims, the location of an object is moving relative to the il, so the object's pronoun label is changing as well. To translate "I see some edible plankton right there; would you like to eat it?" requires knowing the position of the plankton relative to the speaker (to translate "right there" into the appropriate pronoun), the position of the listener ("you") and the position of the plankton by the time the utterance is being completed ("it"). If the listener goes to talk about "it", even if "it" has not moved, he or she would still use a different pronoun to refer to "it", since he or she has to make the reference using his or her coordinate system. So the shifting referents of pronouns as two il communicate are too complicated for humans or even Fithians to process in real time.

A pronoun is "inflected" (the beginning of the electric signal is subtly altered) as one of three pronoun classes: **positive** (beneficial), **negative** (a threat) or **neutral** (not known to be either positive or negative). So a pronoun would be roughly translated as "something [good or bad or neutral] at [distance]."

The pronoun system is further overlaid by three tiers. The first tier is as just described, but the second tier implies **indirect knowledge**; e.g., "I-think-it-is-there-at-(1,2,3)". The indirect tier is used when extrapolating an object's position (for example, if obscured by an intervening object, say a large school of fish) and is therefore always used by blind ils, who automatically and quite sophisticatedly extrapolate the position of objects based on their past known movements, the speed of currents, etc. The third tier is used to refer to something that **had been there**; for instance, the sentence "Remember the moby [English translation for a specific predator] we saw yesterday?" would be more literally expressed as "Remember the moby-like it [giving pronoun of the past coordinates it was seen at] we saw yesterday-ly [adv.]?"

In the ilian languages, all abstract nouns are actually translated as what we would call adjectives, so "some edible plankton right there" would be translated "edible-plankton-like [adj.] it [pronoun]". Pronouns in ilian languages can therefore be modified by adjectives (unlike in human languages). The word "some" would be handled differently; it would be translated with other pronouns to fully cover the coordinates where the plankton can be found; therefore, "it" might be translated as three pronouns covering coordinates (2,2,2), (2,2,3) and (2,3,2) for instance. For truly large objects, sometimes just the coordinates of the edges are referred to: "[1,5,5] and [1,3,3]" (for a two-dimensional object or a thin three-dimensional object).

In summary, an Ilish pronoun refers to the following semantic components: attitude (beneficial, threatening, neutral), location (x, y and z coordinates) and context (seen at that location now, expected to be at that location now, at that location in the past).

Adjectives

The ilian languages have over 50 adjectives describing relative and object velocity and acceleration. Imagine if U.S. motorists had simple words for *55 miles per hour, decelerating at x ft/sec², accelerating at x ft/sec²* and so forth. The il use these words as readily as we use color words. (They of course have no words for color, not perceiving light, but instead have words to describe the texture of echoed sonar signals — try translating those into English!)

The il have a large variety of adjectives to describe animals and plants. The adjectives are used to describe pronouns, as if in English you could not talk about barnyard animals like cows, horses and sheep, but only about "the bovine it, the equine it and the ovine it".

Numbers

The il count using a ternary number system. They have words for zero, one, two and three, which then are combined for larger numbers. For instance, five = 12 (one two), since the first digit represents one occurrence of 3, and six = 20 (two zero).

Decimal	Ternary
0	0
1	1
2	2
3	10
4	11
5	12
6	20
7	21
8	22
9	100
10	101

The il use the word meaning 9 the way English speakers use "hundred" to refer to a large number. So an il that said it saw 9 of something means that it saw a lot of them.

Numbers are always used as adjectives or adverbs. "Can you count to 9?" would be "Can you count 9-ly?" and "I saw 9 of them" would be more literally "I saw 9 its."

Conclusion

The il like to talk! Well, to be as objective as possible, the female il like to electrically shock the male il. It is often difficult to tell if any meaningful communication is always intended by this...

The il use language not only to communicate facts that assist with the necessities of living, but also appear to have discussions and tell stories. Most discussions involve wish fulfillment ("I would really like to see lots of edible-sea-creatures right there, wouldn't you? or would you rather see edible-sea-ferns?"). The stories, on the other hand, are tedious recollections (tedious to Fithians and humans) of a whole day of meals, from the initial identification of each likely meal and its subsequent movements (if plankton, moved by the currents, or if an animate sea creature, any evasive maneuvers it may have taken), to its digestion by the omnivorous il and the path its detritus took to reach the ocean floor.

So even though the il do speak languages, no other sentient creatures really want to learn to speak with them.

Thanks to Frank Mayer for his suggestions on how to improve this write up of the ilian languages.

The Babel Text

This is the start of a verbatim paraphrase of the Babel Text as it would need to be translated into an Ilish language.

1. And ilish beneficial-something-in-entire-field-of-vision-past could communicate together.

2. As ilish beneficial-something-in-entire-field-of-vision-past and I drifted eastward, ilish beneficial-something-in-entire-field-of-vision-past and I found a food-rich, sea-floorish something-below-us-past and hovered above something-below-us-past.

3. Ilish beneficial-something-in-entire-field-of-vision-past and I linked-in-a-communications-chain-and-communicated, "Come, (imperative) eat of sea-floorish something-below-us-now."

4. Then Ilish beneficial-something-in-entire-field-of-vision-past and I communicated-across-a-communications-chain, "Come, (imperative) remain here and eat always of sea-floorish something-below-us-now and let ilish-excrementish beneficial-something-below-us-future settle to the

sea-floorish something-below-us-future. Ilish beneficial-something-in-entire-field-of-vision-past and I will never leave here, so that all the ilish beneficial-something-outside-entire-field-of-vision-now will come here and so that ilish-beneficial-something...

Intermythic English

Inspired by Tamarian, here's a modest proposal for a mythometaphorical model language: Intermythic English. This is simply English with the addition of the vocabulary below.

Sample Sentences

> **Yama can sarasvati Babel.**
> *You can speak Intermythic English.*
>
> **The Minerva of Babel has Castor and Pollux.**
> *The author of Intermythic English has twins.*
>
> **Yama and Nar can ahura mazda new Sarasvatis for Babel.**
> *You and I can create new words for Intermythic English.*

Pronouns

Personal pronouns are not inflected for number, gender or case.

- first person ("I, me, we, us") is **Nar** [from Narcissus]
- second person ("you") is **Yama** [the first mortal in Indian mythology]
- third person ("he, him, she, her, they, them, it") is **Skanda**.

Lexicon

Words separated by a slash are the Greek and Roman forms (Artemis/Diana). Either is acceptable Intermythic.

Achilles [Greek.] - to kill, one killed
Adam [Jewish] - a man, masculine
Adapa [Akkadian] - to think, a wise person, wise
Aditi [Indian] - to bear a child, a mother, motherly

Adonis [Phoenician] - to seduce, a seducer, seductive
Aeneas [Greek] - to worship, a worshipper, worshipful
Agni [Indian] - to ignite, a fire, fiery; to anger, an angry one, angry; to digest, a digester/eater, digestive
Ahura Mazda [Indo-Iranian] - to create, a creator, creative
Amaterasu [Japanese] - to rule, a ruler/monarch/emperor, imperial
Amazon [Greek] - a matriarchy, matriarchial
Amitabha [Buddhist] - to save, a savior, saving
Amun-Re [Egyptian] - to hide, an unknown, hidden
Anahita [Persian] -
Angel [Jewish] - to herald/convey a message, a herald/messenger
Angra Mainyu [Persian] - to die, a dead one, deadly; to rot, filth, rotten
Anna Perenna [Roman] - to feast, a feaster, festive
Anu [Sumerian] - to judge, justice/a judge, judgmental
Anubis [Egyptian] - to embalm, an embalmer
Aphrodite/Venus [Greek] - to beautify, a beauty, beautiful
Apis [Egyptian] - a bull
Apollo [Greek] - time [suggested by Jane Connell]
Ares/Mars [Greek] - to war, a war, martial
Artemis/Diana [Greek] - a virgin, virginal; to hunt, a hunter, venereal [in hunting sense!]
Aten [Egyptian] - to shine, the sun, solar
Athena/Minerva [Greek] - to create art/write/compose/sculpt, an artist, artistic
Baal [Phoenician] - to fight, a fighter, combative
Babel [Jewish] - Intermythic English
Balder [Norse] - to be gentle, one who is gentle, gentle
Castor [Greek] - a twin
Pollux [Greek] - a twin
Centaur [Greek] - to ride a horse, an equestrian
Cernunnos [Celtic] - to run wild, a wild animal, wild
Chac [Mayan] - to rain, the rain, rainy
Demeter/Ceres [Greek] - to farm, a farmer, agricultural
Dionysus/Bacchus [Greek] - to drink alcohol, an alcoholic drink/a drunkard/wino, inebriated
dragon [various] - to hoard, a hoard, miserly
Enlil [Sumerian] - to be true, truth, truthful; to take an oath, oath
Erinye [Greek] - to punish, a punisher, punishing
Eros/Cupid [Greek] - to love, a lover, loving
Eve [Jewish] - a woman, feminine
Freyr [Norse] - to engage in an orgy, an orgy, orgiastic
Gorgon [Greek] - to terrorize, a terror, terrifying
Medusa [Greek] - an ugly one, ugly

Hadad [Assyrian] - to storm, a storm, stormy
harpy [Greek] - to kidnap, a kidnapper
Heimdallr [Norse] - to guard, a guard
Hephastus/Vulcan [Greek] - a blacksmith
Hera/Juno [Greek] - to marry, a married woman
Heracles/Hercules [Greek] - a strong man, strength
Hestia/Vesta [Greek] - to establish a home, a home/hearth, homely
Horus [Egyptian] - sky
Ishtar [Mesopotamian] - to make a really bad movie, a bad movie ☺
Isis [Egyptian] - to make a really bad TV show
Itzamma [Mayan] - a lizard, lizardly
Janus [Roman] - to begin, a beginner
Kami [Japanese] - nature, natural
Kumarbi [Hurrian] - to rival, a rival/rivalry
Leviathan [Phoenician] - a monster, monstrous; a huge one, huge
Loki [Norse] - chaos/disorder, chaotic/disorderly
Maat [Egyptian] - a balance
Mithra [Indo-European] - to make a friend, a friend, friendly
Moerae/Parcae [Greek] - to determine the fate, fate, fatal
Muse [Greek] - to sing, a singer/music [!], musical
Nar Narcissus [Greek] - [first-person pronoun] I, me, we, us
Narcissus [Greek] - self
Njord [Norse] - to fish, a fish, fishy
Odysseus/Ulysses - to travel, a traveler
Orpheus [Greek] - to make poetry, a poet, poetic
Pan [Greek] - to herd sheep, a shepherd/a flock, pastoral
Pandora [Greek] - to hope, one who hopes, hopeful; Esperanto
Poseidon/Neptune - to sail the sea, the sea, maritime
Priapus [Greek] - a chauvinist
Rudra [Indian] - to redden, the color red, red
Sarasvati [Indian] - to speak, a word/a speaker, verbal
Seth [Egyptian] - to cause evil, an evil one, evil
Sin [Sumerian] - the moon, lunar
Skanda [Indian] - [third-person pronoun] he, him, she, her, they, them, it
Soma [Indian] - to drug, a drug
Tezcatlipoca [Aztec] - to sacrifice, a sacrifice
Thor [Norse] - to hammer, a hammer
Thoth [Egyptian] - to writer, a writer/scribe, written
Tlaloc [Aztec] - a mountain
Tlazolteotl [Aztec] - to lust, lust, lusty
Yama [Indian] - [second-person pronoun] you
Yu ["Yu the Great", Chinese] - to engineer, an engineer

The source of the vocabulary and its origins is *The Wordsworth Dictionary of Mythology*.

The Punchline

The punchline of all this is that Intermythic English is not really mythometaphorical. Sure, its vocabulary is derived from mythology, but all the words' meanings will become set and the mythological associations will be lost, just as they are in the eight mytho-etymological words in the following English sentence:

> *Waiting in line to check out* Ishtar *and* Apollo 13, *Jason was annoyed by the sound of sirens in that musical jingle about panicking while deciding between a new Saturn and a used Mazda.*

Kali-sise (Pitakesulina)

Kelu supaka-sunu ke sese kane ke Kali-sise pi nalike se.
Four vowels and six consonants Kalisise has.

Inspired by criticism of the difficulty pronouncing some IALs (International Auxiliary Languages), I have created Kali-sise, an auxlang whose overwhelming goal is ease of pronunciation, regardless of the learner's native language. The design goal of "near universality" means that Kalisise in most cases should only have sound features common to approximately 19 out of 20 natural languages. The real-world data that Kali-sise is based on is **UPSID** (the UCLA Phonological Segment Inventory Database), which profiled the inventories of 317 languages, with one language selected from each family grouping recognized.

Phonology

For a phonological feature to be included in Kali-sise, it must be present in roughly 19 out of 20 languages (92.5%, rounding up 18.5 to 19).

Vowels

Every language profiled in UPSID has three or more vowels, and 94% of the languages in the UPSID survey have four or more vowels.

The minimal vowel system is:

    i u

      a

Languages with this system include Aleut, Classical Arabic, Greenlandic and Quechua.

To make it easy for speakers of such languages to learn a fourth vowel, that fourth vowel is equidistant from the other three, making best use of the vowel space and making it easiest for speakers to distinguish the vowels. This is also identical to the vowel system of Rukai:

```
i  u
 e
  a
```

The **e** is pronounced as a schwa [ə].

Kali-sise does not have an /o/ sound.

Consonants

Stops - Over 99% of UPSID languages have bilabial, dental/alveolar and velar stops. Since voiceless segments outnumber voiced segments (92% vs 67%), we will adopt **p t k** as our stops.

Fricatives - Since 93% of the UPSID languages have at least one fricative, we will have a fricative. About 83% of the languages have some form of **s**, so we will adopt **s** as our single fricative.

Nasals - 97% of the languages have at least one nasal, and in 96% of these cases it is voiced **n**. So /**n**/ is our single nasal.

Liquids — While 96% of languages have at least one liquid, only 72% have more than one, so again we will confine ourselves to one. Since **l** is somewhat more common than **r** (and since **l** is less likely to change over time than **r** is), **l** will be our liquid.

Others - Approximants (**j w**) occur in fewer than 95% of languages and so will be excluded from Kali-sise. Glottalics are also too rare to be included.

```
Stops
        p - as in pot
        t - as in tot
        k - as in cot
Fricative
        s - as in sought
Liquid
        l - as in lap
Nasal
        n - as in nap
```

Syllable Pattern

No syllable pattern is universal.

The CV syllable pattern is the most common, though some languages require it to be pronounced with a tone. This pattern allows 24 (C*V=6*4) types of syllables. It may seem limiting, but in fact there are over 331,000 possible four-syllable words.

The V pattern is at best estimate not found in 95% of languages. It appears that more than 8% of languages require an onset.

The CVN pattern, where N is a nasal, is very common (Chinese, for example, allows it), but fewer than 95% of languages support it, so it is excluded.

Conclusion

Based on this design, clearly, if ease of pronunciation is the number one goal of any IAL, and that goal is defined as only having features common to 92.5% or more natural languages, it is achievable with Kali-sise.

The nickname **Pitakesulina** is a mnemonic that exhaustively exhibits all the sounds and vowels of the language.

Lexicon

Kali-sise has 400 nominal roots that can be freely combined to form compound words. It also has 11 functional roots used for clauses, postpostions and verbs. Over 93% of the vocabulary is derived from natural languages, especially Arabic, English, Hindi, Mandarin, Russian, Spanish and Indo-European; many other natural languages were examined for possible roots.

> *The etymology is often shared with Dublex; if a single word is given, it's a Dublex root. Otherwise, as with Dublex, etymologies are limited to the closest original form(s).*
>
> *If an etymology is missing, it's been forgotten!*

ka [Indo-European *kw-*] {relative clause particle}
kakate action [*cact*]
kaki performance
kaku deficit, shortfall, insufficiency
kakute sharp [*carc*]

kala art [Hindi *kala*]
kalane communication unit [Arabic *kalam*]
kalape change, transformation [Arabic *kalab*]
kalase cross [*cars*]
kale feces, excrement [*cal*]
kalene agent [Hindi *karn*]
kalenu flesh [*carn*]
kalepe carbon [*carb*]
kalese class, kind, type [*cals*]
kaletela road, route [Spanish *carretera*]
kali word [Arabic *kalim*]
kalike throat [*galc*]
kaluka peripheral, auxiliary device [Latin *calc*]
kalusa love [*caras*]
kalute dog [*calot*]
kane sight, vision [Mandarin *kan*]
kaneke shell, outer covering [*canc*]
kanela room, chamber [*camer*]
kanelu camel [*camel*]
kanepuse field [*camp*]
kanete fastener [Hindi *kant*]
kani garment, article of clothing [*cam*]
kanisa shirt [*camis*]
kanuna law, rules [*canun*]
kanune cannon [*canon*]
kapase jump [*cafaz*]
kape coffee [*caf*]
kapina card [Mandarin *kapian*]
kapita leader [*capt*]
kaputa head [*cap*]
kase cas [*gas*]
kasele fraction [Arabic *kasr*]
kasese abstraction [*cah*]
kasu cause [*cas*]
kata cut, cutting [*cat*]
katale dirt, ground [Arabic *kadar*]
katate square [Russian *kvadrat*]
kate heart [*card*]
katipa bar, rod, rail [Arabic *kadib*]
katipe dense something [Arabic *katif*]
katuse cat [*catoh*]
ke {postposition}
keke sibling

kelane family [Russian & English *klan*]
kelepasi celebration, rejoicing, jubilee [Spanish *celebración*]
kelepe play, diversion [*celeb*]
kelesu grass [*gars*]
kelu four [Indo-European **kwetwores*]
kelupe group [*gurp*]
kene hole into something [Mandarin *keng* 'pit']
kesinu science [Mandarin *kexue* + Latin *scientia*]
kesu run, fast movement [*curs*]
kiki measure, measurement
kipele cyberspace [*ciber*]
kipu curve [*cirv*]
kisa story, tale [*cis*]
kisile acid [Russian *kisl*]
kita food [*gid*]
kitala guitar [*gitar*]
kitapa book [*citab*]
ku violence [*curl*]
kukitu knowledge [*cog*]
kuku lightning
kula sphere [Arabic *kura*]
kuleke correct [*corect*]
kulepe oscillation, swinging movement [*coleb*]
kulepu body of water [Spanish *cuerpo de agua*]
kulete string, thread [*cord*]
kulisu wheel [*col*]
kulule color [*color*]
kulupe deep object [*gulb*]
kuna comparison [*comar*]
kunane eating [*comanj*]
kunapale multiplication [Hindi *gunanpal*]
kunase cloth, fabric [*cumah*]
kune opposite extreme [*con*]
kunete condition, state, status [*cond*]
kunune communication [*comun*]
kunuse cone [*conus*]
kupake cup [*cub*]
kupate fight, combat, conflict [*comb*]
kupe cover [*cov*]
kupi copy [*cop*]
kupu edge, boundary [*corb*]
kupute computer [*comp*]
kuse cooking, food preparation [*cos*]

kusete bone [*cost*]
kusulu alcohol [*cohol*]
kusune outer space [*cozom*]
kutane front, forward part [Arabic *kudam*]
kutu eight [Indo-European *okto*-]
kutule control [*cont*]
lala time
lalu iron, Fe
lanase long object [*lang*]
lane face [*lan*]
lanese spear, lance [*lans*]
lani intensity, emphasis [*lam*}
lapati washing [*lav*]
lape lamp [*lamp*]
lati radio [*rad*]
latu loud object [German *laut*]
le {first-person pronoun}
lele male, masculine
lene learning [*lern*]
lepe left (side) [Russian *lev*]
lepeta repetition [*rep*]
lepeti reptile, reptilian [*rept*]
lesune reason, explanation, justification, rationale [*rezon*]
lete little, small; diminutive [*let*]
li {postposition}
liku liquid [*lic*]
lili world
line line [*lin*]
lipe freedom, liberty [*lib*]
lise rice [*ris*]
lisepe reciprocity [*risp*]
lu fall, drop [Mandarin *luo*]
luka rock, stone [*roc*]
luke allium— onion, garlic, leek [*luc*]
luku location, position [*loc*]
lulu excess
luna moon [*lun*]
lune red [*run*]
lunene light [*lum*]
lupete air [*luft*]
luse rough object [*ruch*]
na {postposition}
nala disparagement, pejoration [*mal*]

nalake milk [*malact*]
nale ocean, sea [*mar*]
nalike possession [*malc*]
nalusu outside [Russian *naruju*]
nana electricity
nane mammal [*mam*]
nanepu tuber [*jam*]
nanese meat [*mans*]
nanete command, instruction [*mand*]
nani soft object [*narm*]
nanu paper [*pap*]
napase competition [Arabic *nafas*]
napate increase [Arabic *nabat*]
nape parent [*map*]
napine frequent event [Hindi]
napisu something above [Russian *navirzhu*]
napu obscenity [Sona *apu*]
nasala source, origin [*nahar*]
nase nose [*nas*]
naseke birth [*nasc*]
nasi machine [*mahin*]
nasiku insect [Russian *nasikoma*]
nasine wind [Arabic *nasim*]
nasini vehicle [Russian *mashin*]
nati matter, material, substance [*mater*]
natinu nation, country, state [*natin*]
natu adult [*mat*]
natula nature [*nat*]
ne – 2nd person pronoun [Indo-European *-em*]
nelike deer, cervid [*mirg*]
nelu black [*ner*]
nene nine [*nen*]
nenu egg
nese sheep [*meh*]
nesete site [*mest*]
nesetu nest, house, lair, den [*nest*]
netale metal [*metal*]
nete net [*net*]
neti mind [*ment*]
netu middle, center [*med*]
nike worker, seller, professional [*nik*]
nikule tiny object/event [*micor*]
nila blue [*nil*]

nilite military [*milit*]
nine fish [*min*]
nini whatchamacallit
nu one [Indo-European **oynos*]
nuka limb [*nog*]
nuku mouth [*muk*]
nulute hammer [*molot*]
nune negation [Latin *non*]
nunene name [*nomin*]
nunesu number, numeral [*nomer*]
nunete mountain, mount [*mont*]
nuni absence
nuninali noun [*nomin*]
nunu present, now [*nun*]
nupeti marriage, matrimony [*nupt*]
nupile furniture [*mob*]
nupili noble [*nobil*]
nusika music [*music*]
nusike rodent [*muh*]
nute north [*nort*]
nutipe target, goal [*motiv*]
nutu death [*mort*]
nutule motor [*motor*]
nutuse base, node, station [*nod*]
pa {comparative marker}
pakala hold [pacar]
pakale bovine, cow, bull [*bacar*]
pakute weather [Russian *pagod*]
pala fruit [Hindi *pal*]
palana plant [*pant*]
palasa stripe [Russian *palasa*]
palate part [*part*]
pale blade [Hindi *pal*]
palise digit [Russian *palis*]
pane flag, banner [*baner*]
paneka reserve, supply (*not* the financial institution) [*banc*]
panupu bamboo [*bamub*]
papa fat
papu verb
pasala market [*bazar*]
pasatu past [*pas*]
pata water [Russian *vada*]
patalune pants, trousers [*patuln*]

patate object, thing [Hindi *padart*]
pe person, individual [*per*]
pelane plant organ [Spanish *planta*]
pele interval [pel]
pelene pome, fleshy fruit such as an apple or pear [*pelm*]
pene five [pen]
penesa stylus, pen [*pens*]
penete sale [*vend*]
pepale readiness [Spanish *preparar*]
pepe creation
pesipitasi precipitation: rain, snow, etc. [Spanish *precipitación*]
pete foot [*ped*]
pi {postposition}
piku buttock, cheek [*pig*]
pikuta picture, image [*pict*]
pila feather [*pir*]
pile yellow [Hindi *pil*]
pina plane, surface [*pin*]
pine building, edifice [*bin*]
pinise ending, conclusion [*fin*]
pipi rule, regulation
pisuke high object [Russian *visok*]
pitakesulina alphabet [contains all Kali-sise letters]
pitaku separation [Hindi *pritaku*]
pitina mark [Russian *pyitna*]
pu diagonal, inclined [Mandarin *po*]
pukuse fire [*foc*]
pulape east [Hindi *purab*]
pulase hair [*vols*]
pule brown [*bur*]
pulefe dust [*polv*]
pulitiku politics [*politic*]
puluni full container [*poln*]
puna form, two-dimensional shape [*form*]
pupa an explosive device [*bomb*]
pupi people group, public [*pub*]
pupilike public good, common good [*pubilc*]
pupu file, esp. computer file
pusata mail [*post*]
puse question, query [*pors*]
pusene something late or tardy [Russian *pozn*]
pusi use, usage [*pus*]
pusiti position [*pos*]

putuse future [*bud*]
sa difference, different object [Mandarin *sha*]
sakala form, three-dimensional shape [*hacar*]
sake sack [*sac*]
salana direction [Russian *starana*]
salane decay, something rotten [Hindi *saran*]
salape old object [*salf*]
salata *vegetable* [sald]
sale salt [*sal*]
saluta health [Spanish *salud*]
sanata hand [*hand*]
sanate freezing [*jamad*]
sane sandwich [*sanj*]
sani long event [Hindi *samai*]
sapalane provision, supply [Hindi *sambaran*]
sapali journey, trip [*safar*]
sapili ability [*habil*]
sapite copulation, sexual intercourse [*safid*]
sasa off
sasala event, occurrence, happening [*hasal*]
sasale tree [*hazar*]
sasane government [Hindi *shasan*]
sasape companion, associate; with, accompanied by [*sahab*]
sasi fun [*haz*]
sasila comedy [*hazil*]
sasu risk
sasute container [Russian *sasut*]
sata animal, beast [*jant*]
satale fast object [Hindi *satvar*]
satana side, flank [*sart*]
satasi item, member [Hindi *sadasi*]
sati truth [Hindi *sati*]
satise sitting position [*sadits*]
se {verb, copula}
sekake vertical [Russian *skak*]
seketu secret [*serc*]
sekupe [From English 'scope'] watcher — a close observer
seli series, sequence [*ser*]
senule Mr., Mrs., Ms., Miss [*senor*]
senuse sense [*sens*]
sepata barley [Spanish *cebada*]
sepe pocket [*jeb*]
sepete flower [Russian *svet*]

sepu self [*seb*]
sese six [*sis*]
sesete female, feminine [*ses*]
sesune season [*sezon*]
seta set [*set*]
sete seven [*sem*]
seti emotion, feeling [*sent*]
setina wall [Russian *stina*]
sikala frame [*hical*]
sike search [sic]
sikelu glass [Russian *stiklo*]
sikulu circle [*sirc*]
sikune all sides, all around [Spanish *circundar*]
sila weapon [Arabic *silah*]
sileke silk [*silc*]
silene strong object [Russian *siln*]
silete shield [*hild*]
sili bird [*hir*]
silu zero [*sir*]
siluke wide object [Russian *shirok*]
sine scale (of quantity) [Sona *shin*]
sisana horse [*hisan*]
sise sytem [*sist*]
sisi movement
su {postposition}
sukala thanks [*hucar*]
sukale sugar [*sucar*]
sukesita safety, security [*surc*]
suki happiness [*suc*]
sukulate chocolate [*hocolat*]
sula hour [*hor*]
sulala offspring [*sulal*]
sule sun [*sol*]
suli connection, joint [*jor*]
sulisuna horizontal [*horz*]
suna choice [*hun*]
sunane human [*human*]
sune total, sum [*sum*]
sunu sound [Italian *suono*]
sunuse sleep [*som*]
supaka opening, aperture [*hubac*]
supele superlative [*super*]
supete step [*supt*]

susinu pig, hog [*suvin*]
susite meaning [*suh*]
susitu substitute [sust]
susu responsibility, liability, accountability
sutale thread, filament [*sut*]
sutene suddenness, abruptness [*sud*]
ta {postposition}
taketu touch [*tact*]
tala removal, subtraction [Arabic *tarah*]
tale star [*tar*]
talike way, manner [Arabic *talik*]
tanane worthiness [Arabic *taman*]
tanani expensive object [Arabic *taman*]
tanu injury, damage, harm [Spanish *daño*]
tapaku tobacco [*tabac*]
tapite permanent object [Arabic *tabit*]
tapula board [tabul]
tasale remainder, remnant [Hindi *tahar*]
tata amphibian
tate taut, tight [*tat*]
tatu arachnid
tekale claim, assertion [*delc*]
teke ten to the power of [*des*]
tele far object [*tel*]
telule fear [*teror*]
tena subject [Spanish *tema*]
tenali money [*dinar*]
tene hot object [*term*]
teneta debt [*dend*]
tenete tooth [*dent*]
tepuse time [*temp*]
tesite desire, wish, want [*desir*]
tesu god [*dev*]
tete grains, cereal
ti three [*ter*]
tiketu ink [*tint*]
tikile tiger [*tiger*]

Word-building examples

This is an extract from the full Kali-Sise lexicon, which has over 5000 entries. It's available on the website.

kakate-kalane [action+communication-unit] demand to perform
kakate-kanisa-se [action+shirt] Hawaiian shirt
kakate-kesinu [action+science] kinetics
kakate-kune [action+{opposite}]inaction

kaki-kesinu [performance+science] drama
kaki-sili [performance+bird] manakin

kaku-kupi [deficit+copy] imitation, counterfeit, forgery

kakute-kaputa-tuna-nine [{sharp-object}+head+{augmentative}+fish] sculpin (genus Myoxocephalus)
kakute-kasese [{sharp-object}+{abstraction}] sharpness
kakute-kune [{sharp-object}+{opposite}] dull object
kakute-kune-palana [{sharp-object}+{opposite}+plant] cactus
kakute-kutane-kune-lepeti [{sharp-object}+front+{opposite}+reptile] iguana
kakute-lete [{sharp-object}+{diminutive}] point
kakute-lete-supaka [{sharp-object}+{diminutive}+opening+{verb}] pierce
kakute-nale-sata [{sharp-object}+ocean+animal] sea urchin
kakute-nane [{sharp-object}+mammal] hedgehog
kakute-nasiku-nane [{sharp-object}+insect+mammal] tenrec
kakute-nine [{sharp-object}+fish] porcupinefish
kakute-nuku-sili [{sharp-object}+mouth+bird] sharpbill
kakute-nusike [{sharp-object}+rodent] porcupine
kakute-palise [{sharp-object}+digit] claw, talon
kakute-palise-tata [{sharp-object}+digit+amphibian] clawed
kakute-sila [{sharp-object}+weapon] axe, dart
kakute-sila [{sharp-object}+weapon] sword
kakute-sunu-kaneke-nasiku [{sharp-object} + sound + shell + insect] click beetle

kala-kali-sise [art+word+system] art language, artlang
kala-kesinu [art+science] graphic arts
kala-nasini [art+vehicle] concept car
Kala-natinu-se [art+nation] France
kala-pine [art+building] theatre
kala-pine-nesete [art+building+site] stage

kalane-kalane-kune [communication-unit+communication-unit+{opposite}] oxymoron
kalane-kasese [communication-unit+{abstraction}] communication

kalane-kesinu [communication-unit+science] information theory
kalane-lete [communication-unit+{diminutive}] symbol; idea
kalane-seta [communication-unit+set] record
kalane-tuna-kelupe [communication-unit + {augmentative} + group] file, dossier

kalape-kali-sise [change+word+system] inter-language
kalape-kisile [change+acid] ncatalyst, accelerator
kalape-kune [change+{opposite}] stability
kalape-kune [change+{opposite}+{verb}] keep
kalape-nuni [change+absence] stagnation

kalase-kalane [cross+communication-unit] ritual Christian prayer
kalase-kaletela [cross+road] crossroad
kalase-kasese [cross+{abstraction}] intersection
Kalase-kesinu-se [cross+science] Christology
kalase-kune [cross+{opposite}] parallel lines
kalase-lete [cross+{diminutive}] crisscross
kalase-nupeti [cross+marriage] endogamy, intermarriage
Kalase-nutu-kune-tine-se [cross+death+{opposite}+day] Easter

Grammar

Morphology

The core vocabulary of Kali-sise consists of 400 root nouns, 2 pronouns, 1 verbal marker (*se*), 6 case markers, 1 comparative marker (*pa*) and 1 clause marker (*ka*). New words can be only combined from these roots. With the occasional exception of names, words are never borrowed from other languages into Kali-sise.

Case Markers

Kali-sise has six root case markers:

Nominative	**pi**
Genitive	**ta**
Accusative	**ke**
Dative	**su**
Locative	**li**
Ablative	**na**

Most of the Kali-sise vocabulary is derived from prominent natural languages (e.g., *luna*, "moon", from Latin). The primary exception is that the six case markers form a mnemonic derived from the language's nickname, *Pitakesulina*, a word coined to show all the sounds in the language. *Pitakesulina* is also the Kali-sise word for "alphabet".

The **nominative** specifies the agent (the actor) who performs the verb.

The **genitive** indicates possession as well as number (e.g., *sese ta sili*, "six birds" vs. *sese sili*, "the sixth bird").

The **accusative** specifies the patient.

The **dative** provides the focus or referent of the action expressed by the verb.

The **locative** is used to locate actions in time as well as place (e.g., *sula li*, "in an hour").

The **ablative** acts as a "catch-all" case; it can often be translated into English as "in a ____ manner".

Other notes

The case markers can be modified to indicate more precise semantic roles (e.g., *kasu-na*, "because of").

When the case markers aren't proceeded by noun phrases, they are often translated with third-person pronouns (e.g., *pi kunune se*, "they communicate"). An empty noun phrase has the same referent (antecedent) as the previous instance of that case phrase in the same sentence.

The stock order *pi su* is often used for reflexive actions (e.g., *pi su kunune se*, "they talk to each other").

Articles

The language does not have any definite or indefinite articles.

Pronouns

> **le** - first-person pronoun
> **ne** - second-person pronoun

Possessive pronouns are formed by using the particle *ta*. Demonstratives "this" and "that" are formed from the pronouns (think of them as meaning "this thing near me" and "that thing near you"). Thus *le ta kanisa* means "my shirt" (or "our shirt") and *le kanisa* means "this shirt".

Verbs

Any noun can be converted to a verb by following it with *se* (e.g., *pusi se* ["usage {verb}"], "use"; *kunune se* ["communication {verb}"], "communicate").

If no verb is present, the copula ("to be") is intended and each element of the copula is expressed using the nominative: *Le pi kapiti pi*, "I am a leader"; *Le pi nape pi nike pi*, "I am a parent and a worker".

Serial verbs are ambiguous and can either mean:

1. Two separate actions (e.g., *Pi su kunune se nune sunu-senuse se*, "They speak and do not hear each other").

2. The first verb affects the second (e.g., *Pi pinise se pepe se*, "They finished creating").

An empty verb phrase (*se*) is only used in a question.

Clause Markers

Clauses begin and end with *ka*. Some writers spell the first occurrence as *-ka* and the last occurrence *ka-*.

For relative clauses, a postposition indicates the role the noun would play: *ka pe pi pepe se ke ka pine-tuna*, "people making [*ke*] tower", "tower people were making". In this fragment, *ke* indicates the role the modified noun plays (in this instance, the object being made). Relative clauses cannot be nested.

Subordinate clauses typically leave no phrase unspecified:

> **Le pi kunune se -ka le pi ne ta nape-kasese pi ka- ke.**
> *I said, 'I am your father'.*

Other clause markers can be coined. For instance, long quotations begin and end with *kalane-ka*, "quote/unquote"; *kasu-ka* is used for "because".

As with Japanese, compound Kali-sise sentences require the dependent clauses to precede the independent clause. Unlike Japanese clauses, Kali-sise dependent clauses are terminated by a modified clause marker, which specifies the relation of the dependent clause to the independent clause. For instance, to translate, "I went to lunch early, because I had skipped breakfast" you would have to rephrase it "I *pi* past skip *se* breakfast *ke* cause-clause-marker I *pi* early movement *se* lunch *li*." An empty dependent clause can be interpreted as referring to the previous sentence. For instance, a sentence beginning with *Nune-kasu-ka* would be interpreted as "Not-caused-by-that" (literally) or "Despite that" (figuratively).

Comparisons

The particle *pa* is used for comparisons. It can be modified to indicate the nature of the comparison. It can also be used as an analogue to prepositional phrases.

> **Pa lepeti pi.**
> *There is a greater reptile.*
>
> **Sili pa lepeti pi.**
> *The reptile is greater than the bird.*
>
> **Sili tuna-pa lepeti pi.**
> *The reptile is bigger than the bird. (Literally: The reptile is big in comparison to the bird".)*
>
> **Sili lete-pa lepeti pi.**
> *The reptile is smaller than the bird. (Literally: The reptile is little in comparison to the bird.)*
>
> **Sili tupe-pa lepeti pi.**
> *The reptile is atop the bird. (Literally: The reptile is top in comparison to the bird")*

Prepositions

Kali-sise lacks prepositions or (if it emulated Japanese on this vector) postpositions. The case marker alone specifies the relation. So for something like *setina-kene li* you have to use your judgment to determine if that should be translated "to the window", "out the window", "in the window", "through the window" or "at the window".

Word order

Modifiers precede the words that they modify. Even relative clauses precede the words they modify.

Whether a word is modifying the word immediately after it or the noun before the particle is ambiguous.

The language defaults to SVO but any order is possible thanks to the case markers and verb marker.

Exclamations

The language lacks exclamatory particles. Exclamations are typically terminated with !. Some writers also begin exclamations with ¡.

Questions

The language lacks interrogative particles. Questions must be determined from context.

Questions are typically terminated with ?; emphatic questions are terminated with ?!. Some writers also begin questions with ¿.

An empty phrase (only have a case marker or verbal marker) often indicates what is being asked for. *Ne pi se?* "You did what? What should you do?" The verb isn't specified and is therefore being asked for. "What action did/should you take?"

> **Na ta nunene pi pi?**
> *What is your name?"*

Some expressions of the pattern "What type of...?" in English are expressed used a phrase that is empty except for a relative clause.

> **Ne pi kapita se ka nilite ka ke?**
> *What army do you lead?*

If every phrase is specified, it is probably a yes/no question.

> **Na pi nupili pi?**
> *Are you a noble?*

Acronyms

Kali-sise has a system for creating acronyms. Such acronyms are used more like abbreviations in English, and may have many different meanings; the language lacks permanent acronyms of the *NASA, radar, sonar* type in English. As a result, these acronyms are not used in formal writing. Acronyms are frequent in colloquial writing and in Internet chats, postings, e-mail, IM conversations, etc.

Acronyms are formed by taking the CV- from the beginning of each word in the phrase: The word *putuse-sukala* [future+thanks] "TIA [Thanks In Advance]" becomes PUSU, and *putuse-kunune* [future+communication] "TTYL [Talk To You Later]" becomes PUKU.

Sample Sentences

Kelu supaka-sunu ke sese kane ke Kali-sise pi nalike se.
four vowel(opening+sound) {accusative} six opposite {accusative} possession {verb}
Four vowels and six consonants Kalisise has.

Nasala-tepuse li Kali pi, Kali pi Tesu ta sasape pi, Kali pi se Tesu pi.
beginning(origin+time) {locative} Word {nominative}, Word {nominative} God {genitive} companion {nominative}, Word {nominative} {verb} God {nominative}
In the beginning was the Word, and the Word was the companion of God, and the Word was God. (John 1:1)

Ka pi sisi se nunete ke ka lele pi kune-pinise se sisi se lete luka ke.
{relative-clause} {nominative} movement {verb} mountain {accusative} relative-clause male {nominative} beginning(opposite-end) {verb} movement {verb} little-thing rock {accusative}
The man who moves a mountain begins by moving small stones.

Le pi sisi se lunene-katipa ke li.
I passed the torch to him.

Sample Texts

Senuse-kalane se nala lele sulala-pe su!

Seti na, pasatu sasala se? Sekupe se le ta sulala-pe ke lesune-ka, pasatu-tine sisi se le ta nesetu li sanile kune-sal-ape sesete pi. Kelepe se le ta sulala ke lesune-ka, pi su lete-kelepe se nusika-kalane se ke. Nune-kase-ka, le ta sulala-pe kupate se sesete ke, supele-palate se ke, kita se ke, sisi se tasale ke setina-kene li! Tu le pi se? Le pi se?! Le pi sati nune kukitu se. Kase-ka, kanuna-sekupe pi nune kune-pinise se puse se lete-kune-satisi lete-puse ke lesune-ka, le pi nune kunune se le sasala su.

Pay attention to this bad baby boy!

Oh my, what happened? In order to watch our baby, yesterday a beautiful, young lady came to our house. In order to divert our offspring, she herself played and sang to him. Despite that, our baby fought the lady, tore her apart, ate her and threw the remnants out the window! What should we do? What should we do? I truly don't know. Because of that, and so that the police don't start asking annoying little questions, I won't speak about this happening.

LJ Relay Text

¡Le pi nu-kalane se ne ke kelepasi na!

Le pi pusata-kunune se ne ke suki-tuna na; tune na ne pi suki-tuna se ke putuse li. Tu le pi lene se tuna lili-pupi su sapili na.

Le ta kane-kalane pi:

Le pi -ka pi nalike se tu neti-pe ke ka- kulepu sata pi: nu neti-pe ta nunene pi Laki pi; lete neti-pe ta nunene pi Lwki pi. Le pi suki-tuna se -ka le pi kali-nusika-kalene pi nusika-sise-kalene pi ka- ke. ¿Ne pi suki-tuna se -ka kelepe ka- ke? -Ka Lwki pi sunuse se sune-tepuse li kasu-ka- le pi kunune se satisi pupi ke le kalane su sapili na.

¿Ne pi suki-kune pe pi? Le pi kune satisi-lete-kune pe pi. ¡Supele!

Kunapale sasaki-tesu-kalane ke—

Laki (*;*)

VAKUKA Le pi lete na nune-kukitu se le kalane ke: Le pi kunune se -ka pe pi tu-kali-sise-kalane se le pusata-kunune ke ka- ke. Ne pi lepeta-kukitu se le kalane ke kune tusekale na?

KALI-SISE 201

kali-nusika-kalene [< word+music+agent] Singer, vocalist.

kane-kalane [< vision+communication-unit] Description, commentary.

Laki : A name.

lepeta-kukitu [< repetition+knowledge] recognition, understanding, comprehension

lili-pupi [< world+people-group] world society, world culture

Lwki : A name.

nune-kukitu [< negation+knowledge] forgetting

nusika-sise-kalene [< music+movement+agent] Dancer.

suki-kune [< happiness+{opposite}] unhappiness

suki-tuna [< happiness+augmentative] enjoyment

tu-kali-sise-kalane [< two+word+system+communication-unit] translation — a written communication in a second language having the same meaning as the written communication in the first language

VAKUKA [< va-kune-kalane, one+opposite+communication-unit, postscript] P.S.

Babel Text

1. Sune lili pi pasatu nunu nalike se nu kali-sise ke nu talike kunune ke.
total world {nominative} past possession {verb} one language(word-system) {accusative} public communication way {accusative}.
The whole world then had one language and one way of talking.

2. Pe pi pulape li sisi se Tu-kulepu-natinu li kane-sike se tuna-kanepuse ke pepe se nesetu ke li.
people {nominative} east {locative} movement {verb} Shinar(two-river-nation) {locative} find(opposite-search) {verb} plain(augmentative-field) {accusative} create {verb} home {accusative} {locative}.
People moved eastward and found in Shinar a plain and made homes there.

tuna-kanepuse: plain, plateau

Tu-kulepu-natinu: Shinar — a country on the lower courses of the Tigris and Euphrates rivers

> **3. Pi ka kunune se ka pepe se pine-palate ke se lani pukuse se ka ke.**
> {nominative} {accusative} communication {verb} {clause} creation {verb} intense fire {verb} {clause} {accusative}
> *They said to each other, "Let us make bricks and fire them well."*

pine-palate [building+part]: brick

> **Pi puse se pine-palate ke luka nune-su tasale-liku ke setina-luke nune-se.**
> {nominate} usage {verb} brick {accusative} rock not-{dative} tar {accusative} mortar not-{dative}
> *They used brick instead of stone and tar for mortar.*

tasale-liku [remnant+liquid] pitch, tar — any of various dark heavy viscid substances obtained as a residue

setina-liku [wall+liquid] mortar — used as a bond in masonry or for covering a wall

> **4. Pi kunune se, kalane-ka le pi su pepe se pupi-nesete ke, ka pi nalike se tupe ke tesu-lupete li ka, lupete-pine ke, kasu-ka le pi su sapili pepe se nunene ka nune lepeta sisi se lili ta sune kanepuse li, kasu-ka kalane-ka.**
> {nominative} communication {verb} quote we {nominative} {dative} creation {verb} city(people-group+place) {accusative} {clause} {nominative} possession {verb} top {nominative} heaven(divine+air) {location} {clause} tower (air+building) {accusative} cause+{clause} we {nominative} {dative} ability creation {verb} name {accusative} not repeat move {verb} earth {genitive} total field {locative} cause+{clause} unquote.
> *They said, "Let us build ourselves a city and a tower that has its top in heaven, so that we may make a name for ourselves and not be scattered over all the fields of the earth."*

tesu-lupete [divine+air] heaven

lupete-pine [air+building] tower

kalene-ka: quote, unquote

kasu-ka: because, since, so that

> **5. Nu-tesu pi kune-napisu li sisi se kane-senuse se pupi-nesete ke ka pe pi pepe se ke ka pine-tuna ka.**
> Lord(one-god) {nominative} below(opposite-above) {location} movement {verb} see(visually-sense) {verb} city {accusative} {relative clause} men {nominative} building {verb} {accusative} {relative clause} tower {accusative}.
> *The Lord came down to see the city and the tower that the people were making.*
>
> **6. Tesu pi kunune se kalana-ka, kunete-ka ka pi kunune se kune-sa kali-sise na ka nu pe pi sapili se ke kunete-ka, ka pi tesite se kakate se ka nune kakate pi se sasala-nune-sapili kakate pi su.**
> God {nominative} communication {verb} quote if(condition+clause) {relative-clause} {nominative} communication {verb} same(oppositive+difference) language(word+system) one people {nominative} {condition-clause} {nominative} ability {verb} {accusative} {relative-clause} {nominative} desire {verb} action {verb} {clause} no action {nominative} {verb} impossible action {nominative} {dative}.
> *The Lord said, "If one people who speak the same language can do this, then nothing that they wish to do will be impossible for them.*

kunete-ka: if

> **7. Kunete-ka Le pi sisi se kune-tupe li kalape se pe ta kali-sise ka kunete-ka, pi su kunune se nune sunu-senuse se ta susite ka, kalana-ka.**
> If we {nominative} movement {verb} down {location} change {verb} people {genitive} language {accusative} {condition+clause} {nominative} {dative} communicate {verb} not hearing {verb} {genitive} meaning {accusative} end-quote.
> *If We go down and change their language, they will speak and not hear each other."*
>
> **8. Tesu pi sese se kune-tupe li kalape se ta kali-sise. Kune-kasu-ka pe pi su kunune se nune sunu-senuse se. Kune-kasu-ka pi su telule sisi se lepeta sisi se lili ta sune kanepuse li.**

The Lord came down and changed their language. Therefore, the people spoke and did not hear each other. Therefore, they fled from each other and were scattered over all the fields of the earth.

Kune-kasu-ka: Therefore.

Pi nala-pinise se pepe se lupete-pine ke.
{nominative} stop(pejorative+finish) {verb} creation {verb} tower {accusative}.
They stopped building the tower.

Note: Departs significantly from scriptural text, which has "So the Lord scattered them from there over all the earth, and they stopped building the city."

9. Pe pi nala-kane-sike se ta nunene. Tu-kulepu-natinu li lupete-pine pi kane-sike se ta nunene. Papele.
The people lost their name. The tower at Shinar found its name. Babel.

nala-kane-sike: lose

Note: Departs significantly from scriptural text, which has "That is why it was called Babel — because there the Lord confused the language of the whole world. From there the Lord scattered them over the face of the whole earth."

Scripture taken from the Holy Bible, New International Version. Copyright ©1973, 1978, 1984 International Bible Society. Used by permission of Zondervan Bible Publishers.

History

In 1995, I created my first phonetically simplified language, Sen:esepera; in 1995-6, I designed Simpenga, a simplified Basic English. In 1999, I created a language sketch I called Pitakesulino. The primary intent was to have as few distinct sounds as possible in an auxiliary language; the language didn't progress beyond the description of the sound system, which was dramatically simpler than earlier efforts, with just three vowels and six consonants.

In February of 2004, in order to demonstrate the possibilities of the Dublex etymological compounds, I translated Dublex's 400 roots into Pitakesulina's phonology, in the process expanding the language to include four vowels, generating over 5000 words for the language and coming up with a new name for it (Kali-sise = "word system, language"). I invented the grammar in order to translate the Babel Text. During the summer of 2004, I refined the grammar by participating in a few translation relays and by writing language lessons. I am not encouraging everyone in the world to learn Kali-sise as a second language; I simply created it to see what a phonetically simple IAL would look like.

Karklak (Gnome Tongue)

I developed my first model language in 1982 when I was 13, and I called it Karklak, the Gnome Tongue. It was the language of the gnomes of the land of Wundrian. The impetus for inventing the language was reading an article in *Dragon* magazine that discussed inventing Old Dwarvish (or was it an article on Orcish?).

I didn't type Karklak up on my TRS-80 and save it on cassette tape, but handwrote the language on index cards. I had two sets: one for English to Karklak, and one for Karklak to English. The language never enjoyed any greater existence than those cards, which I've saved, being an inveterate packrat.

I'm disappointed I didn't include the word *bree-yark*, a coinage by Gary Gygax in *The Keep on the Borderlands*, the only adventure module I'd played at the time, where PCs are told that it means "we surrender" while the DM is told it means "hey, rube!"

Nothing remains of the grammar but memories. It was crude and simplistic. The language was VSO because the *Dragon* article, adhering to a strong form of the Sapir-Whorf hypothesis, said orcs would be action oriented and dwarves would be possession oriented (OSV). A "gender" system that was used for nouns and their adjectives had two genders: d., defensive; o., offensive. Verbs and adverbs used this same "gender" system.

Here's the language as it existed in 1982, typos, formatting inconsistencies and all.

aberk n. chain mail, tunic of chain mail [FA hauberk, tunic of chain mail < N hauberc] d.
ak conj. that -
alk adj. each [OE aellc]
arsk adj./adv./n. harsh/harshly/harshness [FA harsk < N.] o.
ban n. warlord [Serbo-Croatian.] o.

barg d.o. prep. her, their, them (o. darg) d.
baron n. baron [FA < N.] o.
barrad n. rabbit d.
beel pn. she, they (feminine) d.
begrinnen v. to begin [ME beginnen < OE bigannan] o.
bik adv. where -
bon v. - irregular bon/bobon/bobun/bon to be - will be, would be (future tense) -
bran n. friend, ally d.
brazzen v. to retreat (from) d.
bregden v. to throw, to turn [OE bregdan.] o.
brekken v. to break (from < M.E. BREKEN < O.E. BRECAN) o.
bren v. to be (present tense) [GT barren < OE aron] -
brog pn. you (all) (o. krog) d.
dal adj./adv. fine -
dar art./pn. - d.o. prep. the, your, you, a, an (o. kar) d.
dar- prefix short, little
darg d.o. prep. his, their, him, them (o. karg) d.
darg d.o. prep. her, their, her, them (d. barg) o.
dargid n. master d.
dark adj./n. dark [ME derk < OE deorc] o.
darkrozzel n. little staff (condescendingly: dangerous little staff) d.
dergrin v. to harness (as in war), to disturb [OE hergian] o.
dez n. lie d.
dezzen v. to lie d.
do pn. I, we (o. ko) d.
dor n. door [ME dor < OE duru] d.
drak n. battle o.
drakken v. to battle o.
drakkenzax n. battle-axe o.
drakon n. dragon [FA dragon < N.] o.
dren v. to be - was, were (past tense) -
dujon n. hilt of a dagger [A dudgeon < FA dogeon < N.] d.
dunor n. thunder; Thunor, God of Thunder; hammer [GT < OA thunor.] o.
dunorkrik n. crossbow [GT dunor, thunder + krik, bow.] o.
durk n. dirk [Sc.] o.
durkken v. to attack or stab with a dirk o.
gar n. hurling spear [OA.] o.
grad n. death o.
gradden v. to die o.
grank n. hour d.
grev n. leg armor [FA greve < N or GT greve < OA reof.] d.

grokken v. to know (word history: from "grok") o.
gron n. gate d.
gronken v. to forget d.
kadd n. a caldron [Backformation < kaddron] o.
kaddron v. to cook (esp. in a kettle cauldron) o.
karg prep. d.o. his, their, him, them (d. darg) o.
Karklak n. The Gnome Tongue o.
karlkraven n. a nightmare creature (literally: fearful men) [ME cravant, cowardly + ME < ON karl, man] [GT < FA cravant, cowardly + karl, man < N] o.
keel pn. he, they (masculine) o.
kirnen v. to fight with a sword [Perh. < kirnizzen, to skirmish] o.
kirniz n. skirmish [FA skirmisshe < N eskirmiss-, to fight with a sword] o.
kirnizzen v. to skirmish o.
klakken v. to draw (a weapon), to get, to take [Imit.] o.
klangen v. to sheathe (a weapon), to put away, to hide [Imit.] [< Lat. clangere] d.
klik adj./adv. quick, quickly [ME quicke, swift < OE cwicu, alive] -
knak adv. not [Perh. OE na, no] -
knord n./adj./adv. north [OE nord] d.
ko pn. I, we (d. ro) o.
konbad n. battle [N combattre.] o.
kor art./pn. - d.o. prep. the, your, you, a, an (d. dar) o.
krad n. enemy, goblin o.
kraken n. kraken [N.] o.
krakken v. to open [ME craken < OE cracian] o.
krangen v. to close d.
kraz n. sword o.
krazzel n. spear - of the thrusting, parrying type (from: kraz+zel = sword+stick) o.
krazzen v. to parry with a sword (from < KROZZEN, to parry + KRAZ, sword) d.
krik n. bow o.
krikken v. to fire a bow o.
krikuk n. bowfire, bow-and-arrow (from: krik+uk = bow+missilefire arrow) o.
kro d.o. prep. my, our, me, us (d. ro) o.
krog pn. you (all) (d. brog) o.
kroz n. a parry (back-formation < KROZZEL - see KRAZZEL) d.
krozzel n. quarterstaff (from: "zel" meaning staff) d.
krozzen v. to parry (esp. with a quarterstaff) (from < KROZ, a parry) d.
rald n. life o.

ralden v. to live o.
ralk adj./n. every/everything [OE aefre+aelk, ever+each] > vralk o.
ralrev n. plunder, especially armor weapons, from the slain [OE wael - reaf.] o.
rard n. guard [OE weard, ward, guardian] d.
rarden v. to guard, to protect [< rard] d.
rarlok n. warlow [OE waerloga, oath-breaker] o.
raven n. raven [GT < OA hraefn] o.
ravenravok n. ravenhawk, or ravinghavoc ("Wings of Night") o.
ravok n. hawk [GT < OA hafoc.] o.
razzen v. to attack with a blade, to kill with a blade (or even a beak or talon) [OT < FA to scrape, rasen] o.
reng n. wing [GT wenge < FA] o.
rengen v. to fly [< reng, wing] o.
renk conj. until -
reven v. to seize forcibly, to plunder [FA < OA reafian.]
revlak n. pillage, plunder [OA reaf-lac.] o.
ro d.o. prep. my, our, me, us (o. kro) d.
ro pn. I, we (now considered archaic) - use do (o. ko) d.
roven v. to shoot arrows at a (practice) target [FA.] o.
uk n. arrow, missile fire o.
urgak n. ogre [Perh. < N - urgach of K.] [K. urgach < N. ogre.] o.
zax n. hatchet, axe [ME sax, knife < OE seax] o.
zel n. staff, walking stick d.

Minhyan

Minhyan /meenn-YAHN/ is the ancient language of the planet Peliaz, still spoken by the forest people of the planet. Minhyan is the precursor of the present Harody language.

Pronunciation

Vowels

Minhyan has just five vowels, each written by a single letter.

    a as in 'father'
    e as in 'pet'
    i as in 'pizza'
    o as in 'Poe' or 'poet'
    u as in 'tutu'

The five diphthongs are:

    ai as in 'aisle'
    au as in 'cow'
    ei as 'bay'
    oi as in 'boy'
    ui as /ooy/ in 'too young'.

Consonants

	Voiceless	*Voiced*
Stops	p - as in 'pot'	b - as in 'bought'
	t - as in 'tot'	d - as in 'dot'
	c /k/ - as in 'cot'	g - as in 'got'
Fricatives	ff /f/ - as in 'fought'	f /v/ - as in 'vote'
	th /θ/ - as in 'bath'	dd /ð/ - as in 'them'

	ss /s/ - as in 'sought'	s /z/ - as in 'zit'
	j /ʃ/ - as in 'shot'	
	ch /x/ - as in 'loch'	
	h /h/ - as in 'hot'	
	Unaspirated	*Aspirated*
Liquids	l - as in 'lap'	ll (aspirated)
	r - as in 'rap'	rr (aspirated)
Nasals		
	m - as in 'map'	mm (aspirated)
	n - as in 'nap'	nn (aspirated)
Approximants	w /w/ - as in 'wing'	
	y /j/ - as in 'young'	

The sounds **h w y** may not end a syllable.

Consonant clusters may begin and end syllables.

Guidelines For English Speakers

As an experienced English speaker, you will need to get use to the following:

The letter **c** by itself is always pronounced /k/.

The letter pair **ch** is never pronounced as in 'church' but is always similar in pronunciation to German *ch* and can be pronounced /x/, i.e. the final consonant in the Scottish pronunciation of *loch*.

As with the spelling of Welsh, **ff** is pronounced /f/, and **f** alone is pronounced /v/ (this sound only occurs at the end of a syllable).

Also as with Welsh, **dd** is pronounced /ð/ (English uses *th* for two separate sounds) as in 'them'; **th** in Minhyan is always pronounced unvoiced /θ/.

The letter pair **ss** is pronounced /s/, and **s** alone is pronounced /z/ (this sound only occurs at the end of a syllable).

The letter **j** is always pronounced /ʃ/. This is odd, certainly, but Latin lacked the /ʃ/ sound altogether.

The letter **r** is actually a trilled /r/ as in Spanish and Russian. If you pronounce it as in English, though, Minhyan speakers are not likely to be bothered.

The aspirated liquids and nasals are pronounced with a puff of air after the consonant. English speakers can safely ignore the distinction between aspirated and unaspirated consonants or can pronounce the consonants long instead (extending the sound).

Every consonant is pronounced, so **lamb** is pronounced /lamb/ not (as in English) /lam/.

Accent

The Minhyan accent system is etymological, with the morphology of the word determining the placement of the primary accent.

The final syllable of an unmodified root word receives the accent:

> **riye** /ree-YEH/ [< *rei-i] n. Peace.

> **esspalas** /ess-pah-LAHZ/ [< *ispalas] n. Starling.

For roots ending with vowels, the final syllable of the root receives the primary accent, even when affixes have been appended.

> **riyema** /ree-YEH-ma/ [< riye, "peace" & -ma-, "loving"] adj. Peace-loving.

For roots ending with consonants, the onset and nucleus of the final syllable of the root receives the primary accent when infixes have been inserted.

> **esspalales** /ess-pah-LAH-lehz/ [< esspalas, "starling" & -le-, "offspring"] n. Starling chick.

In compound words, the first word's primary accent becomes the secondary accent of the combined word.

Proto-Minhyan Pronounciation

Little is known about the ancient ancestral language of Minhyan, but the following observations can be made about how Minhyan evolved from its proto-language:

- Unvoiced stops evolved into voiced stops after vowels.

- Unvoiced front fricatives evolved into voiced fricatives after vowels.
- The aspirated /l/ evolved from a lateral voiceless alveolar fricative as part of a regularization of the aspirated liquids and nasals.
- The front vowels shifted.

Grammar

Minhyan is a VSO inflexional language that grammaticalizes two aspects and seven moods in its verbal conjugation and grammaticalizes definiteness and seven cases in its noun declension, which is active-stative rather than nominative-accusative.

Infixing

Minhyan relies heavily on infixing for declining nouns, conjugating verbs and creating compound words. Infixes are placed before the final consonant cluster of a root (if any); if the word ends in a vowel, then the infix is treated as a suffix and appended.

Word	Infix	Example
tas, "order"	-**he**-, "tendency"	**tahes**, "orderliness"
ach, "snow"	-**ho**-, "small-item"	**ahoch**, "snowflake"
neru, "sand"	-**ho**-, "small-item"	**neruho**, "grain of sand"

Syntax

Minhyan is a VSO language: the standard word order is verb first, then subject, then object.

It is a Place Manner Time language, rather than a Time Manner Place language (see Nouns below for details).

Modifiers follow the words that they modify: *nirr parr*, "grass green" = "green grass". Even relative clauses follow the words they modify.

While the language defaults to VSO, any order is possible in independent clauses thanks to the declensions and conjugations.

Verbs

Minhyan verbs are not conjugated for tense (past, present, future) but for mood and aspect. While Proto-Minhyan had a rich aspect system, by the time of Minhyan this was reduced to just Perfective ("the action is completed") and Imperfective ("action is ongoing") aspects.

Mood	Perfective	Imperfective
Indicative	-re-	
Negative	-no-	-ne-
Optative	-wu-	-we-
Hypothetical	-pu-	-pe-
Conditional	-co-	-ca-
Dubitative	-du-	-di-
Cohortative	-bu-	-bi-

The imperfective affixes typically have a front vowel; the perfective ones typically have a back vowel.

The **imperative** is not expressed by a mood but by repeating the name of person being commanded in both the vocative and agentive cases using the optative mood.

The **optative** is used for hopes or wishes; the **hypothetical** for counterfactual but possible conditions; the **conditions** for possibilities; the **dubitative** for doubtful conditions; and the **cohortative** for encouraging group action.

Serial verbs are ambiguous and can either mean:

1. Two separate actions (e.g., speak + hear = "They speak and do not hear each other").

2. The first verb affects the second (e.g., finish + create: "They finished creating").

All verbs are regular except for the copula, *turi*, which preserves part of an earlier aspect system. Arguments of the copula take the dative.

Mood	Perfective	Imperfective	Progressive
Indicative	-	turiri	turira
Negative	turino	turini	turina
Optative	turiwo	turiwi	turiwa
Hypothetical	turipu	turipi	turipa
Conditional	turico	turice	turica
Dubitative	turidu	turide	turida
Cohortative	turibu	turibe	turiba

Adverbs

Minhyan completely lacks adverbs. Decline a noun using the ablative case instead to indicate the manner of the verb.

Nouns

Minhyan does not have a NOMINATIVE-ACCUSATIVE case system (as most Indo-European languages do) but an ACTIVE-STATIVE system: the agent of the verb is always in the agentive case and the patient of the verb is always in the patientive case. (In a nominative-accusative case system, the patient of the intransitive verb is in the nominative case.)

Minhyan nouns are declined for definiteness and for seven cases. The base form of a noun is the Definite Agentive: *orean*, "the eagle, the eagles", contrasted to *oreahan*, "an eagle, some eagles". The Minhyan declension involves incorporating infixes before the final consonant cluster (if any) of the root word.

Reflecting their evolution from the Proto-Minhyan system for marking singular and plural, the indefinite noun form is assumed singular unless otherwise marked, and the definite form is assumed plural unless otherwise marked. So *orean* would typically mean "the eagles" and *oreahan* would typically mean "an eagle".

		Indefinite	*Definite*
Agentive	Performs the verb	**-ha-**	-
Patientive	Receives action of verb	**-pa-**	**-po-**
Dative	Focus or referent	**-sse-**	**-ssu-**
Locative	Location of verb	**-li-**	**-lu-**
Ablative	Manner of verb	**-we-**	**-wa-**
Temporal	Time of verb	**-ri-**	**-ru-**
Vocative	Addressee of utterence	**-ffi-**	**-ffo-**

The indefinite infixes typically have front vowels, while definite infixes typically have back vowels.

Some notes on cases of special interest:

The ablative also acts as a "catch-all" case.

The temporal case is often used to specify on an as-needed basis information about the verb that other languages express in terms of tense and aspect.

The typical order of the cases and the verb in a sentence is:

vocative verb agentive patientive dative locative ablative temporal

Pronouns

The pronoun declension preserves Old Minhyan's singular and plural distinction.

	Singular	*Plural*
Agentive	**-ha-**	-
Patientive	**-pa-**	**-po-**
Dative	**-sse-**	**-ssu-**
Locative	**-li-**	**-lu-**
Ablative	**-we-**	**-wa-**
Temporal	**-ri-**	**-ru-**
Vocative	**-ffi-**	**-ffo-**

The actual pronouns are nine separate roots that vary for status and person. The pronoun system for Minhyan is, unlike English, concerned with status rather than gender. It depends on the societal status level of the antecedant relative to the speaker: an honorific pronoun, a peer pronoun and a humble pronoun.

Person	*Gloss*	*Honorific*	*Peer*	*Humble*
1	Me	**oridben**	**gara**	**aru**
2	You	**arnodiad**	**calan**	**aba**
3	Them	**trenorn**	**leweg**	**ono**

Actual usage is too complex to be easily summarized. Traditions of Minhyan discourse require the speaker to use the appropriate status pronoun for the situation. It would be considered insulting for a king to address his page using *arnodiad* and considered rebellious of a minor to address a parent using *calan*. A king would say to his betrothed, *Ama oridbehan calapan* ("I love you") if she were a noble and *Ama oridbehan abapa* if she were a peasant. Once she was his queen, he would say, *Ama oridbehan arnodiapad*. (A king could say to his peasant bethrothed, *Abapa ama oridbehan*, "(It's) you I love", if he wanted to place more emphasis on her.)

Possessive pronouns are formed as if they were genitive adjectives. Demonstratives "this" and "that" are formed from the pronouns (think of them as meaning "this thing near me" and "that thing near you"). Thus *echipal aruga* means "my shirt" (or "our shirt") and *echipal aru* means "this shirt" (*echipal aruge* means "a shirt of mine").

Adjectives

Adjectives are never declined for case. However, adjectives can take three endings that must agree in definiteness or indefiniteness with the noun they modify.

	Indefinite	*Definite*
Possessive	**-ge-**	**-ga-**
Comparative	**-me-**	**-mo-**
Superlative		**-sso**

Relative Clauses

The relativization infix *-ba-* marks the word that begins the relative clause, which continues until the first verb is encountered (it precedes any infix marking the declension or conjugation, otherwise it is the last infix in the word).

Relative clauses are typically SOV but order is flexible so long as they end with a verb.

Relative clauses cannot be nested.

Prepositions

Minhyan lacks prepositions. The case alone specifies the relation. So for something like *celumb* [< *cemb*, "window" & *-lu-*, definite locative] you have to use your judgment to determine if that should be translated "to the window", "out the window", "in the window", "through the window" or "at the window".

If more specifics are necessary to specify location in particular, then a preposition can be formed using the comparative.

Questions

The interrogative root *ored* is used to form a question. It can be declined to indicate the case relationship.

	Indefinite	*Definite*	*Gloss*
Agentive	**orehad**	**ored**	who, what?
Patientive	**orepad**	**orepod**	who, what?

Dative	**oressed**	**oressud**	who, what?
Locative	**orelid**	**orelud**	where?
Ablative	**orewed**	**orewad**	how?
Temporal	**orerid**	**orerud**	when?
Vocative	**oreffid**	**oreffod**	who's there?

The interrogative root can be declined as an adjective as well.

	Indefinite	*Definite*	*Gloss*
Possessive	**oreged**	**oregad**	whose?
Comparative	**oremed**	**oremod**	which is greater?
Superlative		**oressod**	which is greatest?

Proto-Minhyan Grammar

The indefinite vs. definite declension evolved out of the singular vs. plural declension in Proto-Minhyan.

Old Minhyan's final aspect system was Perfective/Imperfective/Progressive — it may have had as many as seven aspects, though most scholars believe it had five.

Morphology

Most word building in Minyhan is accomplished using infixes.

> **abo** [< *apo] n. Brother.
> **abocu** [< abo, "brother" & -cu-, "in-law"] n. Brother-in-law.
> **abona** [< abo, "brother" & -na-, "female"] n. Sister.
> **abopi** [< abo, "brother" & -pi-, "half"] n. Stepbrother, half-brother.
> **abossa** [< abo, "brother" & -ssa-, "vice"] n. Stepbrother.

Infixes can be combined:

> **abocuna** [< abo, "brother" & -cu-, "in-law" & -na-, "female"] n. Sister-in-law.
> **abopina** [< abo, "brother" & -pi-, "half" & -na-, "female"] n. Stepsister, half-sister.
> **abossana** [< abo, "brother" & -ssa-, "vice" & -na-, "female"] n. Step-sister.

In fact, quite long words can be created:

litehomigir [< lir, "free" & -te-, "opposite" & -ho-, "small-item" & -mi-, "person" & -gi-, "place"] n. Prison, jail.

Common Infixes

The following 57 infixes are used extensively to form new words.

be	action	**le**	offspring
bo	thing	**lo**	transform
ce	abstraction	**ma**	loving
cha	cause	**mi**	person
che	member	**mu**	tool
chi	aspect	**na**	female
cho	collection	**ni**	worthy
chu	art	**nu**	holder
ci	retro	**pi**	half
cu	in-law	**ra**	doctrine
da	good	**ro**	professional
de	chief	**ssa**	vice
do	separation	**ssi**	capable
ffa	suitable	**ta**	application
ffe	quality	**te**	opposite
ffu	augmentative	**tha**	wrong
gi	place	**the**	negation
go	beginning	**thi**	new
gu	former	**tho**	manner
he	tendency	**thu**	rich
hi	mandatory	**ti**	full
ho	small-item	**to**	thick
hu	similar	**tu**	past
ja	leader	**wo**	return
je	diminutive	**ya**	without
ji	away	**ye**	container
jo	pejorative	**yo**	infix
ju	extreme pejorative	**yu**	male
la	possessing		

Lexicon

The accompanying lexicon is translated from Nichopomm Ssil, *The Royal Word Collection*, which has the virtue of being by far the largest surviving

Minhyan dictionary (14,787 words) and the vice of containing many dubious etymologies. King Idryf commissioned it explicitly to demonstrate that Minhyan was far more regular than Harody, and his lexicographers often overzealously derived words from infixed compounds. For instance, *yajed*, "musket", is described as derived from a compound meaning "small moss" (*yad*, "moss" + *-je-*, "diminutive"), when scholars before and since have classified it as an independent root derived from Proto-Minhyan *i-ashet. Unfortunately, not enough is known of Old Minhyan to determine the accuracy of other etymologies, such as *acholf*, "canary", from *alf*, "reed" + *-cho-*, "collection"; it is possible that *acholf* first meant "collection of reeds", then "bird of the reeds", then "canary", but this is not certain. When reviewing etymologies, therefore, reader beware.

abel [< *abil] n. Idea, invention.
abel [< abel, "idea, invention"] v. Invent, think up.
abell [< all, "service" & -be-, "action"] n. Attendance, waiting, service.
abell [< *abili-] Hundred thousand.
abemurr [< arr, "aviate" & -be-, "action" & -mu-, "tool"] n. Aeroplane.
aberorr [< arr, "aviate" & -be-, "action" & -ro-, "professional"] n. Aviator.
aberr [< arr, "aviate" & -be-, "action"] n. Aviation.
abo [< *apo] n. Brother.
abocu [< abo, "brother" & -cu-, "in-law"] n. Brother-in-law.
abocuna [< abo, "brother" & -cu-, "in-law" & -na-, "female"] n. Sister-in-law.
abona [< abo, "brother" & -na-, "female"] n. Sister.
abopi [< abo, "brother" & -pi-, "half"] n. Stepbrother, half-brother.
abopina [< abo, "brother" & -pi- "half" & -na-, "female"] n. Stepsister, half-sister.
aborn [< arn, "post, mail" & -bo-, "thing"] n. Piece of mail.
abossa [< abo, "brother" & -ssa-, "vice"] n. Step-brother.
abossana [< abo, "brother" & -ssa-, "vice" & -na-, "female"] n. Step-sister.
aceboth [< ath, "refuse dump, dump, tip, rubbish tip" & -ce-, "abstraction" & -bo-, "thing"] n. Refuse, waste, rubbish, clippings, cuttings.
acelf [< alf, "reed, cane" & -ce-, "abstraction"] n. Channel, canal.
aceth [< ath, "refuse dump, dump, tip, rubbish tip" & -ce-, "abstraction"] v. Fall, fall off, tumble down.
ach [< *ach] n. Snow.
ach [< ach, "snow"] v. Snow.
achabent [< ant, "turn" & -cha-, "cause/become" & -be-, "action"] v. Swirl.
achad [< *achad] n. Alcoholic beverages.
achad [< *achad] n. Angina pectoris.
achain [< *achaen] n. Musical instruction.

achainn [< *achaenh] n. Sandwich.
achald [< ald, "bad, rotten" & -cha-, "cause/become"] n. Decay.
achanc [< anc, "lying" & -cha-, "cause/become"] v. Lay.
achanc [< anc, "lying" & -cha-, "cause/become"] v. Lie down.
achant [< ant, "turn" & -cha-, "cause/become"] v. Turn.
achant [< ant, "turn" & -cha-, "cause/become"] n. Turn.
acharn [< *acharn] n. Ticket-window, window.
ached [< *achid] n. Flake.
achedi [< *achite] n. Assembly.
achemm [< amm, "length" & -che-, "member"] n. Longan.
acherio [< *achireo] n. Pleonasm, redundancy.
achil [< *achel] v. Fast.
achil [< *achel] n. Background.
achill [< *acheli-] n. Metaphor.
acholf [< alf, "reed, cane" & -cho-, "collection"] n. Canary.
achond [< and, "of good repute" & -cho-, "collection"] adj. Charitable, benevolent.
achor [< *achor] n. Deficit.
achorr [< *achorh] n. Guinea-pig.
achui [< *achue] adj. Epoch-making.
achuir [< *achuer] n. Self-control; self-rule.
achund [< and, "of good repute" & -chu-, "art"] v. Feel fine, be well.
achund [< and, "of good repute" & -chu-, "art"] n. Well-being.
acthel [< *akthil] n. Office.
ada [< *ada] n. Flow, current, stream.
ada [< ada, "flow, current, stream"] adj. Fluent.
ada [< ada, "flow, current, stream"] v. Flow.
adab [< *atab] n. Middle, mean.
adab [< adab, "middle, mean"] adj. Middle, average, mean.
adab [< adab, "middle, mean"] Average.
adabo [< ada, "flow, current, stream" & -bo-, "thing"] n. Liquid, fluid.
adachan [< adan, "futile, abortive, useless, vain" & -cha-, "cause/become"] v. Thwart, foil.
adaffen [< adan, "futile, abortive, useless, vain" & -ffe-, "quality"] n. Vanity.
adagi [< ada, "flow, current, stream" & -gi-, "place"] n. Watercourse, bed.
adaji [< ada, "flow, current, stream" & -ji-, "away"] v. Flow off, flow down.
adajir [< adar, "abandonment" & -ji-, "away"] v. Desert, quit, forsake, leave, abandon.
adale [< ada, "flow, current, stream" & -le-, "offspring"] adj. Fluid, liquid.
adalebo [< ada, "flow, current, stream" & -le-, "offspring" & -bo-, "thing"] n. Fluid, liquid.

adamun [< adan, "futile, abortive, useless, vain" & -mu-, "tool"] n. Vanilla.
adan [< *atan] adj. Futile, abortive, useless, vain.
adaneth [< *adanith] adj. Orange-coloured.
adann [< *adanh] n. Testament, will.
adann [< adann, "testament, will"] v. Bequeath, make a will.
adar [< *atar] n. Abandonment.
adar [< adar, "abandonment"] v. Allow, let, leave, release.
adawo [< ada, "flow, current, stream" & -wo-, "return"] n. Low tide.
adawo [< ada, "flow, current, stream" & -wo-, "return"] v. Ebb.
add [< *ath] n. Gnat.
add [< add, "gnat"] n. Shorts, short pants.
addel [< *athil] adj. Federal.
addelen [< *athilin] n. Sleigh, sledge.
addelenn [< *athilinh] n. Shoulder-belt, bandoleer.
adder [< *athir] v. Perceive, catch sight of.
adderr [< *athirh] n. Exclamation point.
addren [< *athrin] n. Skirt.
addril [< *athrel] v. Keep back, withhold, hold back.
addrill [< *athreli-] Silently.
addrind [< *athrend] n. Scurvy.
addron [< *athron] n. Sheet.
addronn [< *athronh] n. Apple-sauce.
adeb [< *atib] n. Gist, essence.
adeb [< adeb, "gist, essence"] adj. Essential.
adechal [< adel, "seat" & -cha-, "cause/become"] v. Seat; Sit down.
adel [< *atil] n. Seat.
adel [< adel, "seat"] v. Sit.
adell [< *atili-] n. Quarters.
ademin [< aden, "part, role, rôle" & -mi-, "person"] n. Character.
aden [< *atin] n. Part, role, rôle.
adennill [< *adinheli-] n. Tram stop, streetcar stop.
aderthad [< *atirthat] n. Reply coupon.
adinar [< *atenar] n. Putty.
adinarr [< *adenarh] n. Type.
ado [< *ado] n. Scrabble.
ado [< ado, "scrabble"] v. Scratch.
adog [< *atog] n. Statement.
adog [< adog, "statement"] v. State.
adomi [< ado, "scrabble" & -mi-, "person"] v. Congratulate.
adomi [< ado, "scrabble" & -mi-, "person"] n. Congratulation.
adonno [< *atonho] n. Jurisprudence.
adothui [< *adothue] v. Swell, swell into a roar.

adraith [< *adraeth] Dispassionately.
adregol [< *adrikol] n. Self-defence.
adrein [< *atrien] n. Vocabulary.
adro [< *atro] n. Accusation.
adro [< adro, "accusation"] v. Denounce.
adu [< *adu] n. Music.
adu [< adu, "music"] adj. Musical.
adu [< adu, "music"] v. Make music.
adubo [< adu, "music" & -bo-, "thing"] n. Piece of music.
aduhe [< adu, "music" & -he-, "tendency"] adj. Musical.
aduhe [< adu, "music" & -he-, "tendency"] n. Musicality.
adumu [< adu, "music" & -mu-, "tool"] n. Musical instrument.
adumun [< adun, "pump" & -mu-, "tool"] n. Pump.
adun [< *atun] v. Pump.
adunn [< *adunh] v. Creep in.
aduro [< adu, "music" & -ro-, "professional"] n. Musician.
adurocho [< adu, "music" & -ro-, "professional" & -cho-, "collection"] n. Band.
aduyal [< *adui-al] n. Inscription.
adwen [< *adwin] n. License plate.
adyab [< *ati-ab] n. Agony, death throes.
adyan [< *ati-an] n. Accused, defendant.
adyen [< *ati-in] n. Gabardine.
adyun [< *ati-un] n. Corn-bottle.
afad [< *afat] n. Monk.
afagid [< afad, "monk" & -gi-, "place"] n. Monastery.
afam [< *afam] n. Tangle.
afam [< afam, "tangle"] v. Implicate, entangle.
afanad [< afad, "monk" & -na-, "female"] n. Nun.
afanneth [< *afanhith] n. Maxim, proverb.
afanneth [< *afanhith] n. Ham.
afanno [< *afanho] Under bond, on bail.
afatem [< afam, "tangle" & -te-, "opposite"] v. Take apart, untie.
affado [< *afado] n. Crease.
affadon [< *afaton] n. Olive-tree.
affadonn [< *afadonh] n. Subjunction.
affadrim [< *afadrem] n. Scholarship, stipend.
affadrimm [< *afatremh] n. Tunic.
affemm [< amm, "length" & -ffe-, "quality"] n. Length.
affor [< *afor] Everywhere.
afo [< *afo] n. Tibia, shin-bone.
afoboron [< afon, "wood, timber" & -bo-, "thing" & -ro-, "professional"] n. Cabinet-maker, carpenter.

afohon [< afon, "wood, timber" & -ho-, "small-item"] n. Splinter.
afon [< *afon] n. Wood, timber.
afor [< *afor] n. Prostitution.
afor [< afor, "prostitution"] v. Prostitute.
aforr [< *aforh] Abroad.
afras [< *afras] v. Scald.
afren [< *afrin] n. Thorn.
afrenn [< *afrinh] n. Line.
afro [< *afro] n. Fart.
afro [< afro, "fart"] v. Fart.
agar [< *agar] n. Dust.
agar [< agar, "dust"] adj. Dusty.
agarr [< *akarh] n. Meteoric stone.
agayachar [< agar, "dust" & -ya-, "without" & -cha-, "cause/become"] v. Dust.
ageler [< ager, "frog" & -le-, "offspring"] n. Tadpole, tad-pole.
ager [< *agir] n. Frog.
agerth [< *agirth] n. Caviar.
aginc [< anc, "lying" & -gi-, "place"] n. Lair.
agirn [< arn, "post, mail" & -gi-, "place"] n. Post office, post-office.
aglach [< *aglach] n. Abandonment.
aglach [< *aglach] v. Lisp.
aglan [< *aklan] Previously, ahead; formerly.
aglar [< *aklar] n. Rainbow.
aglechi [< *akliche] n. Social stratum.
aglechio [< *aglicheo] v. Travel through.

The complete lexicon is given on the website.

Translation Tutorial

Sample Translation Exercise #1

"To you belong the stories of eternity."

Step 1: Break the sentence into clauses (subject/verb/object groups).

To you belong the stories of eternity. [just one clause]

Step 2: Join the words in noun phrases and verb phrases with hyphens.

To-you belong the-stories-of-eternity.

Step 3: Translate the sentence into "Minhyan English", using the Minhyan case markers to indicate the role each noun phrase plays in the clause.

> *To-you -po- [Definite Patientive] belong the-eternal-stories -ssu- [Definite Dative]*

Step 4: Re-arrange the phrases into their correct word order for Minhyan: conjunction, vocative, verb, agentive, patientive, dative, locative, ablative, temporal. Not all phrase types will be present. Each type of noun phrase describes the action of the verb in a different way. You can tell the phrase types from the case infixes you decided to apply in Step 3.

> *Belong to-you -po- [Definite Patientive] the-eternal-stories -ssu- [Definite Dative]*

Step 5: Translate pronouns, taking into account the relative status of speaker and listener.

> *Belong aba-po- [Humble 2-Person] the-eternal-stories -ssu-*

Step 6: Translate the verbs.

> *Rufan-re- [Indicative Perfective] aba-po- the-eternal-stories -ssu-*

Step 7: Translate remaining English words.

> *Rufan-re- aba-po- edo-ssu- cur [modifiers follow, so adjectives follow nouns]*

Step 8: Integrate infixes and join clauses with commas.

> *Rufaren abapo edossu cur.*

Sample Translation Exercise #2

"I should have died so long ago, but I have been kept here, on this earth, and I did not know why, until now."

Step 1:

> *A. I should have died so long ago |*
>
> *B. But I have been kept here, on this earth |*
>
> *C. And I did not know why, until now.*

Step 2:

> A. *I should-have-died so-long-ago |*
>
> B. *But I have-been-kept here-on-this-earth |*
>
> C. *And I did-not-know why, until-now.*

Step 3:

> A. *I* -po- [*Definite Patient; killed by old age or something else*] *should-have-died so-long-ago* -ri- [*Indefinite Temporal*]
>
> B. *But I* -po- *have-been-kept here-on-this-earth* -lu- [*Definite Locative*]
>
> C. *And I* — [*Definite Agent, the actor of the verb*] *did-not-know why* -ssu- [*Definite Dative, focus of the verb, what is known*], *until-now* -ru-
>
> [*Definite Temporal*].

Step 4:

> A. *should-have-died I* -po- *so-long-ago* -ri-.
>
> B. *But have-been-kept I* -po- *here-on-this-earth* -lu-.
>
> C. *And did-not-know I* — *why* -ssu-, *until-now* -ru-.

Step 5:

(I'm using the honorific first-person pronoun here.)

> A. *should-have-died oridben* -po- *so-long-ago* -ri-.
>
> B. *But have-been-kept oridben* -po- *here-on-this-earth* -lu-.
>
> C. *And did-not-know oridben* — *why* -ssu-, *until-now* -ru-.

Step 6:

> A. *Dachal* -pu- [*Hypothetical Perfective*] *oridben* -po- *so-long-ago* -ri-.
>
> B. *But mid* — [*Indicative Imperfective*] *oridben* -po- *here-on-this-earth* -lu-.

C. And aur -no- [Negative Perfective] oridben — why -ssu-, until-now -ru-.

Step 7:

    A. Dachal -pu- oridben -po- calonn -ri-.

    B. glero mid — oridben -po- thongail -lu-.

    C. brun aur -no- oridben — edassi -ssu- benn -ru-.

Step 8:

    Dachapul oridbepon calorinn, glero mid oridbepon thongailul, brun aunor oridben edassissu berunn.

Now you give it a try!

Forest People's Rhyme

The following is a version of the rhyme in either Proto-Minhyan or a sister language of Minhyan.

Kevo i sim i
Miko athoni
Kevo rye san rye
Ritho athoni

Here is the Minhyan translation:

Gewel sipom calagan
Bless/OPTATIVE-IMPERFECTIVE day/PATIENTIVE-DEFINITE your(peer)/POSSESSIVE-DEFINITE
May your days be blessed

Tefowen amasse athonisse
Fill/OPTATIVE-IMPERFECTIVE love/DATIVE-INDEFINITE joy/DATIVE-INDEFINITE
Full of love and Joy

Cefowe calan riyeli
Live/OPTATIVE-IMPERFECTIVE you(peer)/AGENTIVE-DEFINITE peace/LOCATIVE-INDEFINITE
May you live in peace

Sirum cefoti calagan ritho.
Day/TEMPORAL-DEFINITE life-full your(peer)/POSSESSIVE-DEFINITE all
All your life filled days

Conversation

Mathi:

Saraffol, ama garaha calapan eruwa garaga rudd.
Xaral/VOCATIVE-DEFINITE I/AGENTIVE-SINGULAR you/PATIENTIVE-SINGULAR heart/ABLATIVE-DEFINITE I/POSSESSIVE-DEFINITE all.
I love you, Xaral, with all of my heart.

Doler garaha calapan erulu garaga molud garaga sirum reddi;
See-again I/AGENTIVE-SINGULAR you/PATIENTIVE-SINGULAR heart/LOCATIVE-DEFINITE I/POSSESSIVE-DEFINITE mind/LOCATIVE-DEFINITE I/POSSESSIVE-DEFINITE day/TEMPORAL-DEFINITE every.
I will see you again, everyday, in my heart and mind;

agonor garaha calapan calalun.
lose/NEGATIVE I/AGENTIVE-SINGULAR you/PATIENTIVE-SINGULAR that/LOCATIVE-DEFINITE.
there I will never lose you.

Xaral:

Mathiffo, ama garaha calapan lubewad.
Mathi/VOCATIVE-DEFINITE, love I/AGENTIVE-SINGULAR you/PATIENTIVE-SINGULAR also/ABLATIVE-DEFINITE.
I love you too, Mathi.

Adajinor garaha calapan dyaril.
Forsake/NEGATIVE I/AGENTIVE-SINGULAR you/PATIENTIVE-SINGULAR ever/TEMPORAL-INDEFINITE.
I'll never forsake you.

Roxhai

The international auxiliary language with the logical vocabulary

Roxhai is a philosophical language (an *a priori* model language), with its vocabulary automatically structured, so that words with longer bases have more narrow definitions than their stems (a stem is a base missing its last letter). For instance:

>**r'o** - sentiment and moral power
>**ro'yo** - religious affection
>**roc'o** - supernatural being or region
>**roca'yo** - Christian supernatural being or region
>**rocac'o** - God.

The base of a word precedes the apostrophe ('). The remainder of the word identifies the part of speech, and uses a variation of the Esperanto word endings: **o** for noun, for instance (preceded by /y/ when the base ends in a vowel).

The core vocabulary of Roxhai is based on nouns. Verbs, adjectives and adverbs are all derived from the nouns. For instance:

>**ro'yo** - noun - religious affection
>**ro'ya** - adjective - having religious affection
>**ro'yi** - verb - to have religious affection (for)
>**ro'ye** - adverb - with religious affection

Even the nouns narrowest in meaning tend to exhibit a polysemy beyond that of natural languages. Because the goal is to keep the vocabulary of Roxhai under 2,000 common nouns, many more specific concepts have to be referred to by using a more general word or paraphrase.

Grammar is for the most part based on a simplification of the grammar of Esperanto.

The initial, tentative conception of the vocabulary follows.

Roxhai was inspired by Solresol, Ro and Esperanto.

Maximizing Redundancy In Vocabulary

FROM: Jeffrey Henning, 74774,157

TO: Conlang, INTERNET:conlang@diku.dk

DATE: 6/7/96 2:34 PM

Re: Re: CONLANG: Roxhai

> From: jim.henry@silver.com (JIM HENRY) Date: Thu, 06 Jun 96
> I wonder how you plan to avoid the problem with Ro which a
> previous poster pointed out a few days ago - namely, that a
> minor typo or noise during conversation could turn a word into
> a plausibly-similar word.

An important problem and one I have given a lot of thought to. As I point out in my summary of Ro [see "Conlangs at a Glance"], if you make a typo [in Ro], a spell checker typically won't catch it, since you'll find it was a valid word anyway. The solution for Roxhai (not implemented, but why I warn the vocabulary will be dramatically restructured) is to have a broad array of phonotactically permissible syllables and not use them all (Ro uses most of its permissible syllables). To do this for Roxhai means having a broader phonology than most IALs — (though the consonant system will probably have fewer consonants than E-o but more than Sen:esepera) this is one reason why I want a 10-vowel system, instead of a five vowel system .

For instance, assume a subtree of the category has two options: under "paternity/maternity" might be words for "mother" and "father"-the only words there. If they differ only by the final vowel (each uses 1 vowel, for 2 vowels total), then only 20% of the possible vowels have been used in that position. So there will be some room for mistakes. A philosophical language will always have lower redundancy than other languages, but I do hope to minimize it in Roxhai.

Another way to make up for this is to have longer words. Roxhai has longer words on average than Ro, and this improves recognizability and redundancy in my opinion. Shorter words are easier to say, but Roxhai would typically be read rather than spoken anyway. And the words are shorter now than in the previous incarnation of Roxhai (an unfinished and unworkable lang. called Minimalex, striving for a minimum number of roots).

> *Perhaps each word in practice could end with a sort of CRC code? :) (Or perhaps you could incorporate that into Fith - the Fithians append an error-detecting-and- correcting code to each utterance. :)*

Actually, the Fithians use a word meaning "check stack depth" [synchronization conjunction]. So they might be talking for a while and then remind their listener, "check-stack-depth 3", meaning, "by the way, you should have three words on your mental stack that I haven't talked about yet". In noisy situations, they will use this phrase a lot; in normal conversation, less often.

> *It would help to reduce the phoneme inventory to the most distinctive sounds, as in Sen:esepera, but that would reduce the number of top-level categories you could distinguish.*

Actually, I think the reverse is true. A broader range of possible sounds for intermediate values is desirable — if you don't use them all, you have the necessary redundancy. "Hmm, I thought he said *rocalam'o*, but that's not a word, he must have said *rocalan'o*." [made up examples]

> *How would one derive prepositions (or might they be postpositions?) in Roxhai? Perhaps three of the top-level categories could deal with "motion," "relation" and "location," and under those headings you could derive adpositions.*

I haven't given any thought to adpositions yet. I did think that they might use a separate initial letter. I've been mainly worrying about nouns for now. Something else to chew on...

Roxhai'ya Naimaici'yo - Initial Lexicon

By the nature of Roxhai, this is not only an alphabetic list, but a classification. E.g. *ca'yo* 'existence' has the subcategories *cac'o* 'abstract being', *caf'o* 'concrete being', *cam'o* 'formal existence', *can'o* 'modal existence', and these in turn have subcategories.

Note: some Roxhai words are glossed twice with the same English word. A subsequent gloss is more narrow than the English term and is colored by words defined from it. Thus *ca'yo*, "existence", is broader in scope than *caca'yo*, "existence".

c'o	**abstract relations**
ca'yo	**existence**
cac'o	being, in the abstract
caca'yo	existence
cacai'yo	inexistence.
caf'o	being, in the concrete
cafa'yo	substantiality.
cafai'yo	insubstantiality.
cam'o	formal existence
cama'yo	intrinsicality.
camai'yo	extrinsicality.
can'o	modal existence
cana'yo	state.
canai'yo	circumstance.
cai'yo	**section ii. relation**
caic'o	absolute relation
caica'yo	relation.
caicai'yo	[want, or absence of relation] irrelation.
caice'yo	[relations of kindred] consanguinity.
caici'yo	[double or reciprocal relation] correlation.
caico'yo	identity.
caicoi'yo	[noncoincidence] contrariety. n. contrariety, contrast, foil
caicou'yo	difference.
caif'o	continuous relation
caifa'yo	uniformity.
caim'o	partial relation
caima'yo	[absence or want of uniformity] nonuniformity.
caimai'yo	similarity.
caime'yo	dissimilarity.
caimi'yo	imitation.
caimo'yo	nonimitation.
caimoi'yo	variation.
caimou'yo	[result of imitation] copy.
caimu'yo	[thing copied] prototype.
cain'o	general relation
caina'yo	agreement.
cainai'yo	disagreement.
ce'yo	**quantity**
cec'o	simple quantity
ceca'yo	[absolute quantity] quantity.
cecai'yo	[relative quantity] degree.
cef'o	comparative quantity

cefa'yo	[sameness of quantity or degree] equality.
cefai'yo	[difference of quantity or degree] inequality.
cefe'yo	mean.
cefi'yo	compensation.
cefa'yo	quantity by comparison with a standard
cefac'o	greatness.
cefaf'o	smallness.
cefai'yo	quantity by comparison with a similar object
cefaic'o	superiority. [supremacy]
cefaif'o	inferiority.
cefe'yo	changes in quantity
cefec'o	increase.
cefef'o	nonincrease, decrease.
cefi'yo	conjunctive quantity
cefic'o	addition.
cefif'o	nonaddition. subduction.
cefim'o	[thing added] adjunct.
cefin'o	[thing remaining] remainder.
cefip'o	[thing deducted] decrement.
cefir'o	[forming a whole without coherence] mixture.
cefis'o	[freedom from mixture] simpleness.
cefish'o	junction.
cefit'o	disjunction.
cefixh'o	[connecting medium] vinculum.
cefixha'yo	coherence.
cefixhai'yo	[want of adhesion, nonadhesion, immiscibility] incoherence.
cefixhe'yo	combination.
cefixhi'yo	decomposition.
cem'o	concrete quantity
cema'yo	whole. [principal part]
cemai'yo	part.
ceme'yo	completeness.
cemi'yo	incompleteness.
cemo'yo	composition.
cemoi'yo	exclusion.
cemou'yo	component.
cemu'yo	extraneousness.
ci'yo	**order**
cic'o	order
cica'yo	order.
cicai'yo	[absence, or want of order, &c] disorder.
cice'yo	complexity

cici'yo	[reduction to order] arrangement.
cico'yo	[subversion of order; bringing into disorder] derangement.
cif'o	consecutive order
cifa'yo	precedence.
cifai'yo	sequence.
cife'yo	precursor.
cifi'yo	sequel.
cifo'yo	beginning.
cifoi'yo	end.
cifou'yo	middle.
cifu'yo	[uninterrupted sequence] continuity.
cifuu'yo	[interrupted sequence.) discontinuity.
cifxh'o	term.
cim'o	collective order
cima'yo	assemblage.
cimai'yo	nonassemblage. dispersion.
cime'yo	[place of meeting] focus.
cin'o	distributive order
cina'yo	class.
cinai'yo	inclusion. [comprehension under, or reference to a class]
cine'yo	exclusion.
cini'yo	generality.
cino'yo	speciality.
cip'o	order as regards categories
cipa'yo	normality.
cipai'yo	multiformity.
cipe'yo	conformity.
cipi'yo	unconformity.
co'yo	**number**
coc'o	number, in the abstract
coca'yo	number.
cocai'yo	numeration.
coce'yo	list.
cof'o	determinate number
cofa'yo	{opp. 100} unity.
cofai'yo	accompaniment.
cofe'yo	duality.
cofi'yo	duplication.
cofo'yo	[division into two parts] bisection.
cofoi'yo	triality.
cofou'yo	triplication.

cofu'yo	[division into three parts] trisection.
cofuu'yo	quaternity.
cofxh'o	quadruplication.
cofxha'yo	[division into four parts] quadrisection.
cofxhai'yo	five, &c.
cofxhe'yo	quinquesection, &c.
cofxhi'yo	{opp. 87} [more than one] plurality.
com'o	indeterminate number
coma'yo	[less than one] fraction
comai'yo	zero.
come'yo	multitude.
comi'yo	fewness.
como'yo	repetition.
comoi'yo	infinity.
coi'yo	**time**
coic'o	absolute time
coica'yo	time.
coicai'yo	neverness.
coice'yo	[definite duration, or portion of time] period.
coici'yo	contingent duration.
coico'yo	[indefinite duration] course.
coicoi'yo	[long duration] diuturnity.
coicou'yo	[short duration] transientness.
coicu'yo	[endless duration] perpetuity.
coicuu'yo	[point of time] instantaneity.
coicxh'o	[estimation, measurement, and record of time] chronometry.
coicxha'yo	[false estimate of time] anachronism.
coif'o	relative time
coifa'yo	time with reference to succession
coifac'o	priority.
coifaf'o	posteriority.
coifam'o	the present time.
coifan'o	[time different from the present] different time.
coifap'o	synchronism.
coifar'o	[prospective time] futurity.
coifas'o	[retrospective time] preterition
coifai'yo	time with reference to age.
coifaic'o	newness.
coifaif'o	oldness.
coifaim'o	morning. [noon]
coifain'o	evening. [midnight]
coifaip'o	youth.

coifair'o	age.
coifais'o	infant.
coifaish'o	veteran.
coifait'o	adolescence.
coife'yo	time with reference to an effect or purpose
coifec'o	earliness.
coifef'o	punctuality
coifem'o	lateness.
coifen'o	occasion.
coifep'o	untimeliness
coim'o	recurrent time
coima'yo	frequency.
coimai'yo	infrequency.
coime'yo	regularity of recurrence. periodicity.
coimi'yo	irregularity of recurrence.
cou'yo	**change**
couc'o	simple change
couca'yo	[difference at different times] change.
coucai'yo	[absence of change] permanence.
couce'yo	[change from action to rest] cessation.
couci'yo	continuance in action.
couco'yo	[gradual change to something different] conversion.
coucoi'yo	reversion.
coucou'yo	[sudden or violent change] revolution.
coucu'yo	[change of one thing for another] substitution.
coucuu'yo	[double or mutual change] interchange.
couf'o	complex change
coufa'yo	changeableness.
coufai'yo	stability.
coufe'yo	present events: eventuality.
coufi'yo	future events: destiny.
cu'yo	**causation**
cuc'o	constancy of sequence in events
cuca'yo	[constant antecedent]. cause.
cucai'yo	[constant sequent] effect.
cuce'yo	[assignment of cause] attribution
cuci'yo	[absence of assignable cause] chance.
cuf'o	connection between cause and effect
cufa'yo	power.
cufai'yo	impotence.
cufe'yo	[degree of power] strength.
cufi'yo	weakness.
cum'o	power in operation

cuma'yo	production.
cumai'yo	[nonproduction] destruction.
cume'yo	reproduction.
cumi'yo	producer.
cumo'yo	destroyer.
cumoi'yo	paternity.
cumou'yo	posterity.
cumu'yo	productiveness
cumuu'yo	unproductiveness.
cumxh'o	agency.
cumxha'yo	physical energy.
cumxhai'yo	physical inertness.
cumxhe'yo	violence.
cumxhi'yo	moderation.
cun'o	indirect power
cuna'yo	influence.
cunai'yo	absence of influence.
cune'yo	tendency.
cuni'yo	liability.
cup'o	combinations of causes
cupa'yo	concurrence.
cupai'yo	counteraction.
f'o	**words relating to space**
fa'yo	**space in general**
fac'o	abstract space
faca'yo	[indefinite space] space.
facai'yo	inextension.
face'yo	[definite space] region.
faci'yo	[limited space] place.
faf'o	relative space
fafa'yo	situation.
fafai'yo	location.
fafe'yo	displacement.
fam'o	existence in space
fama'yo	presence.
famai'yo	[nullibiety]
fame'yo	inhabitant.
fami'yo	[place of habitation, or resort] abode.
famo'yo	[things contained] contents.
famoi'yo	receptacle.
fai'yo	**dimensions**
faic'o	general dimensions
faica'yo	size.

faicai'yo	littleness.
faice'yo	expansion.
faici'yo	contraction.
faico'yo	distance.
faicoi'yo	nearness.
faicou'yo	interval.
faicu'yo	contiguity.
faif'o	linear dimensions
faifa'yo	length.
faifai'yo	shortness.
faife'yo	breadth, thickness.
faifi'yo	narrowness. thinness.
faifo'yo	layer.
faifoi'yo	filament.
faifou'yo	height.
faifu'yo	lowness.
faifuu'yo	depth.
faifxh'o	shallowness.
faifxha'yo	summit.
faifxhai'yo	base.
faifxhe'yo	verticality.
faifxhi'yo	horizontality.
faifxho'yo	pendency.
faifxhoi'yo	support.
faifxhou'yo	parallelism.
faifxhu'yo	obliquity.
faifxhuu'yo	inversion.
faifxh'o	crossing.
faim'o	centrical dimensions
faima'yo	general
faimac'o	exteriority.
faimaf'o	interiority.
faimam'o	centrality.
faiman'o	lining.
faimap'o	investment.
faimar'o	divestment.
faimas'o	circumjacence.
faimash'o	interjacence.
faimat'o	circumscription.
faimaxh'o	outline.
faimaxha'yo	edge.
faimaxhai'yo	inclosure.
faimaxhe'yo	limit.

faimaxhi'yo	front.
faimaxho'yo	rear.
faimaxhoi'yo	laterality.
faimaxhou'yo	contraposition.
faimaxhu'yo	dextrality.
faimaxhuu'yo	sinistrality.
fe'yo	**form**
fec'o	general form
feca'yo	form.
fecai'yo	[absence of form] amorphism.
fece'yo	[regularity of form] symmetry.
feci'yo	[irregularity of form] distortion.
fef'o	special form
fefa'yo	angularity.
fefai'yo	curvature.
fefe'yo	straightness.
fefi'yo	[simple circularity] circularity.
fefo'yo	[complex curvature] convolution.
fefoi'yo	rotundity.
fem'o	superficial form
fema'yo	convexity.
femai'yo	flatness.
feme'yo	concavity.
femi'yo	sharpness.
femo'yo	bluntness.
femoi'yo	smoothness.
femou'yo	roughness.
femu'yo	notch.
femuu'yo	fold.
femxh'o	furrow.
femxha'yo	opening
femxhai'yo	closure.
femxhe'yo	perforator.
femxhi'yo	stopper.
fi'yo	**motion**
fic'o	motion in general
fica'yo	[successive change of place] motion.
ficai'yo	quiescence.
fice'yo	[locomotion by land] journey.
fici'yo	[locomotion by water, or air] navigation.
fico'yo	traveler.
ficoi'yo	mariner.
ficou'yo	transference.

ficu'yo	carrier.
ficuu'yo	vehicle.
ficxh'o	ship.
fif'o	degrees of motion
fifa'yo	velocity.
fifai'yo	slowness.
fim'o	motion conjoined with force
fima'yo	impulse.
fimai'yo	recoil.
fin'o	motion with reference to direction
fina'yo	direction.
finai'yo	deviation.
fine'yo	[going before] precession.
fini'yo	[going after] sequence.
fino'yo	[motion forward; progressive motion] progression.
finoi'yo	[motion backwards] regression.
finou'yo	[motion given to an object situated in front] propulsion.
finu'yo	[motion given to an object situated behind] traction.
finuu'yo	[motion towards] approach.
finxh'o	[motion from] recession.
finxha'yo	[motion towards, actively] attraction.
finxhai'yo	[motion from, actively; force driving apart] repulsion.
finxhe'yo	[motion nearer to] convergence.
finxhi'yo	[motion further off] divergence.
finxho'yo	[terminal motion at] arrival.
finxhoi'yo	[initial motion from] departure.
finxhou'yo	[motion into] ingress.
finxhu'yo	[motion out of] egress.
finxhuu'yo	[motion into, actively] reception.
finxh'o	[motion out of, actively] ejection.
finxha'yo	[eating] food.
finxhai'yo	excretion
finxhe'yo	[forcible ingress] insertion.
finxhi'yo	[forcible egress] extraction.
finxho'yo	[motion through] passage.
finxhoi'yo	[motion beyond] transcursion
finxhou'yo	[motion short of] shortcoming
finxhu'yo	[motion upwards] ascent.
finxhuu'yo	[motion downwards] descent.
finy'o	elevation.
finya'yo	depression.

finyai'yo	leap.
finye'yo	plunge
finyi'yo	[curvilinear motion] circuition.
finyo'yo	[motion in a continued circle] rotation.
finyoi'yo	[motion in the reverse circle] evolution.
finyou'yo	[reciprocating motion, motion to and fro] oscillation.
finyu'yo	[irregular motion] agitation.
m'o	**words relating to matter**
ma'yo	**matter in general**
mac'o	materiality.
maf'o	immateriality.
mam'o	world.
man'o	gravity.
map'o	levity.
mai'yo	**inorganic matter**
maic'o	solid matter
maica'yo	density..
maicai'yo	rarity.
maice'yo	hardness.
maici'yo	softness.
maico'yo	elasticity.
maicoi'yo	inelasticity.
maicou'yo	tenacity.
maicu'yo	brittleness.
maicuu'yo	[structure] texture.
maicxh'o	pulverulence.
maicxha'yo	friction.
maicxhai'yo	[absence of friction. prevention of friction] lubrication.
maif'o	fluid matter
maifa'yo	fluids in general
maifac'o	fluidity.
maifaf'o	gaseity.
maifam'o	liquefaction. -n. liquefaction; liquescence, liquescency;
maifan'o	vaporization.
maifai'yo	specific fluids
maifaic'o	water.
maifaif'o	air.
maifaim'o	moisture.
maifain'o	dryness.
maifaip'o	ocean

maifair'o	land.
maifais'o	gulf. lake
maifaish'o	plain.
maifait'o	marsh.
maifaixh'o	island. n. island, isle, islet, eyot, ait, holf, reef, atoll,
maife'yo	fluids in motion
maifec'o	[fluid in motion] stream.
maifef'o	[water in motion] river.
maifem'o	[air in motion] wind.
maifen'o	[channel for the passage of water] conduit.
maifep'o	[channel for the passage of air] airpipe.
maim'o	imperfect fluids
maima'yo	semiliquidity.
maimai'yo	[mixture of air and water] bubble. [cloud]
maime'yo	pulpiness.
maimi'yo	unctuousness.
maimo'yo	oil.
maimoi'yo	resin.
me'yo	**organic matter**
mec'o	vitality
meca'yo	vitality in general
mecac'o	organization.
mecaf'o	inorganization.
mecam'o	life.
mecan'o	death.
mecap'o	[destruction of life; violent death] killing.
mecar'o	corpse.
mecas'o	interment.
mecai'yo	special vitality
mecaic'o	animality.
mecaif'o	vegetability.
mecaim'o	animal.
mecain'o	vegetable.
mecaip'o	[the science of animals] zoology.
mecair'o	[the science of plants] botany.
mecais'o	[the economy or management of animals] husbandry.
mecaish'o	[the economy or management of plants] agriculture.
mecait'o	mankind.
mecaixh'o	man.
mecaixha'yo	woman.
mef'o	sensation

mefa'yo	sensation in general
mefac'o	physical sensibility.
mefaf'o	physical insensibility.
mefam'o	physical pleasure.
mefan'o	physical pain.
mefai'yo	special sensation
mefaic'o	touch
mefaica'yo	[sensation of pressure] touch.
mefaicai'yo	sensations of touch.
mefaice'yo	[insensibility to touch] numbness.
mefaif'o	heat
mefaifa'yo	heat.
mefaifai'yo	cold.
mefaife'yo	calefaction.
mefaifi'yo	refrigeration.
mefaifo'yo	furnace.
mefaifoi'yo	refrigeratory.
mefaifou'yo	fuel.
mefaifu'yo	thermometer.
mefaim'o	taste
mefaima'yo	taste.
mefaimai'yo	insipidity.
mefaime'yo	pungency.
mefaimi'yo	condiment.
mefaimo'yo	savoriness.
mefaimoi'yo	unsavoriness.
mefaimou'yo	sweetness.
mefaimu'yo	sourness.
mefain'o	odor
mefaina'yo	odor.
mefainai'yo	inodorousness.
mefaine'yo	fragrance.
mefaini'yo	fetor.
mefaip'o	sound
mefaipa'yo	sound in general
mefaipac'o	sound.
mefaipaf'o	silence.
mefaipam'o	loudness.
mefaipan'o	faintness.
mefaipai'yo	specific sounds
mefaipaic'o	[sudden and violent sounds] snap.
mefaipaif'o	[repeated and protracted sounds] roll.
mefaipaim'o	resonance.

mefaipain'o	nonresonance.
mefaipaip'o	[hissing sounds] sibilation.
mefaipair'o	[harsh sounds] stridor.
mefaipais'o	cry.
mefaipaish'o	[animal sounds] ululation.
mefaipe'yo	musical sounds
mefaipec'o	melody. concord.
mefaipef'o	discord.
mefaipem'o	music.
mefaipen'o	musician. [performance of music]
mefaipep'o	musical instruments.
mefaipi'yo	perception of sound
mefaipic'o	[sense of sound] hearing.
mefaipif'o	deafness.
mefair'o	light
mefaira'yo	light in general
mefairac'o	light.
mefairaf'o	darkness.
mefairam'o	dimness.
mefairan'o	[source of light, self-luminous body] luminary.
mefairap'o	shade.
mefairar'o	transparency.
mefairas'o	opacity.
mefairash'o	semitransparency.
mefairai'yo	specific light
mefairaic'o	color.
mefairaif'o	[absence of color] achromatism.
mefairaim'o	whiteness.
mefairain'o	blackness.
mefairaip'o	gray.
mefairair'o	brown.
mefairais'o	redness.
mefairaish'o	greenness.
mefairait'o	yellowness.
mefairaixh'o	purple.
mefairaixha'yo	blueness.
mefairaixhai'yo	orange.
mefairaixhe'yo	variegation.
mefaire'yo	perceptions of light
mefairec'o	vision.
mefairef'o	blindness.
mefairem'o	[imperfect vision] dimsightedness. [fallacies of vision]

mefairen'o	spectator.
mefairep'o	optical instruments.
mefairer'o	visibility.
mefaires'o	invisibility.
mefairesh'o	appearance.
mefairet'o	disappearance.
n'o	**words relating to the intellectual faculties**
na'yo	**formation of ideas**
nac'o	operations of intellect in general
naca'yo	intellect.
nacai'yo	absence or want of intellect.
nace'yo	thought.
naci'yo	[absence or want of thought] incogitancy.
naco'yo	[object of thought] idea.
nacoi'yo	[subject of thought] topic.
naf'o	precursory conditions and operations
nafa'yo	[the desire of knowledge] curiosity.
nafai'yo	[absence of curiosity] incuriosity.
nafe'yo	attention.
nafi'yo	inattention.
nafo'yo	care.
nafoi'yo	neglect.
nafou'yo	inquiry [subject of inquiry. question]
nafu'yo	answer.
nafuu'yo	experiment.
nafxh'o	comparison.
nafxha'yo	[results of comparison. 1] discrimination.
nafxhai'yo	[results of comparison. 2] indiscrimination.
nafxhe'yo	measurement.
nam'o	materials for reasoning
nama'yo	evidence [on one side]
namai'yo	[evidence on the other side, on the other hand] counter
name'yo	qualification.
nami'yo	possibility.
namo'yo	impossibility.
namoi'yo	probability.
namou'yo	improbability.
namu'yo	certainty.
namuu'yo	uncertainty.
nan'o	reasoning processes
nana'yo	reasoning,

nanai'yo	[the absence of reasoning] intuition. [.false or vicious
nane'yo	demonstration.
nani'yo	confutation.
nap'o	results of reasoning
napa'yo	judgment. [conclusion]
napai'yo	[result of search or inquiry] discovery.
nape'yo	misjudgment.
napi'yo	overestimation.
napo'yo	underestimation.
napoi'yo	belief.
napou'yo	unbelief. doubt.
napu'yo	credulity.
napuu'yo	incredulity.
napxh'o	assent.
napxha'yo	dissent.
napxhai'yo	knowledge.
napxhe'yo	ignorance.
napxhi'yo	scholar.
napxho'yo	ignoramus.
napxhoi'yo	[object of knowlege] truth.
napxhou'yo	error.
napxhu'yo	maxim.
napxhuu'yo	absurdity.
napxh'o	intelligence. wisdom.
napxha'yo	imbecility. folly
napxhai'yo	sage
napxhe'yo	fool.
napxhi'yo	sanity.
napxho'yo	insanity.
napxhoi'yo	madman.
nar'o	section vi extension of thought to the past
nara'yo	memory.
narai'yo	oblivion.
nare'yo	expectation.
nari'yo	inexpectation.
naro'yo	[failure of expectation] disappointment.
naroi'yo	foresight.
narou'yo	prediction.
naru'yo	omen.
naruu'yo	oracle.
nas'o	section vii. creative thought
nasa'yo	supposition.

nasai'yo	imagination.
nai'yo	**communication of ideas**
naic'o	nature of ideas communicated.
naica'yo	[idea to be conveyed] meaning. [thing signified]
naicai'yo	[absence of meaning] unmeaningness.
naice'yo	intelligibility.
naici'yo	unintelligibility.
naico'yo	[having a double sense] equivocalness.
naicoi'yo	metaphor.
naicou'yo	interpretation.
naicu'yo	misinterpretation.
naicuu'yo	interpreter.
naif'o	modes of communication
naifa'yo	manifestation.
naifai'yo	latency. implication.
naife'yo	information.
naifi'yo	concealment.
naifo'yo	disclosure
naifoi'yo	ambush [means of concealment].
naifou'yo	publication.
naifu'yo	news.
naifuu'yo	secret.
naifxh'o	messenger.
naifxha'yo	affirmation.
naifxhai'yo	negation.
naifxhe'yo	teaching.
naifxhi'yo	misteaching.
naifxho'yo	learning
naifxhoi'yo	teacher.
naifxhou'yo	learner.
naifxhu'yo	school.
naifxhuu'yo	veracity.
naifxh'o	falsehood.
naifxha'yo	deception.
naifxhai'yo	untruth.
naifxhe'yo	dupe.
naifxhi'yo	deceiver.
naifxho'yo	exaggeration.
naim'o	means of communicating ideas
naima'yo	natural means
naimac'o	indication
naimaf'o	record.
naimam'o	[suppression of sign] obliteration.

naiman'o	recorder.
naimap'o	representation.
naimar'o	misrepresentation.
naimas'o	painting.
naimash'o	sculpture.
naimat'o	engraving.
naimaxh'o	artist.
naimai'yo	conventional means
naimaic'o	language generally
naimaica'yo	language.
naimaicai'yo	letter.
naimaice'yo	word.
naimaici'yo	neologism.
naimaico'yo	nomenclature.
naimaicoi'yo	misnomer.
naimaicou'yo	phrase.
naimaicu'yo	grammar.
naimaicuu'yo	solecism.
naimaif'o	various qualities of style
naimaifa'yo	style.
naimaifai'yo	perspicuity.
naimaife'yo	obscurity.
naimaifi'yo	conciseness.
naimaifo'yo	diffuseness.
naimaifou'yo	feebleness.
naimaifu'yo	plainness.
naimaifuu'yo	ornament.
naimaifxh'o	elegance.
naimaifxha'yo	inelegance.
naimaifxhai'yo	voice.
naimaifxhe'yo	aphony.
naimaifxhi'yo	speech.
naimaifxho'yo	[imperfect speech] stammering.
naimaifxhoi'yo	loquacity.
naimaifxhou'yo	taciturnity.
naimaifxhu'yo	allocution.
naimaifxhuu'yo	interlocution.
naimaifxh'o	soliloquy.
naimaim'o	written language
naimaima'yo	writing.
naimaimai'yo	printing.
naimaime'yo	correspondence.
naimaimi'yo	book.

naimaimo'yo	description.
naimaimoi'yo	dissertation.
naimaimou'yo	compendium.
naimaimu'yo	poetry.
naimaimuu'yo	prose.
naimaimxh'o	the drama.
p'o	**words relating to the voluntary powers**
pa'yo	**individual volition**
pac'o	volition in general
paca'yo	acts of volition
pacac'o	will.
pacaf'o	necessity.
pacam'o	willingness.
pacan'o	unwillingness.
pacap'o	resolution.
pacar'o	perseverance.
pacas'o	irresolution.
pacash'o	obstinacy.
pacat'o	tergiversation.
pacaxh'o	caprice.
pacaxha'yo	choice.
pacaxhai'yo	absence of choice.
pacaxhe'yo	rejection.
pacaxhi'yo	predetermination.
pacaxho'yo	impulse.
pacaxhoi'yo	habit.
pacaxhou'yo	desuetude.
pacai'yo	causes of volition
pacaic'o	motive.
pacaif'o	absence of motive.
pacaim'o	dissuasion.
pacain'o	[ostensible motive, ground, or reason assigned] pretext.
pace'yo	objects of volition
pacec'o	good.
pacef'o	evil.
paf'o	prospective volition
pafa'yo	conceptional volition
pafac'o	intention.
pafaf'o	[absence of purpose in the succession of events] chance. 2
pafam'o	[purpose in action] pursuit
pafan'o	.[absence of pursuit] avoidance.

pafap'o	relinquishment.
pafar'o	business.
pafas'o	plan.
pafash'o	method. [path]
pafat'o	mid-course.
pafaxh'o	circuit.
pafaxha'yo	requirement.
pafai'yo	subservience to ends
pafaic'o	actual subservience
pafaica'yo	instrumentality.
pafaicai'yo	means.
pafaice'yo	instrument.
pafaici'yo	substitute.
pafaico'yo	materials.
pafaicoi'yo	store.
pafaicou'yo	provision.
pafaicu'yo	waste.
pafaicuu'yo	sufficiency.
pafaicxh'o	insufficiency.
pafaicxha'yo	redundance.
pafaif'o	degree of subservience
pafaifa'yo	importance.
pafaifai'yo	unimportance.
pafaife'yo	utility.
pafaifi'yo	inutility.
pafaifo'yo	[specific subservience] expedience.
pafaifoi'yo	inexpedience.
pafaifou'yo	[capability of producing good. good qualities] goodness.
pafaifu'yo	[capability of producing evil. bad qualities] badness.
pafaifuu'yo	perfection.
pafaifxh'o	imperfection.
pafaifxha'yo	cleanness.
pafaifxhai'yo	uncleanness.
pafaifxhe'yo	health.
pafaifxhi'yo	disease.
pafaifxho'yo	salubrity.
pafaifxhoi'yo	insalubrity.
pafaifxhou'yo	improvement.
pafaifxhu'yo	deterioration.
pafaifxhuu'yo	restoration.
pafaifxh'o	relapse.
pafaifxha'yo	remedy.

pafaifxhai'yo	bane.
pafaim'o	contingent subservience
pafaima'yo	safety.
pafaimai'yo	danger.
pafaime'yo	[means of safety] refuge.
pafaimi'yo	[source of danger] pitfall.
pafaimo'yo	warning.
pafaimoi'yo	[indication of danger] alarm.
pafaimou'yo	preservation.
pafaimu'yo	escape.
pafaimuu'yo	deliverance.
pafain'o	precursory measures
pafaina'yo	preparation.
pafainai'yo	nonpreparation.
pafaine'yo	essay.
pafaini'yo	undertaking.
pafaino'yo	use.
pafainoi'yo	disuse.
pafainou'yo	misuse.
pam'o	voluntary action
pama'yo	simple voluntary action
pamac'o	action.
pamaf'o	inaction.
pamam'o	activity.
paman'o	inactivity.
pamap'o	haste.
pamar'o	leisure.
pamas'o	exertion.
pamash'o	repose.
pamat'o	fatigue.
pamaxh'o	refreshment.
pamaxha'yo	agent.
pamaxhai'yo	workshop.
pamai'yo	complex voluntary action
pamaic'o	conduct.
pamaif'o	direction.
pamaim'o	director.
pamain'o	advice.
pamaip'o	council.
pamair'o	precept.
pamais'o	skill.
pamaish'o	unskillfulness.
pamait'o	proficient.

pamaixh'o	bungler.
pamaixha'yo	cunning.
pamaixhai'yo	artlessness.
pan'o	antagonism
pana'yo	conditional antagonism ??
panac'o	difficulty.
panaf'o	facility.
panam'o	hindrance.
panan'o	aid.
panap'o	opposition.
panar'o	cooperation.
panas'o	opponent.
panash'o	auxiliary.
panat'o	party.
panaxh'o	discord.
panaxha'yo	concord.
panaxhai'yo	defiance.
panaxhe'yo	attack.
panaxhi'yo	defense
panaxho'yo	retaliation.
panaxhoi'yo	resistance.
panaxhou'yo	contention.
panaxhu'yo	peace.
panaxhuu'yo	warfare.
panaxh'o	pacification.
panaxha'yo	mediation.
panaxhai'yo	submission.
panaxhe'yo	combatant.
panaxhi'yo	arms.
panaxho'yo	arena.
pap'o	results of voluntary action
papa'yo	completion.
papai'yo	noncompletion.
pape'yo	success.
papi'yo	failure.
papo'yo	trophy.
papoi'yo	prosperity.
papou'yo	adversity.
papu'yo	mediocrity.
pai'yo	**intersocial volition**
paic'o	general intersocial volition
paica'yo	authority.
paicai'yo	[absence of authority] laxity.

paice'yo	severity.
paici'yo	lenity.
paico'yo	command.
paicoi'yo	disobedience.
paicou'yo	obedience.
paicu'yo	compulsion.
paicuu'yo	master.
paicxh'o	servant.
paicxha'yo	[insignia of authority] scepter.
paicxhai'yo	freedom.
paicxhe'yo	subjection.
paicxhi'yo	liberation.
paicxho'yo	restraint.
paicxhoi'yo	[means of restraint] prison.
paicxhou'yo	keeper.
paicxhu'yo	prisoner.
paicxhuu'yo	[vicarious authority] commission.
paicxh'o	abrogation.
paicxha'yo	resignation.
paicxhai'yo	consignee.
paicxhe'yo	deputy.
paif'o	special intersocial volition
paifa'yo	permission.
paifai'yo	prohibition.
paife'yo	consent.
paifi'yo	offer.
paifo'yo	refusal.
paifoi'yo	request.
paifou'yo	[negative request] deprecation.
paifu'yo	petitioner.
paim'o	conditional intersocial volition
paima'yo	promise.
paimai'yo	release from engagement.
paime'yo	compact.
paimi'yo	conditions.
paimo'yo	security.
paimoi'yo	observance.
paimou'yo	nonobservance.
paimu'yo	compromise.
pain'o	possessive relations
paina'yo	property in general
painac'o	acquisition.
painaf'o	loss.

painam'o	possession.
painan'o	exemption.
painap'o	[joint possession] participation.
painar'o	possessor.
painas'o	property.
painash'o	retention.
painat'o	relinquishment.
painai'yo	transfer of property
painaic'o	transfer.
painaif'o	giving.
painaim'o	receiving.
painain'o	apportionment.
painaip'o	lending.
painair'o	borrowing.
painais'o	taking.
painaish'o	restitution.
painait'o	stealing.
painaixh'o	thief.
painaixha'yo	booty.
paine'yo	interchange of property
painec'o	barter.
painef'o	purchase.
painem'o	sale.
painen'o	merchant.
painep'o	merchandise.
painer'o	mart.
paini'yo	monetary relations
painic'o	money.
painif'o	treasurer.
painim'o	treasury.
painin'o	wealth.
painip'o	poverty.
painir'o	credit.
painis'o	debt.
painish'o	payment.
painit'o	nonpayment
painixh'o	expenditure.
painixha'yo	receipt.
painixhai'yo	accounts.
painixhe'yo	price.
painixhi'yo	discount.
painixho'yo	dearness.
painixhoi'yo	cheapness.

painixhou'yo	liberality.
painixhu'yo	economy.
painixhuu'yo	prodigality.
painixh'o	parsimony.
r'o	**words relating to the sentiment and moral powers**
ra'yo	**affections in general**
rac'o	affections.
raf'o	feeling.
ram'o	sensibility.
ran'o	insensibility.
rap'o	excitation.
rar'o	[excess of sensitiveness] excitability
ras'o	[absence of excitability, or of excitement] inexcitability.
rai'yo	**personal affections**
raic'o	passive affections
raica'yo	pleasure.
raicai'yo	pain.
raice'yo	[capability of giving pleasure; cause or source of pleasure]
raici'yo	[capability of giving pain; cause or source of pain].
raico'yo	content.
raicoi'yo	discontent.
raicou'yo	regret.
raicu'yo	relief.
raicuu'yo	aggravation.
raicxh'o	cheerfulness.
raicxha'yo	dejection.
raicxhai'yo	[expression of pleasure] rejoicing.
raicxhe'yo	[expression of pain] lamentation.
raicxhi'yo	amusement.
raicxho'yo	weariness.
raicxhoi'yo	wit.
raicxhou'yo	dullness.
raicxhu'yo	humorist.
raif'o	discriminative affections
raifa'yo	beauty.
raifai'yo	ugliness.
raife'yo	ornament.
raifi'yo	blemish.
raifo'yo	simplicity.
raifoi'yo	[good taste] taste.

raifou'yo	[bad taste] vulgarity.
raifu'yo	fashion.
raifuu'yo	ridiculousness.
raifxh'o	fop.
raifxha'yo	affectation.
raifxhai'yo	ridicule.
raifxhe'yo	[object and cause of ridicule] laughingstock.
raim'o	prospective affections
raima'yo	hope.
raimai'yo	[absence, want or loss of hope] hopelessness.
raime'yo	fear.
raimi'yo	[absence of fear] courage.
raimo'yo	[excess of fear] cowardice.
raimoi'yo	rashness.
raimou'yo	caution.
raimu'yo	desire.
raimuu'yo	indifference.
raimxh'o	dislike.
raimxha'yo	fastidiousness.
raimxhai'yo	satiety.
rain'o	contemplative affections
raina'yo	wonder.
rainai'yo	[absence of wonder] expectance.
raine'yo	prodigy.
raip'o	extrinsic affections
raipa'yo	repute.
raipai'yo	disrepute.
raipe'yo	nobility.
raipi'yo	commonalty.
raipo'yo	title.
raipoi'yo	pride.
raipou'yo	humility.
raipu'yo	vanity.
raipuu'yo	modesty.
raipxh'o	ostentation.
raipxha'yo	celebration.
raipxhai'yo	boasting.
raipxhe'yo	[undue assumption of superiority] insolence.
raipxhi'yo	servility.
raipxho'yo	blusterer.
re'yo	**sympathetic affections**
rec'o	social affections
reca'yo	friendship.

recai'yo	enmity.
rece'yo	friend.
reci'yo	enemy.
reco'yo	sociality.
recoi'yo	seclusion. exclusion.
recou'yo	courtesy.
recu'yo	discourtesy.
recuu'yo	congratulation.
recxh'o	love.
recxha'yo	hate.
recxhai'yo	favorite.
recxhe'yo	resentment.
recxhi'yo	irascibility.
recxho'yo	sullenness.
recxhoi'yo	[expression of affection or love] endearment.
recxhou'yo	marriage.
recxhu'yo	celibacy.
recxhuu'yo	divorce.
ref'o	diffusive sympathetic affections
refa'yo	benevolence.
refai'yo	malevolence.
refe'yo	malediction.
refi'yo	threat.
refo'yo	philanthropy.
refoi'yo	misanthropy.
refou'yo	benefactor.
refu'yo	[maleficent being] evil doer
rem'o	special sympathetic affections
rema'yo	pity.
remai'yo	pitilessness.
reme'yo	condolence.
ren'o	retrospective sympathetic affections
rena'yo	gratitude.
renai'yo	ingratitude.
rene'yo	forgiveness.
reni'yo	revenge.
reno'yo	jealousy.
renoi'yo	envy.
ri'yo	**moral affections**
ric'o	moral obligations
rica'yo	right.
ricai'yo	wrong.
rice'yo	dueness.

rici'yo	[absence of right] undueness.
rico'yo	duty.
ricoi'yo	dereliction of duty.
ricou'yo	exemption.
rif'o	moral sentiments
rifa'yo	respect.
rifai'yo	disrespect.
rife'yo	contempt.
rifi'yo	approbation.
rifo'yo	disapprobation.
rifoi'yo	flattery.
rifou'yo	detraction.
rifu'yo	flatterer.
rifuu'yo	detractor.
rifxh'o	vindication.
rifxha'yo	accusation.
rim'o	moral conditions
rima'yo	probity.
rimai'yo	improbity.
rime'yo	knave.
rimi'yo	disinterestedness.
rimo'yo	selfishness.
rimoi'yo	virtue.
rimou'yo	vice.
rimu'yo	innocence.
rimuu'yo	guilt.
rimxh'o	good man.
rimxha'yo	bad man.
rimxhai'yo	penitence.
rimxhe'yo	impenitence.
rimxhi'yo	atonement.
rin'o	moral practice
rina'yo	temperance.
rinai'yo	intemperance.
rine'yo	sensualist.
rini'yo	asceticism.
rino'yo	fasting.
rinoi'yo	gluttony.
rinou'yo	sobriety.
rinu'yo	drunkenness.
rinuu'yo	purity.
rinxh'o	impurity.
rinxha'yo	libertine.

rip'o	moral institutions
ripa'yo	legality.
ripai'yo	[absence or violation of law] illegality.
ripe'yo	jurisdiction. [executive]
ripi'yo	tribunal.
ripo'yo	judge.
ripoi'yo	lawyer.
ripou'yo	lawsuit.
ripu'yo	acquittal.
ripuu'yo	condemnation.
ripxh'o	punishment.
ripxha'yo	reward.
ripxhai'yo	penalty.
ripxhe'yo	[instrument of punishment] scourge.
ro'yo	**religious affections**
roc'o	superhuman beings and regions
roca'yo	christian deities and powers
rocac'o	deity.
rocaf'o	[beneficent spirits] angel.
rocam'o	[maleficent spirits] satan.
rocai'yo	mythological and other fabulous deities and powers
rocaic'o	jupiter.
rocaif'o	demon.
rocaim'o	heaven.
rocain'o	hell.
rof'o	religious knowledge
rofa'yo	[religious knowledge] theology.
rofai'yo	orthodoxy.
rofe'yo	heterodoxy. [sectarianism]
rofi'yo	revelation.
rofo'yo	pseudo-revelation.
rom'o	religious sentiments
roma'yo	piety.
romai'yo	impiety.
rome'yo	irreligon.
ron'o	acts of religion
rona'yo	worship.
ronai'yo	idolatry.
rone'yo	sorcery.
roni'yo	spell.
rono'yo	sorcerer.
rop'o	religious institutions
ropa'yo	churchdom.

ropai'yo	clergy.
rope'yo	laity.
ropi'yo	rite.
ropo'yo	canonicals.
ropoi'yo	temple.

Simpenga

The International Language For The 21st Century

> *I worked on Simpenga from December 1995 to March 1996. This was one of my early attempts at an IAL, when I was overly concerned about phonetic simplification. Simpenga is a dead project, as I now believe a basic phonology has as many disadvantages (loss of recognizability) as advantages (ease of pronunciation).*

Design Premises

Simpenga is pronounced /sim-PEN-ga/ and is a contraction of Simpela Engelisa, "Simple English." Simpenga is a proposed international auxiliary language (IAL) based on the following premises:

- Those individuals most likely to learn a world auxiliary language will already have made an effort to learn a second language. They will most likely speak English, since English is spoken by between 300 to 900 million people as a second language, having a greater population of second-language speakers than any other language. Therefore, an IAL should be based on English.
- Basic English is the most well known IAL based on English, providing an 850-word subset of English. Unfortunately, Basic English presents serious learning difficulties to speakers of other languages, including an arbitrary orthography, a difficult phonology, a complex grammar, reliance on idioms and a paucity of verbs. An IAL should have a completely regular orthography, a simple phonology, a completely regular grammar, defined idioms and as many verbs as appropriate.

Simpenga is the first IAL that will meet all these objectives:

- **Easy To Read** - Simpenga words are easily spelled, with a one-to-one correspondence between each sound and letter.

- **Easy To Say** - Simpenga words are easily pronounced, with the language using just the five basic vowels (compared to English's 20 or so vowels) and 15 of the most common consonants (vs. English's 24), and with a very simple syllable structure (English *stretched* /stretʃt/ would be pronounced as /setereteta/ in Simpenga, one syllable becoming five).
- **Easy To Use** - Simpenga's grammar is regular, with few rules to remember; Simpenga does without grammatical number, articles, declensions, inflections, and pronouns with gender distinctions.
- **Easy To Learn** - Simpenga will have a basic vocabulary of 1000 words, all based on English, with many words being compounds (e.g., "there" is *dati'wera*, literally "that place"). Simpenga permits neologisms but no extensions to the basic vocabulary; all neologisms must be compounds, for easy learning.

Phonology

Simpenga contains five vowels:

/a/ (as in father)
/e/ (as in bear)
/i/ (as in beat)
/o/ (as in boat)
/u/ (as in boost).

The language has 15 consonants:

stops	/p/ /b/ /t/ /d/ /k/ /g/
fricatives	/f/ /s/ /h/
nasals	/m/ /n/
semivowels	/w/ /j/
liquids	/l/ /r/

Where Esperanto has 23 consonants, Simpenga has only 15 of the most-common consonants, a subset of the 20 most-common consonants identified in the UPSID (UCLA Phonological Segment Inventory Database) survey of 317 languages. Anyone who knows how to speak English will not have to learn any new sounds to speak Simpenga; those who do not speak English may have to learn a handful of new sounds, depending on their linguistic background.

Because Simpenga makes comparatively few distinctions between consonants, most consonants have allophones, of which only the principal ones will be mentioned here. The phoneme /f/ has allophones [f] and [v], and /s/ has allophones [s] and [z] (similar to Old English).

The phoneme /r/ includes any retroflex or any alveolar flap or trill.

As with Esperanto, the accent of a word in Simpenga is always on the penultimate syllable.

Orthography

Every word is spelled phonemically. There is a one-to-one correspondence between letters and phonemes. The alphabet is as follows:

a	b	c	d	e	f	g	h
i	l	m	n	o	p	r	s
t	u	w	y				

The following letters are not used: j, k, q, v, x, z.

The letter **c** always represents the phoneme /k/; **y** represents the semi-vowel /j/.

The roots of a compound word are separated by an apostrophe (e.g., *wati'wera*, "what place (where)").

Phonotactics

Phonotactics is the sequential arrangements of phonemes that are possible in a language. Every syllable in Simpenga follows this pattern:

    [C] V [N]

Where:

    [C] - is an optional non-nasal consonant:

        /p/, /b/ /t/, /d/ /k/, /g/

        /f/ /s/

        /w/ /l/, /r/ /j/ /h/

    V - is a mandatory vowel: /a/ /e/ /i/ /o/ /u/

[N] - is an optional nasal: /n/ /m/

Syllables in Simpenga may not begin with a nasal; thus, English *man* becomes Simpenga *eman*. This is necessary to eliminate ambiguity. If /n/ or /m/ could begin a syllable, a rule would have to be created to define the syllabification of words in ambiguous circumstances, like *mama (/MAM-a/ or /MA-ma/) or *animala* (/an-im-A-la/, /a-ni-MA-la/, or /a-nim-A-la/).

Simpenga has a comparatively small range of syllables, with just 210 (15 x 5 x 3) possible syllables, where Esperanto theoretically has over ten thousand possible syllables. (The exact number is impossible to determine, since Esperanto's vocabulary is not closed and its phonotactics has not been explicitly defined.)

Simpenga's morphology is designed to eliminate complex consonant clusters (e.g., /str/, /bl/, /pr/, /sp/), which are difficult for many speakers of Asian and African languages to pronounce.

Borrowings

When a word is borrowed into Simpenga, it must conform to its phonology and morphology. Thus *English* is borrowed as *Engelisa*.

Grammar

For simplicity, the grammar has been designed to eliminate most features that are not universal to analytic languages. Simpenga lacks number, articles, declensions, inflections, and pronouns with gender distinctions.

Nouns

The language has neither a definite article (*the*, Esperanto *la*) or an indefinite article (*a, an*). Nouns are not inflected for plural, gender or case. The relationship of case is expressed by prepositions.

Pronouns

Personal pronouns are not inflected for number, gender or case.

- The first person pronoun ("I, me, we, us") is *emi*
- second person ("you") is *yu*
- third person ("he, him, she, her, they, them, it") is *di*

All possessive pronouns (e.g., *mine, yours, his*) are formed by appending /n/ (e.g., *emin, yun, din*); possessive pronouns are treated as adjectives.

The reflexive pronouns (e.g., *myself, yourself, himself*) are formed by appending *selifa*, "self", to the possessive pronoun: *emin'selifa*, "myself"; *yun'selifa*, "yourself, yourselves"; *din'selifa*, "himself, herself, itself, themselves".

Adjectives

Adjectives precede the noun they describe. The comparative is always made by using the word *emore*, the superlative by *emosete*. There are no irregular comparatives (English *good, better, best* become Simpenga *guda, emore guda, emosete guda*). With the comparative, the conjunction *dan* is used (e.g., *emore dan*, "more than").

Verbs

The verb undergoes no change with regard to person or number or tense, which are instead conveyed as necessary through context. The verb in each clause is preceded by the word *do*. The passive is rendered by preceding a verb with *be*. The verb *be* is also used for "am, is, are, was, were, to be".

Adverbs

Adverbs follow the verbs they modify.

Correlatives

Esperanto's correlatives are concise but hard to remember. Simpenga instead uses compound words, which provide greater clues for remembering. Thus Esperanto *kiu* [*ki-*, "which" + *u*, "one"] becomes Simpenga's *wati'won*. Sample correlatives are *dise'dinga*, "this thing"; *dati'cinda*, "that kind of"; *som'wera*, "somewhere"; *ano'waya*, "no way"; and *ala'caza*, "for every reason".

A correlative consists of a modifier followed by a context. The six possible modifiers are:

>*wati* "what, which"
>*dise* "this"
>*dati* "that"
>*som* "some"
>*ano* "no"
>*ala* "each, every, all"

The 9 possible contexts are:

> *won* "one"
> *dinga* "thing"
> *cinda* "kind"
> *wera* "where, place"
> *waya* "way"
> *caza* "reason, cause"
> *tim* "time"
> *amonta* "quantity, amount"
> *wonin* "one's"

Correlatives total 54 different words.

Dummy subjects

Constructs with an unreferenced subject pronoun ("It was", "There are") are not acceptable and such sentences have to be rephrased. "It is raining" becomes "See the rain", *Do si rin.*

Tev'Meckian (Galaxy Quest)

I've been a Questarian (not a Questoid! only stupid reporters call us that) since seeing the show's first episode back in 1979. I was ten years old when *Galaxy Quest* premiered, and I loved the optimistic view of the future the show had, such a welcome relief after seeing the Moon ripped away in *Space: 1999* and seeing Starbuck stranded in *Battlestar Galactica*. So I'm a diehard Quest fan, not a newbie "Questerian" (as the folks at DreamWorks SKG keep misspelling it) brought in by the new movie (its about time! thanks DreamWorks, even if you don't know how to spell you had the good sense to buy the rights from the Network That Can't Be Named Because They Canceled The Best Science-Fiction Show Ever).

My favorite character was always Dr. Lazarus of Tev'Meck. In fact, in junior high, one of my nicknames was "Dr. Lazarus" (my other nickname was "Feff", when the stupid yearbook community misspelled my first name — now you know why I'm haunted by misspellings). I know, most people think I'm the Tech Sergeant Chen type, being a programmer and all but Sergeant Chen was good at hardware; I'm no good at hardware (I'm always confused by the difference between the digital conveyor and the molecular conveyor belt, for instance). And Dr. Lazarus was a Mak'tar, last of that wise, reptilian race: cold-blooded warriors when they needed to be, asleep-in-the-sun peacemakers when they could be. Our warrior-diplomat doesn't pinch people in the neck and have them swoon; when roused from his placid nature, he attacks them with the war hammer of Grabthar. The Mak'tar, as you should know, have ridged reptilian foreheads — this look was so successful that *Star Trek* stole this idea for its motion pictures: all of a sudden the Klingons have these bumpy foreheads, when they were just swarthy humans in the original show. The *Star Trek* movies were always stealing ideas from *Galaxy Quest*; don't get me started.

OK, you got me started. This whole Klingon phenomenon was a patent ripoff of Tev'Meckian. *The NSEA Bulletin*, one of the best fanzines of the early 1980s, was the first to start documenting Tev'Meckian in detail. By the third season, any Questarian knew at least a couple dozen words of Tev'Meckian. But, no, that Mork Okra fellow invents this whole goofy Klingon language (they don't have a verb for "to be"! what kind of faked-up language is that?!). I mean, in the original *Trek* series, it was called Klingonese. As in, "We like the Enterprise; we really do. That sagging old rust bucket is designed like a garbage scow. Half the quadrant knows it. That's why they're learning to speak Klingonese." This "Klingon" language they have now had nothing to do with the show; they just made it up.

Where's the consistency that we see with Tev'Meckian? Where are all the Klingon sayings in *Star Trek*? There weren't any. It was only after *Galaxy Quest* showed the Trek copycats how a rugged, guttural and warlike alien language could give an alien race verisimilitude that they started making up Klingon and Vulcan languages for all their silly movies.

Tev'Meckian in the series

There's a ton of Tev'Meckian in *Galaxy Quest*. Here are some highlights. All quotes are from Dr. Lazarus unless otherwise indicated.

La brarnep av sebnak muv. jod von av trut dros pog tud?
These catacombs are surprisingly modern. But why are they full of feline fur? ["The Cthulian Craft"]

Pock trun mek jud pan hen nuv mek av jal.
Verily, the right hand doesn't know what the left hand is doing. ["Split Decision"]

Truz Taggar-ke av brut drex thub.
Half a Taggart was better than two. ["Parallax Premonition"]

Trut av khep Peter-ke.
He's dead, Peter.. [Episode 31]

Fet nul lep wak buz pan paf. jack paf khep rad jux shag zef hot wak fros ses wak vod.
Crewman number six, we hardly knew ye. The vision of your death as the lava monster wobbled towards us will light our hearts. [Episode 31]

Kep mok frutwux av rox for frutzox shev.
Kep-Mok Bloodticks are part of this nutritious breakfast. ["The Scithyan Syndrome"]

Pef trom grabthar trut hom poj shod wak.
By the hammer of Grabthar, they would have nailed me. ["The Bivrakium Element"]

Trut dre fen dan mak'tar fen dan tas.
He who saves the life of a Mak'Tar saves the life of a friend. ["The Bivrakium Element"]

Khax za thack khax gru'tock!
Never give up, never surrender!. ["The Bivrakium Element"]

Bag wak av wak rovmeck tazmoj.
Yes, I am my brother's keeper. ["Friends Never Forget"]

Sheck vuk mek pebmeck sek poj has mak'tar wan brev woj. sheck bax mek dof wur hom poj bok wak thuv wej.
On the one hand, a sister might have meant the Mak'Tar race could continue. On the other hand, the volvac sac would have made me look bloated. ["Friends Never Forget"]

Shaz sheg mak'tar av khax khal trak.
The furrowed forehead of a Mak'Tar is not easily forged. ["The Shape Shifter of Textorian 3"]

Trut dre poj thuv sheck trut khep kux phock poj frer guck sag sa brul.
He who has looked on his death and lived has fallen through a wormhole in time. ["Wormhole In Time"]

Tug wak sok on brarnep mam Cthulaj-ke.
If we only had the catacombs of planet Cthulaj... ["The Hair Shirt"]

Pef trom grabthar pef nof warvan, paf mal av phum.
By the hammer of Grabthar, by the suns of Warvan, you shall be avenged. ["Escape From Tev'Meck"]

Mok av freb pob fev roj kep mok frutwux.
Revenge is a dish best served with Kep-Mok Bloodticks. ["Escape From Tev'Meck"]

Tug hos dred hom buj bug beck kuj mat tev'meckmat jog shoj fujshum jevrut hom drod. wak hom poj zos sa wak brul brusdrov.

If all aliens would learn to speak the logical language of Tev'Meckian, then such unfortunate misunderstandings would cease. We would have peace in our time continuum. ["Escape From Tev'Meck"]

Zar wak hovshef fros khax zar trot ped. roj hos wak pot wab thack, khet av paf dre ban wab bug wak khav trut lox.
The last of our disciples will not last much longer. With all our people preyed upon, it is you who must pray to us for his recovery. [one of the gods of Tev'Meck, speaking through Dr. Lazarus, "Return To Planet Amexon"]

Sok paf gub zog lazzarrus voz. trut drar fros grum trut. paf ban gun trut sa bog Adirolf-ke sheck mam Amexon-ke. nug kux sol.
Only you can prevent Lazarus' fire. His fever will consume him. You must wash him in the spring of Adirolf on the planet Amexon. Rinse and repeat. [one of the Tev'Meck elders, speaking to Lt. Tawny Madison in a dream, "Return To Planet Amexon"]

The Amexon quotes are so different from the rest of Tev'Meckian that they have long perplexed Questarians. Many have argued that they were not in fact phrased in the language of Tev'Meck at all, but were part of the Rulfian ruse. Yet, as I convincingly wrote in "Tawny: Brainy and Brawny," in Issue 43 of the *NSEA Bulletin*, Lt. Madison had full access to the computer, so she would have had the computer translate the quotes.

The Babel Text

It seems the modern proof that any science-fiction language is fully functional is to prepare a Babel Text written in it. Here goes:

Kux hos faj on vuk mat kux vuk wom.
and all earth have one language and one tongue
And all the earth had one language and one tongue.

Kux khet ham eb het sa trut trav hav khef, trut ham bug grep zob neck sa fren Shinar-ke, kux man trut bok trut phock bruj.

and 3n come about that in 3m wander from east / 3m come to stretch flat country in land Shinar-pname / and there 3m establish 3m live place.

And it came about that in their wandering from the east, they came to a stretch of flat country in the land of Shinar, and there they made their living-place.

Kux trut phaz vuk bug e, mun hur wak goj fur, nek trut leck. kux trut on fur khav, kur suz trut drap roj pham faj.

and 3 say one to e, hortative let 1 goj brick / nek trut leck. and 3m possess brick for stone / put 3m together with sticky earth

And they said one to another, Come, let us make bricks, burning them well. And they had bricks for stone, putting them together with sticky earth.

Kux trut phaz, mun hur wak goj rev kux map brock frep fros kes thack rad lul rad bet. kux hur wak goj graz voj khav wak, trem het wak tad khax av travmoj phuj wus faj.

and 3 say hortative let 1 goj town and tower whose top will go up as high as heaven / and let 1 make great name for 1 / so that 1 may never be wander-agtv over face earth

And they said, Come, let us make a town, and a tower whose top will go up as high as heaven; and let us make a great name for ourselves, so that we may not be wanderers over the face of the earth.

Kux fez ham pab bug pex rev kux map jut vuz fef av grur.

and lord come down to see town and tower which child man be build

And the Lord came down to see the town and the tower which the children of men were building.

Kux fez phaz, pex trut av hos vuk pot kux poj hos vuk mat. kux for av sok sal hen trut tad shom. kux hap khet fros khax av khad bug taz trut hav shun khock trut.

and lord say / see 3m be all one people and have all one language. and this be only start what 3m may do / and now 3n will never be possible to keep 3m from any purpose 3m

And the Lord said, See, they are all one people and have all one language; and this is only the start of what they may do; and now it will not be possible to keep them from any purpose of theirs.

Mun hur wak kes pab kux lex leb ruck trut mat, trem het trut fros khax av zom bug goj trut jen bug vuk e.

hortative let 1 go down and take away sense 3m language / so that 3m will never be able to make 3m clear to one another
Come, let us go down and take away the sense of their language, so that they will not be able to make themselves clear to one another.

Trem fez thar un trut leb sa kock rox faj. kux trut za thack grur trut rev.
so lord god send 3m away in every part earth / and 3m give up build 3m town
So the Lord God sent them away into every part of the earth; and they gave up building their town.

Trem khet av voj Babel-ke rem man fez lex leb ruck hos mat. kux hav man fez un trut leb phuj hos wus faj.
so 3n be name Babel-pname because there lord take away sense all language. and from there lord send 3m away over all face earth.
So it was named Babel, because there the Lord took away the sense of all languages; and from there the Lord sent them away over all the face of the earth.

The sounds of Tev'Meckian

Tev'Meckian root syllables take one of the following two forms:

Initial + Vowel + Final: *Tev, Meck, Mak, Tar, Kep, Mok*

Cluster + Vowel + Final: *Grab, Thar*

Here are the sounds indicated by these placeholders:

Initial = B, D, F, G, H, J, K, L, M, N, P, R, S, T, V, W, Z

Cluster = BR, DR, FR, GR, KH, PH, SH, TR, TH

Vowel = A, E, O, U

Final = B, CK, D, F, G, J, K, L, M, N, P, R, S, T, V, X, Z

If the word ends in a vowel, emphasis is on the next to last syllable, otherwise emphasis is on the final syllable.

Every word is pronounced as it is spelt. Surprisingly for an alien language, Tev'Meckian sounds are almost exactly the same as English sounds. Some differences are the distinctions between CK and K and KH, which sound identical to English speakers. Perhaps speakers of other Earth languages can tell the difference, especially those people who spit when they talk: speakers of Scottish or Hebrew maybe. The /k/ sounds distinguish words like *meck* ("sibling") and *mek* ("hand"), and *kep* ("devouring") and *khep* ("death"). Anyway, next time you are watching an episode of *Galaxy Quest* keep an ear out for the differences between these sounds and let me know what it is.

Little known and apparently complex rules govern whether or not to join root words with no punctuation, an apostrophe or a dash; e.g., *Grabthar* ("war+god"), *Tev'Meck* ("world+sibling"), *Kep-Mok* ("devouring+mother"; not only are Kep-Mok blood ticks consumed alive, they are considered to be most delicious when eaten while devouring their own young). We have followed established convention in compiling our lexicon.

The six-and-a-half rules of Tev'Meckian Grammar

Tev'Meckian grammar is so straightforward and logical that it is almost identical to English grammar. It can be summarized in just six-and-a-half rules.

1. **Nouns** - Any word that does not end in a vowel is a noun or proper noun. Unlike English, there are no definite or indefinite articles (*the; a, an*), nor are there different cases (e.g., *he* vs. *him*).

2. **Adjectives** - Adjectives typically proceed the noun they qualify. The superlative is formed by the word *bev*, the comparative by *brom*; "than" is rendered by *drex*.

3. **Personal Pronouns** - The personal pronouns are *wak* ("I, me, we, us"), *paf* ("you"), *trut* ("he, him, they, them"), *los* ("she, her, they, them"), *khet* ("it, they, them"), *bot* ("oneself").

Possessive pronouns have the same forms: *wak* ("my, our"), *paf* ("your"), *trut* ("their, theirs"), etc.

4. **Numbers** - The basic cardinal numerals are *vuk* (1), *thub* (2), *zem* (3), *shan* (4), *phej* (5), *lep* (6), *rug* (7), *khaz* (8), *bras* (9), *haj* (10), *drab* (100), *grez* (1000).

Tens and hundreds are formed by simple junctions of the numerals, e.g. 473 is *shandrab rughaj zem*.

Ordinals are syntatically adjectives and have the same form as the basic numbers (e.g. *phej*, "five, fifth").

Multiples are formed by the use of the suffix *-frez* (*phejfrez*, "five times"), fractions by *-jef* (*phejjer*, "one fifth"), collectives by *-noz* (*phejnoz*, "quintuple"), and distributives using the preposition *ox*.

5. **Verbs** - The copula is *av*.

6. **Adverbs** - Comparison as for adjectives.

6.5. **Names** - Foreign names require the suffix *-ke*. *Peter-ke*, "Peter". Only foreign names are capitalized; native names are not.

Only the first word in the first sentence of a paragraph is capitalized.

A note on the name *Lazarus*

I don't want to hear from any more rabid *Trek* fans about the inappropriateness of the name "Dr. Lazarus". I mean, all the Klingons had K- names (Kor, Koloth, Kras, Kang, et al), and all the Vulcan men had S- names, like Spock, Sarek, Surak, et al. Man, those *Trek* writers didn't know anything about real languages.

It is not true that *Lazarus* is not a standard Tev'Meckian word. In fact, it is simply an English simplification of *Lazzarrus* (both /z/ and /r/ were pronounced long), which was the Tev'Meckian name of Dr. Lazarus, meaning "very last offspring", the prophetic name given him by his mother, foretelling that he would be the sole survivor from the planet Mak'Tar.

The similarity to the name Lazarus from the Gospels is just a coincidence. Trekkies should note that Spock — Spock! — quoted Christ in the episode *The Trouble With Tribbles.*

Trek fans need to get a life, acknowledge that Taggart is better than Picard and stop spending all their time e-mailing me and writing anti-*Galaxy Quest* web sites. Freaks.

Lexicon

av be
avkav before
avkhav after
bag yes
ban must
bax other
bel near

bet heaven
bev most, majority
bog spring (of water)
bok make
bot oneself
brar treasure
brarnep catacomb ['treasure=cave']
brag ceasefire
bras nine
bref drink
brev could
brock whose
brom most
bruj place
brul time
brus whole
brusdrov creation, creature; continuum
brut improve
bug to
buj learn
buk speak
buz hardly
dan life
dep short
di short
dock impossible
dof vulvac
drab hundred
dran gross (144) [*dr*ab shanhaj sh*an*]
drap together
drar fever
dre who (relativization)
dred alien, stranger
drex than (comparative)
drod cease, stop
dros full
e another
eb about
eshor bat-winged lapinoid steed
faj earth
fef man (human?)
fefi humanoid
fen save

fep greetings, hello
fet mate, crewmate
fev serve
fez lord
fon daughter
for of
for this
fren land
frep top
frer fall
frez times (suffix)
fros will
frut blood
frutwux bloodtick
frutzox nutritious ['blood-feed']
fuj star
fujnoz galaxy ['star collective']
fujshum unfortunate
fur brick
gob drain
goj make
goz cause
grab war
grabthar a god ['war god']
graz great
grep stretch
grel million
grez thousand
grum consume
grur build
gru'tock surrender
gub can
guck through; finish, end
gun wash
hab dozen, twelve
haj ten
ham come
hap now
has mean
hav from
hen what
het that
hom would; wood

hos all
hot toward
hov train
hovshef disciple ['train-follow']
hur let
huv left (side)
id fission
ip spouse
ipthun marriage ['spouse union']
jaf sky
jal do, action
jef fraction suffix
jen clear
jev false
jevrut misunderstanding ['false think']
jod but
jog then
jor without
jub forget
juck emotion
jud negative
juf black hole
jut which
jux lava
kaj blind
karal strong, strength
kef west
kax knot
ke suffix marking foreign names
kel ill, sick
kem foot, feet
ken soak
kep devour
kes go
kesh off
ket nothing
khad possible
khak some
khal easy
khat ant; aunt
khav for
khax never
khaz eight

khef east
khep dead
khep death
khes remain
khet it, they, them; its, their
khock purpose
khom celibate
khux soul
kock every
kom father
kuj logic
kur stone
kuv lose, loss
kux and
la this, these
laz very
leb away
leck well
lep six
lex take
lock difficult
los she, her, they, them; her, their
lox recovery
lul high
lun letter, spell
mam planet
man there
map tower, mountain
mak'tar Lazarus's species
mat language
meck sibling
mek hand
moj agentive
mok mother
moz unable
muf forgive
mun come (hortative), arrive
muv modern
nad love
nam here; hear
neck country
nej unclear; fog
nek burn

nep cave, cavern
no want
nof sun, day
nok make
noz collective suffix
nug rinse
nul number
num depart
nup new
nupvuz baby ['new child']
nuv left
on possess
ox distributive
pab down
paf you, your
pam valley
pan know
peb female
pebmeck sister
ped long
pef by; buy
pex see
pham sticky
phaz say
phej five
phep sell
phepmoj salesman
phock live, survive
phockzom habitable
phuj over
phum avenge
pi spend
pock truly, verily
pog feline
poj have
pot people
pref bottom
preg contract
rad while, as
rem because
rev town
roj with
rov male

rovmeck brother
rox part
ruck sense
rug seven
rut with
rus offspring
rut think, thought
sa through
sag wormhole
sal start
sat enemy
sebnak surprising
sek might
ses light
shag monster
shan four
shaz furrow
sheck on
shef follow
sheg head, forehead
shev breakfast
shod nail, destroy
shom do, accomplish
shoj such
shun any
sok only
sol repeat
suz put
tad may
tarath damned
tas friend
taz keep
tazmoj keeper
teb hell
tef officer
tev world
tev'meck Tev'Meck ['world sibling']
tev'meckmat Tev'Meckian language
thack rise,raise; up, upon
thar god
tharat blessed
thub two, second; tooth
thuj score

thun union
thuv look
tock uncle
top animal
trak forge
trav wander
travmoj wanderer
trem so
trom hammer
trot much
truf water
trun right (side)
trut he, him, they, them; his, their
truz half
tud fur
tug if
tur dream, imagine
turrut believe ['imagine think']
un send
veb least, minority
ver civilization
vet nebula
vod heart
voj name
voz fire
von why
vuk one; first
vuz child
wab prey, pray
wak I, me, we, us; my, our
wan race
wej bloated, swollen
woj continue
wom tongue
wur sack
wus face
wux tick
za give
zack slow
zar last
zef wobble; common
zem three, third
zob flat

zog prevent
zom able, ability
zos peace
zox feed, food
zub certain
zuv parent

Denju

> *While I no longer blog about conlangs, I do still conlang: Denju started out as the language I used to name cities in Civilization IV and is now the language of Hexedland, the campaign setting for an OSR-style 5e campaign I run each week.*

Denju, also known as Reg Denju, is the lost language of the Cedreg Empire; the language lives on in names. Denju is close to Proto-Indo-European, which can provide additional vocabulary as needed. Sound changes tend to go in different directions than recorded languages did as they evolved from PIE:

- bhe -> ze
- bh > b
- dh# > d# [word final]
- dh > h
- gh > j /dzh/
- ki > vi
- k > c [orthographic change only]
- kh > c [orthographic change only]
- kw > qu [orthographic change only]
- uV > wV
- wa/i/o/u > fa/i/o/u
- skV > xV

Denju was a pidgin of two sister languages, formed when humans fled into dwarven caverns to escape an invasion. The language formed over the ensuing generation. Denju then became the common second language of the empire, resulting in creolization as the resurgent humans built a continent-spanning empire.

Most of what remains about Denju comes from copper tablets that had imperial messages imprinted on them.

Phonology

All Roman letters except for K are used to transcribe Denju; j corresponds to /zh/.

		labial	alveolar	post-alv	velar
nasals		m	n		
stops	voiceless	p	t		c/qu
	voiced	b	d		g
fricatives	fortis	f	s		x
	lenis	v	z	j	h
liquids			r	l	
semivowels		m̥	n̥/l̥	r̥/y	w

The language does have its own writing system, preserved in copper tables. The copper tablets of the Cedreg Empire were the primary method of record keeping, with runes stamped into the metal. They are typically 5 or 6 inches tall (14 centimeters) and 4 inches wide (11 centimeters) and often paper thin. Some are bent, and most have a patina (green layer). The tablets are usually valueless to anyone not a historian and through the ages most have been melted for creating bronze wares.

Eight iron stamps, long like pokers, were used to indent the tablets with runes. The stamps had shapes that could be rotated four different ways. Most were alphabetic, but a few were numeric.

⌐ P	¬ 2	⌋ J	⌊ L
∧ O	> 1	∨ V	< C
⋏ Z	⋗ Q	⊤ Y	⊰ N
A A	⊳ D	∀ U	⊲ I
⋈ M	≥ B	W W	≤ S
⊓ X	∃ G	⊥ 4	⊨ E
⊓ R	⊐ *	⊥⊥ 5	⊨ F
⊤ T	⊣ H	⊥ 3	⊢ K

The asterisk is the only punctuation symbol; rules about its use seemed to vary over time and aren't well established.

Numbers are written in an odd form of base 5 that starts from one, as there is no rune for zero:

- >> 11 = 1*5+1 = 6
- >⏋ 12 = 7
- >⊥ 13 = 8
- >⊔⊔ 14 = 9
- >⊔⊔ 15 = 10
- ⏋> 21 = 11
- ⏋⊔⊔ 25 = 15
- ⊔⊔⊔⊔ 45 = 25
- ⊔⊔⊔⊔⊔ 555 = 5*25+5*5+5 = 155

Grammar

Declension

Nouns, pronouns, and adjectives are declined.

Case	Singular	Plural
Nominative	*albo*, an elf (subject)	*albos*, elves (subject)
Vocative	*albe*, oh elf!	*albes*, oh elves!
Accusative	*albm̥*, an elf (object)	*albm̥s*, the elves (object)
Instrumental	*albi*, using/by/with an elf	*albis*, using/by/with elves
Dative	*alba*, to/for an elf	*albas*, to/for an elf
Ablative	*albob*, from an elf	*albobs*, from the elves
Genitive	*albu*, of an elf	*albus*, of the elves
Locative	*alboi*, in/at/to an elf	*albois*, in/at/to the elves

The creolization of the imperial language stripped away almost all irregularities, but one that survived is that personal pronouns use different roots for the first- and second-person singular and plural:

- m-, first person singular
- n̥m-, first person plural
- tw-, second person singular
- w-, second person plural
- c-, third person
- toi-, demonstrative (this/that)
- he-, demonstrative (the aforementioned)
- se-, reflexive pronoun
- y-, relative pronoun

- qu-, interrogative pronoun
- qui-, indefinite pronoun

An -r- is inserted before the declensional ending to make a noun an adjective: *albros*, "elven".

In the copper tablets, verbs and adverbs are conjugated for either the perfect or imperfect tense.

Conjugation

		Active	Medio	Stative
Perfective	1	m	ho	he
	2	s	do	te
	3	t	to	te
Imperfective	1	mi	hor	
	2	si	dor	
	3	ti	tor	
Imperative	2	su	swo	
	3	tu	two	
	N/A	ont	heno	wo

The mediopassive (Medio) was often used in a reflective sense, including providing a benefit (e.g., "I gave two coins" (for my benefit).

Other moods:

- Subjective infix *-fa-*
- Optative infix *-ye-*
- Injunctive infix *-vo-*

Syntax

The syntax is typically Subject-Object-Verb, with other arrangements used for emphasis. Notes:

- Noun phrases use postpositions.
- Time, then manner, then place ordering of postpositional phrases.
- A genitive noun phrase appears before the possessed noun phrase.
- Adjectives before the noun they modify.
- Demonstrative adjectives appear before nouns (this is a weak tendency).

- A name appears before a title or honorific.
- Subordinators appear at the end of subordinate clauses.
- Conjunctions are placed after the joined word (as in Latin).
- Relative clauses precede the nouns they modify.
- Auxiliary verbs follow the action verb.

Postpositions and Other Particles

Word	Meaning	Type
apo	from	postposition
bej	without	postposition
ceb	towards, into, at	postposition
ced	to, by, at	postposition
cen	on, upon	postposition
centi	against, at the end, in front of, before	postposition
ceti	from, back, again	postposition
cm̩b	around	postposition
cm̩ti	by, along	postposition
com	with	postposition
cu	off, away, too much, very	postposition
do	to	postposition
de	and, [sentence connector]	conjunction
hegstos	outside	postposition
hegstro	extra	postposition
hej	out	postposition
hen	in	postposition
henter	within, inside	postposition
heti	beyond, over (about quantity), besides	postposition
hopi	near, at, upon, by	postposition
ma	negator for commands	particle
mehi	in the middle	postposition
n̩	privative prefix	particle
hn̩	without	postposition
ne	sentence negator	particle
n̩heri	under	postposition
ni	down, under	postposition
nwu	now	postposition
nu	and, sentence connector	conjunction
o	interjection oh	interjection

pe	with, together	postposition
peri	around, through	postposition
pos	after	postposition
pro	before, forth, in front of, ahead of	postposition
que	and, word or phrase connector†	conjunction
r̥	for (enclitic), for the purpose of	postposition
tr̥cos	through	postposition
uper	above	postposition
upo	under, below	postposition
wai	expression of woe or agony	interjection
we	or, word or phrase disjunctor†	conjunction

†Placed after the second word (the joined word).

Lexicon

As the language is primarily used for role playing, its vocabulary skews towards that common to fantasy RPGs.

> *Denju has over 2600 words; for brevity and general interest, I've listed some RPG-related terms.*

Classes

alura [*alu* + *-ra*] sorcerer
barbara [*bar-bar-* + *-a*] barbarian
blajmen [*bhlagh-men-*] cleric, priest
carera [*kare-* + *-ra*] bard
cladra [< *kladhra*, "alder"] ranger, forester, logger
corosra [*coros* + *-ra*] warrior, fighter
derufid [*deru-* + *fid*] druid
diacorosra [*dia* + *corosra*] paladin, holy warrior
fid [*uid-*] seer
grigra [*grig* + *-ra*] rogue, brigand
gwerera [*gwr̥ə-dh(ə)-o-*, "he who makes praises"] troubadour
legiaz [*lēgjaz*, "one who speaks magic words"] enchanter, spellcaster
lujleuj [*luj* + *leuj*] oathbreaker, warlock, traitor
monwo [*monwo-*, "one who worships alone"] monk, hermit, guru
wegyo [*wegyo*, "one who wakes the dead"] wizard, witch; necromancer

Backgrounds

albo [*albho-*] white, albino, elf
anejomon [*ane + jomon*] djinn
boliyo [*bol-iyo-*] giant
caulra [*caul-* "to make a hole" + *-ra*, "one who"] halfling
druj [*dhuergh-, drugh-*] dwarf
gignosco [*gi-gnō-sko*] gnome
mon [*mon-, man-*] human; person
netṛjomon [*netṛ + jomon*] reptilian (lizard humanoid)
ṇsujomon [*ṇsu- + jomon*] devilman
semialbo [*semi- + albo*] half-elf
semimer [*semi + mer*] half-orc

Monsters

antṛjomon [*antṛ + jomon*] troglodyte
caprocer [*capro*, "he-goat" + *cer*, "horned head"] satyr
comer [*co- + mer*] hobgoblin
cuzhoz [*kuzdho-zd-*, "sitting (over) a treasure"] dragon
cuzhozdu [*cuzhoz + dura*, "dragon worshipper"] kobold
dedialbo [< *de-dia*, "without sun" + *albo*, "elves"] sunless elves
derc [*derk-*] monster; to look with an evil eye
eduno [*ed-un-o-*] man-eating giant, man-eater
epero [*epero-*] boar, wild boar
fai [*uai*] woe; wolf
gulturos [*gulturos*] vulture
gwoucer [*gwou*, "ox" + *cer*, "horned head"] minotaur
jomon [*(dh)ghom-on-*, "earthling"] humanoid, creature
lewontosderc [*lewontos*, "lion" + *derc*, "monster"] sphinx
mer [*mer-, mere-*] goblin; to rub away, wipe; harm; pack, rob
netṛderc [*netṛ + derc*] lizardman
ṇsu [*ansu-, ṇsu-*] ghost, spirit, demon
ṇsuquon [*ṇsu + quon*] hellhound
osthṛg [*osthṛg-*] animated skeleton
pento [< *pent-*] tree-giant, walking tree
pesdemel [*pes + demel*] sandworm
piont [*pī-ont-*] foe, fiend
prica [*par-ikā-*] fate, the Fates
sfardquon [*sfard- + quon*, "laughing dog"] hyena
spenwo [*spen-wo-*, "spinner"] spider
tex [*teks-*, "to weave; to construct"] weaver, web, spider, textile
ulquos [*ulkuos*] wolf
wegmer [*weg- + mer*] orc

Sample Text

The following is an excerpt from the *Ioslojo*, the Law of Copper, the first legal code of the land.

Licru diu iono toira dia pel buti.
each god-gen right.place-nom demonstrative god-dat earn copula-imperfective-indicative-3rd

The right place of each god is to that god to earn.

Conlangs at a Glance

The structure of this section was inspired by Richard Kennaway's classic Constructed Languages List, which unfortunately he has mothballed.

> *These descriptions are mostly based on information provided by the language creators. Sometimes the languages' web pages were consulted. If a date is provided, it's the "Year Began" from the database, or the date of publication if applicable.*
>
> *This list is a snapshot of conlanging in 2007, based on the Langmaker database. Many authors have continued work on their languages, which won't be reflected in these descriptions.*
>
> *Little information is available for some of these; pages on the web vanish like tears in the rain.*
>
> *Very many creators provided source languages, so I've emphasized that here. Typological info is so rare that I leave out relatively common choices— it's not very informative if you have six cases or use postpositions. You can assume every auxlang creator is aiming at aesthetics and ease of use.*
>
> *LM = Langmaker motto: "Prevent language death, create a language."*
>
> —MR.

A

Abakwi is a fictional language and was written by James Finley.

Achaean, an auxiliary language, was designed by Edward Hatfield, based on Minoan.

Achenu (Wil Guilford Jr. — wiki says Wil Pempem, 2005) is an artlang.

Acian (Ace, 2002) is a personal language.

Adam-Man Tongue (Edmund Shaftesbury, 1903) is a philosophical language created for a movement called Ralstonism.

Adare (Asier Gabikagogeaskoa, 2000) is a fictional diachronic language, spoken by the northern Vissar of Sevelorn.

Adawa, a fictional language, was crafted by Bruce Foerster.

Adelic (Scott MacLagan, 1993). With a vocabulary derived from Indo-European roots along lines similar to, but distinct from, the Germanic family of languages, Adelic has a rich internal history, giving it the sound and texture of an old European language and making it well suited for gaming.

> **Vellmöst! dü teed bintde de attlðunges gæmmstadd.**
> *Hello! Welcome to the Adelic Language Page.*

Adin (Nathaniel Knight, 2002) is a fictional language.

Adjuvilo (Claudius Colas, 1908) is an auxlang, a reform of Esperanto.

Adúlad (Trevor Wentworth, 1999) is a diachronic language.

Adûnaic was invented in 1946 by J.R.R. Tolkien. It was the language of the men of Númenor.

Advanced English (Pascal A. Kramm, 2004) is an auxlang and a reformed version of English.

Aeks Nótrï Nódikem (Niki Eve White, 2001) is a fictional language.

> **Il Yae el il Thïelwint elninï en den Laknewinten Jineitornwï, il Thïelwint ekemmï aeterna en in mïpeil Waerfenwï Ët.**
> a spirit is a (think→thought) (embody, passive tense = embodied) in the(acc.) [constrain→constraint][pl.]) [Imagine→Imagination, (/th/+/t/ = /th/ drops out) + possessive suffix (~nwï)], a thought (make, passive tense = made) eternal in a(acc) (hide, progressive tense) (society + possessive suffix ~enwï) script.
> *A spirit is a thought embodied in the constraints of imagination, a thought made eternal in a hiding society's script.*

Ælitian is a fictional language designed by Matthew See.

Aeo (Jonathana Tegire) is an all-vowel fictional language.

Aercant (Michael Bush, 2002) is a Romance-based auxlang.

Aertran (A.B. Basham, 2001) is a fictional language based on Celtic.

Aéstari (Nick Kalivoda, 2002) is a personal language.

Afrihili (K.A. Kumi Attobrah, 1970) was designed as an auxlang for the continent of Africa, with a phonology, vocabulary and grammar all derived from African languages. The grammar will be especially unusual to speakers of European languages. "Good day" was *Zuri lu*.

Ahlimite (John Whatmough, 2004) is a fictional language.

Ahua is the language of the Ahuans, designed by Richard Kennaway.

> **kktsô**
> *zither that sounds like a tree*

Ailurin (Diane Duane, 1999) is a professional fictional language, created for the wizard cats of *The Book of Night with Moon*.

Aingeljã (Ángel Serrano, 1986) is a personal language based on European languages.

Al Bhed (1987) was invented for *Final Fantasy X*; it is mainly a cryptogram of English.

Ålaku was written by Rory as a fictional language.

Alarian (Noby Nobriga, 1999) is a fictional diachronic language based on Finnish.

Aligian (Brandon (Mizenki), 2004) is a personal language, based on European languages plus Japanese.

AllNoun (Tom Breton, 1990). This language attempts to be as true to its name as possible, containing primarily nouns. It does use four operators as part of its grammar. It resembles a simple programming language and in fact has been modified by Breton for use as such. Very atypical, AllNoun is good inspiration for a fictional language for aliens.

Almalinian (Bryant K., 2002) is the language of the two Races of Cardë: Men and Celts.

> **Tol telgael i pennes dónumë éldamor niel lomen ar nomdan élcanen.**

Now the whole world had one language and a common speech.

Alpha Smart is a fictional language developed by Jack Durst.

Alphistian (Tony Skags, 1967) is a fictional language created for the Alphistia micronation, based ion Nordic languages.

> **Ya skanset tat ve skala komen semorne**
> *I said that we will come tomorrow.*

Alrusomanz (Elliot Jackson, 2005) is a personal language based on European languages.

Alurhsa (Anthony Harris, 1977) is the language of the Alurhsa people of the planet Aluria, in the Andromeda galaxy.

> **Vrejónevár zh'Óñenyá — Dweválv!**
> *Proletariat of the World, Unite!*

Alwato (Stephen Pearl Andrews, 1871) is a philosophical language.

Ambarnic (Jordan Lavender, 2003) is a diachronic language, heavily influenced by Welsh.

Amelic was developed by Almirus as the language of *Nazaredi Yeshua, Yehudi no Meoki* (Jesus of Nazareth, King of the Jews).

Americai Speak (Ruby Olive Foulk, 1937) is an auxlang, a phonetic and grammatical simplification of English.

Amerysk (Paal Filssunu, 1979) is an auxlang based on Old Norse and Anglo-Saxon.

Amman-Iar (David Bell, 1990). If you have ever longed to see one of Tolkien's languages brought to completion, you will love Amman-Iar, created in the spirit of Sindarin and Quenya and set in a new continent of Middle Earth. Originally inspired by Elvish, Amman-Iar has grown into something quite different, with a unique flavor of its own and a richly realized grammar.

> **alan életh áni dais cûos erechöiron i daurar.**
> *He killed the tiger with a bow in the forest.*

Amtorian (Edgar Rice Burroughs, 1938) is a professional fictional language, used in *Lost on Venus* and other novels set on that planet.

Anaqaen, (Chris Bouchard, 2002) is a fictional language, based on Sindarin but with inflections modeled on Latin.

> amaenhenel qaeny, qeneny, i aeny lomsath elabeqi Anaqaeny.
> *Go speak, write, and understand the language of Anaqaen thoroughly.*

Anawanda was created by Tommaso Donnarumma for the Anawanda tribes of the Southern-Eastern Archipelago of Elaire.

> ná ágam máttuur tárii, muuníí muun máram addáttirran
> and who? warrior to.win.IMPFCT.3S this.OBL it him chief to.bestow.a.gift.to.OPTATIVE.3S
> *(And) the chief will bestow a gift to the warrior who wins (lit. Which warrior wins, the chief will give him a gift)*

Ancallon (Aran Kuntze, 1990) is a continent created for RPG, with eight different languages.

Ancient Language (Christopher Paolini, 1999) is a professional fictional language, appearing in *Eragon*, and based on Old Norse.

Ancient Tongue of the Wise (Mike Singleton, 1995) is a professional fictional language; fragments are recorded in the manual for his video game *Lords of Midnight: The Citadel*.

Andanese (Andrew Leventis, 2002) is a personal language, in which "everything can be expressed as one word and that one word functions like every other word; all sentences behave as if they were single-morpheme words."

An'dorian (Spence Hill, 1990) While less well known than the officially sanctioned Klingon language, An'dorian is as richly developed and represents the language of the blue-skinned Andorians from the original *Star Trek* TV series. It has eight noun classes and an elaborate TAM system.

> Iit im Thezuraa oth emzireeng.
> (A colloquial expression, the equivalent of "run along and play with some antimatter, kid.")
> *Go ask the Philosophers.*

Anglish (Bryan Ashley James Parry, 2004) is a jargon, based on Germanic languages.

Anglo-Romance (Mattia Suardi, 2004) is a personal language, a reform of English to make it more international.

Anglo-Saxon Computerese (Carl T. Berkhout, 1996). Not every constructed language has to be large and complex. This consists of the hundred or so terms you would need to be able to talk about computers in Old English. Most terms are compounds of real Anglo-Saxon words: for instance, the word for "computer" is *circolwyrde*.

Anikin (Felix Brender, 2003) is a fictional language designed for "easy grammar and nice sound."

Animalic (Mary Incledon and Marjorie Incledon, 1905) is a simple language made by Tolkien's cousins; it was the first of someone else's conlangs that he was exposed to, and it inspired Nevbosh.

Aninese was invented by Andre Steffens. It is the language of Uteged.

> **Azarade alovès, co diomamoiroènibone òsa co dionamoroènine.**
> *One is not King through former deeds, but through continuing ones.*

Anklis (Martin Ferretti, 2003) is a fictional language based on English.

Antapa (Jan Havliš, 1999) is a fictional language based on Arabic and Hebrew using vocalic roots.

Antido (René de Saussure, 1907) is an auxlang, a reform of Esperanto. The name expresses its opposition to Ido.

Antique Lantian (Bucchianeri Marco, 2003) is a personal language.

An'tur (Sander Dieleman, 2003) is a personal language.

Ape or Mangani (Edgar Rice Burroughs, 1912) is a professional fictional language. The most details are in *Tarzan the Terrible*.

Apralios (Christopher Mules, 1999) is a fictional language, based on European languages.

Aqobagena is a personal language. It was crafted by Quentin Read.

Aquitan is a fictional language designed by Frances de Vilalonga.

Arēsæd (Drydic_Guy) is a fictional language.

Aran'Esei (Eric the Best, 2002) is a fictional language.

Arcaicam Esperantom (Manuel Halvelik, 1969) is an "Old Esperanto", allowing Esperanto authors to cite texts in a hypothetical archaic form of their language.

Archeía (Anselm Huppenbauer, 1998) is a fictional diachronic language created for the Ailavundean people.

> **Os· Énos yerquendaǧ' anevende o· δωra, ya ce diá eξanna, ním θenãm lon θainon – ya to· rỹa ye to· viswe oide ní gedeψe oía gúmya os· lŋyas ekoinos.**
> *In the tales of the wind the trees became bare, and if I go out, I woudn't find any apples – and the crimson and the sweet would only remain in one dream of a lost summer.*

Arden was crafted by Tommaso Donnarumma.

> **Þundor nè oyod: Iðilei vi. Eddawe ili alma tavenei lei. Kundo vauroþòu laun. Emà ine fert koppo tikèn te þuri ili nè þundor taumòn to; nè oyodo eneir te aivàl te buloyo gara.**
> *Winter and wine: It rains. Down from the sky the water falls. Brooks are freezing. But throw wood into the fire and drive the winter out; and pour sweet wine without thrift.*

Arêndron (Michael S. Repton, 2003) is the language of the Arêndron Empire. Its ancestor is Proto-Ileuran.

> **Vîat nârdjen Alîsa ghurim zaudenos zilnui hâloi shûmjen telor, orcenosta khauran saunæth.**
> *Alice was beginning to get very tired of sitting by her sister on the bank, and of having nothing to do.*

Arionak (Eric Anger, 2003) is an auxlang.

Arkian (Jan Havliš, 1995) is the official language of the micro-community Ark. Besides its unique set of source languages (Turkish, Finnish, Chinese and Czech), Arkian has a unique script and unique grammatical features like indefinite animate gender and frame clause construction.

> **Mak teks k var bi ge Ten k var bi ent rata ia na, bi k fo na ke ban k id taxt org le, uksa oks eo is xeta ku var bi, dean nam or hist sr ke ralt ven ke Um, ent roum ku id un hez is.**

The North Wind and the Sun were disputing which was the stronger, when a traveller came along wrapped in a warm cloak.

Arlipo (Lubor Vitek, 2003) is an auxlang, which aims to simplify Esperanto and make it more euphonic.

Ar-na-Kamyt was invented by Edward Field as a jargon, based on Akkadian and Sumerian.

Arnira (Kelahäth Ohar, 2002) is a fictional language.

Aronian (Dillon Shaw, 2002) is a diachronic language based on Turkish, Hungarian, and Finnish.

Arulo (Max Talmey, 1925) is an auxlang.

Arvan (Nicola Curat, 1998) is a fictional language based on Savoyard, spoken in a principality named Val-des-Monts.

Arvorec (Deiniol Jones, 2002) is an artlang created as a modern descendent of Gaulish.

â n'ych-chwy dwêwth dyf pon yw ma ovyned, ma'ch plac?
Can you tell me which stop to get off at?

Ascenderati (John Whatmough, 2004) is a fictional diachronic language, created as the court language of Thyrenacia.

Ascian (Gene Wolfe, 1980) is a professional fictional language. It comes from a totalitarian society, and supposedly every utterance must be a quotation from an approved collection of proverbs.

ASD-STE100 (Simplified Technical Engish) is a logical language, a version of English with strict meanings, created by people in the aerospace industry.

Asha'ille (Arthaey Angosii, 2000) is a fictional language, is for the felinoid species that originated in the Central Plains of Cresaea.

Cha'te mirv vel'jas emaen seni! Mish lisev ne asha'ille vae'nesaea.
IMPERATIVE-POLITE come to-online page mine! may read OBJECT Asha'ille LOCATION-there.
Please come to my web page! You can read about Asha'ille there.

Asht (SPH, 2004) is a loglang aiming at "logical construction whilst preserving usability."

Asmeni (Kári Emil Helgason, 2000) is a fictional language.

Ašnaî (Maknas, 2003) is a fictional language.

Asrord-Dânis (Asier Gabikagogeaskoa, 2001) is a fictional language, that of the warrior Phir-Annôn.

Atarel (Seiji Suenaga, 2004) is a personal language.

> **Weyo ra vilu na heim iru. Tes ra cata herna esu.**
> I [particle] want [particle] home to go. It [particle] cold here is.
> *I want to go home. It is cold here.*

Atevi is a fictional language, originating in *Foreigner* (1994) by C.J. Cherryh. It was elaborated by Rodlox R and later Spence Hill.

Atlan or Atlantean (Graham Mabey, 1981) was created by as a diachronic language, based on Germanic and Romance.

Atlango (Richard A. Antonius, 2002) is an auxlang.

> **Qi tu saba ke juste plato esta awtoro di la dikturo ke la ple grana bedaro por homajo estu komuna lango?**
> *Did you know that it was Plato who said that the greatest gift for humanity would be a common language?*

Atlantean (Marc Okrand, 2001) The language of Disney's animated film, *Atlantis: The Lost Empire*.

> **SOH-lesh MAH-toh-noat MY-loh THATCH-toap. Kwahm TEH-red-seh-nen.**
> *All will be well, Milo Thatch. Be not afraid.*

Atlo-Greek (Edward Hatfield) is an auxlang, based on Greek and Egyptian.

Attrendian (Kevin R. VanDenBreemen, 2003) a fictional language, for the people of Attendia.

> **1op tos sa papop leco ohastop xeasx olonop eru.**

1(adj) language and common speaking/speech now(plural animate descriptive) [they were having] entire(plural animate) world.
Now the entire world had one language and common spech.

Aubhárith (Anselm Huppenbauer, 2005) is a fictional diachronic language, derived from Arêndron.

aUI (W. John Weilgart, 1950) is an auxlang for aliens; each of its 7 5 12 18 phonemes is a semantic primitive— aUI means 'space-mind-sound', i.e. "the language of space."

Auld Elvish (Henry Beard & Douglas Kenney, 1969) is a professional fictional language, a parody of Tolkien's elvish languages, found in *Bored of the Rings.*

Aulingese is the language of Uteged and was developed by Andre Steffens.

Oo ploeng aaoïe y ngooie.
The flower is beautiful.

Auxilingua (Jay Bowks, 1979) Is an auxlang.

Avaeran is a fictional naming language.

Avarin - A separate language family from Eldarin (which contains all the other Elvish tongues covered here), Avarin is almost completely unexplored; Tolkien supplied only six words.

Avesta (H. Ellis Ensle, 1974) is a loglang for the fictional Ankanya, the people who fell from a star, the gods (*enkan*) of Atlantean legend..

Ezdu ega avutwe batro vau ezdu hega vutwaxeth lhäntromno abartre fongúleg. Sinaxu uaga?
Used one the-intellect to-choose and used another intellect-greater-own to-justify-only the-choices had-made-already-them-he. Wise-more-was which-of-them?
One used his intellect to choose and another used his stronger intellect only to justify the choices that he had already made. Who was the wiser?

aw'ingiwa was designed by Apollo Hogan as a fictional diachronic language.

Awolang (Daniel Carrasco, 2004) is a stealth language.

Axunašin (Mark Rosenfelder, 1995) is a diachronic language, the language of ancient Axunai, and a sister of Cadinor.

Ayeis (Asier Gabikagogeaskoa, 1994) is a fictional language based on European languages.

Ayeri (Carsten Becker, 2003) is a fictional language.
> **Eri silveváng aibannama padangin. Nivaie evaenain eri ming silvoieváng caparei.**
> TRG=INST see.(2sg.AGT) OBL(ani).good.only heart.TRG
> *One can only see well with one's heart. The essential is invisible to the eyes.*

Ayhan (Barry Garcia, 1999) is a fictional language, inspired by Austronesian languages.

Azak (Christophe Grandsire, 1992) is a personal language, meant for exploring ergativity and agglutination.

B

Baanzish is a fictional language and was created by Rupert A.H. Barnes.

Babalo (Ajin Kwai) is a fictional language with creole-like grammar.

Babm (Fuishiki Okamoto, 1962) is an auxlang.

bac (Matthew Butt, 1997) is a personal language.

Bahasa Tumilenia (Tha Original Penrithian Bandanna Kid, 2001) is an auxlang.

Bahasan (Leo John Moser, 1988) is a personal language with a lexicon derived from a multitude of languages.

Bala-i-balan is a stealth language and was created by Muheddin circa 1550.

Balbylon is an auxiliary language. "To produce phrases of Balbylon you combine words of several languages in a way to get beautiful sensible phrases, as in poetry. In fact, it's multilingual poetry."

Barakhinei (Mark Rosenfelder, 1999) is a sister language to Verdurian and Ismaîn, derived from Cađinor.

Barallen was written by Kevin.

> **Yen'mai daka'ta na Barallen id'mah.**
> *Learn to speak the Barallen language.*

Barmuur (José Martínez, 2003) is a naming language for a text adventure.

Baronh was crafted by Hiroyuki Morioka. It is a professional fictional language, made for the Abh in his *Seikai* (Star World) series (1999+).

Barsoomian (Edgar Rice Burroughs by 1900) is the language of Mars; see the chapter in this volume.

Barushlani (Boudewijn Rempt, 2002) is a fictional language, for Andal.

> **li?yam.e s?.sed**
> sisters_daughter.ERG feed
> *Sister's daughter is feeding it.*

Basic Anglo-Saxon English (Jeffrey Henning, 1995). Jeffrey calls it an "unimaginative derivative of Basic English, replacing all words not of Anglo-Saxon origin."

Basic English (C.K. Ogden, 1930). *Basic*, an acronym for "British American Scientific International Commercial," is a subset of English. Any Basic English text is also a valid English text, but Basic English has just 850 core words (not counting inflectional forms); extensions to the lexicon are permitted for specific subject domains. Ogden hoped Basic English would be used for teaching English as a second language, but because Basic English permits the full complexity of English grammar, this was not practical.

Basple (Kumouri Endriago, 2005) is an auxlang.

Bendeh (Nathaniel G. Lew) was created for a fictional parallel Earth.

> **Muk datilemdef xél tés, lalempag enkudok getorin?**
> *Can you tell me please where I can buy a drink?*

Benjish (Benjamin Bruce, 2002) is a fictional language, for the province of Benjaland in the Republic of Niwic.

Berendt (Alfred Berendt, 1977) is an auxlang.

Bitruscan (Jay Bowks, 1979) is an auxlang designed to be "minimal."

Biyuron, a fictional language, was invented by Pablo Flores.

Blaaninian (Lord Blaa, 1998) is a succinct and flexible language, designed in theory to sound like a cross between ancient Greek and Hebrew.

> **vab mó tsaí loopda elesada ev tubnó geldwanu.**
> [see + past + 1st person] [article: indef plur acc] [glue + acc] [box + inessive] [window + inessive] [art: indef sing gen] [shop + gen] [house + adhesive]
> *I saw some glue in a box in the window of a shop next to a house*

Black Speech was written by J.R.R. Tolkien as a fictional language for the servants of Sauron.

Blaia Zimondal (Cesare Meriggi, 1884) is a philosophical language.

Blissymbolics (Charles Kasiel Bliss, 1949) is an ideographic auxlang, consisting of a set of 120 core graphemes.

Blitz English (Mark Hucko, 1984) is an English-based auxlang.

Bogomol, a fictional language, was developed by Terrence Donnelly.

Bolak (Leon Bollack, 1899) is an auxlang.

Bonjang (Victor Medrano, 2003) is an auxlang with mostly non-European roots.

Bopal (M. Streiff, 1887) is a philosophical language.

Borg was designed by Terrence Donnelly for *Star Trek*'s cyborg culture with a collective consciousness.

> **borgh tve vagh**
> *Borg language*

Brandonian (Jordan Kay, 2003) is an auxlang, based mostly on Romance languages.

Breathanach (Geoff Eddy, 1998) is the first constructed language inspired by Q-Celtic on the Web. It is the "Q" to Brithenig's "P": what might have happened if Latin had been filtered through a Gaelic phonology.

> éificheamh un urbh por nua, cun thuirr ca thaing eall caol, porcha nua faichirmhe u nòimh por nua e non seirmhe dispirse suibhir fàich dia'll mund.
>
> *Come, let us build a city for ourselves, with a tower that touches the heavens, that we make a name for ourselves and are not scattered over the face of the entire land.*

Brithenig (Andrew Smith, 1996) is one of the best of the fictional languages on the web. Brithenig is the language of an alternate history, being the Romance language that might have evolved if Latin speakers had displaced Celtic speakers in Britain. Brithenig has undergone sound changes similar to those of Welsh, and has borrowed from Old Celtic and from Old, Middle and Modern English.

> Gwath, gwan a eddiffigar yn giwdad per nu, cun yn tyr ke dang a llo chel, ke nu ffagen yn nôn per nu e sun ysparied rhen syrs feig lla der inteir.
>
> *Come, let us build a city for ourselves, with a tower that touches the heavens, that we make a name for ourselves and are not scattered over the face of the entire land.*

Broken German (Joshua E. Horn, 2004) is an auxlang based on Germanic and Slavic languages.

Broyan was invented by Boudewijn Rempt.

> Ya yo lyanetan yo yerdat.
> *I and you, we give her a jewel*

Bruceish (Bruce A. Brejta, 2002) is a fictional language.

Brujeric (Gregory H. Bontrager, 2003) is the language of the witches and warlocks of Brujerland. It's based largely on Western Romance.

> Un ĝurno, vendrà un home donte la personalità defiarà la descendença. Ilo so levarà à estir un grando reĝo da Sorceriterra.
>
> *One day, there will come a man whose character will defy his lineage. He will rise to be a great king of Sorcerland.*

Bryatesle (Miekko, 2003) is a personal language based on European languages.

Bucovian (Nicola Curat, 2000) is a personal language, inspired by Albanian and Slavic.

Bvazred (Anselm Huppenbauer, 2004) is a diachronic language, a sister of Archeía.

C

C-14 (Rodlox, 2004) s a personal language.

C-23 and **C-24** (Anthony Docimo, 2004) are personal languages, with a goal of "disambiguating polysemy".

Cacone (Daniel Sacks, 1960) is an auxlang.

Caďinor (Mark Rosenfelder, 1995) is an artlang, created as the ancestor of Verdurian and Barakhinei. In general feel it resembles Latin.

Calénnawn (René Uittenbogaard , 2000) is a fictional language.

Çanil is a fictional language and was invented by Maknas.

Canis (Ron de Leeuw, 2003) is an auxlang with broad sources.

Cannic (Nikhil Sinha, 2004) is a personal language.

Ca'olaeg (2000) is a fictional language.

Ceindian (Jan Havliš, Jim Morgan, 1995) is a personal language, a development of Penguinean.

Ceiteish (Eric Anger, 2004) is an auxlang based on Celtic languages.

Celltiecc (Duke Keenan, Nathaniel Ament-Stone, Dean Powell 1998) is an auxlang based on Celtic languages.

Center (Robert Heinlein, 1963) is a fictional imperial planet whose langauge is descibed as "a pidgin language... uninflected, positional, and flat". It appears in *Glory Road*.

Cepperjoleddicg (Chris Paull (Zeke Fordsmender), 1998) is a personal language, derived from Old Norse, Gaelic, and Gothic.

Ceqli (Rex F. May, 1996) is an auxlang based on languages worldwide.

> **Kyu bwa? Ten pani, biru, kola.**

'?' drink? Have water, beer, cola.
How about a drink? We have water, beer, and cola.

Cetonian (James E.F. Landau, 1998). If you have ever wondered what language whales might speak, you will be interested in Cetonian, the language of the cetaceans of the planet Wuiou. All words are made up out of eight syllables, each approximating a sound that can be made by the cetacean's blowhole: *ha, ho, hui, ma, o, u, wa,* and *wui.*

ohaho . mauo . ha . hoo . wui . wuiuma . ouu . ho . hawui . wuiwui . uu . wawuiho . uha . mauo . ha . waohui . wui . ho . hawui.

although shark it not then(past) be_able_to use towards signal Wuiwui he know that shark it understand then(past) towards signal

Although the shark could not use communication, Wuiwui knew that the shark could understand language.

Chicken (Jack McLaren & Pat Spacek, 1996) is a parody language.

Chickenese (Damon M. Lord, 1996) is a "silly and humorous" language.

Chin'yn-theuk is a logical language. It was created by script.

Ch-m Tlondor (Jeff Lilly, 1004) is a fictional language inspired by Semitic morphology.

Choba (Thomas Leigh, 1983) is a personal language.

Po sato kalëa chë tolëti shiga.
There are some houses on this street.

Choton (Pascal A. Kramm, 2003) is an auxlang based on English, German, and Japanese.

Chovur, (J. Fatula, 2002) is a fictional diachronic language, based on Central Asian languages.

Chunotl (Pablo Barenbaum, 2004) as a personal language, based on Nahuatl, Greek, and Guaraní.

Chusole (Glenn Kempf, 2002) is a fictional language, whose sources include Kazakh, Korean, Japanese, and Russian.

Cilthic (Daniel S. Andersen, 2001) is a fictional language made for the world of Sorukan.

Cinpzy was invented by Shinali as a "parody of every hard thing about natlangs."

Ciravesu is the language of a fictional parallel Earth.

> **Cava tiui chyn chelma fenge unni.**
> man friend 4sm.pp wine.acc draught made
> *The man's friend drank his [the man's] wine*

Cispa (Herman Miller, 1990) is a fictional language made for the rodent-like Zaik people of Mizar.

Clalia (Johannes Hufnagel, 2002) is a fictional language for a small population of nomads on a distant planet.

> **Wevi gane làc, duvi cna'e na, Wevi, ta ja nuh'ate ferç et mart. Qe ta nuhe minlan an luv.**

Classical Yiklamu (Mark P. Line, 1997) is a loglang.

> **Fine yufab tikyika mu yetun yegicak pejyuga yujde.**
> *Colorless green ideas that are hatched by linguists sleep the most soundly.*

Clavis Convenientiae Linguarum (Joachim Becher, 1661) is a philosophical language, where both words and inflections are represented as integers; e.g. 6753:3 is "prince (singular dative)."

cni-vcti (Omid Ghayour, 1999) is an auxlang based on Indo-European languages.

Coastal Zein was invented by Drydic_Guy. It is a fictional language.

Coeniathen (Anselm Huppenbauer, 2003) is a diachronic language.

> **Bhiâ soe nw ânon-nîr, io gies châlw ym- swn cwênon! Giân-Oeryn eisd dyphwn' swn l' ânon nîr.**
> Succeed you.DAT good sequence.OBL-year, and celebrate happy with- your.OBL wife.OBL!
> *Have a good new year, and celebrate happily with your wife!*

Common Germanic (James Johnson, 2002) is a Germanic auxlang.

Comunleng is an auxlang with Germanic and Romance roots.

Çomyopregi (Damátir Ando, 1998) is an artlang, derived directly from Proto-Indo-European.

Conlangs of Destruction is a site by Conrad Cook, featuring Granolish ("the language of romantic relationships"), Gist (with an "ever-changing vocabulary"), and Witness ("A philosophical language gone bad. Based on the inarticulate sounds of Ludwig Wittgenstein").

Conlang #4892 (Justin B. Rye, 2001) is the language of a role-playing campaign.

> **¡Deira·n isija·don jika ak na·da sueker·ap!**
> Sword·2ndFamiliar Earth·NeuterOblique Put·Optative2ndFamiliar Or 2ndFamiliar·Object Kill·1stExclusive
> *Put your sword on the ground or I'll kill you!*

Corint (Daniel Andreasson) is a fictional language.

Cosmian (Wilbur M. Law Beatty, 1922) is an auxlang.

Criollo was designed by Chlewey Thompin as a fictional language.

Cruons (Stefan Lubbersen, 2003) is a personal language.

Cuërna (Jack McNeill, 2001) is a personal language inspired by European languages

Curco (Pablo Flores, 1999) is the language of a fictional parallel Earth.

Cyberyak (Eric Beaubien, 1996) is an auxlang with just 220 roots. It has a variant, Microyak, with just fifty.

Cytrurian (Martin. 1999) is a personal language.

D

Ða difi is a fictional language designed by Jonathan North Washington.

Da Mätz se Basa (Henrik Theiling, 2004) is a personal language.

Dael (Dallin Woolstenhulme, 1993) is a fictional language.

Daimyo, for a creature like a gargoyle, was invented by Muke Tever.

wihi aflicem zinsuam kuri zinsu
Fight linguistic extinction, invent a language.

Daisilingo (Jian Huang, 1997) is an auxlang.

Daléian (Carsten Becker, 2003) is a fictional language.

Dalgarno's Universal Language or *Ars Signorum* (George Dalgarno, 1661) is a philosophical language. Examples: *N* "living being", *Nη* "animal", *Nηk* "quadruped", *Nηka* "horse."

Damin is fascinating and well worth learning about. This language was used by the Lardil tribe of Mornington Island off the coast of Australia. It was used as an initiation language for men and was an unusual variant (or speaking style or slang) of the "everyday" Lardil language.

Danan (Bruce Rimell, 2003) is a personal language, originally based on Basque and Tahitian.

Zadani piroriveton, nezaixaoheonamni ho! *LM*

Danarib (Gary Wann, 1995) is a fictional diachronic language.

Danovën/Arovën (Joshua Shinavier, 1994) is a loglang, intended to be syntactically ambiguous, clear, and precise.

Wilerin endya porvel windïav flëntya.
During-one-time exist farmer horse-owned-whose flee-past.
Once there was a farmer whose horse ran away.

Dapnant (David Durand) is the language of the dawn of humanity.

Shîgitmò'sh òlu'sasp pu pnqòk baghala'th yushlòs
THIS-CLAUSE-PRESUMPTIVE was-happening-at-some-time INT? They the-old-enfeebled-one bit
When did they bite the old enfeebled one?

Darmok is the language of the Children of Tama from *Star Trek*, crafted by Raphael Carter.

Darseni (Libor Sztemon) is a fictional language.

Darynese (Rebecca Harbison, 2004) is a fictional language created for a space opera web comic, *Phoenix Dawn*.

Dashul (Anthony Raymond Bullard, 1996) is a loglang. Its philosophy "rejects both subjectivism and intrinsicism."

Dêbiua (Hans Straub, 2003) is a personal language, inspired by Arabic morphology.

Degaspregos (Tom Wier, 1999) is a personal language derived from Proto-Indo-European.

> **Boreawentoxo e Saweloxo añgapeutabit, hweos galaras bit, hwanose tratoros ambipeliwesas perekaiage werpoge gwamit.**
> *The North Wind and the Sun were disputing which was the stronger, when a traveller came along wrapped in a warm cloak.*

Dekavurian (Geoff Eddy, 2001) is a fictional language, closely related to Gothic.

Delason (Nizar Habash, 1990) is the fictional language of the Mediterranean country of Salamon. Its phonology is "a regularized marriage of Spanish and Modern Hebrew." Its vocabulary is drawn from 20 natural languages.

Delendian (John Shilpetski IV, 2002) is the fictional language of the Dyalinti.

Dementian (Jeremy Boyd. 2004) is a fictional language.

Demonic/Alorian (Kevin Urbanczyk, 2004) is a diachronic language with "ugly, difficult consonant clusters."

Denden (Boudewijn Rempt, 1984) is a fictional-world lingua franca used on the northern continent of Andal, with real-world inspiration drawn from French, Classical Chinese, Classical Tibetan and Nepali.

> **Aya! sémari'ryadhe gabu ni**
> *I wish I was a porcelain cup [the title of a song]*

Denisian (Eric Anger, 2004) is an artlang based mostly on Celtic.

Den'Ksie (Marie Winger) is a fictional language.

Dermensin is a fictional diachronic language by Eugenio M. Vigo.

Derrae (Jotomicro, 2004) is a personal language.

Desa Chat is a loglang developed by Peter Davis.

> **Camisi vigi gojumi.**
> *Tomorrow I will read.*

Descubralía (Shinali, 2033) is a fictional language based on Spanish.

Detbap is for Uteged and was written by Andre Steffens.

> **zyr, RAS, TEQ, FIM, bon, kut, zyr RAS, RAS RAS**
> *zero, one, two, three, four, five, six, seven*

Deviasew (Jonathan North Washington, 1997) is the second language of the Elves, Men, Dwarves and Halflings of the land of Câlnima ("Land"), Deviasew has a Latinate grammar, with a vocabulary derived from Hebrew, English, French and Spanish. The name Deviasew itself is the plural of Devia (from Hebrew *devar*, "word").

Deymual (Jonathan North Washington, 1999) is the language of the Elves of Câlnima.

> **Dda twth leveth, idd twth buaneth**
> *The tide rises, the tide falls.*

Dha-Patu (Karl Jahn, 1993) is completely analytical; it has only two parts of speech, radicals and particles. It has particles that form noun and verb phrases, classify the nouns and define the functions of the verbs. The grammar was conceived entirely on a priori logical principles, and the core vocabulary was generated by random combinations of the given letters; it's expanded by loans from natural languages.

Dhemonh'ka (1990) was invented for AmberMUSH, a MUD, to be the language of Chaosian demons (*Dhemonh'ka* means "demon language"). The orthography and vocabulary were inspired by Klingon.

Di'aleka (Tristan Parker, 2001) is a personal language, based on Hawaiian, Japanese, and San Lorenzan.

Diallic (Blake Adams, 2002) is a fictional language.

Diarenye (Aaron Morse, 2003) is a diachronic fictional language.

Digor (Nicola Curat, 2004) is a personal language.

DiLingo (sUmUs cAcOOnUs, 1990) is a profound English slang with an ever growing vocabulary, and it's full of rhyme. All the time.

> **Ving ding ying ding isink?**
> *Why do you do this?*

Dingwâ (David, 2004) is a personal language based on European languages.

Dinosaur Language (2003) is a professional fictional language.

Diom, a fictional language, was designed by David Stokes.

> **Ampiros aernost sharusae, vi at Enfors Vilandenae, vi je tais zhangoln.**
> *The Empire's greatest strength is not the Iron Army, but its language.*

Diudisk (Raginvard Flut, 2003) is a diachronic language based on Germanic languages.

Divine Language (Luc Besson and Milla Jovovich) is a fictional language, spoken by Leeloo in *The Fifth Element*.

D'ni (Richard Watson, 1994) is the language of the D'ni civilization in the video game *Riven* (sequel to *Myst*).

> **Lihsho kehnehn ehrth nahvah.**
> *Lihsho is a master.*

Doraya, (Adam Parrish, 1991) is the language of an imaginary world consisting of the regions of Mofeva, Doryn and Rooken. The most fascinating part of the language is the relative roles of nouns and verbs. Verbs are invariable, while nouns take special modifiers to indicate tense.

> **Te li'asaran sidor aelae**
> On the next meeting future-star shines
> *I hope to see you again soon.*

Doriathrin is an artlang invented by J.R.R. Tolkien; it was the native tongue of the elf-maid Lúthien Tinúviel.

Dosian (Steve Nickolas (Dosius/Usotsuki), 1994) is an auxlang based on European languages plus Japanese.

Dozhu:n was designed by Apollo Hogan as a fictional language.

Draconic (Sean K. Reynolds & Owen K.C. Stephens, 2001) is a professional fictional language for D&D, appearing in *Dragon Magazine* #284.

Draconic is a fictional diachronic language and was invented by Bryant.

Draconic (Lovarin) (Ikkakujyu, 2003) is a fictional language "designed to be difficult to learn and use."

Draqa (Ajin Kwai) is a fictional langauge spoken by the elf-like draqa.

Draseléq Pablo Flores, 1998) is the language of a fictional parallel Earth; it was designed to be "exquisitely complicated."

> **Be burek "Rei, nam anth", fananval nótasstür thüaq taus donth.**
> if they-say look it's-new this previous in-times it-was also that
> *Is there any thing whereof it may be said, See, this is new? It hath been already of old time, which was before us.*

Dren (Thomas McInturf, 1999) is a loglang.

> **Id i mulso Kithicorim pux'an staf koge's gir i yeb gos, id i pifir ned ad elu wit orm'an.**
> *And the arch-mystic Kithrin outstretched his hands over the ivory alter, and the red jewel of fate was forged.*

Drhaqa was developed by Ajin Kwai.

> **eowijakrsoivandeht**
> *For a long time there had been violence which alternated between high and moderate intensity, was unintentionally perpetuated and has been ended abruptly.*

Drow (Ed Greenwood, 1991) is a professional fictional language, created for the drow (dark elves) of D&D.

Dublex (Jeffrey Henning, 1999) is a langmaking game— think of it as Scrabble for people who like to invent words. Rather than the letter tiles of Scrabble, Dublex has 400 word tiles. You combine the word tiles in as many ways as desired to come up with new words.

Duirún (Arne Duering, 1985) is a stealth language.

Dundein Vega (Gustavo Salvini) is a fictional language.

Dunia (Ed Robertson, 1996) is unique in the scope of its vocabulary, with different parts of speech typically drawn from a single language. Most verbs are from Spanish, most common nouns are from English, most scientific nouns are from Latin, most adjectives are from Hindi/Urdu, most simple adverbs are from Russian, and so forth.

Dunnek was designed by Terrence Donnelly as for the Dun people, who inhabit much of Western and Central Europe on Zyem, an alternate Earth.

Dununmi (Yiuel, 2002) is a fictional, monosyllabic language.

Durdekors (Jeffrey Henning, 1999) is a fictional language, based on Barsoomian and Karklak.

Dutton Speedwords (Reginald J.G. Dutton, 1935) is a shorthand using the Roman alphabet; as it has pronunciation rules it's also an auxlang.

> **Garronum & sep an pas wi perz yzes fovi o c terle u nov dem, ygeni i libs, & diwe a l wee k al on e fony eg.**
> *Four score and seven years ago our fathers brought forth, upon this continent, a new nation, conceived in Liberty, and dedicated to the proposition that all men are created equal.*

Dwarfin, by Martin Greening, is a fictional language created for an RPG.

Dwarven Pidgin (Sean K. Reynolds, 2000) is a professional fictional language created for D&D.

E

E Dashul (Anthony Raymond Bullard, 1999) is a diachronic language intended for an epic fantasy.

ê Èëe (Jonathana Tegire and Jaaaaaa, 2003) is a personal language. It has five phonemes all pronounced /e/ but distinguished by tone.

e2 (Sindelka, 2003) is an auxlang, a reform of Esperanto.

Eaiea (Bruce Koestner, 1990), uses groups of notes to form words. Unlike Solresol, this language uses all twelve notes of the chromatic scale.

Earth Language (Yoshiko F. McFarland, 1988) is an auxlang. It's entirely visual; its 90 symbols can be combined by overlaying.

Eastern (Nik Taylor, 1999). A cousin to Watakassí, Eastern is phonetically far more complex, with more phonemes and more complex syllables. It also has less agglutination, and more isolation and fusion, using auxillary verbs to replace several inflections of Watakassí and its ancestor, and using prepositions to replace some of the cases.

Eastron (Jonathan R Parsons, 2001) is a Welsh-based fictional language.

Ebisédian (H. S. Teoh, 2000) is a fictional language for "people who inhabit a radically different world."

Ebubo (Andrew Nowicki, 2002) is a philosophical language..

Écriture Universelle (Jean Effel, 1968) is a script language.

EDA Arne Arotnow, 2005) is an auxlang with European sources.

Êdhchirriad (Tom Killingbeck, 2002) is a fictional diachronic language based on Sindarin, Welsh, and English.

Egaeic (Edward Field, 2004) is a personal language.

Egren (Tuomo Sipola, 2000) is a fictional diachronic language, based on Latin, Finnish, Germanic languages, and Verdurian.

ehmay ghee chah, (Elmer J. Hankes, 1992) is an auxlang.

Ehxduxadiikootu is a personal language created by many conlangers.

Eklektu 96 (Herman Miller, 1996) is a personal language, whose vocabulary is an eclectic mix of the world's languages.

Ekspreso (Jay Bowks, 1996) is an auxlang with European sources.

Elatoi (John Whatmough, 2004) is a diachronic language.

Elephant's Memory was invented by Timothy Ingen Housz as a fictional language.

Elet Anta (John Fisher, 1997) is the language of the Anta, a hidden subculture that has lived in the British Isles for at least 1,000 years.

> **Sar tal Hishesoy Brufa afat cis parant ya, cren sof varad.**
> Sun and North-from/attrib Wind mutually un- agree ref/acc which-person more be-strong.
> *The North Wind and the Sun were disputing which was the stronger.*

Elkarîl (Mark Rosenfelder, 2002) is an artlang spoken by elcari, a species resembling dwarves. It incorporates non-human features such as continuous phonetic gradation and a five-element sentence structure rather than our subject, verb, object.

Ellandh (Jedrzej Gren, 2000) is a fictional language for elves.

Elleya (Niels van der Plas, 2002) is a "beautiful" personal language.

Eloi (John Logan, 2002) as a professional fictional language, made for the Eloi in *The Time Machine,* one of many versions of H.G. Wells's novel.

Eloram (Daniel Myers, 2002) is a fictional language.

Eloshtan is a fictional language and was written by Josh Roth.

Elven (Sean K. Reynolds, 2001) is a professional fictional language, created for the elves in D&D. It's described in *The Dragon* #279.

Emterz (Edgar c., 2003) is a diachronic language; its parent is Emterezka.

Entish (J.R.R. Tolkien, 1945) is a fictional language, developed for the Ents and noted for its longwindedness: *A-lalla-lalla-rumba-kamanda-lindor-burúmë* is the word for "hill."

Epiq (David J. Peterson, 2003) is a personal language, inspired by Inuvialuktun, an Inuit language.

E-Prime (David Bourland, 1989) is English without the verb 'be', which is held to cause all manner of sloppy thinking.

Eretas (Keith Gaughan, 2001) is a fictional language.

> **Sjesú mjuhlinen eretassan: imarrelló.** *LM*
> Sjesú = 'disputer'/'battler', from the verb 'sjesuin', meaning 'fight(ing)'. Mjuhlin-en = 'of-dying', the genitive form of the verb 'mjuhlin', meaning 'die'. Eretas-(s)an = of-language, genitive form of the noun 'eretas'. Imar(r)-elló = wordmaker, a compound of 'imar' (word) and 'elló', the agent form of 'ellen' (do/make).

Erog (Matt Arriola, 2004) is a personal language based on German.

Erone (Carrie Schutrick, 1996) is a personal language.

> Sec bruc mimuzé, lea egli anfé voc eroné o dlushi hivé aspus.

CONLANGS AT A GLANCE 317

Now the whole world had one language and a common speech.

Esata (Pafu, 2001) is a personal language, in part a creolized English.

Esei (Tuomo Sipola) is fictional language.

Nateri ani waen padao teni ti, terenau mis, ka lede ba so waen kevinavu.
Only god is as wise as you, my king, and that is not sure.

Eseshté-basó (AK Brady, 2003) is a fictional diachronic language.

Esiterato (Sandor Csak, 2003) is a personal language with an agglutinative structure.

Eskimo (Phil James, 1995) is a parody of the 'hundreds of words for snow' meme— e.g. *tlinro* 'snow vapor', *tlayopi* 'snow drifts you fall into and die', *nylaipin* 'the snows of yesteryear.'

Espanzë (Jonathan North Washington, 1998) is the language of the Espans, a European race in 3200 C.E. It's based on Romance.

Ë tuto del mondo era dë una langua ë dë ünë idiomme.
All the peoples of the Earth had one language and one speech.

Esperando (Jay Bowks, 2000) is an auxlang, a reform of Esperanto,

Esperanto (Ludwig Lazarus Zamenhof, 1887) is the most successful constructed language ever, with perhaps a million speakers in the world (estimates vary from 100,000 to 15 million), concentrated in Europe but also with pockets of speakers in Japan and China. Esperanto has more books, periodicals and radio broadcasts using it than any other auxlang. It is a classic and required study for anyone serious about constructed languages. It has spawned more offspring than any other conlang, with many reform projects, the most prominent of which is Ido.

Esperanto de DLT (P. M. Witkam, 1983) is a version of Esperanto used as an intermediate form for machine translation.

Esperanto sen Fleksio (Rick Harrison, 1996) is a non-inflected auxlang.

Esreverian (Dtsdesign, 2004) is a fictional naming language.

Essential World English (Lancelot Hogben, 1963) as an auxlang, a reform of Basic English with 1300 words.

Etrer'aous (Drew Fischer, 2001) is a personal language.

Etwu (1997). The secret organization Eternia has created the international language, Etwu, an extremely regularized language based on French and English.

Eurana (Klaus Dieckmann) is an auxlang.

Euransi was developed by Libor Sztemon.

> **Hur ve o Englensi mitalid?**
> *How do you say this in English?*

Eurolang (Philip Hunt, 1990) is an auxlang, designed for the European Union, with some aggressive goals for ease of learning. Unlike Esperanto, Eurolang has more freely borrowed words from English.

Eurolengo (Leslie Jones, 1972) is an auxlang, mostly based on English and Spanish (but riddled with k's: *menos posabelik le mar-krosants,* "except perhaps the sea crossings").

Europan (Thomas R. Diehl, 1998) is an auxlang based on EU languages.

Europanto (Diego Marani, 1996) is a mock auxlang, parodying the multilingual stew of the European Union and especially the dominance of English. Marani wrote a book of stories in Europanto, *Las adventures des inspector Cabillot* (1999).

Europeano (Jay Bowks, 2002) is an auxlang, a reform of Peano's Latino Sine Flexione.

Eurún (Arne Duering, 2005) is a philosophical language.

Eyahwánsi (René Uittenbogaard, 2004) is a fictional language.

F

Fampónd is the language of vampires, developed by Christopher Wright.

> **Cleraniþan naða fleranað la macílna raln salinditás raleð fláca? Sojiþan naða la Malneþa naþ ríþasnó?**
> *Have you swept the visioned valley with the green stream streaking through it, searched the Vastness for a something you have lost?*

Farlingo (Vladimir Farber & Matvei Farber, 2001) is an auxlang, a reform of Esperanto.

Fasile (B. Egon Breitenbach, 1999) is an auxlang.

Feianovedo (Sander Dieleman, 2003) is a personal language with a Romance vocabulary; it was used by the Feianova micronation.

Ferengi (Timothy Miller, 1990) was has invented for a *Star Trek* alien species. Miller has also created a language for the Cardassians.

Fergiartisch (Johannes Hufnagel) is the language of the Fergiartu continent.

> **varg diskimmèna, hans novud andemmasi**
> *The destroyed city, we will build again.*

Ferismonlaren is a fictional language.

Finnstek is for the Fince, a clan from the planet Pii and was written by N. Gruscha *et al.*

> **Tai finnsa (ingglizsa Fince) paizsaszaiga, tai njaitewè mljaljaa n.gruscaeigaatek. Tai paizsa zsilkana, tai leini mwalga mwe.**
> *The Fince (Finnstek Finns) are a group of tribes from Pii, a planet created by N. Gruscha et al. The Pii are divided up into various tribes, each with an animal totem.*

Fith (Jeffrey Henning, 1996) is the language of aliens of the planet Fithia. It is stack-based — the name is a nod to the computer language FORTH.

> **Tradhruunmh dzheen tyoung ke travwumnh dyimn ke vroinm yan vonh e.**
> fox brown quick the dog lazy the over {past-tense} jump {end-sentence}.
> *The quick brown fox jumped over the lazy dog.*

Fjinnjikulla (Tommaso Donnarumma, 1990) is a game language, which turns Italian text into something that looks like Finnish.

Flaidish (Mark Rosenfelder, 2003) is the language of a humanoid species on Almea. Its phonology is English-like, complete with a version of the Great Vowel Shift, but its lexicon is mostly Hungarian, and it has oddities like measure words and two sets of pronouns based on age.

Flestrin (Maurizio Rovatti, 1999) is a fictional diachronic language, for the kingdom of Flaedin.

Florish (Kata Valinta, 1998) is a fictional language. The sources are mostly Finnish and Quechua.

Folkiske (Quentin Read, 2005) is a personal language based on Germanic.

Folkspraak (Jeffrey Henning, 1995) is an auxlang intended as a pan-Germanic language, easily learned by speakers of English, German, Dutch, Norwegian, Swedish, Danish, Afrikaans, Frisian and other Germanic languages. Folkspraak is an attempt to distill the Germanic languages.

Folksstem was written by Aaron Chapman.

> **Saga til ik anat i fremde sprak.**
> *Say something to me in a foreign language.*

Foneimfin (Simon Mulder, 2003) is a fictional language inspired by European languages.

Forendar (David Bell, 1998) is a fictional diachronic language, a sister of Amman-Iar.

Fortunatian (Marcus Miles, 2002) is a fictional diachronic language.

> **Y nomn de xnenat, tsrat bone naux!.**
> *In the Maid's name, rule us well!*

Frater, (Phạm Xuân Thái, 195) is an auxlang with mostly Greek and Latin vocabulary, but with the roots modified to better suit Asian speakers. It has only five vowels and thirteen consonants (*bdfgjklmnprst*) but permits more consonant clusters than might be expected given Chinese and Japanese phonotactics.

> **O antrop arme-forse, oto re logo surantrop ot mi, na logo futur ili a oto alegro ot ni, kon desir pro beni ni.**
> *Again, O strong-armed one, hearken to my sublime tale, which in desire for thy weal I will recite to thy delighted ear.*

Frater 2 (Paul Bartlett, 1996) is an auxlang, a reform of Frater.

Frionske (Stefan Lubbersen, 2002) is an auxlang based on Dutch dialects.

Fukhian (Henrik Theiling, 1988) is a personal language.

Fungarr (Obar Norrseg, 2002) a fictional language based on Germanic, Finnish, and Hungarian.

Furbish (Dave Hampton, 1998) was designed for the Furby electronic pets. The phonology is simplified for a cheap integrated circuit.

> **Dah a-loh nah-bah. Doo-moh wee-tee kah way-loh.**
> Big light down. Please sing me sleep.
> *The sun's down; please sing me to sleep.*

Futurese (Justin B Rye, 2003) is a fictional language, which checks in on English every 300 years until 3000 AD.

> **Zᴀ kiad w'-exùn ya tijuh, da ya-gᴀr'-eduketan zᴀ da watᴀgan lidla.**
> *We children beg you, teacher, that you should teach us to speak correctly.*

G

Gaciça (Ted Kloba, 1998) is a fictional language.

Gaelish (John Whatmough, 2004) is a fictional language for the nation of Savaiie.

Gälðyr (Luca Galdiolo, 2003) is a personal language.

G'amah (Pablo Flores, 2000) is a fictional language, created for an RPG. The design goal was "a language that is best shouted."

Ganh is the language of the Ganh people, designed by mr professor13.

gá'rDëMy (Geert Rinkel, 2003) is a fictional language, spoken in gá'sTe'f.

Gargish (Herman Miller, 1990) is a professional fictional language, spoken by the Gargoyle race in the video game *Ultima VI*. Syllables from Gargish are used by mages to cast spells.

> **Ánte kódex skríle prí ben esh ver res quí quae.**
> in codex written one well and true answer any problem
> *Within the Codex is written the one right and true answer to any problem.*

Gelveasar (Jon Brase, 2002) is a fictional diachronic language.

Geoglot (Timothy J. Donoghue, 1916) is an auxlang.

Gevey (Rik Roots, 1976) is an agglutinative language for the continent of Ewlah on the planet Kallieda.

> **Mik leprhuu nets pukrhe tem beduu rhou zharhi-skone, man kuu nets te buu rhou zharhi-skone.**
> *If rabbit meat was good enough for my father, then it is good enough for me.*

Giak (Joe Dever, 1986) is the language of the evil Giaks in the *Lone Wolf* gamebooks; details are in *The Magnamund Companion*.

> **Dajo shegtar ash zek hakim kor orgadakim.**
> *Follow the dwarf and hide the humans' bodies.*

Gilish (Jordan Lavender, 2001) is a fictional language based on Hebrew, Greek, and Latin.

Gilo (Alan Giles, 1997), is an auxlang. It uses the categorization of Roget's Thesaurus and a vocabulary based on English.

> **peel ajoma ogoz spidota piskis u du filis eta ovel**
> person+female age+much+(adj.) give+past speed+little+(adverb) fish to two cat small+(adj.) (possessive)+she
> *The old woman slowly gave a fish to her two little cats*

Gladilatian (Dennis Paul Himes, 1997) lacks verbs, with every sentence being a copula. Each conjunction consists of one word before the last conjunct and another before each of the other conjuncts. Syntax is strict. Vocabulary is *a priori*.

> **Fmu rletnapu hrnuzlahrmu hyaxryna hluryt.**
> I [am] for-the-benefit-of.you three.thirty-six.eighteen using.kiss giver.
> *I give you 126 kisses.*

Glaugnea was invented by Michael Helsem as a philosophical language.

Gleeb (Lord Blaa, 2000?) is a fictional language.

> **M'ith odel**
> *It could be worse*

Glide (Diana Slattery *et al.*, 1998) is an animated visual language.

Globish (Madhukar Gogat, 1998) is an auxlang, a reform of English.

Globish (Jean-Paul Nerrière, 2006) is a subset of English with 1500 words, for international use.

Glosa (Wendy Ashby and Ross Clark, 1981) is a reform of Interglossa. The language is generally criticized by conlangers because it has not specified a grammar, relying instead upon English grammar. The vocabulary is Classical (Greek and Latin) and contains about a thousand words.

> **Mi pote qe kompar tu ad estiva di?**
> *Shall I compare thee to a summer's day?*

Goblin (Didier Willis, 1989) is an artlang, inspired by Greek and Quenya.

> **Pú thar-inShtýreinigh phrunen-sawá luethnyalleh, verain-iman thir, ar vekra lýt ire ó fartanen..**
> *Then the sovereign deities all went on the thrones of stone, the very holy gods, and here is what they decided..*

Goesk (James S. Grossmann, 1999) is a personal language.

> **Dus paklinu blablazeus uns dixtueciza.**
> *The boy recited to us a poem.*

Golal Natkali (Betsumei, 2002) is a fictional language.

Golic Vulcan (Mark R. Gardner et al., 1980) – Gardner's Vulcan Language Institute developed Golic Vulcan. Other versions include Marketa Zvelebil's Modern Standard Vulcan and Joel Anderson's Vulcan.

> **Dif-tor heh smusma.**
> *Live long and prosper.*

Gomain (Zack Hart, 2002) is a diachronic language, spoken in Ánhrush.

Góquim is a personal language designed by Nikhil Sinha.

Graatska (Richard Valler (MDR), 2001) is an auxlang based on German and English.

Graod (Dtsdesign, 2004) is a fictional Polynesian-based naming language.

Grooiman (William James Tychonievich) is a fictional language.

gua!spi (Jim Carter, 1991) is a loglang.

> **^:i**

!tara
/vme -crw
!kseo
^vu -tum
!kfor ^fe -fnau
(Start)
(1st parameter) Rat
(Main verb) does activity violently - eats
(2nd parameter) cheese
restrictive coordinate clause - tool
(1st parameter of restrictive clause) fork
and-knife
The rat devours (violently eats) the cheese with a fork and knife

Guask (Iban Etxenaude *et al.*, 2001) is a fictional language based on Basque and Spanish.

Gutisk (Damien Erwan Perrotin, 2000). Alas, no Eastern Germanic language survives in our world, but Perrotin has created an alternate history where Wulfilan Gothic survives. Gutisk, as its speakers call it, is grammatically simpler than its ancestor, but richer in inflexions than modern European languages.

> **Driusands ufta saihvada / ikei filu haba leike. / nsaihvans ik reisa aftra.**
> *I, who have several bodies, / Am often seen to fall. / Unseen I rise again.*

Gweydr (David J. Peterson, 2001) is a personal language.

gzb (Jim Henry) is a personal language.

> **ce hxy-i lq tu-i twax-zox mje-zxa: hoqnx "txlunrana-ram liqw-i liqm-cox tu-i re o runx-zox mje-cox.**
> this [patient] one [agent] says long-ago: that Thlunrana of enemy [agent] there to come awhile-hence.
> *It had been prophesied of old and foreseen from the ancient days that its enemy would come upon Thlunrana.*

H

Hadwan (Muke Tever) is the language of the monsters of Southern Europe.

> **wihi aflicem zinsuam kuri zinsu**
> *Fight linguistic extinction, invent a language.*

Hallon (Paul V. S. Townsend, 2000) is a personal language.

> **Matsaleda soludub'oda sual dima mo uma, valun toja dima mo uma, valun numada dima mo uma.**
> Under-write war-stop-at hour ten and one from day ten and one from month ten and one.
> *The armistice was signed at the eleventh hour of the eleventh day of the eleventh month.*

Hallowese is a fictional language crafted by Robert L. Vaessen.

Hambhukringki (R. Srikanth) is a fictional language for the planet Gliipskandhu in the NGC0888 Galaxy.

Hamdi (K La Touche, 2003) is a fictional language, based on Welsh, Old English, Turkish, and Georgian.

Hänäthlîêr (Shane Hampton, 2002) is a personal language.

> **Fên mo bäïnä nê mäthär**
> cat (subject) pretty (object) is
> *The cat is pretty.*

Hani (C.J. Cherryh, 1998) is a professional fictional language, from the *Chanur* series. Hani has a phonology fit for lions and was inspired by the sounds the author's cats made.

> **Fai-shukh-aarn nai-Terra lin-aarn hen-fhaif chuch hen-fhaan.**
> [prep/all/adj.] [s/Earth] [one/adj] [3psa/language] and [3psa/speech].
> *All the peoples of the Earth had one language and one speech.*

han-taj-tUl-hUt (Aaron Ruimy, 2001) is a personal language, whose design principles are "strangeness, oddness, 90° angles."

Hapoish (James E. F. Landau) is the language of the planet Hapoish in Lehola's Refea slar system.

Harry Potter Magic Language (J. K. Rowling, 1996) is a professional fictional language, used to cast spells; it's largely based on Latin.

Hattic (Jan van Steenbergen, 1996) is a fictional diachronic language, made as a derivation of *kentum* Indo-European.

Heratï (Zingjar ë Gud, 1998) is a personal language.

Hieroglyfic (Rowland Jones, 1768) is a iconic language.

High Speech (Stephen King, 1982) is a naming language, featured in the *Dark Tower* fantasy series.

Hyilté (Robin Morton, 2003) is a fictional language.

Hystudian (Daniel Jewell) is a Slavic-inspired diachronic language.

I

iaPil was created by Peter Mark Garza.

> **mari ga teresa pu altaPu Ke.**
> Mari [subj.] Teresa [more than] tallness-opposite [state].
> *Mari is shorter than Teresa is.*

Ibran (Muke Tever, 2002) is a fictional diachronic language inspired by European languages.

Idjana (Quentin Read, 2005) is a personal language, whose ablaut system is inspired by Semitic.

Ido (Louis de Beaufront, Louis Couturat, 1907) is an auxlang. With a name meaning "derived from" in Esperanto, Ido is a modification of Esperanto.

Idrani (T. Mitchell Pehrson, 1982) is a personal language drawing from Navajo, Chinese, Xhosa and Finnish.

> **Nut, tahmokhtashe'ho, zodiseiv, arnglab kondi in, t'araksoesan.**
> *Come, let us go down and confuse their language so they will not understand each other.*

Ii42hah32reh12man41 is a fictional language by Jonathana Tegire and Jaaaaaa.

Iju Puna (Kevin Goodman, 2004) is a minimalist personal language, influenced by Toki Pona.

Iksto (Keith Mitchell, 2002) a stealth language.

Ilaini (Irina Rempt, 1990) is the language of the kingdom of Valdyas.

> **Biryinan nestyenan sa hyrnena custay ali so myray az dayen sa sumen datay dayan hostea cul brythea lea chalet.**
> *Take almonds or other nuts and grind them with water or wine until the liquid looks white like milk.*

Ilathid'hi (Scott 'Blade' Hamilton, 2005) is a fictional language created for *Ages of Ilathid*, a fan-created game for the *Myst* world.

Ilianóre (Jeff Smith, 1996) is a fictional language created for the Scealdings.

> **Belarest lo. Færa tinwar endlih félwarwe éase ðustre.**
> *Welcome, strangers. Please, stay a while and feed your soul.*

Ilish (Jeffrey Henning, 1996) is the language family of the il, a species of sentient sea creatures of Fithia (see Fith), which communicate by sending electrical shocks to one another. Ilish is unusual in that it has no nouns, but instead uses thousands of pronouns.

Iljanore was written by Jeff Smith as a fictional diachronic language.

Ilkorin (J.R.R. Tolkien, 1917) was an early form of Sindarin.

Illfillin (Uskokovic Vuk) is a fictional language, based on Indo-European languages.

Iltârer is the language of the Iltâr, created by Tom Little (Sêsâmân).

> **Thi Chentirath, ârsilâ essi sâñchiasil.**
> PREP N-ref.sing. V-viv.vol.3 PP-3.abs.coll. N-abs.coll.
> *In Hendir, there are no horses.*

Ilythirri Alurl (Jashan A'al, 20020 is a fictional language, the High Drow alongside Ed Greenwood's (Low) Drow.

Imuttan (Kári Emil Helgason, 2002) is a diachronic language based on Spanish and Tagalog.

Inagalasi (civman2000) is a fictional language based largely on English.

Inda (Gregory Higley) is ergative and features an interesting grammar, with adjectives treated as verbs (as in Japanese). The pronunciation system is also interesting, with consonants undergoing assimilation in different positions.

> **kia gin, ad a gefallay ra eflendeliu, neri ioma lissa ad a Kept-a-Sulelay ra giyay ra hense yontio**
> *From the back of (my) horse, I saw a beautiful young woman standing near the base of the (fortress of) Kept-a-Sulel.*

Indika (Nikhil Sinha, 2003) is a personal language.

Indo-Nugimian (Tony Le, 2001) is a personal language, influenced by Esperanto and Vietnamese.

Inglisj (Stefan Lubbersen, 2002) is an auxlang, a reform of English.

Ini is a fictional language created by Nicole Perrin.

inif Xeuivteles (B. Morgan White, 1998) is a fictional diachronic language based on "beauty and naturalism."

> **Opmeáh rato inifok solteeyok**
> *Strive for the highest comfort and pleasure in life, for life is short and meaningless lest you enjoy it.*

İnlici (ACZ, 2001) is a fictional langauge based on European langauges.

Inrilan (The Inrilan Consortium, 2004) is an auxlang, mostly *a priori*.

Intal (Erich Weferling, 1956) is an auxlang, similar to Interlingua.

Inter Celtic (Makeenan) is a fictional language.

Inter-esperanto, (Greg Hoover, Initiator, 2003) is an auxlang based on Esperanto, Ido, and Mondlango.

Intergermansk (Pascal A. Kramm, 2005) is a Germanic-based auxlang.

Interglossa (Lancelot Hogben, 1943) is an auxlang; cf. Glosa.

InterLang is an international language. It was written by Douglas Green, Kristian Jarventaus, Kevin Albrecht.

Interlingua – The International Auxiliary Language Associationwas founded in New York in 1924 to choose one conlang to support as an auxiliary. In 1951 it published its own language, with a grammar and vocabulary drawn from western European languages. (Not to be confused with Latino Sine Flexione, which was later called Interlingua. The Academia pro Interlingua also had a language with the same name; they later gave Alexander Gode permission to use the name after the IALA had informally adopted it.)

> **Le unic personas qui realmente ha cambiate le historia ha essite illes qui ha cambiate le pensamento del homines a respecto de se mesmes.**
> *The only people who really changed history are those who changed the thought of men about themselves. - Malcolm X*

Intermythic English (Jeffrey Henning, 1996) is a superset language.

International Sign is a Sign auxlang, created World Congress of the World Federation of the Deaf starting in 1951. Earlier called Gestuno.

Intero (Marq Thompson and Johnathan Moore, 2004) is an auxlang, a reform of Esperanto.

Ïpetas (Tuomo Sipola, 1999) is a fictional diachronic language.

Iqalu (Zach McVay, 2005) is a personal language based on European and Anatolian languages.

Irecepte (Eric Remington, 2003) is a personal language based on English, Japanese, and German.

Isirian (Joshua Horn, 2002) is a personal language.

Islandian (Austin Tappan Wright in 1893) is a fictional language.

Islet was developed by Daniel Myers as a fictional language.

Islic Wood Elvish (Curtis Mullings, 2004) is a fictional language, based on Sanskrit, Ancient Greek, and Punjabi.

Ismaîn (Mark Rosenfelder, 1999) is a sister language of Verdurian, derived in a regular process (with historically plausible quirks) from Cadinor, complete with borrowings from Verdurian and Kebreni.

Isotype (Otto Neurath, 1936) is a philosophical language.

Ithkuil (John Quijada, 1978) is a philosophical language, which "utilizes an array of principles from cognitive psychology and cognitive linguistics, including prototype theory, radial categorization, fuzzy logic and semantic complementarity." It reduces the lexicon using a highly productive derivational morphology.

Itlani (James E. Hopkins, 1997) is a fictional diachronic language.

> Tá Miára, tá Várem véy tá Párem — tá Mabugú shéy Dzevárun.
> *Hope, Love, and Respect, the Beginnings of all Journeys.*

J

J'ækatá (Sean Bradt, 2002) is a fictional language based on Old English and Quenya.

Jakelimotu (Lane Schwartz; Ben Rogers, 1998 is a stealth language.

Jamalinaşķ (Jamal Abed-Rabbo, 2001) is a personal language, aggutinative, most influenced by Russian and Arabic.

Jameld, (James Campbell, 1982) is a diachronic language, derived from German, French, Dutch, Frisian and Esperanto. It has "an organic heart and an imaginary history. It is smooth and chocolatey on the outside, with a lovely fluffy centre, and it won't fill you up."

> An laami jors'st guto as an dod' iko.
> *Better a lame horse than a dead one.*

Japanglish (Josh "Jae" Munce , 2002) is a personal language.

Jasminese (Victor Medrano, 2004) is a fictional language, based on Yoruba, Japanese, Tibetan, Indonesian, and Central Pomo.

Jaueqao myys (Zak Keene, 203) is a fictional diachronic language.

Javifo (Daniele P. Morelli, 1000) is a fictional language.

Jechoire (Rubén Ortega, 2004) is a fictional language created for an RPG; it is spoken in Jèquia, which lives in the shadow of Xuàquia.

Jelbazech (Deiniol Jones) is a fictional language.

Jezik Slovianaja (Pawel Ciupak, 2004) is a Slavic-based auxlang.

Tri persteni pro elfaja krali pod nebo.
Three Rings for the Elven-kings under the sky,

Jigwa (Rick Harrison et al., 1990) is an auxlang intended to be more Asian than European.

Jirit (Herman Miller, 1996) is the language of the Mizarian mice people. Interesting for its agglutinative morphology, which makes its grammar very straightforward.

Jleer (2002) is a personal language.

Jovian (Christian Thalmann, 2002) is a fictional diachronic language spoken in Jervaine, part of the Ill Bethisad alternate reality.

Paerde Claestine id Uedun - imminda an lionga! LM

Jynmû (Justin Spahr-Summers, 2004) is a personal language based on Mû.

Alach cinagh'ar nasiet'ra'môrr ra'adhar'cra na!
I am annoyed by these interruptions!

Jytisk (Alex Middleton, 1998) is a Germanic-based fictional language.

K

Kæseran (Alex Alfaro, 2005) is an *a priori* fictional language.

Kagizerin (Nik Taylor) is the language of the Kiz Empire.

Sûkekhenegï, khûmane'e!
Greetings, human!

Kakarak was created by Kaurpin.

chugwus whowholes woyawilayamagøøye wakuup-chapeeka
sick-ATTRIB   dog-ATTRIB   speak-2s_real-wail-PERSIST-CAUSATIVE 1s_real-very_angry-BECOME-BEGIN
The way you wail like a sick dog is starting to infuriate me.

Kalaba-X (Kenneth L. Pike, 1957) is a loglang, nothing more than a formalized grammatical description [verb (modifier) object (modifier) subject (modifier)], yet Pike makes excellent use of it to teach some of the challenges of translation, as he translates material to and from Kalaba-X.

This is a must-read for anyone designing the grammar of a constructed language.

Kaldon (Warmaster, 2000) is a fictional language, for the Bair world.

Kali-sise (Jeffrey Henning, 1999) is an auxlang designed to have no difficult sounds for anyone.

> **Kelu supaka-sunu ke sese kane ke Kali-sise pi nalike se.**
> Four opening-sound ACCUSATIVE six consonant ACCUSATIVE Kali-sise NOMINATIVE possession VERB.
> *Four vowels and six consonants Kali-sise has.*

Kaliso (Jashan A'al, 1999) is a fictional language.

> **Dê rëm osêkal isëtozhëd (?a)?**
> *Do you speak Kaliso?*

Kalonese (David J.S. Boyle, 2003) a fictional language with a grammar similar to Cantonese.

Kamakawi (David J. Peterson, 2001) is a personal language, based on Hawai'ian and another conlang, Zhyler.

> **He, ale ko, ima! A hile lelea!**
> /VOC., go here, EMPH.! New-Sbj. warm water!/
> *Hey, come on in! The water's warm!*

Kankonian (James E.F. Landau, 1997) is an extraterrestrial language is vaguely reminiscent of the tongues of the Middle East, but it is based directly on no human language, with the vocabulary designed according to the author's sense of the most natural set of sounds for each idea.

> **Mahan ar hesias Kankonik?**
> *Do you speak Kankonian?*

Kansu (Dan Morrison, 1998) is a fictional language, partly based on Sumerian, Akkadian, and Proto-Indo-European.

Kar Marinam (Josh Roth) is a fictional language.

Kardasi was invented by Esther Schrager. It is a diachronic language.

Kardasi (Timothy Miller, 1990) is a fictional language, designed for the Cardassians from *Star Trek*.

Kardii (Jayelinda Suridge, 1994) is a fictional language.

> **Manike namasa iilkana - niteinke rru!** LM

Karis (Maknas) is a fictional language.

Karklak (Jeffrey Henning, 1982) is a fictional diachronic language, spoken by gnomes.

Kash (Roger Mills, 1975) is a fictional language, based on Indonesian and Spanish.

> **aposimim tolisa ri tambranipan.**
> nom'lizer+sail+our visit*+past LOC (place)+acc.
> *Our ship called at Tambranipa..*

Kattoelai (J.T. Antley, 2004) is a fictional language.

Kaupelanese (Paulo Eduardo França Padilha, 1970) is the language of the Austronesian kingdom of Kaupelan.

> **Au aman na au dahuk wita sèngurita rau lau hi hami paliman**
> *My father and me saw two little girls in our hamlet.*

Kebreni (Mark Rosenfelder, 1998) is the language of Kebri, which is near Verduria on the planet of Almea. Its grammar is designed to differ from that of English in nearly every way possible: for instance, the verbal system depends on categories like aspect, politeness, desire, and volitional impact, and not at all on person, number, or tense, and conjugation depends on metathesis and vowel change rather than inflection.

Kel (Robert Jung, 2003) is a logical languagem inspired by Latenkwa.

Kēlen (Sylvia Sotomayor, 1980) is the language of the Kēleni of Tērjemar; it was designed to do without verbs.

> **p'ja naer maruw il-alle an tashaon anyth an a soreñ aneñ**
> rel. +art. "whole" "earth" time- phr. "now" obj. part. "language" "one" obj. part. pl. part. "speech" "one together
> *Now the whole earth had one language and one speech.*

Kelenala (David J. Peterson, 2003) is a personal language designed as a creole.

> **Sayanawsa sisi ki li eni yu wakawiyoko.**
> weather cold PRED. give 3sg. GEN. wrinkle
> *Cold weather gives you wrinkles.*

Kemilas (Robert L. Brown III) is a fictional Pan-African language.

Kerno (Padraic Brown) is a fictional diachronic language, for Ill Bethisad.

Kesh (Ursula K. Le Guin, 1985) is a professional fictional language, described in *Always Coming Home*. The book is pseudo-anthology, a study of the post-apocalyptic Kesh people living in what is now California.

Khangaþyagon (Pete Bleackley, 2003) is a magical langauge used by the Wizards of Huna.

> **ærkriuflt kriariþon glæstæpontol**
> ærkr-i-uf- lt kria- riþ- on glæs- tæp- ont-ol heal-3-pass-imp blood-flow-PrP spirit-command-PrP-by
> *Let the bleeding be healed by conjuration.*

Khikeng (Apollo Hogan, 2004) is a fictional language derived from Kinfa.

Khundruzn (Nicole Perrin) is a fictional language.

Khuzdul (J.R.R. Tolkien, 1940) is a professional fictional language, the secret language of the dwarves.

Kiadin (DarkHorizon, 2001) is a fictional language.

Kiffish (C.J. Cherryh, Spence Hill, 1998) is a professional fictional language. Science-fiction author Cherryh sketched out Kiffish for the villains in her *Chanur* series. With her permission, linguist Spence Hill added details to the language, based on her documentation of the anatomy and culture of the Kiff themselves. Besides being ergative, Kiffish is a synthetic language, rather than an agglutinative or order-bound language.

> **Ginkt-ku umankt-kkt Tera-kta kkisf-ok ruk-ku kkoiskk-otk ruk-ku trakk-ska, tha.**
> [all/adj] [human/pl] [Earth/gen] [speak/past] [one/adj] [language/abs.] [one/adj] [way/instr] [reported]
> *It is reported that all humans of Earth spoke one language in one way.*

Kika Olelo (Eclipse/Turquoise) is a fictional language.

Kingifa (Pete Bleackley, 2004) is a fictional language, the basis for derivations by other conlangers: **Kimva** by Bleackley, **kimwa lilyeho** by Alex Fink, **Kinfa** by Sven Lotz, **Kingfa** by Apollo Hogan, **Kingiwa 'Awiwasa** by Alex Fink.

Kine (Daniel Myers, 2001) is a personal, "cattle-centric" language.

Kìn-Sang is a fictional language developed by Kári Emil Helgason.

Kinsi Rorotan (Robert Wilson, 2002) is a fictional diachronic language.

Kinya (Maurizio Gavioli, 1995) is a fictional language.

Kioshu (Jeff Goguen, 1996) a fictional language.

Kir (Jashan A'al, 1999) is a language from the same world as Psharádi.

Kirda-han (Shane Hampton, 2002) is a personal language.

Kiromi (Raphael Singing Wolf) was created for the amusement of the author's friends and as an enjoyable way of learning more about linguistics. It has the most informal definitions I have encountered in a constructed language, with words such as *batra* (defined as "drums, poundable instruments of rhythm") and *bejke* (defined as "belch, burp, suddenly emit").

Kirumb (Muke Tever, 2000) is a fictional language made to be a protolanguage.

Klaatu's Language (Edmund H. North, 1951) is a professional fictional language, used in the film *The Day the Earth Stood Still*.

Klingon (Marc Okrand, 2000) is the most popular fictional language today, with more speakers and more enthusiasts than even Tolkien's Quenya. It uses OVS for alienness, but also features of Native American languages. Okrand used some of the Klingon dialog devised by James Doohan for the first *Star Trek* movie (1979).

> **nuqDaq yuch Dapol. QuchlIj vIyach vIneH.**
> *Where do you keep the chocolate? I would like to stroke your forehead.*

Klingonaase (John M. Ford, 1984) is a professional fictional language, used in the *Star Trek* RPG and in several novels.

Knarwaz (Pablo Flores) is the language of a fictional parallel Earth.

KNSL (David J. Peterson, 2005) is a constructed Sign language.

Ko e Vagahau he Motu (Philip Newton) is a personal language.

Kobaïan (Christian Vander, 1970) is a professional fictional language used in the songs of the French band Magma

KOD (Johann Vielberth, 2000) is an auxlang. A speaker uses their own grammar with the KOD lexicon. E.g. an Italian speaker expresses 'with' *oke* using a preposition, but a Russian uses it as a case ending.

Kokipopi (Eric Sleator McGill, 2000) is a parody auxlang with only four phonemes (**k p o i**).

kolaqadock (martin) is a fictional naming language.

Konya (Larry Sulky, 2004) is an auxlang whose sources include Indonesian, Loglan, and Ceqli.

Kordron (Jeffrey Henning, 1997). Kordron was created as a naming language, to be used to name orcs (goblins) in a campaign in a fantasy RPG.

Kor'ekhani (J. Matthew Saunders, 1998) is a diachronic language based on European languages.

Korpesk is a fictional language developed by Shawn C. Knight.

Kosi was invented by Robert Jung as a fictional language.

Kosmal Idioma (José Guardiola, 1893) is an auxlang.

Kot (Marco Bucchianeri, 2005) is a fictional language, for an imaginary island on Earth.

Kótèsä was designed by Justin Spahr-Summers. It is a personal language.

> **mùrè jin'vy'twänúvä mèkótè nót känätè**
> this me(possession) three(rd) language is !(particle)
> *This is my third language!*

Kramxelian (Dtsdesign, 2004) is a fictional naming language.

Kriegsprach (Jeffrey Henning, 1996) is the language of a fictional Germanic race featured in the war game Donnerkrieg.

Krithnag (Alex Middleton, 2004) is a Gaelic-based personal language.

Kronokayjin (Tyler Hogan, 2001) is a European-based artlang.

Kugzogak (Tom Killingbeck, 2002) is a fictional language.

Kushan (Rob H., 2003) is a a European-based personal language.

Kusthü is the language of the world of Endra.

> **dirae kunla lirana elé sasa baku-sumba lisora**
> past-we escape the-city just-as it-itself start-to-flood the-river
> *We escaped the city just as the river started to flood.*

Kvaaplaang (Tom Curtis, 2004) is a personal language.

Kwaadakw (Victor Medrano, 2002) is a fictional language based in part on Haida.

Kwendyngu is a fictional language created by Ceisiwr Serith.

Kya'terrian (Dtsdesign, 2004) is a Polynesian-based naming language.

Kyran (Kian, 1996) is for the alternate Earth known as Taris.

> **Tep pehehl snem dedlaak gahraev aav srihen ahk.**
> *The ancient readings and writing form were made clear to me.*

Kzinti (Roger Kuiper *et al.*, 1984) is a professional fictional language, used in the *Man-Kzin Wars* series begun by Larry Niven in 1988.

L

L17 (Victor Medrano, 2005) is a fictional language based on the Pama-Nyungan languages.

Láadan (Suzette Haden Elgin, 1982). Elgin created Láadan as an experiment to test the Sapir-Whorf hypothesis. Specifically, she felt that English and most natural languages were better suited for expressing the views of men than women. She designed Láadan to enable women to better give voice to their viewpoints, and the lexicon of Láadan, more than any other constructed language, has many unique concepts that are expressed in Láadan in one word but cannot be easily expressed in natural languages. It was first described in her *Native Tongue* science-fiction trilogy.

Lacue (Eirik Olsen, 2003) is a personal language.

Ladekwa is a loglang written by Rick Morneau.

Lahabic (Marcus Miles, 1996) is a fictional language based on European languages plus Hawai'ian.

Laikath is a fictional language.

Lakal/Saradic (Certic, 1994) are fictional languages created for an RPG.

Lalortel (Robert N. Yetter, 1959) is an auxlang.

Langue Nouvelle (Faiguet de Villeneuve, 1765) is an auxlang, described in the *Encyclopédie*.

Langue Universelle (Charles Letellier, 1855) is a philosophical language.

LANGUST (Grigoriy Korolev, 1998) is an auxlang, based on Earth Language, Blissymbolics, and aUI.

Lannu den gental was created by Morris.

> **Triste varra vus vad.**
> *Sad to see you go.*

Lano (M. Martin, 2003) is a philosophical language.

Lanrohidh'il (Alison Fisher, 2004) is an *a priori* fictional language.

Lapine (Richard Adams, 1972) — *Watership Down* is one of the classic works of xenofiction, set among and between the warrens of rabbits in the English countryside. Lapine, the language of the rabbits, is arguably the best naming language ever created, and is a minimalist virtuoso performance, a haiku of a language compared to the sonnet of Sindarin. It's amazing how much can be accomplished with how little. Lapine went a long way towards establishing the verisimilitude of the rabbits' culture and in the process making Watership Down a bestseller.

> **Hoi, Hoi, U embleer Hrair, M'saion ulé hraka vair!**
> A kind of rabbit's nursery rhyme. The word *hrair* is the Lapine for any number over four and is frequently translated as "thousand". In this case it refers to "The Thousand" which is the term applied to all the rabbits' natural enemies. *Hraka* is the Lapine for droppings.
> *Hey, Hey, the stinking Thousand, They attack us even as we stop to pass droppings!*

Lara (Alessandro Pedicelli, 1991) is an auxlang.

Larenti Tergush (Tiogshi Laj, 2000) is a fictional language.

Larua (Darrell Manrique, 1999) is a fictional diachronic language.

> **Foi din ollan la harha, ganau tzunnu rau matz?**
> Q NEG intend you garden, although still exist rain?
> *You don't intend to garden even though it's still raining, do you?*

Lashkos was created by Christopher Wright.

> **Priskel, jundech pershisti ish akmenau khad. Shis tu vindaras?**
> *Ancient one, you have followed the judge to the battle line. What have you seen?*

Latalmish (Ian Burleson, 2004) is an auxlang, based on European languages with a bit of Arabic.

Latineo (Jay Bowks) is an auxlang.

> **Patro nosa, kuo estas en la cielo, sankta estu tua nomino; venu regno tua; estu facita volo tua, tal en la cielo sike anke in la tero.**
> *(The Lord's Prayer)*

Latino Moderne (David Th. Stark, 1994) is an auxlang based on IALA Interlingua. The vocabulary is the that of Interlingua, but Stark has rejected Interlingua's grammar, which he views as oversimplified and hard to use in practice, especially in regards to pronouns. The grammar is instead a distillation of ancient Latin and modern Romance.

> **In le principio era le Verbo, e le Verbo era con Deo, e le Verbo era Deo.**
> *In the beginning was the Word, and the Word was with God, and the Word was God.*

Latino Sine Flexione (Giuseppe Peano, 1903) is an auxlang. Peano felt that — while the Latin vocabulary is known to many people — its inflexional system and syntax were too complex. The vocabulary consists of all Latin words (including borrowings of Greek terms) and the growing collection of common "international" words. He later changed the name to Interlingua, but it is usually referred to by its original name to avoid confusion with the IALA's Interlingua.

Latinvlo (Stephen Houghton, Paul Bartlett, 2001) is an auxlang, a modification of Magistri Linguio.

Latötsc (Brian Suchsland-Gutiérrez, 2003) is a personal language.

> **Ken sunt jeg, o sunt jeg; jeg sunt ker aint d'est mi—aine zait perdeten, jec trouveten.**

Laval (M. Martin, 2003) is a fictional language created for a micronation named Lavalon.

Laxonomasoljomijodo (Quentin Read, 2005) is a personal language.

Leibniz's Characteristica Universalis (Gottlieb W. Leibniz, 1677) is a philosophical language.

Lemurian (Sander Dieleman, 2004) is an *a priori* personal language.

Lengua Universal (Bonifacio Sotos Ochando, 1851) is a philosophical language.

Lengua Universal (L. Selbor, 1988) is a philosophical language.

Lepidopteran or Ze (Shinali, 1998) is a fictional language. The people are not insects, but have wings like lepidopterans.

Lesdekan (David Johnson (Sonib), 1995) is a fictional language based on Magyar, Welsh, Basque, and Finnish,

Lesko (Shawn C. Knight) is the language of aliens known as Lesu.

Leturian (Patrick Pfeaster) i the language of Leturia.

Ley Arah (Jashan A'al, 1993) is the language of the Tsara, the warrior-sect of the Tsendashai. It developed into Psharádi.

> **Náho, oslésh sa ché tlís sa vo.**
> Sorry/apologies, [neg]-intend I that insult I you.
> *I'm sorry, I didn't mean to insult you.*

Li' Anyerra-Tarah (Wesley Parish, 2002) is a fictional language based on Tok Pisin and Māori.

Liaden (Sharon Lee, Steve Miller, 1988) is a professional fictional language, appearing in the Liaden series beginning with *Agents of Change*.

Life Sound (mikulzqm, 1995) is a loglang with 30 basic concepts.

Lijou (collaborative, 2004) is a personal, English-based language.

Lilipu (Victor Medrano, 2002) is a personal language with just 9 phonemes, based on Polynesian languages plus Japanese.

Limciela (Jim Taylor, 2004) as a fictional language.

> **Impertí le bic ocult - imbentá una lim!** LM

Lin (Skrintha, 1996) incorporates nine-fold polysemy ("enneasemy") in its lexicon, where vocabulary is disambiguated through inter-word morphology. This, and the use of single- and double-letter words for the most commonly used concepts, makes Lin spatially compact.

> **$-Dz1ln~pf**
> no-without-imperfection-I(1,1)-lang-COPULA-perfect
> *No language without imperfections is perfect.*

LINC was designed by Igor Garshin.

Lincos (Dr. Hans Freudenthal, 1960) is designed to be broadcast in space; its 'phonemes' are radio signals.

Linear A/Minoan (Edward Hatfield, 2003) is an auxlang based on ancient languages.

Lingo (inventor unknown) is a fictional language.

> **Thilinosemen ak plako ak grocerines.**
> *The men went to the store to get groceries.*

Lingua Franca Nova (C. George Boeree, 1965) is an auxlang based on European languages.

Lingua Ignota "Unknown Language" (Hildegarde of Bringen, 1150), is considered to be the first constructed language (or the first that we have record of). Its inventor, an abbess, created it as a secret, mystical tongue.

> **Aigonz, Aieganz, Zuuenz, Liuionz, Dlueliz, Ispariz, Inimois**
> *God, Angel, Saint, Savior, Devil, Spirit, Man*

Lingualumina (Frederick William Dyer, 1875) is a philosophical language.

Liniyai-Karmisa (Eric Anger, 2004) ias a fictional language, based on Finnish and Tolkien's languages.

Linka Romànika (Dana Hadar, 2004) is a personal language based on European and Semitic languages.

Liñxî (Andrew J. Meilstrup, 2003) is an auxlang based on French/English.

Liotan (Geoff Eddy, 1991) is a diachronic language. It is the principal member of the Central branch of the Sunovian family.

Lips Kith (Joseph Scarisbrick, 1919) is an auxlang.

Lipu'onai (Amanda Smith, 2003) is a personal language, based on English, Spanish, and Hawai'ian.

Liva (Claudio Gnoli, 1995) is a loglang.

> **a kwxo kuça ni k'sa rw kase**
> *Three persons go from the water that I know towards the building.*

Livagian (And Rosta, 1985) is a loglang.

Llàtec (Nicola Curat, 2004) is a Romance-based jargon.

Llathos (Pharazon) a fictional language.

Loglan (James Cooke Brown, 1955) was designed to test the Sapir-Whorf hypothesis through use of a language that followed the concepts and structures of symbolic logic, while striving for a thoroughly unambiguous grammar. See also gua!spi and Lojban.

Logli (Marcos Cramer, 2003) is a personal language, based on Ceqli, Loglan, and Esperanto.

Logopandectesion (Thomas Urquhart, 1651) is a philosophical language.

Logsan (Filip Skwarski, 2004) is a loglang based on Lojban, Sanskrit, Mandarin, and Latin.

Logulos (Shawn C. Knight) is a loglang.

Lojban (Bob LeChevalier, John Cowan, et al., 1987) is a continuation of Loglan, It is the most professional and thought-provoking of the modern logical languages, with a fascinating methodology for deriving its root words from Arabic, Chinese, English, Hindi, Russian and Spanish. For the sheer joy of it, you should check out how Tolkien's Tengwar alphabet can provide "a romantic orthography for Lojban."

> **mi viska le mlatu ku poi zo'e zbasu ke'a loi slasi**
> I see the cat(s) such-that something-unspecified makes it/them (the cats) from-a-mass-of plastic.
> *I see the cat(s) made of plastic.*

Lojsk (Ariano Reyes, 2002) is a loglang based on other conlangs.

> **kve sv3v ri lojsk**
> *Overview of Lojsk*

Lone (Risto Kupsala, 2002) is s an auxlang.

Long Wer is a fictional language written by Sophia Abraham (Ábrahám Zsófia) a.k.a Mau Rauser.

Loroi Trade (Jim Francis, 1997) is a fictional language of "simple clarity."

Low Orkish (Merle D. Zimmermann, 1999) has but eleven different letters in its alphabet, and the language freely borrows words from other languages (such as English). The language was designed to give the author's MUD personas more flavor, and to annoy the other players.

Lrahran (Adam Walker) is the language of aliens of the Commonwealth.

Lûá (Fen Yik, 1997) is an *a priori* fictional language..

> **Hââ raá-lëï Müù-fhûù hâì-höà - hââ hïé-raú lûá.** LM

Ludireo (Herman Miller, 1996) is a fictional language.

Ludycian is an artlang invented by Alex Beaverstone.

Lugasuese (Jurre Lagerwaard, 1999) is a fictional language based on English, Dutch, and Tolkien's languages.

Luinin (Boomajoom, 2003) is a fictional diachronic language.

Luni, an IAL, was designed by Florent Garet.

Lusane (Luis Sainz Lopez-Negrete) is an auxlang.

Lusiaquía is an auxlang developed by Stefan Lubbersen.

M

Machi (Terrence Donnelly) is the language of the insectoid race of Epsilon Indi II.

Mærik, a fictional language crafted by Benct Philip Jonsson.

Magistri Linguio (Stephen Chase Houghton, 1907) is an auxlang based on Latin. It uses English word order in place of the Latin declensional system. Houghton did not actually develop a dictionary, instead specifying how existing Latin words would be transformed.

> **Isti quia parata a aliqui un surpensi propositio.**
> *This may seem to some a startling proposition.*

Maktalu was designed by Nik Taylor for the Great Valley on the planet Yord.

> **Mìfànbis fàumà misó bá mìfàsbitshe fàaktabo.**
> It:him/her:may:kill acc:human nom:what that it:him/her:certainly:cause-to:live Native
> *What nourishes a Native may kill a Human.*

Malacandrian (C. S. Lewis, 1938) is a fictional language, used in *Out of the Silent Planet*.

Malknarh (Maknas, 2000) is a fictional *a priori* diachronic language, descended from Mekhael.

Maltae was invented by Kuanye. It is a personal language.

Mamseunsci was written by Andrew McKenzie.

> **Lelaic epillas foneusci sa semmas galsceut mines.**
> **lelaic e-pill-as fon-eusci sa, semma galsc-eu mines.**
> since [not-you-nom] [call-past+expletive] conj. diff subj.
> we-nom [miss-past+motive] film-acc
> *Since you didn't call, we missed the film.*

Manaki (Yann Kiraly, 2004) is a personal language designed for "simplicity, beauty, and efficiency."

Manaža (Shane Hodgson, 2005) is a personal and stealth language.

Mango - Inspired by Sanskrit, Hindi-Urdu and other Indian languages, Mango is the language of the Tiger people of planet Pii, featured in a personal RPG. Tigers' respect for nature, women and agriculture rules the Mango language. Their disgust for crimes of violence, the Leopard people and their sneering attitude for literacy and studying are also reflected in their language.

> **Zoij zrufranti vasruhu - ronodosso nogihi!** *LM*

Mannish (J.R.R. Tolkien) is a fictional language.

Mänti is a philosophical language invented by Daniel Tammet.

Mapalgetian Continental Basic Language (Greg Johnston, 2003) is an auxlang based on French and Spanish

Matsui (Ray Flores, 2003) is a loglang.

Megdevi (David J. Peterson, 2000) is a personal language based on Arabic, designed to "cover every semantic idea imaginable."

Meghean (Andreas Johansson) is a fictional language.

Meiko (Florent Garet, 2003) is a European-based auxlang.

Mekhael (Maknas, 2003) is a fictional diachronic language.

Mekhael was invented by Maknas. It is a fictional diachronic language.

Melani (Michael Mechmann, 1998) is a personal language, created for the "keepers of the Lower Plains."

Melindaran (Randal L. Lanning, 2004) is a personal language based on several languages including German and Klingon.

Mellyrn (Alex Bolton, 2002) is a personal language based on Quenya and Sindarin.

Mentolatian (Padraic Brown, 2003) is a fictional language.

> **Qua erufaguz rauni, durem fomandu dauv!** *LM*

Merahai (Mia Soderquist) is a fictional language.

Merdian (David Dynes, 1995) is an artlang.

Mêriale Nunérim was written by Eugenio M. Vigo as an artlang.

Merian is a naming languages crafted by David Kirschner.

Mêriate et Darae (Eugenio M. Vigo, 2001) is a fictional diachronic language based on European languages.

Merilareth (Chris Rohan, Christian Hansen, 2001) is a fictional language based on Norwegian, Quenya, and English.

Mesogeoika, a fictional language, was developed by Alex Katsaros.

Meth (Shawn C. Knight) is the language of a fictional race.

> **ya ja'aja mal ja'nikur; nu lesu.**
> *I am Aja Nikur; we are les.*

Mhigiwipian (Simon Whitechapel, 2004) is a personal language.

Microlang 1.0 is a philosophical language crafted by James.

Midikan (Curtis Mullings, 2004) is a fictional language.

Mikiana (Rebecca Bettencourt, 2002) is the language of the Mikianans.

> **Na Mi~kana Cithra erra sha mes personem tith gardella diyana tath thea sabren evra denna. — Xenymmenen**
> *In Mika City there are many people with blonde hair that they brush every day. — Anonymous*

Mineng (tli-ze, 2004) is a European-based auxlang.

Mingjiese (YongDeok Cho, 2001) is a fictional language.

Minhyan (Jeffrey Henning, 2004) is a language for the planet Peliaz, still spoken by the forest people of the planet.

> **Cefowe calan riyeli sirum cefoti calagan ritho.**
> Live/OPTATIVE-IMPERFECTIVE you(peer)/AGENTIVE-DEFINITE peace/LOCATIVE-INDEFINITE Day/TEMPORAL-DEFINITE life-full your(peer)/POSSESSIVE-DEFINITE all.
> *May you live in peace all your life-filled days.*

Minyeva (Garrett Jones, 1997) is a loglang designed to be "the most logical a language can be." Its lexicon is *a priori*.

> **oL tes iLe asek iLe anek**

> I sing-to him kick her, injuring.
> *I sing to him, making him kick her, injuring her.*

Mjuteità Inglisja (Tomas Magath) is a fictional language.

> **Yú gouésji givésju þetéd mened kissef.**
> *You go to give to that man a kiss.*

Møkobi was developed by Joseph W. Mynhier as a diachronic language.

Molvanian (Santo Cilauro, Tom Gleisner, Rob Sitch, 2004) was invented for the travel guide parody *Molvanîa: A Land Untouched by Modern Dentistry*. It features a quadruple negative: "Can I drink the water?" is expressed "Is is not that the water is not not undrinkable?"

Mondlango (He Yafu, 2002) is an auxlang.

Moonshine (Andrew Leventis) is a naming language.

Mornaë (Emily Bisset, 2004) is a fictional language.

> **Mhiro sprís ílcar ír fwíros.**
> *You run like a salmon. [insult]*

Moten (Christophe Grandsire) is a fictional language.

Mowhan is the language of the Mowameddo Regime, a Canadian micronation.

Mua (Valentin Koulikov) is a loglang.

> **GoaAr aljA aAa / Ha Ol gail aAa / aAa gail jaAa / Ma guguid aAa / Miiim gail jaAa / imi aAa. Vu aAa Aa.**
> *While travelling through time / Do not try to kill it. / Time kills itself. / Our brave time warriors / Always fight themselves. / Everything ends. / And so does the time.*

MUL (Michael Cartier, 2002) is a loglang.

> **av de dug god maak de himx en de erd en de erd is ge vid en ding na en merk is ge af de dup zix.**
> *In the beginning God made the heavens and the earth and the earth was emptiness and nothing and darkness was on the face of the deep.*

Mundo-Lingue, an auxiliary language, was crafted by Julius Lott.

Musbrek was designed by Jashan A'al as a stealth language.

Mushroomese (Lee Wilson) is a fictional language.

N

Nabel (Damon M. Lord, 2004) is an auxlang.

Nadsat (Anthony Burgess, 1961) is the language (slang, actually) used by gangs of violent English teenagers in the now-classic book and movie *A Clockwork Orange*. It serves a serious purpose in the book, which is to help keep the violence of the protagonist (who rapes, murders and steals) from becoming unbearable to the reader. Nadsat is the best slang ever invented, with over 300 words, many of them cleverly derived from Russian (e.g, Russian *nadsat*, "-teen").

> *And they skazzed odin to another, "Itty to, let us make bricks, and burn them dobby." And they had brick for stone, and cal they had for mortar.*

Naffarin (J.R.R. Tolkien, 1905). The first of Tolkien's constructed languages for which we have any information, though even that is sparse. But it already foreshadows Quenya.

Nakiltipkaspimak (Daniel Andreasson) is a fictional language.

ñakiw pym wifiw kingewhàwwas (Pete Bleackley, 2004) is an artlang.

Nalona (Douglas Green, Kevin Albrecht, Kristian Jarventaus, 2002) is an auxlang.

Nalonin (Boomajoom, 2003) is a fictional diachronic language.

Nalosya (Kuanye. 2005) is a personal language.

Namarin (Renli Marek) is a fictional language.

Namek (Akira Toriyama, 1990) is a naming language.

Nandorin (J.R.R. Tolkien) is a fictional language.

Nanigani (Kaihsu Tai) is the language of the Asteroid Commonwealth.

Nanon (Matt Scott) is a fictional language.

Naqu (Kevin Albrecht) is the language of the planet Naqu.

Naracze (Yoon Ha Lee) is a fictional language.

Naranis (Maknas) is a fictional language.

Nari (Thomas Slawson, 2003) is a fictional language, based on English, Hebrew, and Russian.

Narish (Jordan Lavender, 2002) is the language of the Narian Elves.

Nartrean (Edward Field, 2004) is a personal language based on Atlantean and Greek.

Nassian (Jan Havliš, 2001) is the language of the Ossers, a north Slavonic people in an alternate timeline of Ill Bethisad.

Natu-Khuzdul (Siewurd S. Wendau, 2003) is a fictional naming language.

Nedertæl (Stefan Lubbersen, 2003) is an auxlang based on Dutch.

Neelan (Neil Buckley) is a fictional language.

Neitetar (Jashan A'al) is a fictional language.

Nemeritvie (Luciano Nicolás Parisi, 1996) is an auxlang, based on Eseperanto and Latin.

Neo (Arturo Alfandari, 1937) is an auxlang designed to encourage conciseness of expression.

> **Si o no si, em lo qestyon: sar it plu nobla / Lo fleshos e l'atak subi d'un suert oltraga, / O kontra un ocean de penos preni l'armos, / Ze nili, z'endi?**
> *[The opening of Hamlet's 3rd soliloquy.]*

Neo-Dalmatian was invented by Ferenc Gyorgy Valoczy.

> **Úna krestomátia da la langa neodalmátika ku úna deskripsión gramatikál da la lánga, ku úna glosúra, e ku des tékstas, túti ku traduksiónes in-a la langa engléza.**
> *A chrestomathy of the Neo-Dalmatian language with a grammatical outline, a glossary, and texts with English translations.*

Neo-Khuzdul (David Salo, 1998) is an expansion of Tolkien's Khuzdul, based on Semitic.

Neove (Theodore Carras, 2002) is a philosophical language.

Nesupian (Dacian, 2001) is an auxlang based on Russian and French.

Nevbosh (Mary Incledon, 1905). Tolkien made some modest contributions to his cousin's language, Nevbosh ("New Nonsense").

Nevokanyi (Nicole Perrin) is a fictional language.

New Avaeran (Eric Sortun, 2002) is a diachronic language spoken in Elyria, used in an RPG.

New English (Jeffrey Henning, 1986) is a fictional language, mostly a repository of proposed new words.

Newahon (John Whatmough, 2004) is a fictional diachronic language.

Newspeak (George Orwell, 1948) is a simplified form of English from the dystopian *1984*. The language is based on the destruction of words rather than their creation. It seeks to control philosophical outlooks by controlling the parameters through which they can or cannot function.

Ngolopalnec (John Whatmough. 2004) is a fictional diachronic language.

Nickish is a fictional language.

Nihilosk (Nikhil Sinha, 1003) is a personal language inspired by Esperanto.

Niline lale (Chris Bates, 2002) is a fictional language.

Nimyad (Thomas Thurman, 1987) is a fictional diachronic language, where nouns reflect five states (creation/birth-before-birth, birth, growth, strength, peace) that every entity is assumed to pass through.

Nirdaen (Reinhart Keim, 1997) is the language of the land of Vaenthyr.

> **Shenid lort iadhro Knaar em teur-nas ar, loetras nari Vaenthyr noeg lac innecorat saer lac imegen Dhamog raun.**
> *When Knaar fell in 441, the land of Vaenthyr barely survived the destruction by the northern kingdom of Dhamog.*

Njaama (David J. Peterson, 2002) is a personal language.

Noceltaeh (Allen Squires) is a fictional language.

Nômík Sprøk (Connor Becker) is a fictional language.

Noraan (Noraa J. Suiralc, 2005) is a stealth language based on Indonesian, Dutch, and Hawai'ian.

Nordálien (Gabe Bloomfield, 2002) is a fictional language based on Quenya and Spanish.

Nórdicg (Ywlyan Rott, 2002) is a Germanic-based fictional language.

Nordien (Aaron Chapman) is a fictional language.

> **Eg spreke neet Nordien so gud.**
> *I don't speak much Nordien.*

Northern Griffin Script (Zylom, 1997) is an artlang.

Nova (Brad Coon) is spoken on the island of Pan and the contiguous nation of Nowapan.

Novial (= New International Auxiliary Language, Otto Jespersen, 1928) was designed by) is a auxlang based on Ido and Occidental.

Novial 98 (NOVIAL-L, 1997) is an auxlang, a reform of Novial.

Novial Pro (Marcos Franco, 1997) is an auxlang reforming Novial.

Nowapan is a fictional language.

Noxilo (MIZUTA Sentaro, 1996) is an auxlang which allows multiple word orders (e.g. SVO or SOV).

Nóyahtowa (J. S. Burke, 1995) as a fictional diachronic language, based on Cheyenne and Mohawk.

Nóyanla (Maknas) is a fictional language.

Nu Aves Khara-Ansha (Wesley Parish) is a fictional language.

Nuatic (Daniel Day, 2002) is a fictional language.

Nuirn (Steve Gustafson) is a jargon.

Nunihongo (Jeffrey Henning, 2004) is a diachronic language based on English and Japanese.

Nüreqio (Cristián Cuevas, 2002) is a fictional language for the world of Nüreq.

Nuspic (Przybylowicz, 2003) is an English-based auxlang.

O

Õingææ (Alex Fink, 2004) is a fictional diachronic language derived from Aw'ingiwa.

Obrenje (Christian Thalmann, 2000) is a fictional language used for an RPG.

Lembe i samprose cynje - xyna chesse! *LM*

Occidental (Edgar von Wahl, 1922) is a Romance-based auxlang. The language is so naturalistic that Don Harlow says, "a linguist unfamiliar with it might be forgiven for assuming it to be a minor Romance dialect that had grown up after the collapse of Rome." Inspired by Mundo-Lingue, Occidental itself served as an inspiration for Novial.

Oda Zginzgala (Bradford Morgan White, 2001) is a fictional language.

ODODU (Jere Northrop, 2002) is a loglang.

Odonien (Steve Oostrom, 1981) is spoken by the Odonans, aliens introduced in the author's *Star Trek* fan fiction. Creating the language, he intentionally violated as many language universals as possible in order to produce a more alien language. The aim of Odonien is to make sentences as succinct as possible.

Ok (Duke Keenan, 2002) is a loglang inspired by Speedtalk.

Jagonxnwm Udokslem
I welcome you to the Oksite

Okaikiar (Mark Reed. 2003) is a fictional language.

Olaetian (Herman Miller, 1979) is a language of the Kolagian universe.

Old Dwarvish (Clyde Heaton, 1982) is a professional fictional language.

Old Kandar (Tim Hall) is a fictional language.

Old Rashurish (Ikkakujyu, 2002) is a fictional diachronic language.

Old Sindarin (J.R.R. Tolkien) is presented as intermediate between Primitive Quendian and Sindarin.

Old Southern (Laurie Gerholz) is the language of Arvandra.

Old Tongue (Robert Jordan, 1990) is a professional fictional language, used in the *Wheel of Time* series.

O'lelic (Curtis Mullings, 2004) is the language of the Akinokans.

> Komáhu Pá. Kusa vá ko'ána komáhu-ni Mokoatá'eth 'e Lonáka. vá hiko Lonáka kinonèka 'e kona. hilává kálipomè ko'epál-átá'e. Kusa Nuhánimè vá pá mokutálè má noáko-atá'e.
>
> Beginning The. God create (Past t.) beginning-in up-overs and Earth. become (past t.) Earth formless and empty. surface deep (G.C.) Darkness-over. God Spirit (G.C.) stay-fly (past/present) waters-over.
>
> *In the beginning God created the heaven and the earth. And the earth was formless and empty; and darkness was over the surface of the deep. And the Spirit of God hovered over the waters.*

Olijad (Robert Hill, 2001) is a personal language.

Olvardeth (Victor Yuri Gevirtz, 1006) is a personal language.

Omnesian (Jordan Kay) is an auxlang.

Omnial (Elx Amnial, 2003) is a Romance-based auxlang.

Oneirien (Collectif Oneira, 2001) is the language of the world Oneira.

Ongaki (ACZ, 2004) is a fictional language designed for making music.

Oopee (Kelly Kozlowski/ Carmen St. Jean, 2002) is a fictional language.

Oou (Sonja Elen Kisa) is an artlang designed to be hard to understand: "acts of communication become trippy idea-art."

Opus-2 (Chris Pressey, 2001) is a non-speech-based artlang.

> deep red
> F, tympani roll, forte
> F, french horn, piano
> *The building glorifies the woman.*

Oraq (Mason Fraley, 2002) is the language of Oraq.

Orcish (Clyde Heaton, 1982) is a professional fictional language.

Oro Mpaa (Christian Thalmann, 2002) is a fictional language related to Obrenje, spoken in Tao Ttoua.

Otg (Spencer Sturgeon, 1960s) is inspired by Celtic and Turkic languages, Otg has word-initial case markers, vowel contrast and harmony for grammatical function, and a contorted use of the Latin orthography. The language is mainly agglutinative, with the inflected nouns allowing free word order.

> **Naal slyryt uo borthoth boraca te Otg tioul iar garbygyr te gacoth mydhdoun.**

Ouranian-Barbaric (Peter Carroll et al., 1980) is a fictional language. It lacks a verb "to be", has only plural pronouns, and has no expressions of certainty or causality.

Oz (Charles Milton Elam, 1932) is an a priori philosophical language, with a vocabulary derived not from natural languages but from a classification structure. The vocabulary was to be based on Roget's Thesaurus, but does not seem to have been worked out in its entirety.

Ozay (Daniel Myers, 2002) is a personal language designed to "violate normal rules of language."

P

P@x'àãokxáã (Eddy Ohlms, 2004) is a fictional naming language.

> **N|òp@òõkàtsúũ tũo p'ààkàtsàò shikhàònè.**
> Large-rotating-place poss workers unite-volitive
> *Workers of the world, unite!*

Pabappa (Andrew Leventis, 2004) is a fictional language.

Pacarian (Sander Dieleman, 2001) is a personal language for the micronation of Pacary.

Pailodd (Jeremy Graves, 2000) is a fictional language.

Pakitani (Paco "España", 12001) is a personal Baltic-based language.

Pakuni (Victoria Fromkin, 1974) is a professional fictional language, used in *Land of the Lost*.

Pala-kalloejna (Christopher Reid Palmer, 1997) is a personal language. . The lexicon, once it has been generated, will consist of a set of names in a non- or super-hierarchical namespace (a web), with names (nodes) fuzzily linked to other names. Any name can have any number of links to any other names. The form the pattern takes will be malleable - indeed, every expression in pala-kalloejna will reshape the web - and will in itself define the names (i.e., describe usage patterns for the lexemes).

Paleneo (Leslie Charteris, 1972) is a universal sign language.

Pamrul (José Martínez, 2003) is a fictional diachronic language based on Pamryr.

Pamryr (José Martínez, 2003) is a fictional diachronic language, based on Quenya, Sindarin, and Spanish.

Pan-kel (Max Wald, 1907) is an auxlang.

Panovese Kal is a stealth language, a Pig Latin-like alteration of Dutch created in the early 20th century by the workers in a tile factory.

Pantato is for a fictional parallel Earth.

Parseltongue (J.K. Rowling, 1999) is the language of snakes in the Harry Potter books. It was fleshed out in the movies.

Pasilalion (Mojsije Paic, 1864) is a script language.

Pasilogia (Edward Groves, 1864) is an auxlang.

Patrienish (Mike Brooker, 1975) is the language of Antarbhumi Ramrajya, the Inner Realm of Patria, a micronation.

> **Períful delivrán ísí santanán, fecamortán ísí malefítorán, remontán rítambarulítor, ín omnís epoquís ímí nasquïtí.**
> *To deliver the holy men, to destroy the evil-doers and to restore righteousness (dharma), I take birth in every age. – Bhagavad-gita*

Paulic was created by Paul Smith.

> **Egaugnal Ciluapa ebbaki lacitsiugnil aedi, taht aputhguohtbakbei Luapo Htimso.**

The Paulic Language is a linguistical idea, that was thought up by Paul Smith.

P'bankian (Dtsdesign, 2004) is a fictional naming language based on Arabic and French.

Pélénne (Tom Killingbeck, 2004) is a personal language based on Quenya and Welsh.

Pe'Ma'De (Eric the Best, 2000) is a personal language.

Perilo (Horváth Róbert, 2004) is an auxlang, a "simpler Esperanto."

Perio (Mannus Talundberg, 1904) is a philosophical language.

Phaleran (Thomas Wier, 2001) is the language of Gelenê, a large satellite orbiting the second planet of Upsilon Andromedae.

phonetic picture-writing (Leonhard Heinzmann, 1998) is a philosophical language.

Piat (John Cowan, 1996) is a language for a fictional Central European country, based on Finnish and German.

Dwo pitii de fiatwnwe, li giann-giann mieso puhio.
In leaf-falling season, bears catch sick.

Pictban (Dtsdesign, 1999) is a Celtic-based auxlang.

Picture Language (Wally Flint, 1989) is an auxlang based on pictures.

Pig Elvish (Bicoherent, 2004) is a personal language, formed by permuting English text.

Pig Latin is the most famous English language game. The earliest example from Wikipedia dates to 1919.

Pikachu (Aneel Nazareth, 2000) permutes input text to "Pikachize" it.

Pikutu (μ, 2005) is a personal language.

Pil'koska (Tom Killingbeck, 2005) is a personal language based on Desa Chat, Basic English, Quenya, and Esperanto.

Pisina (Mathias, 2004) is an auxlang with just 10 phonemes.

Plan B (J. Prothero) is a loglang.

Plan C (Jacques Guy, 1992) is a loglang.

Platio (J Carbajal, 2003) is a Romance and English-based auxlang.

Plefande (Pablo Barenbaum, 2001) is a personal language.

Pokémon (Nintendo, 1995) is a professional fictional language.

Poliespo (Nvwtohiyada Idehesdi Sequoyah or Billy Joe Waldon, 1992?) is an auxlang based on Esperanto and Cherokee.

po'P'kp (Xhin, 2005) is a personal language based on Kokipopi.

Poþi (Joseph W. Mynhier) is a fictional language.

Prajiþiast (Eric Anger, 2004) is a fictional language based on the Elvish tongues and Basque.

Primal (Trickster) is a personal language designed for furries.

Prime Lexicon (Chris K. Caldwell) is a personal language.

Primitive Elvish (J.R.R. Tolkien, 1915) is a fictional diachronic language.

Progressiva (Mattia Suardi, 2002) is an auxlang, used for a fictional South American state called Elyria.

Projet d'une langue universelle (Jean Delormel, 1795) is an auxlang.

Proslava (George (Juraj) Doudy, 2002) is a Slavic-based auxlang.

Proto-Drem (Kevin Urbanczyk, 2003) is a diachronic language.

> **Lìêĝiṣýèĝâgdidlpep**
> TAMVmarker+3S+bird+adj+verbalizer+v. To fly.
> *The bird (habitually) just flew again.*

Proto-East-Arakhelian (Maknas, 2003) is a fictional diachronic language.

Proto-Eastern (Mark Rosenfelder, 1994) is the ancestor of Caďinor, Verdurian, Barakhinei, Axunašin, and many other languages of Almea.

Proto-Hambah (Tom Little (Sêsâmân, 2004) is a fictional language.

Proto-Liotan (Geoff Eddy, 1993) is a Celtic-based diachronic language.

> **Do biod shuibhisin fasgas am ghaod feod sheaineisin llabh sheuphar rreul a morraisin al-eaidhiuisin dae chamh rreabh.**
> *When you are visiting a friend, it is an act of the greatest courtesy to speak to him in his own language, rather than to require him to learn yours.*

Prototype Worlds (Eric Raymond, 1996) is a superset language— a glossary of SF coinages used across many fictional worlds.

Psharádi or Modern Tsaran (Jashan A'al, 1993) is a fictional language, originally developed as a stealth language.

Ptokan (Ryan Eakins, 2003) is a personal language.

Purdik (Steffen M. Turnipseed, 1997) is a European-based auxlang.

Pushakian (Dr X, 1999) is a European based auxlang.

Q

q~'u^pl! (Adam Walker) is the language of aliens of the Commonwealth.

> **d~'ihq! th~y^l! m#c~'u?! p#r~iw!**
> Man road walked-with-purpose was-traveled.
> *The man walked down the road.*

Qa (Tregetour Yare) is a fictional language.

Qatama (Carl Buck) is a personal language.

> **nga nuda ta tomo uq ta muja m'ha otara**
> *That which doesn't kill me, will make me stronger.*

Qelvietu (Robbie, a.k.a. Zoqaeski, 2005) is a fictional language.

Q'en|gài (Henrik Theiling, 2003) is a personal language.

Qenya (J.R.R. Tolkien, 1915) is a diachronic language derived from Primitive Elvish.

Qhalite (John Whatmough, 2004) is a fictional diachronic language.

Qilmanian (Jordan Lavender, 2002) is a fictional language based on Narish and Greek.

Qtwyqp Qly (Marq Thompson, 2000) is an *a priori* personal language.

Quebh (Jake Zeroth, 2004) is an auxlang based on Irish Gaelic.

Quenya (J.R.R. Tolkien, 1917) is the chief of Tolkien's Elvish languages, used mainly in *The Lord of The Rings* and *The Silmarillion*. The beauty of Quenya has inspired many to take up the hobby of model languages. Unfortunately, it was never a primary goal of Tolkien's to finish the design of Quenya, and his death left the vocabulary and grammar incomplete. This incompleteness has dampened the fires of enthusiasm for many who would have liked to have learned the language. At present there exists no single authoritative reference to the meta-history (the history of the creation of the fictional history) of Quenya. This gap will be filled eventually, when some unknown among us rises to the challenge of analyzing the editorial efforts of Tolkien's son Christopher, who has prepared a series of volumes relating the history of Tolkien's invention of Middle Earth. [Since I first wrote that in 1995, Helge Kåre Fauskanger has come close to achieving this.]

Quya (Ricardo Pinto & David Adger, 1998) is a professional fictional language, appearing in *The Stone Dance of the Chamelon* series.

R

Rachovian (Geoff Eddy. 2004) a diachronic language derived from Liotan.

Radilu (Chris Collins, 1995) is a personal language intended to have "a very complicated grammar."

> **survate, ute fara gat i vukedute vono nu:mt, ha fa ingegovot lo munamo yuta.**
> *Go to, let us go down, and there confound their language, that they may not understand one another's speech.*

Rahha (James Campbell) is for an agricultural people.

> **Visti u deheba izever-sata tistbibi!**
> *I don't know, but I think I bought a pregnant mouse.*

Ranamemi (Terrence Donnelly, 1999) is the language of the Ranamemi people of Zyem.

Rav Zarruvo (Bob, 2002) is the language of non-humans who live in a jungle in a fantasy world.

'î zhïzàl zàzìl dä zhög
This is the writing's appearance.

Ravenloftish (Eric Anger, 203) was created for the Shadow Elves.

Raxanakoa (Jonathana Tegire, 2004) is a fictional language.

Rayatako (Michael Mechmann, 2000) is a Chinese-based fictional language.

Rèaniano (Giovanni Angelo Doveri, 2004) is a European-based personal language.

Regelluga (Ben Poplawsk, 2003) is a personal language.

Reman (Christophe Grandsire, 1995) is a Romance-like diachronic language.

Reñim (Martin F., 2002) is a personal language.

Retehitu (Alex Middleton, 2005) is a personal language based on Māori.

Réziko (J.T. Antley, 2004) is a fictional language inspired by Japanese, Cherokee, and Flaidish. It has a derived form, **Late Réziko**.

Rhean (Mike Ellis, 1998) is a fictional language.

C'ipir anokz g'azuye - izkan sazdvye! LM

Rhyllan (Andrew J. Meilstrup, 2002) is a fictional language.

Rigavie Sutanio (Nate and Steve, 2004) is a personal language based on Japanese and Latin.

Ie iru sanimeru se temini via iru honinoru se sumini surimeru. -General Rigavi
And the blood flowed through the streets as though it was wine.

Rikchik (Denis Moskowitz, 1996) is the language of aliens known as rikchiks.

Rinya (Daniel Andreasson, 1996) is a personal language.

Risan (Kári Emil Helgason) is a fictional language.

Rivaansa (Thomas Schorreel, 2004) is a Finnish-based fictional language.

Ro (Rev. and Mrs. Edward Powell Foster, 1906) is, like Solresol, a pasigraphy (an *a priori* philosophical language), with a vocabulary derived not from natural languages but from a classification structure. You can roughly guess the sense of a word by recognizing its initial letters; for instance, in Ro, *bo-* is the category of "sense-affecting matter"; color words begin with *bofo-*. e.g. *bofoc* "red", *bofod* "orange", *bofof* "yellow". Unfortunately, if you make a typo in Ro, you've probably just spelled another word, and your spell checker is not going to catch the mistake..

Rodlox's Unnamed Conlang (Rodlox, 2004) is a personal language.

Rokbeigalmki (Steg Belsky, 1997) is a fictional language.

Romana (Dan Tohatan, 2003) is a Romance-based auxlang.

Romanico (1991) is a Romance-based auxlang.

> **Fácila Orgasmos: Quale Façar Olos Halucinifanta et Multe Mena Laboro**
> *Easy O's: How to Make Them Mind-Blowing and a Lot Less Work*

Romanid (Zoltán Magyar, 1956) is a Romance-based auxlang.

Romanova (David Crandall, Robert Hubert, Michael Edwards, 1999) is a Romance-based auxlang.

Romulan or Rihannsu (Diane Duane, 1984) is the language of *Star Trek*'s Rolumans, as developed in *My Enemy, My Ally* and other works.

Rootian English (Joris Bollen, 2004) is an auxlang influenced by Esperanto, Ido, and others.

Rosakeat (Maknas, 2004) is a fictional diachronic language.

Roxhai (Jeffrey Henning, 1996) is a philosophical language, with its vocabulary automatically structured, as with Ro. For instance: *r'o* means "sentiment and moral power"; *ro'yo*, "religious affection"; *roc'o*, "supernatural being or region"; *roca'yo*, "Christian supernatural being or region"; and *rocac'o*, "God". The core vocabulary of Roxhai is based on nouns, with verbs, adjectives and adverbs derived from these. Roxhai was inspired by Solresol, Ro and Esperanto.

Rrldha (Tom Corcoran, 2002) is a fictional language.

Rúmeann (jú) is a diachronic language.

Rusakui (Maknas, 2003) is a fictional language.

Rúvuk (Robert, 2003) is a fictional language.

S

Saakha (Adam Parrish) is for the desert nomads of the planet Endra.

Safo (Andreas Eckardt, 1956) is an auxlang.

Saiwosh (Frank Legros, 2002) is a diachronic language based mostly on Chinook Jargon.

Sakatda Ka Kadomo (Barry Garcia, 1999) is one of the few conlangs based on an Austronesian Language, Tagalog, It is also the fictional language of the Jakautdok people of the Sierra Madre Mountains in the northern Philippines.

Salanjan (Drydic_Guy) is a fictional language.

San Corrado Langue (Jan Skrob, 2004) is a European-based auxlang.

Sap'e'o (Jonathon Bly, 2004) is a fictional language.

Saphah (Anton Kemmeren, 2005) is a fictional diachronic language based on Aramaic, Hebrew, and Persian.

Sarkelean is a fictional language.

Sarminath (Edward Field, 2003) is a personal language based on Sarmanuin and Sindarin.

SASXSEK (Dana Nutter, 2003) is an auxlang based on over 200 languages.

Sathir (David J. Peterson, 2003) is an Austronesian-based personal language.

Satritain (Luther Blissett, 1999) is a fictional language.

Saurian (James Gurney, 1992) is the language of the dinosaurs in the *Dinotopia* series.

Scallin was invented by Kaurpin.

> **Clideð ða kaurpin næ sryk, ðuca spæccer's sam.**
> *The raven doesn't speak back, even though I speak to him.*

CONLANGS AT A GLANCE 363

SCSL (Shanya Spiritskunk) is a personal language.

Sea Elvish (Curtis Mullings, 2005) is a fictional language.

SedoNeural (Merle D. Zimmermann, 1999) is a stealth language.

Seimi (Daniel Andreasson, 2000) is a personal language.

Sen:esepera (Jeffrey Henning, 1996) is a reform of Esperanto to make it easier to pronounce. Where Esperanto has 23 consonants, Sen:esepera has only the 14 most commonly used consonants; where Esperanto permits complex consonant clusters (e.g., *spr*), Sen:esepera only permits clusters using nasals. It is also noteworthy for its kinship terms, capable of concisely expressing thousands of familial relationships.

Senu Yivokuchi (Pablo Flores, 2003) a fictional language.

Senyecan was invented by Charlie Brickner as a fictional language.

Serasraes (Rodlox, 2005) is a personal language.

Sermo (Jose Soares Da Silva, 2003) is an auxlang based on Interlingua and other neo-Latin languages.

Seversk (Libor Sztemon) is the language of a North Slavic people.

> **Atece når, ketri jesi na nevaror, ta jâst fasvestøn namet 'âr.**
> *Our Father, who art in heaven, hallowed be thy name.*

Sevorian (James Campbell, 1992) is the language of a North Slavic people.

Seyekoneth (Michele C., 2003) is a personal language.

Shaelic (Scott Hutton, 2002) is a diachronic language for the conworld Eshraval.

Shaleyan (James) is for the planet Shaleya in the Refea Solar System.

Shan is the language of the Shan Cannibals.

> **Yeközä Dijtsland namumurüguk täyuxile mawal korölünire kuzipe pinake.**
> *Back in Dijtsland I wondered why pork tasted so different here.*

Shaquelingua (Remi Villatel, 1986) is a fictional language designed to be as "alien as possible."

Sharioléh (Eugenio M. Vigo, 2002) is a fictional language.

Sheli (David J. Peterson, 2001) is a personal language designed for maximally free constituent order.

> **Man3 as1 ğwos6 nèm3 os2this3 šen3.**
> /animate-demonstrative Class-21-classifier fish-GEN. swim(of an animal) against flow/
> *This fish swims upstream.*

Shilgne S'drawkab C'navdair (Tom R., 2005) is a stealth language. Try reading the language name backwards. (But *-ir* marks past participle.)

Shinoarnii (Shiari, 2002) is a personal language.

Shkanshej (Pablo Flores, 1999) is the language of the winged people of an alternate Earth.

Shoa (J. Harness, 2006) is a fictional language.

Shondan (David C. Morrow, 1986) is the language of Shondar on the planet Pandalar, spoken by centauroids.

Sialy (Aaron Morse, 2005) is a fictional language..

Sidonian (Dtsdesign, 2002) is a naming language for a war game.

Signuno (1991) is a constructed Sign language, bearing the same relation to Esperanto as Signed English does to English.

Silarg (JP Mallaroni, 2004) is an auxlang with wide sources.

Silindion (Elliott Lash, 1997) is a fictional language.

> **A ilë, të ophosis ë, yulda olotma, ilkoimiesis no koimanna.**
> *Oh, god, who is above me, gleaming like a diamond, lay me down to bed.*

Simlish (Maxis Games, 1999) is a professional fictional language, used in *The Sims* to convey emotion without being tied to any human language.

Simpekso (Jonathon Grimes, 2005) is a European-based auxlang.

Simpenga (Jeffrey Henning, 1996) is a contraction of *Simpela Engelisa*, "Simple English." The language is just a phonetically simpler version of Basic English. Yawn.

Simpla (Samuel Fredrickson, 2002) is a European-based auxlang.

SIMPLE (1990) is a simplified English, with about a 500-word vocabulary. Unlike Basic English, SIMPLE does not aim to be a grammatical subset of English, but attempts to simplify the rules. The SIMPLE language is not so simple, for it does not formally specify its grammar (which appears to consist of some arguable but complex subset of English), it idiomatically forms new words that have to be learned (a'other, there-for), it ignores the issues of polysemy, and it permits a full range of verbal idioms (verb-preposition pairs: give up, put up, go in, etc.).

Sinampaiton (Paul Hoffman, 1978) is a fictional diachronic language.

Sindarin (J.R.R. Tolkien) is the tongue of the Grey-Elves, itself descended from Old Sindarin and from Primitive Elvish, which is also the ancestor language to Quenya.

Sinnish (Scott 'Blade' Hamilton, 2002) is a personal language.

Skerre (Doug Ball, 1994) is for hunter gatherers of the Western Interior Range.

> **Etsosin tsa Karak tsique ya tseris-ta.**
> PERF-kill-TR ERG (name) deer DAT family=3SG.POSS
> *Karak killed a deer for his family.*

Slavëni (Libor Sztemon) is the language of a North Slavic people.

> **Je as cesta er as pravda er as zeveta em.**
> *I am the Way and the Truth and the Life.*

Slavisk (Libor Sztemon) is the language of a Slavic people.

> **Ó Fódär myn, kojyn o nóvesa es, asvétist as nóme Tyn.**
> *Our Father, who art in heaven, hallowed be thy name.*

Slezan (Jan van Steenbergen, 2004) is a diachronic language, the language of Silesia on Ill Bethisad.

SLOVIO (Mark Hucko, 1999) is a Slavic-based auxlang.

Slvanjec (Benct Philip Jonsson, 2002) is is a diachronic language, the language of Slevania on Ill Bethisad.

> **Popol szne ljadzva jej popol szne kore**

A people without a language is a people without a heart

Sohlob (Benct Philip Jonsson, 1990) is a diachronic language, the daughter of Kijeb.

Solresol (Jean François Sudre, 1830) is the cleverest philosophical language, the earliest constructed language to be successful and the most likely to be learned by Julie Andrews. Solresol is based on the musical scale and has just seven syllables: *do, re, mi, fa, sol, la, si*.

Somerish (Bo Bernvill, 1995) is a fictional diachronic language based on Old English and Welsh.

Somish (Aaron Chapman, 2003) is a personal language.

Sona (Kenneth Searight, 1935) is an *a priori* auxlang. Sona is an isolating and agglutinative language. There's a very minimal lexicon -- Searight mentions Roget's Thesaurus— but unlike similar tiny languages, Sona seems to be complete enough for real usage: 375 words.

Sorgalo (Carlos Cervera, 2003) is a European-based diachronic language.

Speedtalk (Robert Heinlein, 1949). In "Gulf", supermen of the future used a language called Speedtalk. This "verbal shorthand" assigned every word a unique phoneme, so that resultant sentences were as short as a few English words. Use of the language enabled the superman to think more quickly and to experience more in less time. See aUI, which attempted to actually implement this idea.

Spelin (Georg Bauer, 1889) is an auxlang.

Spet (ACZ, 2003) is an auxlang with worldwide sources.

Spocanian (Rolandt Tweehuysen) is for Spokanië, a group of islands in the Atlantic Ocean, southwest of Iceland.

> **Ef spooksoliy lângâr tiffe divers terat generâl ki wuftas, mitÿr ef etymolôiy knôfe noi ur quoss.**
> *The Spokaans language contains some very common words whose etymology is not exactly known.*

Spokil (Adolphe Charles Antoine Marie Nicolas, 1890) is an auxlang which is a reform of Volapük.

Stālāg (Pablo Flores) is a fictional language.

Stitch Words (Disney, 2002) is a professional fictional language, used in *Lilo and Stitch*.

Straifpin'r (Dtsdesign, 2004) is a Celtic-based personal language.

Streich (Tommaso Donnarumma, 1980) is the language of the Helu of the Archipelago of Elaire.

> **Luer mui wichsan muinam wythmene uuhih thru!**
> *It was my wife's/husband's idea to come here for vacation!*

Strelwidhan (Pyter Voeros) is a fictional language.

Strom (Stephen Fry, 1987) is a personal language which first appeared on *Saturday Night Fry*.

Sturnan (Christopher Wright) is a fictional IE-based language.

> **Kerit hentalge huri a turek.**
> *A chicken attacked the king.*

Suma is an a priori language, but is unusual for the category in that its vocabulary does not use a systematic classification system. The language allows only CV (consonant+vowel) syllables, for easy-to-pronounce words.

Sunset Elvish or Pinuidan (Curtis Mullings, 2004) is a fictional language based on Welsh.

Suoníppomí (Eric Anger) is a fictional language.

Susachi (Bradford L. Lewis, 1970) is a personal language intended to use roots from "every language I can find."

Svargó (Stefan Lubbersen, 2003) is a personal language.

Swa-di (Bradford Morgan White, 2003) is a fictional language based on Esperanto, English, German, Latin, and D'ni.

Syldavian (Hergé (Georges Rémi), 1938) was invented by the Belgian comic artist for the Tintin series, notably *King Ottokar's Sceptre*. Mark Rosenfelder has created a 200-word dictionary and has translated the sample texts, and developed a grammar to explain them, based on Dutch grammar, commenting, "As in restoring a fresco, a bit of invention was needed to form a coherent picture."

Szkev (zbihniew, 2003) is a fictional language.

T

Tá à p'u (Eddy Ohlms) is a fictional language.

Ta Pémish Shprochna (Jan Havliš, 2002) is a diachronic language based on German and Czech, used on Ill Bethisad.

Ta Ti (Marq Thompson, 2004) is a stealth language.

Taeisan (Geoff Tuffli, Shai Strouse, B.G. Moser, *et al*, 1992). is a language family consisting of Drgn, Iniel, Ohs and Petrocea, and used in RPGs.

Taki (Jerry Mings) is a fictional language.

Talhata (David Stewart-Candy, 2002) is a personal language.

Talossan (R. Ben Madison, 1980) was invented for the imaginary country of Talossa (located in Milwaukee). Talossan is a Gallo-Romance language, inspired by French, Provençal and Occitan. With over 30,000 words, it is one of the most detailed fictional languages ever invented. A weakness of the language is that it has no fictional derivation from Latin, with forms having been invented arbitrarily rather than regularly.

Talumena (F.A.Fabian, Sr., 1989) is a personal language.

Tamarian (1991) is a professional fictional language, appearing in the "Darmok" episode of *Star Trek: The Next Generation*. The Tamarians speak by means of mythic references, e.g. "Darmok and Jalad at Tanagra." Though this seems impossible, it's a sly way of introducing linguistic confusion in a setting that contains a Universal Translator.

Tanach-a Shile (Doug Ball, 2002) is an *a priori* fictional language.

Taneraic (Javant Biaruja, 1968) is a stealth language.

Tarnese (Etak, 2004) is a fictional language.

Tarnif (Nik Taylor) is a fictional language.

Taruven (taliesin, 1992) is the "lingua franca of a vast area spanning several universes."

Tasratal (Yoon Ha Lee) is a fictional language.

Tatari Faran (H. S. Teoh, 2004) is a fictional language based on several Asian languages.

Tatsique (Nicola Curat, 1995) is a personal language.

Tazhi (Makeenan) is a fictional language.

Tech (Danny Wier) is a fictional language.

Telerin (J.R.R. Tolkien) is the language of the Sea Elves.

Telpuilkoc (Eddy Ohlms, 2003) is a personal language.

Tēlvo (Jonathan North Washington, 2002) is a diachronic language, spoken by the Pinclans.

Telyana (Adam Parrish) is the language of the Telyani Empire.

> **fi-fu malis nyi-ujiari u-hap**
> nom2-it travels across acc3-waters dat1-harbor
> *It travels across the waters to the harbor.*

Tenctonese (Kenneth Johnson, Juliet Johnson, Van Ling, Scott Mislan, 1988) is a professional fictional language, largelly based on Russian and English; it appeared in *Alien Nation*.

Teonaht (Sally Caves, 1962) is a personal language, Much is unique about it, from its word order to its verbal system to its affixing. Teonaht distinguishes between volitional and non-volitional verbs and subjects, so that the nominative has two forms, agent and experiencer, It has the Law of Detachment, whereby affixes can switch from final to initial position for rhetorical or prosodic purposes; this allows the tense suffix to detach and prefix the pronoun.

> **Eskkoat ol ai sendran, rohsan nuehra celyil takrem bomai nakuo.**
> *My shadow follows me, putting strange, new roses into the world.*

Tepa (Dirk Elzinga, 1990) is a unique personal language, professionally designed and presented, and rightfully highly regarded among the Internet community of language modelers. It is simply the most professional treatment of an artlang on the Internet. has two annotated texts well worth reading: *Coyote Eats Rocks* and *Two Otters*. His frame story about his sources is excellent; because of it, some innocent web surfers probably think Tepa is a real language. By the time you finish reading about Tepa, you may think it's a real language too!

> **alekku pilii hatuuta-n tea esuhusatte ateka yuqea numa ehumu ekami hunumupu.**
> *The North Wind and the Sun were disputing which was the stronger, when a traveller came along wrapped in a warm cloak.*

Terran (Josh Brandt-Young) is a fictional language.

Tev'Meckian (Jeffrey Henning, 2002) is a fictional language. Barsoomian inspired the phonology. Esperanto inspired the grammar. Klingon was a counter-inspiration. Tenctonese was a cautionary tale.

> **Pu wex datgrud bok mat.** *LM*

Tharan (Dan Cole, 2003) is a diachronic language.

Thauliralau Triyk (Jim Henry, 1998) is a language of alien mammals.

Thequm (Sami Kleit, 2005) is an auxlang based on Arabic and Tolkien.

Thereskeya (Ben Poplawski, 2003) is for a female-dominated warrior society ruled by their queen the Candace.

> **Thonath belo khelbit auriswelespit.**
> *I soar over sunlit lands.*

Thh:tmaa (Matt Pearson, 1996) is a professional fictional language created for the *Dark Skies* TV series.

Thiazic (Chris Paull (Zeke Fordsmender), 2000) is a diachronic language based on Germanic and Slavic.

Tho-Kyi (Karl Jahn, 1999) is a diachronic language.

Thosk (Dean Easton, 1992) is the language of a fictional Indo-European people.

> **Hur Vejen i Solen buv no hontaht u je hi go to bu moi aber, hutu sotend ukumev noludun no gurm falt.**
> *The North Wind and the Sun were disputing which was the stronger, when a traveller came along wrapped in a warm cloak.*

Tiemish (Stephen Mulraney) is a Mandarin-based fictional language.

Tigerian (Jonathana Tegire, 2001) is a fictional language which religiously avoids consonant clusters.

Tikasako (Chris Paull (Zeke Fordsmender), 2002) is an auxlang with just 13 phonemes and a lexicon derived from proto-languages.

Tilya (Herman Miller) is a loglang.

tinico (Alexandre Xavier, Casanova Domingo.) is an auxlang.

Tinxirean (Accard, 2003) is the language of the Eternally Glorious, Ever-Honoured Everlasting Empire of The Thousand Falling Feathers.

Tirelat (Herman Miller, 1999) is a personal language.

Tisjelán (Jonathan North Washington, 2000) is a fictional language.

Tjelwu, a fictional diachronic language, was designed by Jonathan North Washington.

Tlön (Jorge Luis Borges, 1940) is described in a story in *Ficciones*. It is a language of Berkeleyan idealists who reject the idea of the continuity of objects; its primary units are all adjectives. A concept may be combined of any simultaneous sensations: e.g. "the sun and the water on a swimmer's chest, the vague tremulous rose color we see with our eyes closed, the sensation of being carried along by a river and also by sleep."

> **Hlör u fang axaxas mlö.**
> upward beyond the onstreaming it.mooned
> *The moon rose above the river.*

Toaliralolo (Jim Henry, 1996) is a fictional diachronic family.

Tokana (Matt Pearson) is a personal language, with an emphasis on syntax.

> **Niokteh telanku! Ma tuiaku ietiehu ulumotihi sule Tokana.**
> *Thank you! I don't speak Tokana very well.*

Toki Pona (Sonja Elen Kisa, 20010 is a personal language.

> **O kama pona lon toki awen pi toki pona!**
> *Welcome to the Toki Pona site!*

Tomato (Catty) is an auxlang.

> **Tao fo yeli bo rido bi Tao nau lefa.**
> *The Tao described in words is not the real Tao.*

Tomoulini Ganmaa is the language of a fictional parallel Earth.

> **damaa luurai, looi ganumaanye, looi mitemaa, kaalare milinmaa choonlinjoonrunyei.**
> all-of the-world the-thing-just-mentioned language-the-possessed-in-the-past the-thing-just-mentioned a-oneness the-thing-first-mentioned use-of-equal-words-in-the-past
> *All the world had the same language and used the same words.*

Torrin (Jeff Hopkins, 2004) is a personal language, partly a loglang.

TRAN (Andrei Burago, 1996) is an unusual language, with two very interesting features: first, a unique morphology for cases, and second, unusual formation of noun/verb pairs. Cases are marked on the end of preceding words (so, *Vagu gat* is "A cat sitting", where -*u* marks the case of *gat*, "sit"); this is well suited for forming compound words, e.g., *tanosharasvanak* is *tan* ("house") *o-shar* ("of selling", genitive) *a-svanak* ("drugs"), "pharmacy". Finally, verbs are formed from nouns by TRANsposing the initial and final consonants: e.g., *tran*, "speech", becomes *nrat*, "to speak".

Transcendent Algebra (J. Linzbach, 1921) is a philosophical language.

Transitional English (John Lihani) is an auxlang.

Triparik (Carrie Schutrick and Shawn Knight, 1998) is the language of a micronation, Septempontia. Most of the root words are Romance or Germanic. Designed to be fun but useful, the initial joke was that Triparik was "what Roman centurions used to chat up Gaulish barmaids."

Trurian (Jona J. Fras, 2003) is an artlang.

Tsolyáni (M.A.R. Barker, 1978) is one of the languages of Tekumel, the world of Barker's fantasy RPG *Empire of the Petal Throne* and novels (*Man of Gold, Flamesong*). Though all these works are out of print, Tekumel, Tsolyani and the other Tekumelani languages have a loyal following. Tsolyani was inspired by Urdu, Pushti and Mayan.

Tsuhon (Yoon Ha Lee, 2002) is a European-based fictional language.

Tsumhetyan (Exu Yangi) is a fictional language.

Vastsamxanbiltehen kaftsumtyantefat. *LM*

Tukbeyo (Dtsdesign, 2004) is a personal language based on Beothuk.

Tulari was developed by Rialian.

> **faladar**
> *A sense of something impending, either something about to happen or something that needs to be done.*

Tulinx (J. Valler) is a personal language.

Tundrian (Gábor Sándi, 1966) is for Tundria, an island off the western coast of France, similar to French and Catalán.

> **Non cognousco una soula persouna en celâ çutat.**
> *I do not know a single person in this city.*

Tunu (Mathias, 2000) is an auxlang.

> **Raki hopisong tumu henakang yaruma.**
> *The man cuts the plant inside the house.*

Tutonish (Elias Molee, 1902) was designed as an "Anglo-German union tongue" and actually intended for it to be not just an international auxiliary language but the new mother tongue of the Germanic-speaking peoples, supplanting their native languages. Tutonish has a phonetic spelling, a simplified grammar and a vocabulary drawn primarily from German and English.

Tvernel (Adam Walker) is the language of aliens of the Commonwealth.

Tydash was created by NA.

> **ði:næferetvë ?æ**
> *He is handsome.*

Tyl Sjok (Henrik Theiling, 2000) is a personal language.

Tymat (Shane Hodgson, 2004) is a personal language.

> **Nokasapêkomerongalola**
> *Will you not have been eating it?*

U

Uajiren (Steven Collins) is a fictional language.

Ubbi Dubbi is a stealth language, made by inserting "ub" into each syllable.

UberLingua (Jonathan Hayward, 2002) as a miscellaneous language.

Ukhik (Pablo Flores) is for a fictional parallel Earth.

Ummo (Jean-Pierre Petit) is a stealth language.

Ungil (Dean Easton, 2000) is a fictional diachronic language.

UNI (E. Wainscott) is an auxlang.

Uni Mar (J Harness) is a fictional language.

Unideo (Cattelain Eric) is a universal writing system.

Unipix (Cindy Drolet, 1982) is a pictographic reference that tourists could point at to make their meaning clear.

Unish (Language Research Institute, Sejong Univ., 2000) is an auxlang.

Unitario (M. Pleyer, 1987) is a Spanish-based auxlang.

Universal (G. I. Muravkin, L. I. Vasilevskij, 1923) is an auxlang.

Universal Character was crafted circa 1657 by Cave Beck as a philosophical language.

Universal Cipher Language (Charles Stewart, 1874) is a philosophical language.

Universal Networking Language is a fictional language.

> **aoj:01(tired(aoj>thing,mod-move(agt>thing,gol>place,src>place)),:01)**
> *If you are tired, we will go straight home.*

Universala Lingva Kodo (Linxiang Wang) is a fictional language.

Universalglot (Jean Pirro, 1868) is an auxlang.

Un'ky'ok (Jordan Lavender, 1995) is a personal language based on Latin and Hebrew.

CONLANGS AT A GLANCE 375

Unstränng (Scott 'Blade' Hamilton, 2005) is a Norse-like fictional language used in an RPG.

Üqoi (Bruce V. Bracken, 1996) is the language of the Zhoooonaïï of the planet Kaj'eevdhuz.

> **Qlhüüz'i tthajuvoen dhnuuthlhumed.**
> Glass outside injury I eat.
> *I can eat glass; it doesn't hurt me.*

Uropi (Joël Landais) is an auxlang.

Utésalañé (Jordan Lavender) is a personal language.

Uusisuom (Daniel Tammet, 2001) is a Finnish-based auxlang.

uuteib eafeis (David Caveney) is the language of the elves on Faya.

V

Vabungula (Bill Price) is a personal language.

> **Olar mala galasê bana sikili zafêne, i del mala aman Flopsi, Mopsi, Framivêm-tajope, i Peter.**
> *Once upon a time there were four rabbits, called Flopsy, Mopsy, Cottontail, and Peter.*

Vadhawian (Curtis Mullings) is for the Desert Wanderers of the Southeastern Desert.

Vaior (William S. Annis, 1999) is a personal language.

> **Sand-ai Din ach Rhith Auhal, tha mie-far-o, thildu achurler-anthal-o faonal od-o-l síathe-n.**
> dispute-PAST sun and wind north, who MORE-strong-PRESENT when near-come-BY=CHANCE-PRES traveler wear-PRES-PART cloak-ACC.
> *The North Wind and the Sun were disputing which was the stronger, when a traveller came along wrapped in a warm cloak.*

Valarin (J.R.R. Tolkien) is the language of the Valar. It's known mostly for borrowings into Quenya, e.g. *Manwë* < *Mânawenûz*. *Nazg* 'ring' in the Black Speech may derive from Valarin *naškad*.

Valavya (Mariana Lo, 2001) is a fictional language used for magic.

Valmelind (Asier Gabikagogeaskoa, 2000) is a fictional language.

Vamperr (Bradford Morgan White) is a fictional language.

Var'aq (Brian Connors) is a loglang.

Vardhastani (Anselm Huppenbauer, 2004) is a diachronic language influenced by Sanskrit.

> **Thuva anadiyadan bâjaya joah" - jakva kunasi ya balinasitvan.**
> *"You only must change the direction" - said the cat and eat it up. (Franz Kafka)*

Varro (Jurre Lagerwaard, 2005) is a fictional language based on Quenya, Sindarin, Latin, and Greek.

Vash (Peter Ramsey, 1958) is a fictional language.

Vayaun (Andrew Smith, 2004) is an IE-based diachronic language.

Ve Segelm A Laighödhét (Carsten Becker) is a fictional language.

Veltsin (T. A. Wieb) is a fictional diachronic language.

Vendi (Chris Ashton) is a personal language.

Venyárin (Ikkakujyu, 2002) is a fictional language with an "intricate grammar", featuring 23 cases.

Verdurian (Mark Rosenfelder, 1978) not only has a large vocabulary (over 5,500 words) and a linguistically informed grammar, but a fully worked-out family tree, going back two levels: to its ancestor, Cadinor, and to its ultimate origin, Proto-Eastern, with sister languages at both levels. It is naturalistic, with irregularities, sound changes, dialect differences, and interesting etymologies.

> **Ac esce řo e niš ak gintrovelecán? —cuesnai.**
> but is-it-that isn't zero against sash-stealer? ask-past-I
> *"But can nothing be done against a usurper?" I asked.*

Verlan is a French language game dating to the 1930s, formed by reversing syllables (*basket* 'running shoe' > *sketba*) or sounds (*femme* 'woman' > *meuf*).

Vihal (Jonathana Tegire) is a fictional language.

Viikqnnosf (Jan Havliš, 1999) is a fictional language based on Inuit.

Viku (Victor Medrano, 2001) is a loglang.

Vilani (Kenji Schwarz, 1997) is a fictional language used in an RPG.

> **Sheshmanenemnuriini kakarik kameliliish.**
> *I hope I'm going to stop keeping on finding you in the garden by [listening to] your screaming.*

Vinlandic (Tony Senn, 2005) is a Germanic-based auxlang.

Vixen (Curlyjimsam) is a personal language.

Vling (Victor Medrano) is an auxlang.

VOA Special English, (United States Information Agency, 1959) is a simplified English: 1500 words, no idioms, and a slow reading speed.

Vogu (Terence Donnelly) is a fictional language.

Vogukadanë (Teresh) is the language of the Kadanë people of the planet Zyem.

> **kihgu'k aha'thuchataglu di, nastu'gotebkri syech u'pul thaki'zn**
> was-not-saying our-guide that in-this-place now occurs revolution
> *Our guide did not tell us that there was a revolution going on in this country.*

Voidä is a personal language and was developed by Kaspars Ozolins.

Voksigid was invented by Bruce Gilson; et al. It is a loglang.

Volapük (Johann Martin Schleyer, 1879), with a name meaning "world speech", became a fad in the late 19th century and was the second international auxiliary language to win thousands of adherents (after Solresol); it was the precursor to Esperanto in popularity. It has a vocabulary based primarily on English and German roots that have been somewhat simplified for ease of pronunciation and morphological analysis. Its grammar was difficult enough that enthusiasts were rarely able to actually learn to speak the language. The language was successfully reformed in the 1930s. If Esperanto is the GUI (Graphical User Interface) of auxiliary languages, than Volapük is the DOS of the field. The language is primarily of interest now for historical reasons.

Volapük Revised (Arie de Jong in 1931) is an auxlang.

Völkerverkehrssprache (C. Dietrich, 1902) is an auxlang.

Von Morath Pasigraphy (Joseph de Maimieux, 1797) is a philosophical language.

Vônánà (Curlyjimsam) is a personal language.

Vong (Victor Medrano) is a personal language.

Vorlin – Rick Harrison is approaching the design of Vorlin very professionally, and you can read his opinions about the requirements of an international language in an excellent essay on his web site. Harrison is the editor of the *Journal Of Planned Languages* and has prepared a detailed bibliography of constructed languages. He is arguably the foremost scholar of constructed languages working on the Internet today. Vorlin is most noted for its use of words with three letters for its base vocabulary. The language has changed significantly over the years and still has far to go, as Harrison restructures its vocabulary.

Vosh (Daniel Myers, 2002) is the principal language for Monolothic Games' fantasy world Albarelis. Since Vosh is intended primarily for gaming, the goal was as simple a set of grammatical rules as possible, while still being realistic.

Vozgian (Jan van Steenbergen, 1996) is a diachronic language primarily baed on Uralic, used for a fictional Vozgian Republic.

W

Waldzell Conlang (Mark P. Line) is a fictional language.

Wamen (Pablo Flores) is the language of the Dahaite.

Wapadja (Thomas Schorreel) is a fictional language.

Wasabi (David J. Peterson et al.,, 2002) is an attempt at creating a pidgin in a class at UC Berkeley.

Watakassí " (Nik Taylor, 1998) is a diachronic language.

WDFDspeak or Ostopian (Jon, 2002) is a jargon.

Wede:i (Mark Rosenfelder, 1995) is an ancient language of Almea. It is agglutinative, with no strict division into parts of speech, meaning a single Wede:i word can express quite a lot of English verbiage. Other unusual aspects, for a constructed language, include its logographic writing system and its base 6 number system. Finally, it fits into the history of Almea; its writing system and much of its lexicon were adopted by Axunašin.

Wenedyk (Jan van Steenbergen, 2002), based on Latin and Polish, is for the Republic of the Two Crowns on Ill Bethisad.

> Nacoń sień lęgwy jest nacoń sień krodzi.
> *A nation without a language is a nation without a heart.*

Wessisc (Damon M. Lord, 2000) is a Celtic and English-based fictional diachronic language.

Western Zein (Drydic_Guy) is a fictional language.

Westron, (J.R.R. Tolkien) is the language of men and the common speech of Middle Earth, represented by English in *Lord of the Rings*.

Wilawossian (Dtsdesign, 2003) is a fictional naming language based on Basque and Hopi.

Wilkins' Analytical Language (John Wilkins, 1668) is a philosophical language.

WittyWordWork (Quentin Read, 2005) is an English-based jargon.

Woznackh (Eirik Wixøe Svela, 2000) is a fictional language.

> Weikomalin ekwaqueth weitalinos womalindo womsalandoth dapos wisantolinde tål wacasonith quisor wosontrimloth, tål quåh Gandalv ai wepotaru wisomtockh.
> *[a sentence from The Lord of the Rings]*

X

X (David J. Peterson, 2003) is a pasigraphy, with a grammar based on Tagalog and glyphs mostly from Middle Egyptian.

Xail (Sampo Taito Louke) is a personal language.

Xap II (Andrew Leventis) is a fictional language.

Xapqt (Nick Summers, 1995) is a loglang.

Xara (Jim Taylor) is a personal language.

> **xeon hojer Bilbo Baggins Bag End-ar ha samivas xe lixforafoler tartanan asan na salajas xo saleyej jilidejar helixan, ha oros melidev xu gexil purim do Hobbiton.**
> *When Mr. Bilbo Baggins of Bag End announced that he would shortly be celebrating his eleventy-first birthday with a party of special magnificence, there was much talk and excitement in Hobbiton.*

xathmel (Paul Blake) is the language of the planet Xa?n orbiting Ar.

> **keld im ar, im xtero kelisset ek'**
> *keld under sun and under the swift moons [conventional greeting]*

Xianese (John Whatmough, 2004) is a diachronic language.

Xliponian (Ronald Kyrmse, 2000) is a Romance-based diachronic language.

Xt! (Adam Walker) is the language of aliens of the Commonwealth.

xuxuxi (John Cowan) is an auxiliary language.

Y

Yahina (Dtsdesign) is a personal language.

Yathor (Jurre Lagerwaard, 2005) is a fictional language based on Quenya, Sindarin, Latin, and Greek.

Yeaji (Edward Field) a personal language.

Yeishan (Keolah) is a fictional language.

Yeledumel Thanusil (Eric Anger) is a personal language.

Yerti (Andy Helber) is a stealth language.

Yf Rgalin (Mark E. Shoulson, 1995), inspired by Lojban and Klingon, was developed to explore some features that were "amusing" to the author, while maintaining simplicity and regularity. It's a verb-first ergative language, with some attempt at Lojban-like regularity (but without quite so much rigor). There's some attempt to derive everything from verbs (except nouns). The phonology is slightly unusual; its sentence structure may be unique, as well as its verb structure (inspired by a feature in Basque).

Ygyde (Andrew Nowicki) is a philosophical language.

Yihhian (Simon Whitechapel, 1980) is a fictional language.

Yiirabarhi (Robert Eaglestone) is a fictional language.

Yilanè (T.A. Shippey, 1984) is the langauge of the intelligent saurians from an alternative timeline in Harry Harrison's *West of Eden;* see p. 17.

Y-irril (Jeremy Marshall, 1995) is a personal language..

Yivrian (Jesse Bangs, 1994) is a fictional diachronic language.

Ylhäällä (Lang Boy, 2004) is a fictional language.

Yorlakesian or Mok'yorlak'ol (Jörg "paleface" Burkel) is the language of the Yorlakesian Empire.

> **moq vequk ' nor dál rem yenorom par mok yorlakól**
> *I hope you enjoy learning the Yorlakesian language.*

Ypsìlònsk (Yulyan Ròt) is a personal language.

Ystheron (Patrick Littell) is a loglang.

> **Dhos Vos Pherdhas spheron Zhulos shen Boshos shen mariom.**
> If or (weak) is-green ball is-blue ball is-belonging-to ball Mary.
> *If the ball is either green or blue, it belongs to Mary.*

Ýtádý (Ren Willocks) is a personal language.

Z

Zadri (Vionau Raitak) is the language of the Zadarans.

Zan (Edrik, 2001) is a naming language.

Zaynktooks (spence5000) is the language of the Zanktooksians.

> **aBelDac marqla Ulueq bo dUcqa zanqDUqZu**
> ah-pel-tach mar-klah ool-uh-ek boh dooch-kah zahnk-tooks-uh
> *I like to annoy people by speaking in Zanktooks.*

Zdekkite (Tom R., 2005) is a Latin-based diachronic language.

Zegzolt (Toni Keskitalo, 1995) is a personal language.

Zelknaym (Dtsdesign, 2004) is a Selk'nam-based personal language.

Zengo (Rick Harrison, 1990) is a language that allows the author to indulge his interest in words with five letters. The small vocabulary contains an eclectic mix of such words from different languages. Zengo was formerly called Penta (until Intel made him change the name :-).

Zhakish (Keolah) is a fictional language.

Zharranh (Herman Miller) is for the furry four-foot Kireethin.

Zhong Ying is a jargon. It was created by A Forrest.

Zhyler (David J. Peterson, 2003) is a personal language.

> **Volanaz petti ÿlðavay nönjo, ÿlðalay nönjo.**
> /time-INE. king-NOM. people-SUB. speak-3sg., people-SUP. speak-3sg./
> *When the king speaks on behalf of the people, he speaks without the people.*

Zim (Stefan Koch, 2000) is a personal language, used in an RPG.

Ziotaki (Shihali Ramichu) is a diachronic language.

Zireenka (Herman Miller, 1990) is the language of some furry aliens, the Zireen, who dwell on the planet Reeshai, in the general direction of Ursa Major.

Zjivalian (J. R. Mauro, 2005) is a diachronic language based on Egyptian, Quenya, and Russian.

Zoggian (Jan Havliš, 2003) is a diachronic language based on Chinese and Tibetan, spoken on Ill Bethisad.

Zoinx (Roger Espel Llima, 1993) is a fictional language.

Zurbian (Torbjoern Andersson, 1981) is a fictional language originally based on the Black Speech.

Zurvár (James Nicholls, 1993) is the language of the nomadic, maritime Zurvár (Surf) people.

Peveliskàet msà barat pevsubilim, subilim lòtò holateláet toklas. Dò pevre'loklet lâraz barat, sà pevramaskátá talabon.
(past)dream-I us sea (past)on, on boat (transitive)sink fast. You (past)sail across ocean, I (past)tie-up(experience) mast.
I dreamt that we were at sea, on a boat that was sinking fast. You sailed across the ocean, I was tied to the mast.

Zusayan (Necralitor, 2000) is a naming language, based on Tolkien and Egyptian; it's used in an RPG.

Zyem (Terence Donnelly) is a fictional language.

Index

See also "Conlangs at a Glance". Conlangs are listed here only if they are referred to on another page. Natural languages that are liable to be referenced all over, like German and Latin, are omitted.

!Xũ, 25
A'al, Jashan, 327, 332, 335, 340, 348, 349, 358
Abed-Rabbo, Jamal, 330
Abraham, Sophia, 343
Accard, 371
Ace, 291
active-stative, 215
ACZ, 328, 353, 366
Adams, Blake, 311
Adams, Richard, 124, 338
Adger, David, 359
Æthelthýrth, 51
Afrikaans, 320
Akkadian, 177, 298, 332
Albrecht, Kevin, 328, 348
Aleut, 25, 181
Alfandari, Arturo, 349
Alfaro, Alex, 331
Almirus, 294
Alvish, 103
amelioration, 53, 60
Ament-Stone, Nathaniel, 305
Amharic, 39, 41
Amman-Iar, 294, 320
Amnial, Elx, 353
Andersen, Christopher, 32
Andersen, Daniel, 307
Andersson, Torbjoern, 382
Ando, Damátir, 308
Andreasson, Daniel, 308, 348, 360, 363
Andrews, Stephen Pearl, 294

Anger, Eric, 297, 305, 310, 342, 357, 360, 367, 380
Anglo-Saxons, 42, 48, 53
Angosii, Arthaey, 298
Annis, William, 375
anthroponomastics, 38
Antley, J.T., 333, 360
Antonius, Richard, 299
apocope, 28
Arabic, 39, 41, 42, 43, 132, 133, 181, 183, 296, 310, 330, 339, 342, 345, 356, 370
Aramaic, 362
Arotnow, Arne, 315
Arriola, Matt, 316
Ashby, Wendy, 323
Ashton, Chris, 376
assimilation, 27
Athey, Kevin, 9
Attobrah, K.A. Kumi, 293
Auden, W.H., 93
aUI, 300, 338, 366
auxlangs, 49, 181, 261
Axunašin, 301, 357, 379
Babel text, 8
Ball, Doug, 365, 368
Bangs, Jesse, 90, 381
Barenbaum, Pablo, 306, 357
Barker, M.A.R., 372
Barnes, Rupert, 301
Barsoomian, 112, 314, 370
Bartlett, Paul, 320, 340
Basham, A.B., 293

Basic English, 204, 261, 302, 317, 356, 364, 365
Basque, 357
Bates, Chris, 350
Bauer, Georg, 366
Beard, Henry, 300
Beatty, Wilbur, 308
Beaubien, Eric, 308
Beaufront, Louis de, 326
Beaverstone, Alex, 343
Becher, Joachim, 307
Beck, Cave, 374
Becker, Carsten, 301, 309, 376
Becker, Connor, 351
Bell, David, 104, 294, 320
Belsky, Steg, 361
Beothuk, 373
Berendt, Alfred, 302
Berkhout, Carl T., 296
Besson, Luc, 312
Betsumei, 323
Bettencourt, Rebecca, 346
Biaruja, Javant, 368
Bicoherent, 356
Bierwisch, Manfred, 67
Bisset, Emily, 347
Blaa, Lord, 303, 322
Blake, Paul, 380
Bleackley, Pete, 334, 335, 348
Bliss, Charles, 303, 338
Blissett, Luther, 362
Bloomfield, Gabe, 351
Bly, Jonathon, 362
Bob, 359
Boeree, C. George, 341
Bollack, Leon, 303
Bollen, Joris, 361
Bontrager, Gregory, 304
Boomajoom, 343, 348
Borges, Jorge Luis, 371
Bostonian, 22, 25
Bouchard, Chris, 295
Bourland, David, 316
Bowks, Jay, 300, 303, 315, 317, 318, 339
Boyd, Jeremy, 310
Boyle, David, 332
Bracken, Bruce, 375
Bradt, Sean, 330
Brady, AK, 317
Brandt-Young, Josh, 370
Brase, Jon, 321
Breitenbach, B. Egon, 319
Brejta, Bruce, 304

Brender, Felix, 296
Breton, Tom, 293
Brickner, Charlie, 363
Bringen, Hildegarde of, 341
Brooker, Mike, 355
Brown, James Cooke, 342
Brown, Padraic, 334, 345
Brown, Ray, 144
Brown, Robert, 334
Bruce, Benjamin, 302
Bryant, 313
Bucchianeri, Marco, 296, 336
Buck, Carl, 358
Buckley, Neil, 349
Bullard, Anthony, 310, 314
Burago, Andrei, 372
Burgess, Anthony, 17, 46, 47, 348
Burke, Jeff, 351
Burkel, Jörg, 381
Burleson, Ian, 339
Burroughs, Edgar Rice, 112, 294, 296, 302
Bush, Michael, 293
Butt, Matthew, 301
C., Michele, 363
Campbell, James, 330, 359, 363
Carbajal, J., 357
Carpenter, Humphrey, 102
Carras, Theodore, 350
Carrasco, David, 301
Carroll, Lewis, 20, 354
Carter, Jim, 323
Carter, Raphael, 309
Cartier, Michael, 347
case, 86
Catalán, 373
Catty, 372
Caveney, David, 375
Caves, Sally, 369
cellar door, 30
Ceqli, 305, 336, 342
Certic, 338
Cervera, Carlos, 366
Chapman, Aaron, 320, 351, 366
Charteris, Leslie, 355
Cherokee, 357, 360
Cherryh, C.J., 299, 325, 334
Cheyenne, 351
Cho, YongDeok, 346
Cilauro, Santo, 347
Ciupak, Pawel, 330
civman2000, 328
Claiborne, Robert, 23

Clark, Ross, 323
clitic, 87
cluster simplification, 28
Colas, Claudius, 292
Cole, Dan, 370
Collins, Chris, 359
Collins, Steven, 374
componential analysis, 68
contradative, 90
contronym, 62
Cook, Conrad, 308
Coon, Brad, 351
Corcoran, Tom, 361
Coren, Michael, 102
Couturat, Louis, 326
Cowan, John, 145, 342, 356, 380
Crandall, David, 361
Crystal, David, 25
Csak, Sandor, 317
Curat, Nicola, 298, 305, 311, 342, 369
Curlyjimsam, 377, 378
Curtis, Tom, 337
Czech, 297, 368
Da Silva, Jose Soares, 363
Dacian, 350
Dalgarno, George, 309
Danish, 69, 80, 92, 320
DarkHorizon, 334
David, 312
Davis, Peter, 311
Day, Daniel, 351
Delormel, Jean, 357
Denju, 283
Derzhanski, Ivan, 144
Dever, Joe, 322
diachronic language, 17
Dickey, Ethan, 9
Dieleman, Sander, 296, 319, 340, 354
Dietrich, C., 378
dissimilation, 27
Docimo, Anthony, 305
Domingo, Casanova, 371
Donnarumma, Tommaso, 295, 297, 319, 367
Donnelly, Terrence, 303, 314, 344, 359, 377, 383
Donoghue, Timothy, 321
Doohan, James, 335
Doudy, George, 357
Doveri, Giovanni Angelo, 360
Dragon, 103, 206, 313, 316
Drydic_Guy, 296, 307, 362, 379

Dtsdesign, 317, 323, 336, 337, 356, 364, 367, 373, 379, 380, 382
Duane, Diane, 293, 361
Dublex, 127, 183, 204
Duering, Arne, 313, 318
Durand, David, 309
Durst, Jack, 294
Dutch, 69, 83, 92, 133, 320, 330, 343, 349, 351, 355, 367
Dutton, Reginald, 314
dwarves, 98, 206, 316, 334
Dyer, Frederick, 341
Dynes, David, 144, 345
Eaglestone, Robert, 381
Eakins, Ryan, 358
Earth Language, 314, 338
Easton, Dean, 370, 374
Eckardt, Andreas, 362
Eddy, Geoff, 303, 310, 342, 357, 359
Edgar, 316
Edrik, 381
Edwards, Michael, 361
Effel, Jean, 315
Egyptian, 379, 383
Elam, Charles, 354
Elgin, Suzette Haden, 337
elision, 28
Ellis, Mike, 360
elves, 23, 42, 66, 94, 103, 311, 313, 316, 375
Elzinga, Dirk, 369
Endriago, Kumouri, 302
engelangs, 8
Ensle, H. Ellis, 300
epenthesis, 28
Eric the Best, 297, 356
Esperanto, 10, 11, 13, 17, 47, 49, 133, 229, 262, 263, 264, 265, 292, 296, 297, 298, 314, 317, 318, 326, 328, 329, 330, 342, 350, 356, 357, 361, 363, 364, 367, 370, 377
Etak, 368
Eternia, 318
Etxenaude, Iban, 324
Eurolang, 49, 318
F., Martin, 360
Fabian, F.A., 368
Fatula, Joe, 306
Fauskanger, Helge Kåre, 359
Ferengi, 49, 319
Ferretti, Martin, 296
fictional language, 17
Field, Edward, 298, 315, 349, 362, 380

INDEX

Filssunu, Paal, 294
Fink, Alex, 335, 352
Finley, James, 291
Finnish, 88, 91, 293, 315, 319, 320, 326, 342, 356
Fischer, Drew, 318
Fisher, Alison, 338
Fisher, John, 315
Fith, 8, 10, 146, 231, 327
Flaidish, 319, 360
Flint, Wally, 356
Flores, Pablo, 303, 308, 313, 321, 335, 345, 363, 364, 366, 374, 378
Flut, Raginvard, 312
Foerster, Bruce, 292
Ford, John, 335
Forrest, A., 382
Foster, Edward, 361
Foulk, Ruby Olive, 294
Fraley, Mason, 354
Francis, Jim, 343
Franco, Marcos, 351
Fras, Jona, 372
Fredrickson, Samuel, 365
Freudenthal, Hans, 341
Fromkin, Victoria, 355
future language, 48
Gabikagogeaskoa, Asier, 292, 299, 301, 376
Galaxy Quest, 267
Galdiolo, Luca, 321
Garcia, Barry, 301, 362
Gardner, Mark, 323
Garet, Florent, 343, 345
Garshin, Igor, 341
Garza, Peter, 326
Gaughan, Keith, 316
Gavioli, Maurizio, 335
generalization, 55
Gerholz, Laurie, 353
Gestuno, 329
Gevirtz, Victor, 353
Ghayour, Omid, 307
Giles, Alan, 322
Gleisner, Tom, 347
Glosa, 323, 328
Gnoli, Claudio, 342
Gode, Alexander, 329
Gogat, Madhukar, 322
Goguen, Jeff, 335
Goodman, Kevin, 327
Gothic, 92, 93, 305, 310, 324
Grandsire, Christophe, 301, 347, 360

Graves, Jeremy, 354
Green, Douglas, 328, 348
Greening, Martin, 314
Greenwood, Ed, 313, 327
Gren, Jedrzej, 316
Grimes, Jonathon, 364
Grossmann, James, 323
Groves, Edward, 355
Gruscha, N., 319
Guardiola, José, 336
Gud, Zingjar ë, 326
Guilford, Wil, 291
Gurney, James, 362
Gustafson, Steve, 351
Guy, Jacques, 357
Gygax, Gary, 206
H., Rob, 337
Habash, Nizar, 310
Hadar, Dana, 342
Haida, 337
Hall, Tim, 352
Halvelik, Manuel, 297
Hamilton, Scott, 327, 365, 375
Hampton, Dave, 321
Hampton, Shane, 325, 335
Hankes, Elmer, 315
Hansen, Christian, 346
haplology, 28, 44
Harbison, Rebecca, 309
Harness, J., 364
Harody, 210
Harris, Anthony, 294
Harrison, Harry, 17
Harrison, Rick, 73, 145, 378, 382
Hart, Zack, 323
Hatfield, Edward, 299, 341
Hatfield, James, 291
Havliš, Jan, 296, 297, 305, 349, 368, 377, 382
Hawaiian, 24, 77, 80, 311, 332, 338, 342
Hayward, Jonathan, 374
He Yafu, 347
Heaton, Claude, 103
Heaton, Clyde, 103, 352, 354
Hebrew, 24, 41, 42, 273, 296, 303, 310, 311, 322, 349, 362, 374
Heinlein, Robert, 305, 366
Heinzmann, Leonhard, 356
Helber, Andy, 380
Helgason, Kári Emil, 299, 327, 335, 360
Helsem, Michael, 322

Henning, Jeffrey, 302, 313, 314, 319, 320, 327, 329, 332, 333, 336, 346, 350, 351, 361, 363, 364, 370
Henry, Jim, 170, 230, 324, 370, 371
Hergé, 367
Higley, Gregory, 328
Hill, Robert, 353
Hill, Spence, 295, 299
Himes, Dennis Paul, 322
Hindi, 88, 132, 133, 183, 314, 342, 345
Hodgson, Shane, 344, 373
Hoffman, Paul, 365
Hogan, Apollo, 300, 313, 334, 335
Hogan, Tyler, 337
Hogben, Lancelot, 328
honorific, 40
Hoover, Greg, 328
Hopkins, James, 330
Hopkins, Jeff, 372
Hopper, Grace, 57
Horn, Joshua, 304, 329
Horváth Róbert, 356
Houghton, Stephen, 23, 102, 340, 344
Housz, Timothy, 315
Huang, Jian, 309
Hubert, Robert, 361
Hucko, Mark, 303, 365
Hufnagel, Johannes, 307, 319
Hungarian, 40, 43, 298, 319, 320
Huppenbauer, Anselm, 297, 300, 305, 307, 376
Hutton, Scott, 363
IAL. See auxlangs
Icelandic, 41
Ido, 296, 317, 326, 328, 351, 361
Ikkakujyu, 313, 352, 376
Ilish, 171
Ill Bethisad, 331, 334, 349, 365, 368, 379, 382
Incledon, Mary & Marjorie, 296, 350
Indonesian, 330, 333, 336, 351
Interglossa, 323, 328
Interlingua, 10, 49, 328, 329, 339, 363
Intermythic English, 177
Inuit, 44, 316, 377
IPA, 11
Jaaaaaa, 314, 326
Jackson, Eliot, 294
Jahn, Karl, 311, 370
James, 346, 363
James, Phil, 317
Janton, Pierre, 11
Japanese, 11, 24, 25, 40, 56, 78, 79, 80, 133, 197, 293, 306, 311, 312, 320, 328, 329, 330, 341, 351, 360
Jarventaus, Kristian, 328, 348
Jespersen, Otto, 351
Jewell, Daniel, 326
Johansson, Andreas, 345
Johnson, James, 307
Johnson, Juliet, 369
Johnson, Kenneth, 369
Johnston, Greg, 345
Jon, 378
Jones, Deiniol, 298, 330
Jones, Garrett, 346
Jones, Leslie, 318
Jones, Rowland, 326
Jong, Arie de, 378
Jonsson, Benct, 344, 365, 366
Jordan, Robert, 353
Jotomicro, 310
Jovovich, Milla, 312
jú, 361
Jung, Robert, 9, 333, 336
K., Bryant, 293
Kali-sise, 10, 181, 332
Kalivoda, Nick, 293
Karklak, 206, 314
Kaurpin, 331, 362
Kay, Jordan, 303, 353
Keenan, Duke, 305, 352
Keene, Zak, 330
Keim, Reinhart, 350
Kempf, Glenn, 306
Kennaway, Richard, 291, 293
Kenney, Douglas, 300
Keolah, 380, 382
Keskitalo, Toni, 382
Kevin, 302
Khuzdul, 334, 349
Kian, 337
Killingbeck, Tom, 315, 337, 356
KinDEEP, 76
King, Stephen, 326
kinship terms, 68, 76
Kiraly, Yann, 344
Kirschner, David, 346
Kisa, Sonja Elen, 353, 371
Kleit, Sami, 370
Klingon, 13, 47, 267, 268, 295, 311, 335, 345, 370, 380
Kloba, Ted, 321
Knight, Nathaniel, 292
Knight, Shawn, 336, 340, 342, 346

INDEX 389

Koch, Stefan, 382
Koestner, Bruce, 314
Korean, 43
Korolev, Grigoriy, 338
Kozlowski, Kelly, 353
Kramm, Pascal, 292, 306, 328
Kuanye, 344, 348
Kuiper, Roger, 337
Kuntze, Aran, 295
Kupsala, Risto, 343
Kwai, Ajin, 301, 313
Kyrmse, Ronald, 380
La Touche, K., 325
Laj, Tiogshi, 339
Landais, Joël, 375
Landau, James, 306, 325, 332
Lang Boy, 381
Lanning, Randal, 345
Lapine, 124, 338
Lash, Elliott, 364
Latino Sine Flexione, 318, 329, 339
Latvian, 88
Lavender, Jordan, 294, 322, 349, 358, 374, 375
Le Guin, Ursula, 45, 334
Le, Tony, 328
LeChevalier, Bob, 342
Lee, Sharon, 340
Lee, Yoon Ha, 349, 368, 372
Leeuw, Ron de, 305
Legros, Frank, 362
Leibniz, Gottlieb, 340
Leigh, Thomas, 41, 306, 313, 318, 342, 349, 350, 356, 360, 378
lenition, 26
Letellier, Charles, 338
Leventis, Andrew, 295, 347, 354, 379
Lew, Nathaniel, 302
Lewis, Bradford, 367
Lewis, C.S., 344
liaison, 28
Lihani, John, 372
Lilly, Jeff, 306
Line, Mark, 307, 378
Ling, Van, 369
Linzbach, J., 372
Littell, Patrick, 381
Little, Tom, 327, 357
Llima, Roger Espel, 382
Lo, Mariana, 375
Logan, John, 316
Loglan, 336, 342
Lojban, 132, 133, 342, 380

Lord, Damon, 306, 348, 379
loss, 28
Lott, Julius, 347
Lotz, Sven, 335
Louke, Sampo Taito, 379
Lubbersen, Stefan, 308, 320, 328, 343, 349, 367
Mabey, Graham, 299
MacLagan, Scott, 292
Madison, R. Ben, 368
Magath, Tomas, 347
Magyar, Zoltán, 340, 361
Maimieux, Joseph de, 378
Makeenan, 328, 369
Maknas, 299, 305, 333, 344, 345, 349, 351, 357, 361, 362
Malay, 80
Mallaroni, JP, 364
Manrique, Darrell, 339
Māori, 340, 360
Marani, Diego, 318
Marek, Renli, 348
Marshall, Jeremy, 381
Martin, 308
Martin, M., 338, 340
Martínez, José, 302, 355
Mathias, 356, 373
May, Rex, 305
Mayer, Frank, 175
McFarland, Yoshiko, 314
McGill, Eric, 336
McGrath, Mark, 145
McKenzie. Andrew, 344
McLaren, Jack, 306
McNeill, Jack, 308
McVay, Zach, 329
Mechmann, Michael, 345, 360
Medrano, Victor, 303, 330, 337, 341, 377, 378
Meilstrup, Andrew, 342, 360
Meriggi, Cesare, 303
metaplasmus, 51
metathesis, 27
micronation, 294, 319, 340, 347, 354, 355, 372
Middleton, Alex, 331, 336, 360
Miekko, 304
mikulzqm, 341
Miles, Marcus, 320, 338
Miller, Herman, 307, 315, 321, 331, 343, 352, 371, 382
Miller, Steve, 340
Miller, Timothy, 49, 319, 332

Mills, Roger, 333
Mings, Jerry, 368
Minhyan, 210
Mislan, Scott, 369
Mitchell, Keith, 327
Mohawk, 351
Molee, Elias, 373
Morelli, Daniele, 330
Morioka, Hiroyuki, 302
Morneau, Rick, 145, 337
Morris, 338
Morrison, Dan, 332
Morrow, David, 364
Morse, Aaron, 9, 311, 364
Morton, Robin, 326
Moser, B.G., 368
Moser, Leo, 145, 301
Moskowitz, Denis, 360
Moss, Norman, 59
Múharafic, 45
Muheddin, 301
Mulder, Simon, 320
Mules, Christopher, 296
Mullings, Curtis, 329, 346, 353, 363, 367, 375
Mulraney, Stephen, 370
Munce, Josh, 330
Mundo-Lingue, 347, 352
Muravkin, G.I., 374
Myers, Daniel, 316, 329, 335, 354, 378
Mynhier, Joseph, 347, 357
Nadsat, 17, 47, 348
Nagada, 36, 37, 73, 74
naming language, 20, 47
Nate, 360
Navajo, 326
Nazareth, Aneel, 356
Necralitor, 383
Negasi, 73
Nepali, 310
Nerrière, Jean-Paul, 323
Neurath, Otto, 329
Nevbosh, 93, 94, 296, 350
Newton, Philip, 336
Nicholls, James, 382
Nickolas, Steve, 312
Nicolas, Adolphe, 366
Niven, Larry, 47, 337
Njamal, 80
Nobriga, Noby, 293
Norrseg, Obar, 320
North, Edmund, 335
Northrop, Jere, 352

Norwegian, 42, 92, 320, 346
Nostratic, 22
Novial, 133, 351, 352
Nowicki, Andrew, 315, 381
Nunihongo, 11
Nutter, Dana, 362
Occidental, 351, 352
Oðblgshezi, 12
Ogden, C.K., 302
Ohar, Kelahäth, 298
Ohlms, Eddy, 354, 368, 369
Okamoto, Fuishiki, 301
Okrand, Marc, 47, 299, 335
Okrent, Arika, 11
Old Alvish, 104
Old English, 24, 25, 27, 28, 32, 50, 51, 53, 55, 57, 62, 69, 77, 92, 94, 95, 96, 98, 263, 296, 325, 330, 366
Olsen, Eirik, 337
onomastics, 38
onomatopoeia, 30
Oostrom, Steve, 352
orcs, 97, 103, 206, 336, 354
Original Penrithian Bandanna Kid, 301
Ortega, Rubén, 330
Orwell, George, 350
Ozolins, Kaspars, 377
Paco "España", 354
Padilha, Paulo, 333
Pafu, 317
Paic, Mojsije, 355
Palmer, Christopher, 355
Paolini, Christopher, 295
Parish, Wesley, 340, 351
Parisi, Luciano, 349
Parker, Tristan, 311
Parrish, Adam, 312, 362, 369
Parry, Bryan, 295
Parsons, Jonathan, 315
patronymic, 40
Paull, Chris, 305, 370, 371
Peano, Giuseppe, 339
Pearson, Matt, 370, 371
Pedicelli, Alessandro, 338
Pehrson, T. Mitchell, 326
Pei, Mario, 11
pejoration, 50, 61
Perrin, Nicole, 328, 334, 350
Perrotin, Damien, 324
Persian, 362
Persson, Matthias, 9

Peterson, David J., 7, 9, 168, 316, 324, 332, 333, 336, 345, 350, 362, 364, 378, 379, 382
Petit, Jean-Pierre, 374
Pfeaster, Patrick, 340
Phạm Xuân Thái, 320
Pharazon, 342
philosophical language, 229
phonotactics, 24
Pike, Kenneth, 331
Pinto, Ricardo, 359
Pirro, Jean, 374
Pitakesulina, 181
Pitjanjatjara, 80
Plaz, Niels van der, 316
Pleyer, M., 374
Polish, 38, 40, 379
Pomo, 330
Poplawsk, Ben, 360
Powell, Dean, 305
prepositions, 87
Price, Bill, 375
professor13, mr., 321
Prothero, J., 356
prothesis, 28
proto-language, 22
prototypes, 71, 74
Przybylowicz, 352
Psharádi, 335, 340
Punjabi, 329
Quechua, 91, 320
Quenya, 13, 18, 22, 92, 94, 95, 103, 104, 294, 323, 330, 335, 345, 346, 348, 351, 355, 356, 359, 365, 375, 376, 380, 382
Quijada, John, 330
R., Tom, 364
R., Tony, 382
Radiation, 58
Raitak, Vionau, 381
Ramichu, Shihali, 382
Ramsey, Peter, 376
Raymond, Eric, 358
Read, Quentin, 296, 320, 326, 340, 379
Reed, Mark, 170, 352
Remington, Eric, 329
Rempt, Boudewijn, 302, 304, 310, 327
Repton, Michael, 297
Reyes, Ariano, 343
Reynolds, Sean, 313, 314, 316
Rhiemeier, Jörg, 170
Rialian, 373
Rimell, Bruce, 309
Rinkel, Geert, 321

Ro, 10, 230, 361
Robert, 362
Robertson, Ed, 41, 314
Rodlox, 299, 305, 361, 363
Rogers, Ben, 330
Roget's Thesaurus, 322, 354, 366
Rohan, Chris, 98, 346
Room, Adrian, 34
Roots, Rik, 322
Rory, 293
Rosenfelder, Mark, 8, 9, 301, 302, 305, 316, 319, 329, 333, 357, 367, 376, 379
Rosta, And, 342
Ròt, Yulyan, 381
Roth, Josh, 316, 332
Rott, Yẃlyan, 351
Rovatti, Maurizio, 319
Rowling, J.K., 326, 355
Roxhai, 229
Ruimy, Aaron, 325
Rukai, 182
Russian, 39, 40, 41, 43, 56, 64, 72, 92, 131, 132, 133, 134, 183, 306, 314, 330, 336, 342, 348, 349, 350, 369, 382
Rye, Justin, 308, 321
Sacks, Daniel, 305
Sainz Lopez-Negrete, Luis, 343
Salo, David, 349
Salvini, Gustavo, 314
Sándi, Gábor, 373
Sanskrit, 27, 86, 88, 139, 140, 142, 329, 342, 345, 376
Sapir-Whorf, 206, 337, 342
Saunders, J. Matthew, 336
Saussure, René de, 296
Scarisbrick, Joseph, 342
Schleyer, Johann Martin, 377
Schrager, Esther, 332
Schutrick, Carrie, 316, 372
Schwartz, Lane, 330
Schwarz, Kenji, 377
Scott, Matt, 348
script, 306
Searight, Kenneth, 366
See, Matthew, 292
Selbor, L., 340
semantemes, 67
semantic primitives, 67
semantic reversal, 61
Sen:esepera, 82, 204, 231
Senn, Tony, 377
Serith, Ceisiwr, 337
Serrano, Ángel, 293

Shaftesbury, Edmund, 292
Shaw, Dillon, 298
Shiari, 364
shift, 59
Shilpetski, John, 310
Shinali, 307, 311, 340
Shinavier, Joshua, 309
Shippey, T.A., 17, 381
Shoulson, Mark, 145, 380
Sign, 329, 336, 364
Simpenga, 204, 261
Sindarin, 18, 22, 92, 94, 95, 103, 104, 124, 294, 295, 315, 327, 338, 345, 353, 355, 362, 365, 376, 380
Singing Wolf, Rachel, 335
Singleton, Mike, 295
Sinha, Nikhil, 305, 323, 328, 350
Sipola, Tuomo, 315, 317, 329
Sitch, Rob, 347
Skags, Tony, 294
Skrintha, 341
Skrob, Jan, 362
Slattery, Diana, 322
Smith, Amanda, 342
Smith, Andrew, 304
Smith, Jeff, 327
Smith, Paul, 355, 356
Soderquist, Mia, 345
Solly, David, 9
Solresol, 10, 230, 314, 361, 366, 377
Sortun, Eric, 350
Sotomayor, Sylvia, 333
Sotos Ochando, Bonifacio, 340
Spacek, Pat, 306
Spahr-Summers, Justin, 331, 336
specialization, 55, 58
spence5000, 381
SPH, 299
Spiritskunk, Shanya, 363
split, 27
Sproson, C.J., 9
Squires, Allen, 350
Srikanth, R., 325
St. Jean, Carmen, 353
Star Trek, 49, 267, 295, 303, 309, 319, 332, 335, 352, 361, 368
Stark, David, 339
Steenbergen, Jan van, 326, 365, 378, 379
Steffens, Andre, 296, 300, 311
Steve, 360
Stewart, Charles, 374
Stewart-Candy, David, 368
Stokes, David, 312

Straub, Hans, 310
Streiff, M., 303
Strouse, Shai, 368
Sturgeon, Spencer, 354
Suardi, Mattia, 296, 357
Suchsland-Gutiérrez, Brian, 340
Sudre, Jean François, 366
Suenaga, Seiji, 299
Suffield, Ronald, 50
Suiralc, Noraa, 351
Sumerian, 178, 179, 298, 332
Summers, Nick, 380
sUmUs cAcOOnUs, 312
Suridge, Jayelinda, 333
Svela, Eirik Wixøe, 379
Swedish, 28, 29, 77, 80, 92, 320
syncope, 28
syncretism, 91
Sztemon, Libor, 309, 318, 363, 365
Tagalog, 327, 362, 379
Tai, Kaihsu, 348
taliesin, 368
Talmey, Max, 298
Talundberg, Mannus, 356
Tamarian, 177, 368
Tammet, Daniel, 345, 375
Taylor, Nik, 315, 331, 341, 344, 368, 378, 380
Tegire, Jonathana, 292, 314, 326, 360, 371, 376
teknonym, 41
Teoh, H.S., 315, 369
Teresh, 377
Tev'Meckian, 8, 267
Tever, Muke, 308, 325, 326, 335
Thalmann, Christian, 331, 352, 354
Theiling, Henrik, 308, 320, 358, 373
Thompin, Chlewey, 308
Thompson, Marq, 329, 359, 368
Tibetan, 310, 330, 382
tli-ze, 346
Todas, 45
Tohatan, Dan, 361
Tok Pisin, 340
Toki Pona, 327, 371
Tolkien, Christopher, 99, 359
Tolkien, J.R.R., 11, 13, 14, 17, 18, 22, 30, 46, 65, 66, 92, 93, 103, 105, 292, 294, 296, 300, 303, 312, 316, 327, 334, 335, 342, 343, 345, 348, 349, 350, 353, 357, 358, 359, 365, 369, 370, 375, 379, 383
toponomastics, 38
Toriyama, Akira, 348

INDEX 393

Townsend, Paul, 325
translation, 72
Trickster, 357
Tuffli, Geoff, 368
Turnipseed, Steffen, 358
Tweehuysen, Rolandt, 366
Tychonievich, William, 323
Uittenbogaard, René, 305, 318
UPSID, 181, 262
Urbanczyk, Kevin, 310, 357
Vaessen, Robert, 325
Valinta, Kata, 320
Valler, Richard, 323, 373
Valoczy, Ferenc, 349
VanDenBreemen, Kevin R., 299
Vander, Christian, 336
Vasilevskij, L.I., 374
Vega, Suzanne, 67
Verdurian, 302, 305, 315, 329, 357, 376
Vielberth, Johann, 336
Vietnamese, 328
Vigo, Eugenio, 310, 345, 346, 364
Vilalonga, Frances de, 296
Villatel, Remi, 363
Villeneuve, Faiguet de, 338
Vitek, Lubor, 298
Volapük, 49, 366, 377, 378
Vuk, Uskokovic, 327
Vulcan, 323
Wahl, Edgar von, 352
Wainscott, E., 374
Wald, Max, 355
Waldon, Billy Joe, 357
Walker, Adam, 343, 358, 373, 380
Wan, Felix, 9
Wang, Linxiang, 374
Wann, Gary, 309
Washington, Jonathan, 308, 311, 317, 369, 371
Watakassí, 315, 378
Watson, Richard, 312

Weferling, Erich, 328
Weilgart, W. John, 300
Wells, H.G., 316
Welsh, 18, 33, 39, 40, 43, 57, 92, 95, 294, 304, 315, 325, 340, 356, 366, 367
Wendau, Siewurd, 349
Wentworth, Trevor, 292
Whatmough, John, 293, 298, 315, 321, 350, 358, 380
White, B. Morgan, 328, 352, 367, 376
White, Niki Eve, 292
Whitechapel, Simon, 346, 381
Wieb, T. A., 376
Wier, Tom, 310, 356, 369
Wilkins, John, 379
Willis, Didier, 323
Willocks, Ren, 381
Wilson, Lee, 348
Wilson, Robert, 335
Winger, Marie, 310
Wolfe, Gene, 298
Woolstenhulme, Dallin, 308
Wright, Christopher, 318, 329, 339, 367
X, Dr., 358
Xavier, Alexandre, 371
Xhosa, 326
Yangi, Exu, 372
Yare, Tregetour, 358
Yetter, Robert, 338
Yiddish, 24, 29
Yik, Fen, 343
Yiuel, 314
Yivrian, 90, 381
York, 35
Yoruba, 330
Zamenhof, L.L., 17, 317
zbihniew, 368
Zimmermann, Merle, 343, 363
Zoqaeski, 358
Zylom, 351
μ, 356

Printed in Great Britain
by Amazon